Rules of the Game for Sustainable Business

Rules of the Game for Sustainable Business

Laws, Contracts, and Morality

David Frydlinger

Wolters Kluwer

Published by:
Kluwer Law International B.V.
PO Box 316
2400 AH Alphen aan den Rijn
The Netherlands
E-mail: lrs-sales@wolterskluwer.com
Website: www.wolterskluwer.com/en/solutions/kluwerlawinternational

Sold and distributed by:
Wolters Kluwer Legal & Regulatory U.S.
920 Links Avenue
Landisville, PA 17538
United States of America
E-mail: customer.service@wolterskluwer.com

ISBN 978-94-035-2828-1

e-Book: ISBN 978-94-035-2838-0
web-PDF: ISBN 978-94-035-2848-9

Cover design: Daniela Cristofori

To my children Oskar, Rebecka and Klara

About the Author

David Frydlinger is a distinguished lawyer and partner at Cirio law firm in Stockholm, Sweden. For over twenty years, he has been a trusted legal business advisor to companies and governmental agencies across the Nordics and beyond. David is the author and co-author of seven books, including two notable works in English on relational contracting. His expertise has also been featured in the *Harvard Business Review* through co-authored articles. Currently, David guides clients through the transition to sustainable finance, sustainable business operations and sustainable supply chains, ensuring compliance with the intricate EU sustainability regulations.

Table of Contents

Foreword

Society's institutions and rules have long been highlighted as important for sustainable development. Now, we are in the precarious position that six out of nine planetary boundaries have been crossed. Not only are we at risk of even more socially and economically damaging shocks, such as extreme heat waves, droughts, floods and diseases. We also risk destabilising Earth itself, with far-reaching consequences for all future generations of the world.

So, new rules of the game are needed for the economy, business and society, and new formal and informal institutions that consider the well-being of all people and their relationship with nature.

Businesses play a key role in this reorientation. That all companies must be part of the sustainability transition is no longer just good advice, but has in recent years been established in the extensive regulations dealt with in the emerging area of sustainability law, which is becoming more urgent every second and to which all companies are now forced to relate. In a world that is also so interconnected that what happens at the local level today is dependent on and influenced by what happens in other parts of the world, the rules of the game in global markets and institutional frameworks (such as the global climate agreements) become even more important for achieving sound business operations and long-term social and economic development.

That is why David Frydlinger's book is so important. It is not only a solid introduction to sustainability law but can also be read as an instruction manual for sustainable business in general. And this is exactly what is needed if we are to build a strong and successful economy in an increasingly turbulent and challenging future in the long term.

In addition to dealing with existing laws and regulations, Frydlinger also discusses conclusions from Earth system science and the understanding of Earth as a self-regulating system, which can buffer disturbances if the systems are environmentally healthy, but which through self-reinforcing processes can be destabilised (and stop supporting humanity) if the biophysical systems are depleted. This understanding has its origins in research conducted in the latter part of the twentieth century and which in this century is consolidated in many observations.

The foundation for this insight was laid over fifty years ago through the Gaia theory, which was developed by biochemist James Lovelock and biologist Lynn Margulis. Their conclusions were contemporaneous with the development of system dynamics under Jay W. Forrester, who was active at MIT University, and with the development of the World3 model led by Dennis Meadows and presented by Frydlinger in Chapter 1. It was this model that supported the report *The Limits to Growth* (Donella Meadows et al.), which was sent to all the world's political leaders. In the report, written in 1972, the researchers warned that continued conventional growth could lead to resource scarcity, increasing environmental degradation and possible economic collapse in the twenty-first century. The measures proposed by the researchers were seen by many social actors as far too far-reaching and radical, but in recent years, they have been confirmed as necessary to meet human welfare. We are in a very troubling situation where humanity needs to act vigorously to safeguard the opportunities for a good life on Earth.

My and several other researchers' work on the Earth4All project and the new Earth4All model (which is an update of the World3 model) has been about staking out a rescue plan for humanity and the planet.[1] We have built an agenda to, together with the pressing environmental problems, also tackle the growing inequality and rising social tensions. We see dealing with these as a prerequisite for implementing the measures needed for sustainable development. The Earth4All model simulates options for the continued well-being of humans and the economic and environmental development of the rest of the century. We note that too few governments and companies have taken up and are acting against both environmental degradation and socio-economic problems. In some regions, poverty has been significantly reduced, but overall development is still too slow, and inequality is growing in most societies. Unfortunately, the efforts being made today are clearly inadequate.

Today's developments can be defined as 'too little, too late'. It is characterised by the well-being of people in general decreasing – measured as the overall impact of disposable income, public services, equality and quality of the living environment. Social tensions risk is rising due to a mix of rising inequality, persistently deep poverty in many countries, and increasing pressures on our societies due to warming and biodiversity loss. However, our conclusion is that it is possible for the entire world's population to achieve a good quality of life within the planetary boundaries. But then we must break with the development that has led to increasing economic disparities, overexploitation of many vital ecosystems and excessive emissions of greenhouse gases. What is needed is a full-scale change in the institutional rules of the game and sweeping changes in five areas:

(1) Poverty must be vigorously tackled through a combination of alternative development strategies.
(2) Growing inequality must also be tackled vigorously – for reasons of fairness, but also to avoid rising social tensions.

1. The Earth4All model and the survival guide is presented in the book: Dixson-Decleve, S., et al., Earth for All: A Survival Guide for Humanity, New Society Publishers, 2022.

(3) Empower women by making sure more women in positions of power are promoted globally through increased investments in education and health.
(4) Transform the world's food production. Invest in regenerative agriculture, changing diets and reducing food waste.
(5) Accelerate the decarbonisation of energy. Invest in rapid electrification and increased energy efficiency to enable a halving of CO_2 emissions every decade until 2050.

Frydlinger's book can be said to be a contextualisation and operationalisation of what these conclusions mean for businesses – large and small. The book is an important guide for lawyers, business leaders, sustainability officers, auditors, sustainability advisors and others and provides a necessary basic understanding to do what is required to transform today's business into a sustainable business – and thus contribute to the future of humanity on Earth.

Johan Rockström
Professor in Earth System Science
at the University of Potsdam
August 2023

Acknowledgements

Of all the books I've written, this one has been the hardest. While it is held together by some basic moral principles, it spans a wide variety of areas. Since I am not an expert in all the areas covered, I have depended on help. My thanks go first and foremost to David Collste, PhD and researcher at the Stockholm Resilience Center and, together with Jörgen Randers, one of the main creators of the Earth4All model. David has been responsible for important fact-checking of all parts of the book that concern the Earth4All model. My thanks also go to my friend and former colleague Erik Linnarsson, not only for his ever-encouraging comments but also for very valuable comments on Parts IV and V on contracts and supply chains. I would also like to thank my colleague Erik Engström for equally valuable comments on the same parts. Thanks to my colleague Alexandra Linusson and former colleague Sebastian Iso-Kamula for contributing to raising the quality of Part II on sustainable finance. Thanks also to Markus Ekelund, CEO and sustainability expert at the consulting firm 2050 Consulting, for doing an important review of Part III of the book.

Further thanks to Professor Johan Rockström. Had there been a Nobel Prize in Environmental Science, he would have been its first recipient. The origin of this book was a visit to a bookstore in Stockholm in the winter of 2022. I bought Johan and Owen Gaffney's book *Breaking Boundaries*. I was immediately shocked because it was actually only then that the scale of the climate crisis dawned on me. In addition to getting a shock, I was inspired by Johan's impressive combination of scientific thinking and the ability to explain the difficult in simple ways. I am, therefore, of course, extremely grateful to him for wanting to write the foreword to this book. Although I have a long way to go, I have still tried to follow in his footsteps in writing this book.

I also want to take the opportunity to thank two anonymous reviewers of an early manuscript of this book. I then submitted it to two other publishers, both with their main audience in the academic space, who then sent the manuscript for review to two academics. To summarise, they did not like the book. This is okay of course, the book is mainly addressed to practitioners. However, I do have academic ambitions with the book, and their input gave me good ideas on how to improve the text, which was possible only after my ego had returned from a quick tour to the pit. Based on their input, I have made the interpretive legal theory underlying the entire book much more explicit, and while doing that, I realised just how important this choice of theory is not only for legal theory but also for sustainable business. This has been made explicit in the much more elaborated Chapter 6 on corporate purpose.

As regards Chapter 6 and also Part IV on contracts, I want to thank professor and Nobel laureate Oliver Hart at Harvard University for valuable comments and several years of fruitful collaboration. Our collaboration regarding formal relational contracts has changed my professional life forever. Recently, our paths have crossed on the difficult question of corporate purpose, and as always, Oliver has shown, totally disregarding all prestige, that being a Nobel laureate matters little, but what is important is to find the best solutions to make the world a better place. Oliver personifies academic integrity, in combination with being brilliant and a very nice person. Thanks, Oliver.

Finally, thanks to my partner, Daniela Cristofori. Her many years of work as a graphic designer for the UN's various organisations and other NGOs, all of which work for a better and more sustainable world, have been very inspiring to me. Like Johan Rockström, she has the ability to make the difficult and very important simple and understandable, whether it is to illustrate refugee flows from Ukraine, women's right to land or the emergence and spread of pandemics. Without Daniela, there would have been no book. Thanks.

Introduction

In this book, an attempt is made to embrace a somewhat new and emerging area of law - sustainability law. The focus here is on sustainable business. The book rests on an underlying idea that what determines whether humanity is moving towards an unsustainable or sustainable world depends to a large extent on the *rules* applicable to business. The rules, herein referred to as the rules of the game, include laws, contracts, policies and informal social norms, which affect how people act within companies and how companies act on the market. Moving from unsustainable to sustainable business is about clarifying and changing these rules in essential respects.

Ultimately, the purpose of the book is purely practical, namely to:

- enable companies to conduct sustainable business in compliance with EU law, and
- assist companies to report these activities under EU law requirements for sustainability reporting.

The book is aimed at several categories of readers. It is aimed at business leaders who want to transition to sustainable business, sustainability professionals, people who work practically with sustainability reporting, in-house counsels and attorneys who support their companies and clients in the transition to sustainable business, to actors in the financial sector moving towards sustainable financing, and to people who work with contracts where sustainability matters are actualised. But it is also aimed at more academically oriented lawyers, as there is also an ambition in the book to embrace a new and emerging area of law.

The simultaneously practical and theoretical ambition of the book naturally affects the presentation. Some readers who primarily want to use the book for their practical sustainability work may find the book's more theoretical parts difficult to access, although attempts have been made to make the presentation easy to understand. Hopefully, this doesn't deprive the book of too much practical value. It's only the practicalities that matter - transforming all businesses into sustainable ones.

1 OUTLINE OF THE BOOK

The book is divided into five parts each having a different scope.

Part I deals with overarching issues of sustainability, law and morality. The overall purpose of this part is to provide readers with some fundamentals as to what sustainability is and what it means to conduct a sustainable business. These are insights that seem important for the in-the-end practical purpose of the book.

Sustainability is first discussed from an empirical perspective, using the powerful Earth4All model launched in 2022 in collaboration with a large number of researchers, including Earth system scientist Professor Johan Rockström. This is followed by an overview of the entire sustainability legal framework; from this overview, it is made clear that the EU sustainability laws aim to implement two overarching norms, stemming ultimately from the international treaties of human rights and environmental protection as well as the Agenda 2030: the norms of positive contribution and due diligence.

An attempt is then made to show the normative, ultimately moral, basis for what sustainability is all about, including sustainability law. The last chapter of Part I then deals with the fundamental subject of corporate purpose. An attempt is made to show that, in the move towards sustainable business, it is critical to free oneself of the apparently necessary shareholder-stakeholder dichotomy. Focus should instead be put on the 'ground rules of the game': the corporate purpose as a general idea of how the company generates value for its customers and corporate values basically meaning that everyone affected by the company's business should be treated as equals.

Part II deals with the wide subject of *sustainable finance*, with the main focus on the EU laws regulating various forms of disclosure requirements on actors in the financial market, such as the Sustainable Finance Disclosure Regulation (SFDR) and the EU taxonomy. This part builds directly on the first part of the book in that it shows how those laws should be interpreted as the EU legislator's attempt to implement the norms of positive contribution and due diligence into the financial markets. The core of this implementation is a basic concept of 'sustainable investments' as investments in a business which contribute to environmental or social objectives without harming such objectives and also follow good governance practices.

Part III is the most comprehensive part of the book, dealing with the topic of *sustainable business operations*. The main legal rules dealt with are the directives on Corporate Sustainability Due Diligence (CSDDD) and Corporate Sustainability Reporting (CSRD). It is shown how the EU legislator has set up what is referred to as an 'ideal image of sustainable business', again implementing the norms of positive contribution and due diligence. An attempt is then made to show how this ideal image can be used by companies to shift to sustainable business while at the same time complying with applicable sustainability laws. This covers the three areas of environmental, social and governance sustainability.

Part IV deals with the important subject of *contracts and sustainability*. An unsustainable business is largely so because of the way all the contracts that underpin a company are written. Through the rules of the game that the contracts create, peoples' and organisations' incentives to act in different ways are shaped, actions that can lead to sustainable or unsustainable results. Implementing the norms of positive contribution and due diligence often requires a rather fundamental shift from traditional views about contracts and how they should be written. Various business models and contracting models are described, as well as how they can be combined to obtain optimal results, also from a sustainability perspective.

There are many types of contracts, some of which are more relevant in business operations and others in various forms of financing. In Part IV, financing contracts are discussed, while customer-supplier contracts are left to the fifth part of the book.

Part V thus deals with *sustainable value* chains. Since the sustainability of the value chain is very much about how the contracts in the value chain are written, this part rests heavily on Part IV. However, Part V describes how contracts in the value chain are easily written with unsustainable results, after which an overall description is made of the importance of contracts in transforming the value chain into a sustainable one.

The book is deliberately limited in that it only deals with legislation adopted or at least politically agreed upon at the time of the book's publication. The European Commission is moving at a fast pace in delivering on its Green Deal. This means that new legislation is being adopted at the EU level, in particular, at a high pace. At the time of writing – in the spring of 2024 – there are several ongoing legislative processes where new legislation will likely be adopted just months after the book is published. So, it is important to remember that the book only deals with legislation that has been adopted and not with legislative proposals.

The book is also limited in that it does not address important areas of sustainability law such as environmental law, labour law, consumer law or data protection. These are areas of law, many with their roots in EU law, which all, I would argue, are based on the normative foundations of sustainability law – the protection of equality and freedom of humans. But at least in this edition of the book, they will not be dealt with.

2 SUSTAINABILITY AS A FIELD OF LAW

Sustainability law is not a reasonably well-defined area like other areas of law, such as corporate law, contract law or tort law. Sustainability law is based on a fundamental question, namely what sustainability law *should be* to serve its purpose. What is this purpose? Nothing less than to create and maintain rules of the game in the economy and society that make sure humanity can continue to live within boundaries that respect the dignity of every human over time and generations. This may seem surprising. However, this is what sustainability is ultimately about, which will be explained in more detail in the book.

Sustainability law encompasses areas of law that have existed for a long time, such as human rights, environmental law and labour law. It also includes the new EU regulations on corporate sustainability due diligence, sustainability reporting and related rules adopted as a result of the European Green Deal. Sustainability law encompasses both the mandatory and dispositive areas of law. It thus covers both mandatory statutory provisions and contract law.

The unifying element of all these sets of rules is a normative basis that deals with the right of all people to equality and freedom, which will be described below. Sustainability is often discussed in terms of global average temperatures, pollution, biodiversity loss, and so on. The matter is discussed in factual terms. However, as described in the book, sustainability is ultimately a moral issue. The moral equivalent of data that shows a climate crisis is widespread violations of human equality and freedom, where countries, companies and individuals have created negative effects on their surroundings without carrying the costs of them and having not taken the necessary actions to avoid such effects. This is, it will be argued at least, what the European Court of Human Rights established in its important ruling in *Verein Klimaseniorinnen Schweiz and others v. Switzerland* on 9 April 2024.

Ultimately, this is the normative basis of sustainability law. It runs like a red thread through human rights treaties, sustainability reporting requirements, environmental law standards of care, labour law, contracts with actors in the value chain, financing contracts regarding equity and debt, and so on. Through EU sustainability law, an attempt is being made to reshape how business is carried out by inducing them to act respect and contribute to human freedom and equality.

The claims made here about the normative basis of sustainability law are not necessarily uncontroversial. This will become clear, for example, when the question is discussed as to whether it is possible to achieve the EU law ideal image for sustainable business and at the same have profit maximisation as the company purpose.[2] The claims of a moral basis for sustainability law imply a legal theory, not least a theory that there is a close connection between law and morality. A supporter of so-called legal positivism could protest because legal positivism, in principle, denies that moral principles are needed to interpret the law unless there is an explicit reference to such principles in the law. Supporters of law and economics could also object, as this school of thought argues that the law should be interpreted in terms of how it contributes to socio-economic efficiency. The author, therefore, wishes to be clear that this book is largely based on what is usually called interpretivist legal theory, which is described in the next section. The section is mainly addressed to lawyers, in particular lawyers with a theoretical interest. Readers who are not interested can skip directly to Part I of the book. It should be emphasised, however, that the question of which theory of law to apply is in itself a matter of sustainability with important practical consequences. This will hopefully become clear, not least in Chapter 6 on the discussion about corporate purpose.

3 ON INTERPRETIVISM AS A THEORY OF LAW

Interpretivism, as a theory of law, is basically a practical theory of how judges judge and should adjudicate cases. In this way, it is a practical tool for any practising lawyer

2. *See* Chapter 13.

who interprets the law. If a judge in a case finds himself or herself in a situation where the legal text is not entirely clear about what the applicable law says, what does a judge do then? Here are some examples of situations that may arise:

- A company has applied for an environmental permit for a new plant. Has the company been able to demonstrate that it will use *the best available technology* for the plant it intends to build?
- A representative of the same company has offered a gift to the County Administrative Board to speed up the processing of the case regarding the same facility. All the facts are clear, but is the offered gift an *undue* benefit?
- The company has marketed products that will be produced in the proposed facility as 'climate-smart'. Consumers have reacted and consider it greenwashing. Is this *unfair* marketing according to the marketing legislation in the relevant jurisdiction?
- The company has published a sustainability report. It has now been alleged that the company has failed to comply with the reporting requirements because it has not disclosed all of its material impacts, risks and opportunities relating to sustainability matters. But what does the concept of *materiality* mean?

How does a judge act when this type of assessment is to be made? How *should* a judge act? This is basically a question of what the law is and how to go about finding that. These are practical questions, but to be able to answer them, a legal theoretical basis is required.

There is also a wider issue in the background, namely the question of the legitimacy of the law. The state has a monopoly on legislation, administration of justice and exercising force. In a democratic society, the question arises as to by what right the state can demand its citizens to follow laws, to follow court rulings and to accept being deprived of their liberty. The judge who is to interpret the bribery legislation has the power to sentence a person to imprisonment, and that person's freedom or lack of freedom can depend entirely on the interpretation of this legislation. Similarly, an administrator or judge may decide that a company should not be allowed to run a new large-scale business based entirely on the interpretation of the concept of best available techniques. How can this be justified? This is also a question of legal theory.

In order to understand interpretivism, it is appropriate to first briefly consider two other influential theories of law: legal positivism and utilitarianism, the latter represented mainly by law and economics.

3.1 Legal Positivism

One type of answer to the question of what is valid law and what legitimises the law comes from *legal positivism*.[3] Proponents of this school, which exists in a number of

3. For an overview of this theory, *see, e.g.*, Mindus, P. and Spaak, T., Cambridge Companion to Legal Positivitism, Cambridge University Press, 2021. The foremost representative of this theory

varieties, see law and the administration of justice as an empirical question, in principle separate from moral or normative judgments. To find out what the law says is, in simple terms, to make a retrospective factual investigation of what has happened from a legislative point of view and to assess the current situation in light of these facts. The legislature has, at some point in time, adopted a particular legal text, which describes the facts in which the legal text is applicable and the consequences if the facts are covered by the legal text. There are often preparatory works that needs to be taken into account. Furthermore, there may be a number of previous judgments of the courts, which a judge must relate to in the same way as to the legal text. Thus, when the judge is to determine whether a company has used the best available technology or whether a benefit is undue, it is simply a question of whether the description of the facts in these authoritative texts – legal texts, preparatory works and judgments – matches the facts of the case and based on that adjudicate the case. If, however, it is unclear what the current law says, then the judge will have to make his or her own judgment, which will essentially be a political judgment. Whatever you think about the appropriateness of this, according to the legal positivist, this is what happens – the judge makes an assessment based on what he or she thinks is best.

No legal theory can avoid dealing with the question of the legitimacy of law, i.e., the question of how law and the judge enforcing laws can rightly claim authority over citizens subject to the rules of law. There are many rules in society, from laws to rules of chess to informal rules about appropriate behaviour and only some of those rules are viewed as laws and thus have the authority of laws. A defining characteristic of much of legal positivism is the claim that this authority is *not* taken from some kind of underlying morality. Most laws can claim to be valid as laws because they have been adopted using processes laid down by other laws.[4] But what makes those other laws valid? Since morality is taken out of the picture by legal positivism, it must be something empirical that ultimately makes all laws valid. Some positivists here refer to an implicit *rule of recognition* used by judges.[5] Ultimately, laws are valid not because of their normative foundations but simply because judges and lawyers have developed a practice of recognising some rules as laws and other rules as not being laws.

3.2 Utilitarianism and Law and Economics

Another type of answer to what is law comes from *utilitarianism*. This theory also exists in a number of variants. If the legal positivist looks backwards to history to assess what a valid law is, then the utilitarians ultimately look into the future. They ask

of law is H.L.A. Hart. *See* Hart, H.L.A., The Concept of Law, Oxford University Press, 2012. Another important, more contemporary representative is Joseph Raz. *See*, *e.g.*, Raz, J., Between Authority and Interpretation, Oxford University Press, 2009. The presentation of the meaning of legal positivism is, of course, simplified, not least because there are many representatives of this trend who do not all agree on all issues. Legal positivitism, like utilitarianism below, is presented in a simplified way to make interpretivist theory more understandable.

4. Hart makes an important distinction between primary and secondary rules, where the latter are rules about adopting the former rules.
5. Hart, *ibid.*, p. 103.

themselves which ruling will create the greatest possible benefit to society in the future and judge accordingly.

The dominant variant of utilitarianism is law and economics, where the thought models of economics are used to analyse law.[6] The law is then seen as a tool for achieving economically efficient results for society. There are various views within law and economics on what efficiency criteria to use, but a common approach is to say that a socially efficient outcome is when economic resources are allocated to those who value them the most. Such allocations arise in a market where exchanges can take place without transaction costs, i.e., without costs for buyers and sellers to find each other, to assess the value of what is exchanged, to negotiate and enter into contracts, to monitor compliance with contracts, and so on. This idealised state can be said to constitute a model that a judge must relate to, which means that the judge should judge so that the same result occurs as would have occurred in the idealised state.

A concept such as the *best available technology* should, under this theory, be interpreted as the technology that means maximum social efficiency is obtained. To interpret anti-corruption legislation, a benefit is to be considered *undue* if it leads to decisions being taken that differ from the decision that would have been taken in a fully efficient economy, where no extraneous remunerations are paid.

3.3 Legal Interpretivism

What legal positivism and law and economics have in common is that they see the question of what is valid law as an empirical question, as a question of what is a fact, either historically or in the future. Interpretivism – the legal theory adopted in this book and, in the author's view, the only theory that can make sense of sustainability law – does not dismiss these legal theories but sees them as incomplete and incapable of explaining how judges actually act and how they should act where the legal text needs to be interpreted.[7]

It is impossible to deduce, based on empirical facts alone, what is the best available technique, what is undue in a benefit, what kind of marketing is unfair, when an impact on sustainability matters is material and so on. Facts about the past and the future are important for the assessment of what the law says, but in the end, the question of law is a normative question. It is ultimately about the basic norms that make legislation, the administration of justice and the exercise of executive power

6. The literature in law and economics is vast. For an overview, *see, e.g.*: Parisi, Francesco (ed.), The Oxford Handbook of Law and Economics: Volume 1: Methodology and Concepts (online edn, Oxford Academic 2017). The foremost proponent of law and economics is probably Richard Posner. *See, e.g.*, Posner, R., The Economic Analysis of Law, Wolters Kluwer Law Business, 2014. Other important proponents are Ronald Coase and Guido Calabresi. It could be argued that law and economics is not a form of utilitarianism, but some other form of consequentialism. The basic features of law and economics are, however, the same as in utilitarianism, why it still seems highly relevant to claim that law and economics is a variant of utilitarianism.
7. The foremost representative of interpretivism is Ronald Dworkin. *See, e.g.*, the books Dworkin, R., Taking Rights Seriously, Bloomsbury Academic, 2013, Law's Empire, Harvard University Press, 1986 and Justice for Hedgehogs, Harvard University Press, 2011. Other proponents of interpretivism, different from Dworkin, are Mark Greenberg and Nicos Stavropoulos.

legitimate. The legislative text, preparatory work and case law must be *interpreted* (hence interpretivism) based on the normative principles that also justify the exercise of state power.

Interpretivism gives a fundamentally different answer to the question of how a judge arrives at what the law is. Every ruling claims to be correct. You could say that it claims to be 'true'. A positivist and utilitarian then argues, simplified, that this truth claim is the same as when one says that the Earth is round, that the sky is blue, or that inflation amounted to 8.5% last year. It involves making claims and comparing them to reality to verify whether or not claims are true. Of course, we also make claims that something is true and correct in a variety of situations where it is not something that can be verified against an empirically observable reality. Every time a person says that a party was nice, a movie was good, a concert was bad, a poem is a masterpiece, one person is good, another person is evil, and so on, the person making this claims to be saying something that is in some sense true. But of course, that does not mean it is true in the same sense that the Earth is round or that inflation reached a certain level.

Someone may say here (and many have said) that there is no basis for claiming that a statement about the quality of a poem, the pleasantness of a party, and so on is true and correct. Precisely because these are not statements that can be verified against an empirical reality, all such things are subjective and, therefore, relative. However, anyone who says this immediately falls into a trap, illustrated by the following example. A Swede says: 'All Swedes lie all the time.' Since the person who says so is Swedish, they probably mean they are lying. But he/she is making a truth claim, so he cannot reasonably claim that all Swedes lie all the time. Anyone who says that all claims of a moral or aesthetic nature are relative or subjective because they cannot be empirically verified is making a corresponding claim. This statement cannot in itself be empirically verified and must, therefore, be a statement of value that, by definition, cannot be true. A claim that all morality is relative is in itself a moral claim since the practical consequence is that all actions are permitted.

However, this type of paradox only affects those who believe there is only one way to make claims of truth, namely by saying something that can be verified against an empirical reality (that the Earth is round, that inflation has reached x%, that the legislature has adopted a law with the text content y on a certain date, and so on). As soon as you abandon that idea and start thinking as people usually do, you realise there is more than one way to make claims about truth. To interpret something means to engage in a different kind of truth-seeking. Here, truth is about coherence – lack of contradiction and existence of coherence – and less about the correspondence between statement and reality.

Why this emphasis on the importance of coherence in the interpretation of the law? Fundamentally, the state can only legitimise the exercise of its monopoly to use force and interpret the law by treating all citizens as equals. A state that provides benefits to half the population at the expense of the other half cannot legitimately claim obedience from its citizens. This obedience can only be demanded if the state treats everyone as equals. To treat everyone as equals is to consistently treat all citizens according to a set of norms and principles, which apply equally to everyone, rich and poor, male and female, employee and employer, and so on.

Thus, when concepts such as 'unfair', 'best available technique', 'undue', and so on are to be interpreted, the judge must seek help from the normative principles that underpin, legitimise and bind the rules of the legal system. In this book, there is a strong emphasis on some of the most fundamental norms of the legal system – equality and freedom. Through an interpretivist approach, I have tried to show that there is a normative, moral connection between widely different areas, such as the rules on sustainability reporting, bribery, environmental law, labour law and consumer law.

Although there is a strong emphasis on sustainability morality in the book, this should not be mistaken for the book taking a so-called natural law perspective. According to the old natural law, there was a morality instilled in humans by the Christian God, and the law expressed this morality. This, of course, was pure metaphysics and alien to modern legal theory. Law is best viewed as part of a wider *political morality*.[8] This perspective implies a hierarchical tree structure, which is worth keeping in mind. Political morality should be distinguished from personal morality. Personal morality is transformed into a political morality between people who are part of the same political community, such as the EU. While personal morality is concerned with what people owe each other, political morality is concerned with what people who are part of this political community owe each other, precisely as members of that community.

Here, the rights of personal morality are transformed into political rights. The most fundamental political right is the right to be treated with dignity, expressed in the principles of equality and freedom. As shown in the book, this is expressed, for example, in the UN Declaration of Human Rights. However, no individual can rely on this declaration to enforce a right in court. Only political rights that have been transformed into legal rights can be enforced in this way.

What is referred to in the book as 'sustainability morality' is thus a political morality based on the rights to equality and freedom. These political rights and accompanying obligations have been partially transformed into legal rights and obligations. As an example, the ILO's conventions lay the foundation for workers' political rights, which are then partly transformed into legal rights through national labour law.

The interpretivist perspective here means that the legal rights and obligations expressed in legislation, case law and so on must be interpreted in light of the broader political morality or the more fundamental political rights that the legal rights and obligations express. It is basic political morality that constitutes the common basis for interpretation of, for example, concepts such as 'unfair', 'undue', 'the best available technology', and so on.

8. *See* Dworkin, R., Justice for the Hedgehogs, Harvard University Press, 2011, pp. 327 ff. and 400 ff.

3.4 Does It Matter?

These may seem to be questions of theory and of little practical importance for a sustainable business. Unfortunately, the opposite is true. The three legal theories presented here - legal positivism, law and economics and interpretivism - are three different ways of looking at the world, forcefully shaped by mental models which have profound effects on how the world is analysed, what problems are viewed as relevant and, most importantly, what policies to adopt, how to interpret the law and how to adjudicate cases. As indicated above, the choice of legal theory is, in fact, also a sustainability question. In which ways will be discussed in various parts of the book.

PART I Sustainability, Law and Morality

CHAPTER 1

An Unsustainable World

What is sustainability really about from an overall perspective? There is no simple answer to this question. The flow of information about elevated average temperatures, biodiversity loss, supply chains where people work under inhumane conditions, corruption of public sector officials and so on is massive. So, too, is the flow of information on investments and technological initiatives linked to the 'green transition', social investments and so on. There are 17 global development goals broken down into 169 sub-goals – in other words, the picture is complex, to say the least. The mix of massive amounts of scientific and unscientific information makes it difficult to get a grip on sustainability. It should also be added that the whole issue is highly politicised and that different initiatives or lack of initiatives linked to, for example, greenhouse gas emissions, are a weapon in new and old party-political confrontations.

So, of course, there is no uniform definition of what sustainability or sustainable business is. It is common to use the abbreviation ESG in the context of sustainability – Environmental, Social and Governance. The acronym points to three dimensions of sustainability. Environmental sustainability is about the exploration and consumption of Earth's resources, greenhouse gas emissions, and so on. Social sustainability is about people – poverty, equality, gender equality and so on. Governance-related sustainability includes bribery and corruption. So far, so good, but it helps little to get an overview.

Reference is often made to the Brundtland Report's definition of sustainable development: development that meets the needs of the present without compromising the ability of future generations to meet their own needs. There is power in this definition, but it serves little to specify what sustainability is all about.

As a preliminary definition to create an overview, sustainability is about the fact that humanity – states, companies, organisations, and people – use nature's and society's resources in a way that exceeds nature's and society's capacity for restoration and stability. Eventually, it is about an undermining of nature and society that leads to their collapse and, at the same time, also drags the economy and the market with it in the fall. The unsustainable path embarked on by humanity is not the result of conscious and coordinated action by humanity. But it is also not something we have stumbled upon by chance. It results from certain types of behaviour patterns repeating over and over again, year after year, decade after decade – until collapse occurs unless there is a change of course. That behaviours are repeated depends on the rules of the game that are followed. Thus, there is a logic here, and it is necessary to capture the most important aspects of this logic to understand what has happened and what is happening.

A powerful tool for understanding sustainability and sustainable business is the Earth4All model, which was launched in 2022.[9] In this book, the Earth4All model will serve as a starting point for descriptions of and discussions about sustainability law, the meaning of the concept of sustainability, and so on. Of course, I don't claim that the Earth4All model is the only way to understand what sustainability is about, but the model presents a coherent and scientifically based framework that makes something very complex understandable.

Earth For All is a collaboration between the Club of Rome, the Potsdam Institute for Climate Impact Research, the Stockholm Resilience Center and the Norwegian Business School.[10] The model is a further development of two earlier powerful models for understanding economic and environmental development from a sustainability perspective: the World3 model described in the book *Limits to Growth*[11] and the model of the nine planetary boundaries.[12] The Earth4All model is also based on a wealth of research on the links between economic inequality and environmental degradation, social unrest and other negative phenomena.

1.1 THE NINE PLANETARY BOUNDARIES

One of the greatest difficulties in understanding sustainability is that there are so many mutually influencing factors that together create the systematics in society and economy that have today set humanity on a course towards the collapse of nature and society. When everything is connected, where do you start?

A good place to start is in nature, on Earth. Nature is a prerequisite for any society and economy. Most people know that the climate, biodiversity, the world's oceans and so on are endangered. That they are endangered implies there is a limit to what they can handle. If nature's resources and resilience were infinite, there would be no environmental crisis. So, where are the limits to what nature can handle? Is it even possible to identify them? And what is meant by 'nature'? It is an umbrella term for an enormous number of disparate phenomena: forests, seas, mountains, weather, wildlife, vegetation, air, land, waterways, and so on. Are there common limits for all these

9. *See* Dixson-Decleve, S., et al., Earth for All: Survival Guide for Humanity, New Society Publishers, 2022.
10. *See* www.earth4all.life.
11. Meadows, D., et al., Limits to Growth: The 30 Year Update, Chelsea Green Publishing Co., 2013.
12. Rockström, J., Steffen, W., Noone, K., et al., A Safe Operating Space for Humanity. 461 Nature 472-475 (2009).

disparate phenomena? Or is it necessary to find an enormous number of different limits for widely different parts of nature?

Today, many of these questions have been answered, although intensive research is still ongoing. In 2009, a research report was published in the journals *Nature* and *Ecology and Society* by, among others, Johan Rockström - today world-famous, then relatively unknown - and a large number of other researchers. Somewhat surprisingly, they found that nature can be divided into nine major so-called Earth system processes.[13]

- **The climate system**, which, among other things, regulates Earth's average temperature.
- **Stratospheric ozone depletion**, which regulates, among other things, the amount of dangerous ultraviolet radiation from the sun that reaches Earth's surface.
- **Ocean acidification**, which endangers biodiversity and controls the exchange of value between the Earth's surface and the atmosphere.
- **Biosphere integrity**, i.e., biodiversity, which, among other things, affects Earth's ability to cope with changes and shocks.
- **Land system change,** forests, wetlands, arable land, urbanisation and so on, which not only control Earth's uptake of carbon dioxide from the atmosphere but also biodiversity.
- **Freshwater use,** fresh water is described as the 'bloodstream of the biospheres' - crucial for life on Earth.
- **Biogeochemical flows,** where nitrogen and phosphorus are important substances for Earth's biochemical flows, but where human interference with these processes already has serious consequences today.
- **Novel entities,** chemicals and other substances that do not exist naturally but have been produced by humans. These include plastics, air pollutants, such as emissions, water vapour and so on, affect the planetary processes.

For most of these systems or processes, the researchers identified the boundaries to what the Earth system can handle without undermining the conditions for human life and development. Beyond these boundaries, there is a risk of changes that could lead to nature going from being friendly to being non-friendly to humans. In the worst case, it can lead to various forms of collapse. The nine planetary processes have been stable for millennia. For about 12,000 years - roughly from the time humans became settled until 1950, the average temperature on Earth rose and changed by at most 1 °C. This epoch is referred to by scholars as the *Holocene*. Although changes occurred, Earth remained relatively stable, measured in terms of, for example, average temperature, ozone layer thickness, ocean acidity, and so on. Since the Industrial Revolution in the 1800s, however, humans have changed these processes and Earth's conditions for life

13. For a good description of the model of the nine planetary boundaries, *see* Rockström, J. and Gaffney, O., Breaking Boundaries: The Science of Our Planet, DK, 2021.

through increased use of Earth's resources, the burning of fossil fuels, and so on. In the 1950s, a point was reached where the impact of humanity had become so great that the most important processes of the Earth system no longer existed independently of humans. Instead, humans became the driving force behind virtually all changes in the Earth system. This is considered so important that some scientists say that Earth has thus entered a new geological epoch - *Anthropocene* (from the Greek word for man: *anthropos*).

For each of these nine planetary processes, the researchers have identified the factors that govern each process and how they are related to the other processes, as well as where the boundaries are for each process's self-sustaining ability. It has been shown that in six of the nine systems, the boundaries have been crossed: the climate system, biosphere integrity, freshwater use, land use, novel entities and biochemical flows.[14]

1.2 LIMITS TO GROWTH

Nature and the planet are thus in a serious crisis and are in danger of no longer supporting human life as we know it. How did it get to this point? What has happened?

To answer this question, it is necessary to broaden the perspective and include nature, society and the economy in the analysis. Already in the early 1970s, one of the most important documents on the theme of sustainability was published - the report *The Limits of Growth*, published by the Club of Rome. The report was revised in 1992 and 2004 with updated data. The purpose of the report was to shed light on the limits of population growth and economic growth since Earth's resources and its ability to absorb pollutants are limited. One of the main reasons for the crossing of the planetary boundaries is that humanity is over-exploiting nature's resources and, as a result, disposing of the waste from this resource exploitation in the same nature.

As part of the report, four MIT researchers developed a computer-based system dynamics model called World3. Such a model makes it possible to study and understand complex systems - such as the social-ecological system - by identifying the most important parts and how these affect each other, often in so-called reinforcing feedback loops.[15]

Like many system dynamic models, the World3 model is not designed to make precise predictions about the future, but to increase understanding and analyse different conceivable future scenarios based on knowledge of relationships in the systems studied. By definition, the concept of sustainability includes a temporal dimension. That something is unsustainable means that something cannot continue without something else eventually breaking. That the World3 model is system dynamic means it can be used to analyse developments over time.

14. Rockström and Gaffney, *ibid.*, p. 108.
15. A good understanding of sustainability requires a good understanding of systems theory. A good introduction to the subject is: Meadows, D., Thinking in Systems, Chelsea Green Publishing, 2008.

The logic of the World3 model is simple and complex at the same time. It is simple in its premise. It describes a tension between factors that drive growth on the one hand and factors that limit that growth on the other. At the same time, all these factors also affect each other, which makes the model complex.

1.2.1 The Growth Factors

The fundamental growth factors that form the basis of the World3 model are population growth and economic growth. Both of these show so-called *exponential growth*, i.e., the growth rate increases the greater the growth. Population growth is a function of birth rates and mortality rates. Let's ignore the mortality rates for the time being and assume that only new children are being born. Let's imagine a population of 1 million people, half of whom – 500,000 men and women – have one child together. 250,000 new children will be born. The population then increases to 1.25 million, i.e., by 25%. Given the same proportion, i.e., that half of the population are men and women who have one child together, 312,500 new children will be born, which is about 25% more children born than when the population was 1 million individuals. The population then increases to 1,562,500 people. When half of this population – 781,250 men and women – give birth to one child per couple, the population increases by 390,625 individuals, again about 25% more than when the population was 1,562,500 individuals. The growth here is exponential. A growth rate of 25% means that more children are born in each generation.

The economy too, as it stands today and when the World3 model was created, shows exponential growth, measured in gross domestic product (that is, the value of all goods and services produced). Regarding population growth, it's about more people giving birth to more children. In the case of the economy, it is instead a matter of increasing the amount of capital used to produce goods and services (which would correspond to the number of men and women in the previous example), which means that the volumes of goods and services produced increase. Economic growth is mainly a function of the amount of capital used to produce goods and services minus depreciation. Let us ignore write-downs for the moment and assume that EUR 1 billion worth of goods and services are produced with the help of factories and machinery worth EUR 100 million. Not all the goods and services produced will be consumed. A certain proportion of the goods and services produced are factories and machines, which are used to produce other goods and services. Assume that 5% of the value of the goods and services produced is such capital, i.e., EUR 50 million. In the next round, if we disregard write-downs due to wear and tear, factories and machinery worth EUR 150 million will be used for production, which, all else being equal, gives a GDP of EUR 1.5 billion. In the next round, factories and machinery worth EUR 225 million will be used instead, resulting in a GDP of EUR 2.25 billion. And so on.

This is simple math. However, exponential growth is a surprising phenomenon. The creators of the World3 model refer to the old story of the farmer who invented the chess game and who was promised by the king that he would receive as much rice as would be given if, on the chessboard, one grain of rice was first placed and then doubled the amount of grain on each of the remaining 63 chess squares. All in all, it sums up to 18.4 trillion grains of rice, i.e., an absurdly large amount of grains of rice – larger than the entire world's current production in one year already on the 54th square.[16]

1.2.2 Limits

How long can exponential growth of population and economy continue, given that Earth is not inexhaustible of resources? This was one of the main questions in *Limits to Growth*. The World3 model includes several limits that growth will encounter. Food and water are obvious examples. Fresh water and land are limited resources. Another limitation is energy sources, not least non-renewable ones such as oil, coal and gas. Other natural resources, such as minerals and metals, are also limited, non-renewable resources. Another type of limit is the emissions that Earth can absorb and manage in a broader sense without leading to increased death rates and increased wear and tear on productive capital or passing tipping points.

Already with the two growth factors of population growth and economic growth and the three limiting factors of food and water, non-renewable resources and emissions, it is possible to understand an essential part of the logic of the World3 model. As the population and economy grow, the need for food and water will increase, more energy will be consumed, and more emissions will end up in the atmosphere. If we assume there is no technological development, the costs in the economy will increase. It will become more and more expensive to produce energy, emissions will increase the cost of replacing and maintaining productive capital, and it will become more and more expensive to produce food and other necessities. At the same time, emissions and the difficulty of feeding the growing population will increase mortality. Growth will run out of boundaries. Which limits come into play first – whether they are restrictions on food production, energy costs or something else – depends on various factors, but the important thing is that the limits will eventually come into play.

1.2.3 Scenarios: Collapse and Stabilisation

The description above is a major simplification of the World3 model but still captures the essence. The creators of the model entered assumptions into the model based on historical data about natural resources, how emissions affect the health and consumption of fixed capital, growth rates, birth and mortality rates, and so on. By varying the assumptions in the model, they created different future scenarios. In the majority of these scenarios, the model shows an important pattern, namely that a more or less strong growth in the latter part of the twentieth century would turn into collapse in the

16. *See* https://www.mathscareers.org.uk/the-rice-and-chessboard-legend/.

twenty-first century. In one scenario, however, the world achieves stability. Below, four such scenarios are presented:[17]

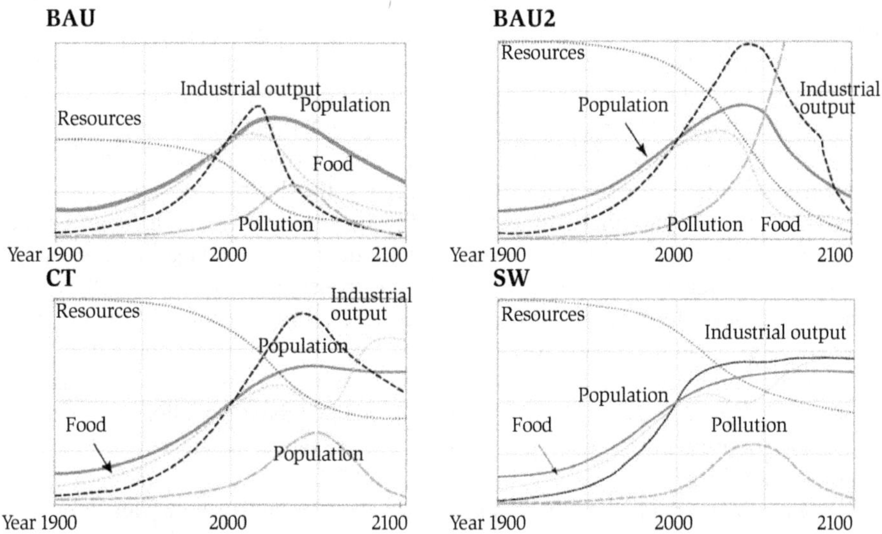

In the BAU scenario (BAU = business as usual), economic and population growth accelerates to a point where natural resources begin to run out, after which production turns sharply downward into collapse. In the BAU2 scenario, the researchers instead assumed that Earth has twice as much resources – for example, oil – as in the BAU scenario. This shifts the point when the constraints of natural resources begin to affect the economy. But in this scenario, the production of non-renewable energy leads to a steep rise in pollution, which today is perhaps most clearly illustrated by global warming, to a point where this begins to affect maintenance of fixed capital and health so much that collapse once again occurs.

In the CT scenario, the researchers made assumptions about the introduction of a large number of technological innovations in, for example, food production, prevention of air pollution, and so on. As shown in the figure above, this is a better scenario than the previous two, but it still ultimately leads to sharply negative economic growth (i.e., contraction). The reasons for this are discussed in the next section. In SW (stabilised world), collapse is avoided, but economic and population growth levels off. In this scenario, the researchers assumed voluntary restrictions on childbearing (which was an important focus at the time of writing the report) and general acceptance to reduce consumption and exploitation of Earth's resources.

It is important to understand why three of the four scenarios above and most of the other scenarios in *Limits to Growth* lead not only to stagnation but to collapse. This

17. Taken from Herrington, G. Update to Limits to Growth: Comparing the World3 Model with Empirical Data, 25(3) Journal of Industrial Ecology, June 2021, 614-626 DOI: 10.1111/jiec.13084.

is about the consequences of crossing the limits. For a car driver, there is a limit where it is too late to brake to avoid colliding with a rock wall in front, a limit that depends on speed, whether there are slippery conditions and so on. In the same way, there is a limit beyond which, for example, natural fish stocks have declined so much due to fishing that they cannot recover, as has happened in many parts of the world. The World3 model illustrated that similar dynamics can be assumed to exist at the global level regarding the extraction of natural resources and the pollution that production entails.

Both economic growth and population growth are a function of self-reinforcing and balancing forces or feedback loops. Population growth is a function of birth rates and mortality rates. If the mortality rate exceeds the birth rate, the population decreases. Economic growth is a function of investments in, for example, factories and machinery (which create a positive feedback loop) and of wear and tear on this capital (which creates a negative feedback loop). If the positive side dominates, growth will be exponential unless there are factors that limit growth. In the case of the World3 model, this could be a question of voluntary restrictions on childbearing or consumption. If the negative side dominates, there is a risk of a sharp decrease unless there are forces that counteract the decrease. If the value of maintenance of fixed capital begins to exceed the value of investments in productive capital, negative economic growth occurs. This is pure mathematics.

The reason for collapse in the majority of the World3 model's scenarios is that the growth in population and economy causes such damage to nature that the countervailing forces cannot prevent a sharp decline in production capacity and population numbers. When, for example, the level of pollution reaches a certain limit, the damage to productive capital (such as machinery and factories) will be so great that there will not be enough money and resources to both limit capital destruction and reduce wear and tear *and* to invest in new productive capital *and* invest in the technologies necessary to reduce further pollution.

The phenomenon is not uncommon in business, and when it occurs, it often leads to bankruptcy. When costs start to exceed revenues, the trend can often be reversed through increased investments in, for example, marketing, better products or services, and so on. But there will come a point where the company's equity will start to run out, at which point it must either borrow or ask the shareholders for more equity. However, the loans increase interest costs, which risks reinforcing the downward trend. In the end, shareholders will not want to inject more capital either because it is believed that the contributions will not be enough to make the revenues exceed the costs. The whole thing leads to bankruptcy unless you can restructure the company by writing down the debts and reducing interest costs and other costs.

For companies, there are legal rules on, for example, corporate restructuring. That doesn't exist in nature. If Earth is seen as a bank that injects natural resources, as capital then nature has a point where it can no longer recover on its own (pay its own interest and amortisation) and help the economy to limit costs and spiral downwards. It is when this occurs that the World3 model predicts that collapse will occur.

1.2.4 The Importance of Technology

The World3 model includes several elements of technological development. However, the researchers behind the model also show the risk of having overconfidence in technology's potential to solve the problems created by exponential growth in the economy and population. In *Limits to Growth*, the authors describe several scenarios in the World3 model, where different technologies are introduced to manage the limits regarding, for example, food production or pollution. Still, most of these scenarios lead to collapse.

This is due to several reasons. If only one technology is introduced, for example for pollution prevention, it only means that growth encounters another of the model's limits, such as food production. If many technologies are introduced, the model shows that the total costs may eventually be so high that the economy simply cannot cope with it. Another important reason is there are important delays in both the World3 model and in the real world. If growth hits a certain limit, such as global warming, it will take time for people to react, before political decisions are made, before the research has begun and yielded results, and before the results of the research have been commercialised on a broad front, and so on. In the World3 model, some scenarios assume that it takes twenty years for a technology to spread widely from the laboratory stage.

The point is not that technology cannot help solve problems. The point is that technology that does not address the roots of the problems - exponential growth of the economy and population - is not enough. In addition, technological development can, in many cases, be downright counterproductive. This is called Jevons' paradox and is because increased efficiency through technology often leads to increased resource utilisation.[18] For example, the development of technology in the world over the past fifty years has taken place in parallel with a sharp increase in emissions and material footprint.[19]

1.2.5 Accuracy of the World3 Model

The World3 model has been discussed here in some detail not only because it creates a good understanding of the Earth4All model, which will be used more in this book but also because later measurements have shown that the World3 model, despite all the criticism the model and its creators received at the time of its publication, has proven to be remarkably accurate. In one of several studies that have been done, updated data has been entered long after (fifty years) when the original model was created. The study showed that the world's actual development matches the BAU and BAU2

18. https://en.wikipedia.org/wiki/Jevons_paradox.
19. Wiedmann, T., et al., Scientists' Warning on Affluence, 11(1) Nature Communications, 2020, 3107.

scenarios relatively well and that the matching with the hopeful SW scenario is low.[20]

1.3 RESEARCH ON ENVIRONMENTAL DEGRADATION AND ECONOMIC INEQUALITY

In parallel with the increasingly developed understanding of the planetary systems and the limits of growth, research has been conducted that shows the connection between environmental degradation and economic inequality. This is an extensive area of research, which can only be outlined here briefly. However, it is central to understanding sustainability, not least because social sustainability is very much about equality.

1.3.1 Data on Economic Inequality

Inequality can be measured in many ways. It is becoming more common to measure the distribution of income and assets between, on the one hand, the 10% of the population that earns/owns the most and, on the other hand, 50% of the population that earns/owns the least. The World Inequality Report 2022 presents data on inequality in the world and in each individual country.[21] The report states that:

- The richest 10% of the world's population receives 52% of revenue, while the poorest 50% receives 8.5% of revenue.
- The richest 10% of the population owns 76% of global wealth, while the poorest 50% owns 2% of global wealth.
- Globally, inequality in the world is about as high as it was in the early 1900s.
- Inequality *between* countries has been declining since 1980. However, inequality *within* countries has increased since 1980, after having had a long period of decline from the end of World War II.
- The richest 10% generates 48% of global greenhouse gas emissions. The poorest 50% generates 12% of global emissions. In the US, the numbers are more extreme, with the richest 10% accounting for 73% of emissions. In Europe, the richest 10% are responsible for 32% of emissions.

1.3.2 Economic Inequality and Sustainability

Whether economic inequality is a problem or not depends to a large extent on political beliefs or normative starting points. However, there are several interrelated links

20. Herrington, G., Update to Limits to Growth: Comparing the World3 Model with Empirical Data, 25(3) Journal of Industrial Ecology, June 2021, 614-626. *See also* Turner, G., A Comparison of the Limits to Growth with 30 Years of Reality, 18(3) Global Environmental Change, 2008, 397-411 *and also* Turner, G., Is Global Collapse Imminent? Melbourne Sustainable Society Institute, The University of Melbourne, 2014.
21. Chancel, L., et al., World Inequality Report 2022.

between economic inequality and environmental degradation that are difficult to ignore, regardless of political persuasion. A common argument against politically initiated redistribution policies, for example through taxes, is that in a growing economy, everyone benefits, even the poorest. This is true; the number of poor people in the world has radically decreased since 2000, partly because of economic growth. The problem, apart from the fact that almost half the world's population still lives on less than EUR 4 a day,[22] is that the world's population annually consumes far more of Earth's resources than Earth can naturally regenerate. This leads to climate change that manifests itself as extreme weather, natural disasters, etc., which mainly affects the poorer population groups, which increases inequality. In other words, it is a question of poverty-reducing growth based on the fact that a minority of the population has engaged in the unsustainable consumption of resources. This resource consumption then hits the poorest and returns them to poverty. The poverty-reducing growth turns out to be based on 'loans' from nature, and when nature demands 'repayment', poverty and inequality increase again. Such growth cannot reasonably be considered to solve the issue of poverty.

It is also worth noting that inequality as such is contributing to climate change. Research shows that increasing inequality increases consumption aimed at showing social status.[23] Furthermore, inequality undermines trust in society,[24] increases violence,[25] and so on. Societies with lower social capital and trust function less well in a democratic sense, i.e., have a poorer capacity for collective decision-making.[26] This affects the possibility of adopting legislation on, for example, measures to combat climate change. The yellow vest protest movement in France, which had its origins in the proposed increases in petrol prices, is often cited as an example of social resistance to climate improvement measures motivated by feelings of injustice and inequality.

The insight into the connection between economic inequality, climate change, and social unsustainability has, of course, not escaped the attention of the business community. The World Business Partnership for Sustainable Development (WBCSD) is a global coalition of leaders of over 200 of the world's most sustainable companies. The organisation's purpose is to accelerate the transition to a sustainable world by making sustainable business operations more successful. The WBCSD has set up the Business Commission to Tackle Inequality (BCTI), which comprises CEOs and other senior executives from companies such as Unilever, HSBC, Equinor, Manpower, Bain & Company, Nestlé, Hitachi, Mercedes-Benz, IKEA and representatives of several non-profit organisations. In the report *Tackling Inequality: An Agenda for Business Action,* BCTI first refers to the data from the World Inequality Report 2022 reported above.[27] It

22. Dixson-Declève et al., Earth for All, p. 59.
23. *See, e.g.*, Loughnan et al. Economic Inequality Is Linked to Biased Self-perception, 22(10) Psychological Science, 2011, 1254-1258.
24. *See, e.g.*, Fehr, D., et al., Inequality, Fairness and Social Capital, 120 European Economic Review, 2000, 103566.
25. *See, e.g.*, Elgar, F.J. and Aitken, N., Income Equality, Trust and Homicide in 33 Countries, 21(2) European Journal of Public Health, 2021, 241-246.
26. *See, e.g.*, Putnam, R., Making Democracy Work: Civic Traditions in Modern Italy, Princeton University Press, 1994.
27. BCTI, Tackling Inequality: An Agenda for Business Action, 2023.

states that economic inequality poses a systemic risk to society, the economy and businesses. With reference to the research in the field, six consequences of economic inequality are listed:

- Erosion of trust in the political and economic system.
- Increased polarisation in society leads to lower trust, reduced willingness to improve the living conditions of others, increased likelihood of crime and belief in conspiracy theories.
- Fuelling civil and political unrest, including riots and strikes.
- Increased damage caused by crises, i.e., inequality, usually exacerbates damage caused by climate crises, pandemics, etc.
- Limiting economic growth, including through reduced consumption and investment in human capital.
- Undermining the collective capacity to create sustainable development, as those affected by inequality will resist necessary changes that are perceived as unfair.

The BCTI also points to the clear commercial risks that economic inequality can pose to companies and to measures that companies can take to manage the risks. Some of these analyses and proposals are presented later in the book.

1.3.3 The Dynamics and Logic of Inequality

What is the reason for the increase in economic inequality? This, too, is now a well-studied area. Although not all connections are clear, many of the overall features are.[28] It is important here to look separately at the two forms of economic inequality: differences between incomes from different types of labour and differences between income from capital and labour. Although inequality in these areas is often due to common causes, there are also important differences.

When explaining *differences between incomes from different forms of labour,*[29] the main explanatory factor is simply the supply and demand of different skills. If there is a strong demand for software programmers, for example, but supply is limited, salaries for this category will rise. In particular, they will rise more relative to other categories – such as warehouse workers – where demand will fall due to technological developments that replace the need for these skills. The example shows that differences between wage incomes will largely be a function of the education system – which affects the supply side – on the one hand, and technological developments – which affect the demand side – on the other.

28. The following is based on Piketty, T., Capital in the Twenty-First Century, The Belknap Press, 2017. Piketty's theories of inequality have of course been met with criticism and I don't claim that Piketty is right about everything. The purpose here is to provide the reader of a good understanding of some of the key mechanisms explaining societal inequality. For an overview of some of the criticism against Piketty: *see* https://en.wikipedia.org/wiki/Capital_in_the_Twenty-First_Century.
29. *See* Piketty, Chapter 9.

Another perspective on the same phenomenon is to see it as a matter of differences in economic productivity. Technological development often leads to increased productivity and lower demand for tasks previously performed by humans, but that can now be performed with higher productivity through technology. More education and training also lead to increased productivity, and as long as people can perform tasks with higher productivity than technology, education will lead to higher demand for labour and higher wages.

However, these fundamental forces - the supply and demand of talent and skills - are not enough to explain wage differences between countries. Two other important factors are the existence of minimum wage legislation and the balance of powers in the labour market. These factors are important to explain, not least the lowest wage levels. However, they are of less value to explain differences in the highest wages, with the United States often cited as an example of countries where CEOs have salaries that exceed those of other employees by huge sums. These 'differences at the top' are explained by a combination of factors. The classic explanation that there is a low supply of managers with the right skills and a high demand for such skills does not seem likely, given the size of the wage gap. A more plausible explanation (at least for the US) is that such salaries are largely set by the company managers themselves or by people in remuneration committees with comparable salaries and basic norms and values about what constitutes reasonable wage differences.

An equally important dimension of economic inequality is *the difference between income from capital and labour.*[30] The former refers to income from dividends, interest, the sale of real estate and securities at a higher value than the purchase value, and so on. There are at least two factors to be considered here: on the one hand, external factors through which such differences arise and, on the other hand, factors inherent in the economic system that can reinforce or weaken fundamental differences.

As for the external factors, differences in the holding of capital wealth can be influenced by a variety of phenomena. Some examples are wars (which can lead to massive capital destruction) and business cycles. Other factors are the market value of capital assets - such as real estate and shares - which in turn depend on several factors such as interest rate policy, housing construction and so on. In times of so-called asset price inflation - general increases in the prices of capital assets - economic inequality between those who have assets (such as real estate and shares) and those who do not can increase sharply.

The basic distribution between capital and labour income can then be strengthened or weakened depending on mechanisms that are more or less inherent in the economic system. In *Limits to Growth,* the exponential growth of the population and the economy was the starting point. Economic growth is an exponential growth of capital. In books about everyday finances or stock saving, the example of an interest-bearing savings account is often used. The compound interest effect causes the holdings in the savings account to grow exponentially. This is the case with capital in

30. *See* Piketty, Capital in the 21st Century, Chapter 10.

general – as long as part of the return is reinvested in more capital assets, the value of the capital and the return from the assets will grow exponentially.

A driving force behind growing inequality is when the exponential growth of capital is higher than the exponential growth of the economy. This happens if the return on capital exceeds the rate of growth.[31] Suppose that every year, two individuals – a capital owner and a worker – share a cake. The cake results from two factors: the worker's cake-making (labour) and the capital owner's purchase of kitchen, baking equipment and ingredients (capital). When the cake is made, it is sold on the market, and the proceeds are to be distributed. The capital owner's share of income is his income from capital. Let us say it is 10%. As the capital owner invests part of his return in more equipment and ingredients, the pie will get bigger and bigger every year (it grows exponentially). Let us say the pie also grows by 10% every year. Thus, the return on capital equals the rate of growth. The relative fortunes of the owner and the worker of capital will then not change. Both get richer, but neither gets richer in relation to the other. But let us say instead that the return on capital is 15%, i.e., the return exceeds the rate of growth. The owner of capital can continue at the same rate of investment each year but can also save the excess 5%, which can be invested in other ways that also lead to exponential growth. In this scenario, not only will both get richer every year but also the owner of the capital will get richer than the worker. The inequality between them is exacerbated every year.

Thus, if capital is unequally distributed in society from the outset and the return on capital exceeds growth, this original inequality will be reinforced. What this looks like in the actual economy depends on how growth and return on capital have developed over time, which also varies in different countries. An important explanation for increasing inequality, however, is precisely that growth is lower than return on capital.

This means that a natural mechanism to counteract increased inequality is to reduce the return on capital, which can be done through capital taxation. However, the introduction of this taxation is a political matter in which economic interests have a great deal of influence over policy. The more the money concentrated in the hands of the owners of capital, the greater their influence over political decisions, including decisions over taxation. Thus, instead of increasing taxes, they gain the power to remove capital taxes. This is happening and has been done with the argument that it will increase growth because the capital owner's increased capital can be invested thanks to the removal of taxes and increased growth. However, if the return on capital increases more than the growth because of the tax, inequality will increase even more.

The admittedly simplified description above shows that economic inequality is not given by nature but that very strong forces in the economy drive society towards inequality. Important explanations for the sharp increase in inequality since the 1980s are due to asset price inflation in combination with a lower growth rate, weakened power of trade unions, removal of taxes on capital income, and more. An inequality that thus also increases climate-changing consumption while reducing society's ability

31. Piketty expresses this in the formula $r > g$ (return on capital > growth).

to make collective decisions to adopt rules to reduce environmental degradation and more.

1.4 THE EARTH4ALL MODEL: THE LIMITS OF HUMAN WELL-BEING

The crossing of more and more planetary boundaries seriously threatens the conditions for human life on the planet as we have known it so far. The World3 model and the report *Limits to Growth* show that this is largely due to the overexploitation of natural resources, which is due to exponential growth in the population and economy. Research on economic inequality shows that strong forces in the economy easily create self-reinforcing correlations where the economy's exponentially growing pie at the same time increasingly goes to those who already have large ownership and large incomes, which in turn increases the rate of environmental degradation.

The Earth4All model is a further development of the World3 model and the model of the nine planetary boundaries, with a focus on what changes are needed to transition to a more sustainable development. It also integrates research on the interconnection between negative environmental impacts and inequality. The Earth4All model is also a system dynamics model. An important difference is the focus on what the model should explain. In the World3 model, it is about the limits of economic growth and population growth. The model of the nine planetary boundaries is precisely about these boundaries. Both of these models can contribute to good discussions about sustainability. But ultimately, sustainability is about what is sustainable for humanity.

The starting point of the Earth4All model is therefore a definition of human well-being, measured in terms of a *well-being index*. The focus of the Earth4All model is on the well-being of the vast majority of the world's population, who spend about as much as they earn in a year. This vast majority are referred to in the model as 'workers'.[32] The others, about 10% of the world's population who have money left over, are referred to in the model as 'owners'. The well-being index is built on five variables:

(1) Dignity
(2) Nature
(3) Connection
(4) Fairness
(5) Participation.

Dignity: The researchers measure this criterion based on workers' disposable incomes, based on the assumption that human well-being increases with increasing disposable income but at a gradually decreasing rate.

Nature: To measure the impact of the environment on human well-being, the researchers have chosen global warming as a variable for environmental degradation since the ability to make predictions is better for this variable than for many others. But

32. Randers, J. and Collste, D., The Earth4All Model of Human Wellbeing on a Finite Planet Towards 2100, September 2022. Available on www.earth4all.life.

global warming can also be seen in the model as representative of other types of environmental degradation.

Connection: Connection refers to a person's sense of belonging to a society and that society has institutions that serve the common good. The researchers measure this in the model in terms of public spending on education, health, transport, infrastructure and more.

Fairness: The researchers assume that an unequal society has a lower level of well-being than an equal one, which is strongly supported by other research discussed above. Inequality is measured as the owners' total after-tax income divided by the workers' total after-tax income.

Participation: The researchers have assumed that if well-being has risen in recent years, people are happier and have more hope for the future than if well-being has remained stable or has decreased. In the latter case, they will be less willing to support collective decision-making that increases well-being in the long run. The participation factor, therefore, measures how well-being has changed over the past five years.

By combining the World3 model and the model of the nine planetary boundaries, as well as adding more factors to the model, the researchers behind the Earth4All model have made it possible to test different scenarios and what they mean for human well-being by varying basic assumptions about future developments.

1.4.1 A Simplified Overview of the Model

A simplified overview of The Earth4All model is shown below:[33]

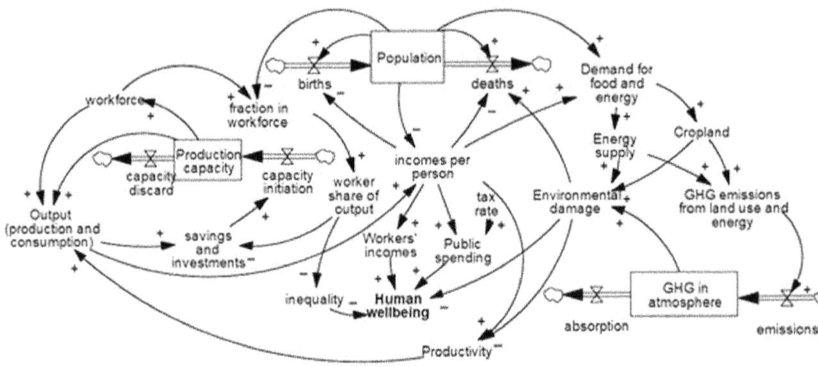

The logic of the Earth4All model is, like the World3 model, complex due to all the possible relationships, yet simple in its basic structure. One challenge in understanding a system dynamics model is that all the constituent factors are interconnected and affect each other. Human well-being cannot be explained by a chain of causality with a beginning and an end.

33. Thanks to David Collste at Stockholm Resilience Center for this overview of the model.

A good way to understand the Earth4All model is to start with the World3 model and the simplified description above with the two growth factors, population growth and economic growth, and the three limits of food production, pollution and access to natural resources. In several scenarios presented in the *Limits to Growth*, collapse occurred due to a combination of excessive pollution, the depletion of Earth's resources, and insufficient food to feed the population. The model showed that technological development is, with a legal expression, a necessary but not sufficient condition for achieving a stable world. It wasn't until the researchers behind the World3 model made assumptions about voluntary restrictions on childbearing (which was the focus of the 1970s) and consumption that the model generated a scenario that led to a stable world.

These were assumptions that pointed to the root causes of the problems that the World3 model focuses on - exponential economic growth and population growth. However, it can be seen from the Earth4All model that the way to tackle these root causes does not necessarily have to go via difficult political decisions on birth control or voluntary renunciation of consumption. With regard to the first part, demographic change, the Earth4All model shows that population growth is already coming to a halt.

This is where the complex relationships between social and environmental sustainability become apparent. An exponentially growing population will eventually over-exploit Earth's resources (and is already doing so). However, it is a well-established fact that there is a clear correlation between a society's birth rate and poverty. Richer people, measured in terms of not only income but also education, access to healthcare, etc., give birth to fewer children. In the Earth4All model, the relationship between GDP per capita and population growth is important. When people have more disposable income, access to education, better healthcare, and so on, the mortality rate falls, but the birth rate falls even more, as shown by the modest population growth of the rich world. This is one of several reasons, in addition to being morally required, why combating poverty is one of the most important ways of avoiding an environmental catastrophe through the overexploitation of Earth's resources. Through higher disposable incomes, more education, healthcare, etc., for the poor, exponential population growth will decrease, which is *one* of several important prerequisites for avoiding overloading Earth's resources. The relationship between the well-being index variables dignity (measured in terms of disposable income per capita), connection (measured in terms of public spending in, for example, education and healthcare) and nature (measured in terms of global warming) is clear here.

Inequality is also important in the Earth4All model. In the model, inequality has not only a direct negative impact on human well-being but also an indirect impact through the increased inability to make political decisions to counteract climate change. There is also a self-reinforcing connection - a feedback loop. The Earth4All model measures the feeling of participation in perceived increases or decreases in well-being over the past five years. Declining experiences of participation increase tensions in society and reduce the ability to make collective decisions about reforms. Global warming will then continue, which will lead to increased energy and food costs in the long term, which will mainly affect lower-income workers, increasing inequality and social tension, and so on in self-reinforcing loops.

1.4.2 Two Scenarios: Too Little Too Late and Giant Leap

Like the World3 model, the Earth4All model makes it possible to outline different future scenarios, which is done by varying basic assumptions regarding, for example, technological development, political decisions, tax levels and so on. The researchers behind the Earth4All model present two main future scenarios. In both of these scenarios, data from the period 1980–2020 is fed into the model, whereby the current state of the world with a crossing of several planetary boundaries, falling poverty but rising inequality, increasing renewable energy production, technological development in agriculture and so on are being recreated.

In the Too Little Too Late scenario,[34] assumptions are then made that people and states will act much as they have done so far, both in a positive and negative sense. The well-being index will fall below the 1980 level around 2030 and continue to decline thereafter, mainly due to increased inequality and environmental degradation. Earth's average temperature will rise to 1.5°C above pre-industrial levels even before 2030, even though greenhouse gas emissions will begin to fall, and then to 2°C around 2050 and then upwards to land well above the Paris Agreement's commitments to stay within 2°C of warming by 2100. Technological development will continue, accelerating the transition to renewable energy sources and increasing the efficiency of machines, etc. However, as in the World3 model, technological development cannot prevent the development towards collapse because other forces act in the opposite direction. Technology, as such, often leads to increased resource use, increased emissions and increased inequality when workers are replaced by technical solutions.[35] As measures to counter rising inequalities are not sufficiently taken, e.g., through tax transfers, social tensions are growing. This means that political decisions required for technical and other solutions to have a major impact are not made. The same factors also mean that states lack sufficient funds for education, healthcare, etc., which leads to population growth slowing down but not fast enough for Earth's resources to suffice.

The scenario leads to environmental disasters and severe impacts on human well-being because of a degraded environment and severe economic inequality in a reinforcing relationship.

In the second scenario – the Giant Leap – humanity achieves a stable Earth and a stable society. This is done through a variety of political measures: poverty reduction, redistribution of income and capital for greater equality, strong measures to reduce inequality between men and women, technological revolutions in agriculture, changing eating habits, exponential increase in renewable energy, and so on.

34. Dixson-Declève et al., pp. 35 ff.
35. *See* section 1.2.

1.5 DECOUPLING BETWEEN GROWTH AND ENVIRONMENTAL IMPACT

Recital 1 of the EU directive 2022/2464 as regards corporate sustainability reporting, i.e., the CSRD, states almost in passing that the European Green Deal[36] 'aims to decouple economic growth from resource use'. This expresses a theory of so-called decoupling between growth and environmental impact, which is central to the transition to a sustainable world. The Earth4All model is based on the assumption that this decoupling is possible, otherwise the Giant Leap scenario cannot be realised. It should be underlined that decoupling and its potential is a highly debated issue.[37]

There are two forms of decoupling - relative and absolute. Relative decoupling means that, for example, emissions indeed increase with growth, but not to the same extent as growth. Absolute decoupling means that emissions are reduced even if the economy grows. Relative decoupling is relatively common and is due to improved and more environmentally friendly technology, energy efficiency improvements and more. There are also good examples of absolute decoupling, but only at the local level in different countries and in certain industries.

The European Green Deal, like the Earth4All model, is based on the assumption that absolute decoupling is possible. However, this is not an obvious assumption. There are researchers and others who believe that the issue is uncontroversial: as countries get richer, the environmental footprint will also decrease.[38] Others, however, argue this is an illusion - even if absolute decoupling were possible, it would never be sufficient to save the climate.[39] Because the connection between growth and environmental impact is so strong, they believe that the opposite of growth - degrowth - is the only alternative.

Both of these views, however, appear to be ideological. There is nothing to suggest that absolute decoupling would occur by itself. At the same time, there are examples of how it is possible to reconcile economic growth and absolute decoupling - Sweden is one example, at least regarding greenhouse gas emissions. In the end, it is a political question, i.e., what collective efforts are made in a society to bring about decoupling. This is the view expressed in the European Green Deal. However, it is not very clear *exactly how* the regulations and investments that are adopted as part of the Green Deal will lead to absolute decoupling.

---

36. *See* section 4.3.
37. *See, e.g.*, Jackson, T., Prosperity Without Growth, Routledge, 2016, Hickel, J., Less Is More, Penguin Books, 2020, Terzi, A., Growth for Good, Harvard University Press, 2022. *See also* the highly influential book: Raworth, K., Donut Economics, Random House UK, 2018.
38. Often referred to as the environmental Kuznets curve.
39. *See, e.g.*, Jackson, T., Prosperity without growth, Routledge, 2016.

CHAPTER 2
The Legal System and Sustainability

What is the significance of the legal system for whether society and the economy are sustainable or not? The legal system does not feature explicitly in the Earth4All model. But that it is still important is evident in the description of the Giant Leap scenario, which is based on reforms of the intellectual property regime to give more people access to important technology, changes in property rights to create citizen funds, and regulations of the financial markets to ensure that investments are made for increased sustainability. By implication, this also means that the legal rules that underpin the Too Little Too Late scenario contribute to maintaining a system that risks leading to environmental disasters and societal collapse. The data between 1980 and 2020 fed into the model includes the deregulation and re-regulation of the markets that have taken place since the 1980s, including important free trade agreements that have limited the ability to prioritise the environment over profit, which is important because about half of all the greenhouse gas emissions since the Industrial Revolution have taken place since 1990.

Still, the Earth4All model includes no formal theory of the relationship between the legal system and the overall system of economic, social and natural subsystems that the Earth4All model is based on. This book is not the place to develop this formal theory. For the rest of the presentation, however, it is appropriate to outline the place of the legal system in the Earth4All model at a general level.[40] The legal system is a fundamental part of the rules of the game for business activities that affect the sustainability of the business.

The research on the relationship between the legal system on the one hand and the economy and society on the other is comprehensive. Over the years, important contributions have been made in various disciplines such as legal history, sociology of

40. It should be pointed out here that this is an economic and sociological perspective of law, which must be distinguished from the perspective of legal theory. In principle, the former perspective has no bearing on how the law is to be interpreted. Instead, it is the legal theoretical perspective that affects the interpretation of the law. In the introduction to the book, I describe the interpretivist theory that forms the basis of the book from a legal theory perspective.

law, economics and economic history. A suitable scientific model for understanding the role of the legal system in the Earth4All model is the model developed by the economist and economic historian Douglass North, who received the Prize in Economic Sciences in Memory of Alfred Nobel in 1993.[41] North is behind this book's fundamental idea of the importance of the rules of the game for the sustainability or unsustainability of a business.

North was active in the economic sub-discipline of new institutional economics. An important focus of his research was to try to explain why some countries and economies achieve growth and prosperity while others get stuck in stagnation and poverty. North found an important part of the answer in what he calls the *institutions*. By this, he meant the rules of the game in society, that is, the restrictions that people set for themselves to regulate how they interact with each other. At any given moment, every human being is faced with an infinite number of choices, which theoretically leads to a high risk of human inability to cooperate with each other. The institutions – the rules of the game – reduce this uncertainty by limiting the number of courses of action and setting the incentives to act in certain ways. Without institutions, there is no society.

2.1 INFORMAL AND FORMAL INSTITUTIONS

North made a fundamental distinction between *informal* and *formal institutions*. Informal institutions are cultural and social norms for how people act in relation to each other. Formal institutions are legal rules and contracts, the former of which can be roughly divided into political and economic legal rules. The political rules set the structures for political decision-making. The economic rules set the framework for property rights and for the exchange of goods and services.

Institutions are thus the rules of the game in society and in the market. The players are organisations, such as corporations, states and other political entities. Which organisations emerge and how they function is greatly influenced by the institutions, but the impact is also in the opposite direction – organisations may want to influence the institutions to their own advantage.

2.2 TRANSACTION COSTS

It is the institutions, combined with the technology used, that determine the cost of companies to operate. The costs are divided into production costs and transaction costs. Technology sets the production costs. However, transaction costs are also important. Transaction costs are, in simple terms, the costs of exchanging goods and services, which include finding buyers or sellers, determining the value of the goods or services, negotiating prices, drawing up contracts, following up on contractual

41. This section is primarily based on North, D., Institutions, Institutional Change and Economic Performance, Cambridge University Press, 1990. For a good overview of the importance of North's theories: *see* Galliani, D. and Sened, I., Institutions, Property Rights and Economic Growth: The Legacy of Douglass North, Cambridge University Press, 2014.

compliance and, if necessary, going to court to enforce them. In a market with clear property rights and rules on transferring such rights, transaction costs will be much lower than in a market with weak or non-existent property rights, for example, in societies where there is violence and no rule of law.

Institutions are not designed to be effective, for example, to achieve an ideal distribution of society's resources or to achieve sustainable results. Above all, the formal institutions are created to benefit those with such a strong bargaining position that they can design new rules of the game. This means that these rules rarely benefit the vast majority. In history, however, there are examples of combinations of rules of the game that mean that what is best for those who have designed the rules of the game is also best, or at least good for society. What Adam Smith called an invisible hand that made the good of all be served if everyone best served themselves is a product of the formal and informal rules of the game in a particular historical context. In other historical contexts, a system in which everyone serves themselves first can lead to results far from beneficial to everyone.

This, in turn, implies a theory of human behaviour, which is shaped by and shapes institutions. North is clear (and correct) in saying that the idea of human behaviour in traditional economic theory – called expected utility theory – is far too restricted to capture the nuances of why people act as they do. People show what other economists have referred to as 'bounded rationality' and 'bounded self-interest'.[42] Their mental models for understanding and navigating the world are far from perfect. And people are not wealth maximisers but show complex patterns of self-interested and altruistic behaviours.

2.3 INSTITUTIONS AND THE SUSTAINABILITY OF THE ECONOMY

According to North it is this – the institutions and the incentives they create – that explains why some countries and economies grow and prosper while others stagnate and impoverish.[43]

North did not focus on sustainability but on economic growth and prosperity. However, his theories are arguably equally applicable in this field. The Earth4All model is, as mentioned, a system dynamic model, where the results of the combined actions of billions of people are captured in key variables such as population growth, economic growth, public spending, the level of trust in society, the production and use of fossil and renewable fuels, and so on. Based on North's relatively simple but powerful model, it is possible to understand that both the elements of the Earth4All model and their connections result from the underlying institutional infrastructure – the formal and informal rules of the game.

42. *See, e.g.*, Jolls, C., Sunstein, C. and Thaler, R., A Behavioral Approach to Law and Economics, Stanford Law Review, July 1998.
43. *See also* Acemoglu, D. and Robinson, J., Why Nations Fail, Profile Books Ltd, 2013 where the authors explain, not least based on North's theories, differences between successful and failing countries based on whether nations have inclusive or extractive institutions.

For example, it is not the rules on property rights and the security they create that enable exponential growth in the economy, which were already described in the World3 model. Without secure property rights, the incentive to invest part of the output in additional productive activities is reduced, as a return on such investment cannot be expected. It is a combination of technology and regulations that governs whether it is more or less attractive to use fossil or renewable fuels. It is not least the political rules of the game that determine whether, for politicians and civil servants, it pays to act for the common good or, through corruption, appropriate public funds for one's own good. It is the rules of the game that determine whether those who emit greenhouse gases must also bear the costs of doing so (for example, through a carbon dioxide tax) or not.

Furthermore, it is the rules of the game that determine whether people, society and the economy get stuck in various types of social dilemmas to the detriment of the environment. A common example is called *the Tragedy of the Commons*.[44] It is an example of a social trap where it is rational for everyone to act for their own good while leading to an outcome which is bad for everyone. The fish stock in a sea is a commons, a resource no one owns but that many people have access to. It is rational for every fisherman to try to fish as much as possible to get as much income as possible. But if every fisherman does this, it leads to the fish running out, and then there is no fish for anyone. This is exactly what has happened in many places on Earth. At the same time, there are many examples of when people have avoided this trap.[45] This has been done through a combination of formal and informal rules of the game - institutions - that drive people to cooperate in a way that lets them take advantage of the common asset without overusing it.

As we have seen above, the legal system - the formal institutions - is thus of crucial importance in a model such as the Earth4All model. In fact, it is impossible to fully understand why the logic of the model is the way it is without understanding the underlying institutional framework.

44. Hardin, G., The Tragedy of the Commons, 162(3859) Science, 1968, 1243-1248.
45. *See, e.g.*, Ostrom, E., Governing the Commons: The Evolution of Institutions for Collective Actions, Cambridge University Press, 1990. *See also* Ellickson, R., Order Without Law: How Neighbours Settle Disputes, Harvard University Press, 1991.

CHAPTER 3

The Role of Companies

The Earth4All model, presented in Chapter 1, has not been developed to explain and analyse the role of companies in the scenarios that the model enables analysis of. But still, it can easily be done. Through their activities, companies influence several factors and sectors on which the Earth4All model is based, which are also linked to the morally shaped well-being index. In addition, it is the companies that, to a large extent, must be responsible for the decoupling between growth and resource use and environmental impact that must take place to avoid the Too Little Too Late scenario. Corporate actions linked to the Earth4All model will be dealt with in more detail in later parts of the book. Here, however, an overall description will be made, linked to the three areas of nine planetary boundaries, limits of growth and inequality.

3.1 POSITIVE AND NEGATIVE IMPACTS

Companies play an important role in the ongoing crossing of six of the nine planetary boundaries. Through the extraction and use of natural resources and later emissions of greenhouse gases and other pollutants into the air, water and soil, as well as inadequate waste management, companies contribute to climate change, biodiversity loss, water acidification and so on. In the Earth4All model, this is mainly exemplified by global warming, which forms part of the well-being index.

Companies contribute greatly to growth and prosperity and give workers wages and other benefits, which is positive for well-being. At the same time, it is also companies that are largely responsible for the exponential economic growth that ultimately risks leading to economic, environmental and social collapse. The Earth4All model is based on the assumption that decoupling between growth and negative environmental impacts is possible to some extent. It is largely companies that need to be responsible for this decoupling. This needs to be done by phasing out capital assets that cause environmental degradation and by investing in assets that do not cause environmental damage. An important reason why decoupling does not take place at a higher rate is probably companies' reluctance to abandon previously made environmentally harmful capital investments.

Companies also have a major impact on the social factors found in the Earth4All model. In the model, public spending and the capacity for collective decision-making are important factors in achieving a stable world. Corruption and money laundering among companies counteract both of these factors, partly by limiting the state's resources and partly by reducing trust in society.

Furthermore companies have a major impact on economic equality in society. For example, companies can increase or decrease equality through how they remunerate their employees, what differences in compensation levels between management and staff are accepted, whether they offer training and education to increase staff productivity, in which countries they locate their production, and so on. Furthermore, companies affect conditions in the labour market if they promote or oppose collective agreements.

Thus, companies influence, directly and indirectly, all the factors in the well-being index on which the Earth4All model is based: dignity, nature, connection, fairness and participation. It is important to underline how the environmental, social and governance (ESG) aspects of sustainability are closely interlinked. A service company with limited greenhouse gas emissions can be as sustainable or unsustainable as an industrial company through its impact on inequality, fairness and so on – factors that greatly affect society's ability to prevent environmental disasters. Socially inclusive companies that have switched to low-carbon production can still destabilise society by bribing politicians. And so on. The Earth4All model is a tool to understand the complexity of unsustainable actions and activities.

3.2 COMPANIES AS PLAYERS OF THE GAME

It is, however, one thing to understand companies' positive and negative impacts in the Earth4All framework. It is another thing to understand *how* these impacts are generated. What is the cause? It is only based on such understanding that it is possible to transform business into a more sustainable business.

In Douglass North's framework, presented in the previous chapter, companies are not the rules of the game but *players* of the game whose actions are shaped by the rules. Such a view on companies is insufficient, though, since companies' actions are obviously shaped by more factors than formal laws, contracts and informal social norms. The economist Ronald Coase famously asked why companies exist in the first place if the market mechanism hailed by economists is so efficient.[46] The activities *within* a company are carried out outside of the market. The price mechanism, which fulfils, among other things, an important role in coordinating market activities, is not switched on within a company. The coordination mechanism of the market is handed over to the managers of the company. Why?

46. Coase, R., (1937), The Nature of the Firm, 4(16) Economica, 386-405.

Coase's answer was simple but profound. Being an economist, he claimed that activities are organised in firms when it is more economically efficient to do so than organising them through transactions on the market. The same transaction costs, discussed in section 2.1, that, according to North, give rise to institutions also give rise to companies. Companies exist, according to this view, since the transaction costs are lower when all the individuals building up the company do not have to all the time negotiate and enter into new contracts about what they shall do.

This is a powerful perspective on what a company is – a mechanism for organising activities cheaper than on the market. It is a perspective that, as we will see, underlies the law and economic view of corporate law.[47] It is also this perspective that provides much of the logic and force of the claim that the purpose of a business is to maximise shareholder value, an idea that some claim is the single biggest obstacle against a shift to sustainable business.

An equally important problem with the transaction cost optimising view of companies is that it is limited in how much help it can provide in understanding why companies act as they do. While a focus on transaction cost can put light on questions such as the relationship between the company and its shareholders, creditors and others, it will not provide much understanding of questions regarding business model, strategy, corporate culture and other factors. Those factors very much shape how companies act and, of course, ultimately lead to transactions, for example, with customers, employees, suppliers, creditors and others. While the costs of those transactions can be optimised, the business model and strategy are not themselves the result of transactions but of planning, trial and error, leadership, etc.

Therefore, the transaction cost view on companies is much too limited to understand how and why companies generate positive and negative impacts that ultimately show in the Earth4All model. Another perspective is necessary, and probably the best perspective is then the same system dynamics perspective on which the Earth4All model is based.

We are surrounded by phenomena that can be understood as systems: technical systems such as cars or the internet, ecological systems such as forests or lakes, biological systems such as the human body, and human systems such as the entire society, the market, political parties and, of course, companies. Saying that they 'can be understood as systems' means that there, of course, are other perspectives to adopt on cars, lakes, political parties and companies, but that a systems perspective is a powerful way to understand how they work.

What is a 'systems perspective'? It is a perspective for understanding events and behaviour as caused by an underlying set of related and interacting factors over time. In systems theory, it is common to describe a system using the metaphor of an iceberg.[48] As everyone knows, only approximately 20% of the iceberg is visible above the surface, with the other 80% lurking beneath the surface. The following illustration can be used:

47. *See* Chapter 6.
48. *See, e.g.*, Stroh, P., Systems Thinking for Social Change, Chelsea Green Publishing, 2016, 63.

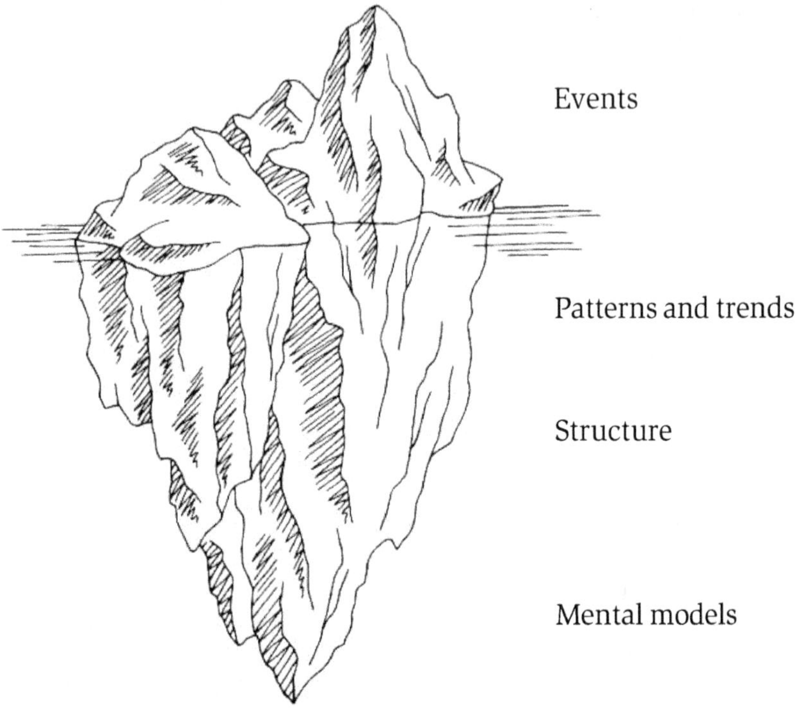

What we see above the surface are events – a heating system heating a room to a certain temperature, a car running at a certain speed, global temperatures rising towards 1.5 °C, a company generating certain profits and so on. Such 'events' must, from a system dynamics perspective, first be understood as caused by factors which cannot be seen above the surface. First of all, any event is typically part of a larger 'pattern' or a 'trend'. These patterns and trends must, in their turn, be understood as generated by the fundamental system structure. At the deepest level, we have mental models. Those are models and perspectives that shape people's views of the world. Those models shape and reinforce the higher levels of the hierarchy, starting, of course, with the structure. To view, like Coase and others, the company as a mechanism for economising on transaction costs is a powerful mental model.

In the iceberg metaphor, the core of the system dynamics perspective is at the structure level. That is the level where a system starts to behave like a system, generating repetitive behaviour over time according to its own inner 'laws'.

The details of systems dynamic theory will not be further elaborated on here. However, the iceberg view of a company is highly useful for the purpose of this book, where the aim is to guide companies in the transition to sustainable business while at the same time complying with EU sustainability law. In Part III of the book, I describe the European Sustainability Reporting Standards (ESRS), which companies to whom the CSRD is applicable shall use when reporting on sustainability impacts, risks and opportunities. The ESRS do not use a systems dynamic approach, but their various components can easily be included in such approach. We will look into the details of this in Part III, but now, it is good to illustrate the perspective of a company that will be applied throughout the book:

In this illustration, we have a company's both financial and sustainability results - social and environmental impact above the surface, along with its process for corporate reporting. Those should, in this perspective, be viewed as *symptoms* of what is going on beneath the surface. Most immediately, those symptoms are results of human behaviour shaped by contracts between the company and others and also internal processes and routines. Those would be the patterns and trends. These are, in turn, to a large extent, a result of what is going on at the structural dimension below, where the company's business model is executed in a strategy through a certain governance organisation, where management and others have certain incentives. At the deepest level, we find the corporate culture and, finally, the corporate purpose.

As will be further discussed in later chapters of the book, these factors - from corporate purpose to contracts - together with market forces and laws and regulations, are what cause a company's environmental and social impact as well as its economic results. They all belong to what I here refer to as the rules of the game that companies play on the market in the game of winning customers.

CHAPTER 4

The Levels of Sustainability Law

In light of the description in the previous chapters of the role of the legal system in the Earth4All model and of a company as a system, it is appropriate to provide an overview of the general framework of EU sustainability law, i.e., the *legal* rules of the game for sustainable business. As mentioned in the book's introduction, sustainability law is not an established area of law. It consists partly not only of new legislation, such as the EU taxonomy but also of traditional areas of law, such as environmental law, labour law and so on. In line with the interpretivist legal theory adopted in this book, it is appropriate to view the various legal acts of sustainability law as the transformation into a law of wider political morality. What unites the different parts of sustainability law is an underlying and cohesive normative logic that deals with how people's equality and freedom can be violated or protected through unsustainable and sustainable actions.

Sustainability law is best viewed as consisting of several levels, where the lower levels affect the higher levels. This is illustrated in the following image:

Each of these levels is further described in the following section.

4.1 TREATIES ON HUMAN RIGHTS AND PROTECTION OF THE ENVIRONMENT

On the first level of sustainability law, we find the fundamental treaties on human rights and protection of the environment.

4.1.1 Human Rights

Human rights form the foundation of sustainability law. According to Article 2 of the Treaty on the European Union, the Union is founded on the values of respect for human dignity, freedom, democracy, equality, the rule of law and respect for human rights, including the rights of persons belonging to minorities. According to Article 3, the internal market shall work for the sustainable development of Europe based on balanced economic growth and price stability, a highly competitive social market economy aiming at full employment and social progress, and a high level of protection and improvement of the quality of the environment.

The Charter of Fundamental Rights of the European Union has been in force in the EU since 2010, where Article 1 says that human dignity is inviolable and that it must be respected and protected. However, according to the EU Treaties and European Court of Justice (ECJ) case law, the union is also bound by the treaties of international law.[49] These would then include the UN's Universal Declaration of Human Rights, which has been in force since 1948 and which forms the basis for, among other texts:

- The International Covenant on Economic, Social and Cultural Rights (1966)
- The International Covenant on Civil and Political Rights (1966)
- The Convention on the Elimination of All Forms of Discrimination against Women (CEDAW) (1979)
- The Convention on the Rights of the Child (1989), and not least
- The European Convention for the Protection of Human Rights and Fundamental Freedoms of 1950 (ECHR).

In its ruling in *Verein Klimaseniorinnen Schweiz and others v. Switzerland*, the European Court of Human Rights (ECtHR) found that Article 8 of the ECHR regarding the right to protection of private and family life encompasses a right for individuals to effective protection by state authorities (including legislative, executive and judicial branches) from serious adverse effects on climate change on their life, health, well-being and quality of life.[50]

In addition, there are a large number of international conventions drawn up by the ILO – the International Labour Organization – which is a trade union body within the UN. At its core are eight so-called core conventions, which establish human rights for workers. The eight core conventions are:

- Forced Labour (29)
- Freedom of Association and the Right to Organise (Convention 87)
- Right to Organise and Collective Bargain (Convention 98)
- Abolition of Forced and Compulsory Labour (Convention 105)
- Equal Remuneration (Convention 100)
- Abolition of Forced Labour (Convention 105)
- Discrimination (Employment and Occupation) (Convention 111)
- Minimum Age (Convention 138)
- Elimination of the Worst Forms of Child Labour (Convention 182).

4.1.2 International Declarations and Conventions on the Protection of the Environment

The sustainability legal framework also includes several international declarations and conventions that aim to protect the environment and natural resources. Below is a brief description of some of the more important texts adopted.

49. *See, e.g.*, C-366/10, Air Transport Association America and others, section 101 and C-308/06, Intertanko, section 42.
50. Section 519 of the ruling. *See* section 5.1 for an analysis of this important case.

4.1.2.1 *The Stockholm Declaration*

At a UN conference in Stockholm in 1972, the Stockholm Declaration was adopted in the form of twenty-one principles. Through this declaration, the environment was given international legal status, clearly linked to the right of human beings to a dignified life. The first principle states that humans have a fundamental right to freedom, equality and adequate living conditions in an environment that enables a dignified and fulfilling life. The responsibility of humanity to protect and improve the environment for present and future generations was underlined. The twenty-first principle established the right of each state to exploit its own natural resources and, at the same time, the so-called no harm principle - the responsibility not to harm the environment of other states at the same time.

4.1.2.2 *The Rio Conference*

The Stockholm Conference was followed up in 1992 by the Rio Conference - Earth Summit. Prior to that, the UN had appointed an independent Commission on Environment and Development, which in 1987 presented the Brundtland Report.[51] The report established the definition of the term *sustainable development:* A development that meets the needs of the present without compromising the ability of future generations to meet their own needs.

The Rio Declaration was yet another declaration of principles. The declaration establishes humans' right to a rich life in harmony with nature. The 'no harm' principle from the Stockholm Declaration is reiterated. The seventh principle emphasises the special responsibilities of the developed countries because of the pressures they put on the global environment in terms of their technological and financial resources. The fifteenth principle lays down the important precautionary principle: where there is a threat of serious or irreversible damage, the absence of scientific evidence must not be used as an excuse to postpone cost-effective measures to prevent environmental damage. The sixteenth principle establishes the equally important principle that the polluter must pay for the damage caused by pollution, or in other words, internalise the environmental costs caused.

During the Rio Conference, the United Nations Framework Convention on Climate Change (UNFCCC) - the Climate Convention - was also adopted. The background was the growing awareness of the contribution of greenhouse gas emissions to global warming and the damage this would cause. Article 2 states that the purpose of the convention is to ensure that concentrations of greenhouse gases in the atmosphere are stabilised at a level that prevents dangerous anthropogenic interference. According to the convention, states should protect the climate system, taking into account, again, the differences between developed and developing countries. There are no concrete emission limits, but there is a duty for each country to publish reports on its emissions.

51. The Chairman of the Commission was the Norwegian Prime Minister Gro Harlem Brundtland.

In 1997, a supplement to the UNFCCC was adopted: the Kyoto Protocol. Here, more concrete climate targets were set, namely, that annual global greenhouse gas emissions should be reduced by at least 5.2% from 1990 to the period 2008–2012, targets that were far from being achieved.

In addition to the UNFCCC, the Rio Conference also adopted the Convention on Biological Diversity. The goals of this convention are the conservation of biological diversity, the sustainable use of its components and the equitable sharing of the benefits generated. In December 2022, the Kunming-Montreal Global Biodiversity Framework was adopted under this convention.

Finally, the Rio Conference also adopted the United Nations Convention to Combat Desertification in countries affected by severe drought and/or desertification, in particular, in Africa.

4.1.2.3 The Paris Agreement

In 2015, the well-known Paris Agreement was adopted, which replaced the Kyoto Protocol. Under the agreement, each country commits to contributing to keeping global warming well below a 2 °C increase compared to pre-industrial levels by the year 2100. An intention is expressed to make further efforts to limit global warming to 1.5 °C. Another aim of the agreement is to make finance flows consistent with low greenhouse gas emissions and climate-resilient development.

4.1.2.4 Agenda 2030 and the Sustainable Development Goals

One of the most important international frameworks for sustainability and sustainable development is the UN resolution Agenda 2030, the 17 Sustainable Development Goals (SDGs) and the 169 targets of the SDGs. Agenda 2030 is an agreed strategy document on what the constituent states commit to do in sustainability by 2030 and is frequently referred to in the texts of EU sustainability law.

The 2030 Agenda is based on a shared vision, namely a world without poverty, hunger, disease or deprivation, where everyone can read and write and have access to education, where human rights are protected and equality between women and men prevails, where every country enjoys sustainable economic growth with decent work for all, and where the environment is managed sustainably.

After noting that there are too many poor people in the world, that inequality within and between countries is high and that the consumption of Earth's resources is too high, while development also creates a lot of opportunities, the 17 global sustainability goals are listed:

- **Goal 1**. End poverty in all its forms everywhere.
- **Goal 2**. End hunger, achieve food security and improved nutrition, and promote sustainable agriculture.
- **Goal 3**. Ensure healthy lives and promote well-being for all at all ages.

- **Goal 4.** Ensure inclusive and equitable quality education and promote lifelong learning opportunities for all.
- **Goal 5.** Achieve gender equality and the empowerment of all women and girls.
- **Goal 6.** Ensure availability and sustainable management of water and sanitation for all.
- **Goal 7.** Ensure access to affordable, reliable, sustainable and modern energy for all.
- **Goal 8.** Promote sustained, inclusive and sustainable economic growth, full and productive employment and decent work for all.
- **Goal 9.** Build resilient infrastructure, promote inclusive and sustainable industrialisation and foster innovation.
- **Goal 10.** Reduce inequalities within and among countries.
- **Goal 11.** Make cities and human settlements inclusive, safe, resilient and sustainable.
- **Goal 12.** Ensure sustainable consumption and production patterns.
- **Goal 13.** Take urgent action to combat climate change and its impacts.
- **Goal 14.** Conserve and sustainably use the oceans, seas and marine resources for sustainable development.
- **Goal 15.** Protect, restore and promote sustainable use of terrestrial ecosystems, sustainably manage forests, combat desertification, halt and reverse land degradation and halt biodiversity loss.
- **Goal 16.** Promote peaceful and inclusive societies for sustainable development, provide access to justice for all, and build effective, accountable and inclusive institutions at all levels.
- **Goal 17.** Strengthen the means of implementation and revitalise the global partnership for sustainable development.

The Earth4All model described in Chapter 1 makes it possible to understand how these 17 economic, social and environmental goals are interrelated and affect and support each other.[52]

The EU is a party to the Agenda 2030. Many legal rules about sustainability are about governments, companies and others refraining from doing harm. They thus set forth what can be called 'negative obligations', mainly expressed in the due diligence norms discussed further below. But Agenda 2030 and similar legal texts important for EU law also establish 'positive obligations', i.e., obligations to take actions to contribute to improved sustainability. While it can be discussed to what extent there is a real difference between those negative and positive obligations, it is clear in the EU legislation that there is what here will be referred to as a 'norm of positive contribution' in addition to the due diligence norm.

52. *See, e.g.*, Bernstein, J., et al., SDGs For All: Strategic Scenarios. Earth4All System Dynamics Modelling of SDG Progress, Working Paper version 1.0, September 2023.

4.2 NON-BINDING PRINCIPLES AND GUIDELINES FOR RESPONSIBLE BUSINESS CONDUCT

The international treaties on human rights and protection of the environment are not binding for companies. They apply between the parties to the treaties and sometimes also between the state and the individual. They neither apply between individuals nor between companies and individuals. At the same time, companies can have a huge impact on people's ability to live their lives according to the principles of equality and freedom that underpin human rights and environmental treaties. At the next level of sustainability law, we, therefore, find two fundamental internationally agreed, but still non-binding, documents which can be said to translate what the international treaties on human rights and the environment should mean for business: the United Nations Guiding Principles on Business and Human Rights and the OECD Guidelines for Multinational Enterprises.

4.2.1 UN Guiding Principles on Business and Human Rights

In 2011, the UN adopted its Guiding Principles on Business and Human Rights. These principles are, as said, not legally binding, but the UN wants to guide how states make sure companies in their territories respect human rights and how the companies themselves work to respect them. The UNGPs have now acquired legal status within the EU, as these principles form part of the minimum requirements for what is considered environmentally sustainable investments under Article 18 of the Taxonomy Regulation.

The first part of the UN Guiding Principles regulates how states should make sure they protect the population in their territory against human rights abuses by third parties, including companies. The second part is about the responsibility of companies to respect human rights. Principle 11 requires businesses to respect human rights, which means that they should avoid violating the human rights of others and should address any adverse human rights impacts in which they are involved. According to Principle 12, the human rights that businesses are expected to respect are internationally recognised human rights, including those expressed in the Universal Declaration of Human Rights and the ILO's core conventions described above. According to Principle 16, the starting point for exercising a company's responsibilities should be a policy adopted by the company's highest decision-making body.

Principle 17 is important because, together with its equivalent in the OECD Guidelines for Multinational Enterprises, it lays the foundation for sustainability law's fundamental *due diligence norm*. According to the principle, companies should conduct human rights due diligence to identify, prevent, mitigate and account for how they address their adverse human rights impacts. The process should include assessing actual and potential impacts on human rights, incorporating and acting on these findings, following up on actions taken, and communicating what actions are being taken. The details are elaborated in Principles 18–21. This is work that should be done on an ongoing basis and includes the company's value chain.

Principle 22 further states that if companies conclude that they have caused or contributed to an adverse impact, they should, individually or through cooperation, remedy the violation through legitimate processes.

4.2.2 OECD Guidelines for Multinational Enterprises

The OECD Guidelines for Multinational Enterprises were first adopted in 1976 and last updated in June 2023. Like the UNGPs, these guidelines are not legally binding but have acquired legal status as compliance with them is a minimum requirement for environmentally sustainable activities under Article 18 of the EU Taxonomy. There are eleven overarching guidelines, with more specific advice and recommendations under each guideline.

General Policy. Multinational enterprises should take fully into account established policies in the countries in which they operate and consider the views of other stakeholders. Key advice in this area includes that multinational enterprises should contribute to economic, environmental and social progress with a view to achieving sustainable development, respect the human rights of those affected by their activities, support and uphold principles of good corporate governance, and develop and apply good governance practices throughout enterprise groups. A recommendation is that multinational companies should carry out risk-based due diligence and avoid causing or contributing to adverse impacts on matters covered by the guidelines through their activities and manage them when they arise.

Disclosure. Multinational enterprises should take into account established disclosure policies in the countries and sectors in which they operate and consider the views and informational requirements of shareholders and other relevant stakeholders. Disclosure policies should include material information on, e.g., financial and operational results, enterprise objectives and sustainability-related information, capital structure, major share ownership and remuneration of members of the board and key executives. They should also publish information about the company's values or ethical guidelines.

Human rights. Multinational enterprises should respect human rights, which means that they should avoid infringing the human rights of others and address adverse impacts in which they are involved.

Employment and Industrial Relations. Multinational enterprises must respect the rights of workers, including the right to organise and join trade unions and collective bargaining. Companies should contribute to eliminating child labour and forced labour. They should also be guided by the principles of equal opportunities and equal treatment in the workplace.

Environment. One of the more important updates in the 2023 edition of the guidelines is about the environment. Multinational enterprises should conduct their activities in a manner that takes due account of the need to protect the environment and, in turn, workers, communities and society more broadly, avoids and addresses adverse environmental impacts and contributes to the wider goal of sustainable development. Enterprises should establish and maintain an environmental management system appropriate for the company, including risk-based due diligence. The system shall include identifying and assessing adverse environmental impacts associated with the enterprise's operations, establishing and implementing measurable objectives, targets and strategies to address these impacts, regularly verifying the effectiveness of the strategies, informing the public, employees and other stakeholders, and taking measures to address adverse impacts caused by the enterprise.

Combatting Bribery and Other Forms of Corruption. Multinational enterprises must not engage in any act of corruption, including the offering, promising or giving of any undue pecuniary or other advantage to public officials or employees of persons or entities with which an enterprise has a business relationship. The recommendation includes the development and implementation of adequate internal controls, ethical guidelines and programmes in the area.

Consumer Interests. When dealing with consumers, multinational enterprises should act in accordance with fair business, marketing and advertising practices and should take all reasonable steps to ensure the quality and reliability of the goods and services that they provide. The recommendation includes making sure the company's goods and services follow all agreed and legal standards for the protection of consumers' health and safety, that accurate, verifiable and clear information is given, and that consumers are given access to fair, easy-to-use and effective dispute resolution, and that their personal data is processed with respect for consumers' privacy.

Science, Technology and Innovation. Multinational enterprises should contribute to the development and national innovative capacity. The recommendation includes carrying out scientific and technological development work in host countries to address local market needs.

Competition. Multinational enterprises should operate in accordance with the applicable competition law in the jurisdictions in which they operate, refraining from entering into anti-competitive agreements with competitors in order to, for example, fix prices or share markets.

Taxation. Multinational enterprises should contribute to the public finances of host countries by paying their taxes on time and by complying with both the letter and the purpose of tax laws.

As in the UN Guiding Principles, it is recommended that companies conduct risk-based due diligence. This due diligence process is, as already said, a central element of sustainability law. The OECD Guidelines define due diligence as the process through which companies repeatedly identify, prevent, mitigate and account for how they address actual and potential material adverse impacts as part of their decision-making and risk management systems. Both the company's own operations and the supply chain are covered. Of the eleven guidelines, human rights, employment and industrial relations, the environment, bribery and corruption, disclosures and consumer interests are covered by the recommendation on due diligence.[53]

53. OECD, OECD Due Diligence Guidance for Responsible Business Conduct, 2018.

4.3 EU LAWS ON SUSTAINABLE FINANCE

The first two levels of sustainability law can, within the interpretivist theory adopted in this book, be said to provide the political morality underpinning the European Union and Member State laws on sustainability. As said, the UNGPs and OECD Guidelines can be viewed as translations of what international treaties on protection of human rights and environment mean for business. Those documents establish the fundamental due diligence norm for responsible business conduct. This norm is primarily negative in the sense that its intention is to restrict harmful behaviour. The global sustainability goals of Agenda 2030 and similar documents, instead, provide a positive direction, promoting certain behaviour and not restricting it. For lack of better terms, the norm expressing this positive direction will hereinafter be referred to as the 'norm of positive contribution'.

The other levels of sustainability law can, to a large extent, be viewed as the legislator's attempt to transform the restrictive due diligence norm in combination with the positive contribution norms coming from Agenda 2030 into law, providing frameworks and incentives for companies to follow.

At the next level of sustainability law, we find the EU rules on sustainable finance, which form a key component of the European Green Deal.

4.3.1 Action Plan on Financing Sustainable Growth

Even before the European Commission launched the Green Deal, discussed in the next section, the Commission had published an 'Action Plan on Financing Sustainable Growth'.[54] The Action Plan was adopted as part of the EU's efforts to comply with the Paris Agreement and meet the goals of Agenda 2030. The Commission concluded that the role of the financial system is key. The objectives of the Action Plan are to:

- reorient capital flows towards sustainable investment in order to achieve sustainable and inclusive growth;
- manage financial risks stemming from climate change, resource depletion, environmental degradation and social issues; and
- foster transparency and long-termism in financial and economic activity.

The Commission stated that 'sustainable finance' generally meant that environmental and social considerations are taken into account in investment decisions. By environmental considerations, the Commission meant 'climate change mitigation and adaptation, as well as the environment more broadly and related risks (e.g., natural disasters)'. By social considerations, the Commission meant 'issues of inequality, inclusiveness, labour relations, investment in human capital and communities'.

54. COM(2018) 97.

In the Action Plan, the European Commission declared its intention to propose, as a first step, a uniform classification system for the types of activities to be considered 'sustainable'. The declared ambition was then to include both climate, environment and social responsibility. So far, the EU taxonomy only covers sustainable activities from an environmental perspective. A so-called social taxonomy is a long time coming.

4.3.2 The European Green Deal

In December 2019, the European Green Deal was launched.[55] The Green Deal is a strategy to transform the EU into a sustainable economy and society and includes actions in a wide range of areas. The stated ambition is to transition to a modern, resource-efficient and competitive economy where there are no net emissions of greenhouse gases by 2050, economic growth has been decoupled from resource consumption, and no people or places are left behind. The Green Deal is part of the Commission's strategy to implement Agenda 2030 and the Sustainable Development Goals.

The Green Deal consists of several strands, some of which are and are to be achieved through legislation:

- Increasing the EU's climate ambitions for 2030 and 2050.
- Supplying clean, affordable and secure energy.
- Mobilising industry for a clean and circular economy.
- Building and renovating in an energy and resource-efficient way.
- Accelerating the shift to sustainable and smart mobility.
- From 'Farm to Fork': designing a fair, healthy and environmentally friendly food system.
- Preserving and restoring ecosystems and biodiversity.
- A zero-pollution ambition for a toxic-free environment.

In addition, in the Green Deal, the European Commission communicated several mechanisms that will need to be used to mainstream sustainability in all EU policies:

- Pursuing green finance and investment and ensuring a just transition.
- Greening national budgets and sending the right price signals.
- Mobilising research and fostering innovation.
- Activating education and training.
- A green oath: 'do no harm'.

On the first mechanism, the Commission stated that the private sector will be key in financing the green transition. In this context, the Commission declared its intention

55. Communication from the Commission to the European Parliament, the European Council, the Council, the European Economic and Social Committee and the Committee of the Regions, The European Green Deal, 11 December 2019.

to adopt a sustainable finance strategy, following on from the action plan described in the previous section, which has since led to the adoption of several important pieces of legislation. Four of those belong to the third level of sustainability law.

4.3.3 EU Climate Law

As part of the first point of the Green Deal, in 2021, EU Regulation 2021/1119 establishing the framework for achieving climate neutrality was adopted, commonly called the *European Climate Law*. Article 2(1) of the Regulation states that Union-wide greenhouse gas emissions and removals shall be in balance by 2050. In other words, the goal is net-zero emissions. Article 4(1) further states that by 2030, the EU is to reduce its net greenhouse gas emissions by at least 55% compared to 1990 levels.[56] Article 6 states that every five years, starting in 2023, the Commission shall assess the collective progress of all Member States towards achieving the 2050 climate-neutrality goal.

4.3.4 Regulation 2018/2088 on Sustainability-Related Disclosures in the Financial Services Sector (SFDR)

To increase the investments made to transform the EU economy into a sustainable economy, requirements are set for how companies in the financial sector disclose sustainability-related information. The requirements are set out in Regulation 2018/2088 on sustainability-related disclosures in the financial services sector (SFDR). The regulation applies to financial market participants and financial advisers, both of which are defined in Article 2 of the regulation. The specific requirements of the regulation are described in Chapter 8 of this book.

The regulation contains an important definition of the term *sustainable investment* – defined in Article 2(17) – which means an investment in an economic activity that contributes to an environmental or social objective, provided that the investments do not cause significant harm to any of those objectives and that the investee companies comply with good governance practices, in particular with respect to sound management structures, employee relations, remuneration of staff and tax compliance. This expresses, on the one hand, the positive contribution norm coming from the Agenda 2030 and, on the other hand, the due diligence norm coming from the UNGPs and OECD Guidelines.

The regulation gives the Commission a mandate to adopt certain so-called delegated acts. For example, Delegated Regulation 2022/1288 sets out regulatory technical standards that specify how to comply with the information requirements set out in the regulation.

56. The package is therefore referred to as Fit for 55.

4.3.5 Regulation 2020/852 on the Establishment of a Framework to Facilitate Sustainable Investment (EU Taxonomy)

Regulation 2020/852 on the establishment of a framework to facilitate sustainable investment - known as the EU Taxonomy - is directly linked to the SFDR. As mentioned, Article 2.17 of the SFDR contains a definition of what constitutes a sustainable investment. The EU taxonomy clarifies which investments can be referred to as *environmentally sustainable investments*. An investment is, according to Article 3, environmentally sustainable if the economic activity in question:

- contributes substantially to one or more of the environmental objectives set out in Article 9;
- does not cause significant harm to any of the environmental objectives set out in Article 9;
- is carried out in compliance with the minimum safeguards laid down in Article 18, and
- complies with the technical screening criteria established by the Commission.

The environmental objectives set out in Article 9 are:

- climate change mitigation;
- climate change adaptation;
- the sustainable use and protection of water and marine resources;
- the transition to a circular economy;
- pollution prevention and control; and
- the protection and restoration of biodiversity and ecosystems.

Of course, the environmental objectives are directly linked to the nine planetary boundaries, as described in Chapter 1. The technical screening criteria referred to in Article 3(d) constitute the taxonomy itself. The content of the EU Taxonomy is described in more detail in Chapter 9 of this book.

4.3.6 EU Regulation 2023/2631 on European Green Bonds

The most recently adopted legislation on sustainable finance is EU Regulation 2023/2631 on European Green Bonds. The regulation is closely related to the EU taxonomy and requires issuers of green bonds named EU Green Bond to use the proceeds for taxonomy-aligned business activities. The regulation is described in Chapter 10 of this book.

4.4 EU LAWS ON SUSTAINABLE BUSINESS

Through the regulations on sustainable finance, the EU legislator intends to meet the objectives of the Action Plan on Financing Sustainable Growth. Those regulations are naturally focused on actors on the financial markets and will only indirectly affect the conduct of businesses. To meet the requirements of the SFDR and the EU taxonomy, the financial actors are dependent on data from the businesses in which investments are made. Also, many companies can and do have significant positive and negative impacts on sustainability matters regardless of financing. At the next level of sustainability law, we, therefore, find laws directly regulating the conduct of business in all other markets.

4.4.1 Corporate Sustainability Reporting Directive (CSRD)

Since 2014, the Directive 2014/95/EU on disclosure of non-financial and diversity information by certain large undertakings and groups (NFRD) applies. The directive has been updated by Directive 2022/2464 on corporate sustainability reporting, often (and in this book) called CSRD (Corporate Sustainability Reporting Directive). The directive and the accounting standards adopted in response to it largely shape the structure of Part III of this book. Article 19a of the directive requires large undertakings to disclose information necessary to understand the undertaking's impacts on sustainability matters, and information necessary to understand how sustainability matters affect the undertaking's development, performance and position. The requirements for sustainability reporting are then gradually introduced to an increasing scope of companies.

4.4.2 The Directive on Corporate Sustainability Due Diligence (CSDDD)

As will be further described in the book, SFDR, the EU taxonomy and CSRD establish obligations for companies to report about their investments and business operations from a sustainability perspective. The EU legislator has set up an ideal image of what it means to be a sustainable investor and to conduct sustainable business, based on the fundamental due diligence norm set out in the UNGPs and OECD guidelines and the positive contribution norm coming from Agenda 2030. The reporting frameworks require companies to report how they perform in relation to this ideal image.

Through the Directive 2024/1760/EU on Corporate Sustainability Due Diligence, the sustainable due diligence norm is transformed into direct legal obligations for those large companies to which the directive will apply. Article 1 of the directive lays down rules on obligations for companies regarding actual and potential human rights adverse impacts and environmental adverse impacts with respect to their own operations, the operations of their subsidiaries, and the value chain operations carried out by entities with whom the company has an established business relationship as well as on liability for violations of these obligations.

According to Article 5, companies are obliged to conduct human rights and environmental due diligence by carrying out the following actions:

(a) integrating due diligence into their policies;
(b) identifying actual or potential adverse impacts;
(c) preventing and mitigating potential adverse impacts, bringing actual adverse impacts to an end and minimising their extent;

(d) establishing and maintaining a complaints procedure;
(e) monitoring the effectiveness of their due diligence policy and measures; and
(f) publicly communicating on due diligence.

The content of the Due Diligence Directive will be described in further detail in Chapter 14.

4.5 OTHER SUSTAINABILITY-RELATED EU AND NATIONAL LAWS

The SFDR, EU taxonomy and other regulatory frameworks referred to in the previous sections are all coming as a direct result of the EU Green Deal. But it would be too limiting to say that sustainability law only encompasses these regulations. Sustainability law also covers areas of law existing before the EU Green Deal, such as environmental law, labour law, marketing law, consumer law and data protection law. These areas of law are all based on the same normative ground regarding protection of human dignity in accordance with the principles of equality and freedom, e.g., the Corporate Sustainability Due Diligence Directive, even though they were adopted in another context.

This book only covers EU law and not national legislation. But, of course, national legislation constitutes an important part of sustainability law. The EU directives referred to in previous sections have to be implemented in national legislation to become effective.[57] Furthermore, the EU may only adopt legislation within the legislative powers given to it in the EU treaties, meaning that important areas of law are not at all regulated at the EU level. Often, there is a complementary relationship between EU law and national legislation.

4.6 CORPORATE POLICIES

With the previous level, we leave the area of adopted laws. At the next level, we instead find corporate policies, which form a natural part of the rules of the game, influencing whether a business is sustainable or not.

Through the Corporate Sustainability Due Diligence Directive, adoption of such policies is mandatory for companies to which the directive applies. Under the disclosure rules of, e.g., SFDR and CSRD, companies should instead just report if and to what extent they have sustainability-related policies and similar corporate documentation.

4.7 CONTRACTS

The final level of sustainability law is the level of contracts. Contracts form an obvious and crucial part of the rules that shape companies' behaviour and, hence, whether a business is conducted in a sustainable manner or not. Almost all of a company's

57. EU regulations become effective upon adoption by the EU legislative bodies and may not be implemented into national legislation.

revenues and costs pass through a web of contracts and contractual rules. In practice, the contracting level may be the most important level to focus on in the transition to a sustainable economy.

Part IV of this book, therefore, deals with the matter of contracts and sustainability and, more specifically, how contracts can be written to implement the norms of due diligence and positive contribution. The perspective in that part is more general. A key distinction must, however, be made between contracts related to corporate value chains and contracts related to corporate finance. The latter is dealt with in more detail in Part IV, whereas the former is dealt with in Part V – sustainable value chains.

CHAPTER 5

Sustainability, Economics and Morality

As explained above, the EU laws of sustainability should be viewed as a transformation of the due diligence norm in the UNGPs and OECD Guidelines, as well as the positive obligations to promote, for example, the SDGs into binding legal obligations. This is a simplified view, but it should at least serve as a starting point for interpreting the laws. The due diligence norm requires companies to systematically identify, prevent, mitigate and account for how they address actual and potential material adverse impacts as part of their decision-making and risk management systems. Adding the positive contribution norm to this, companies shall use the same process to identify and implement positive contributions to the environment or society. The norms of positive contribution and due diligence form the basis of a political morality, which is converted into laws.

It is important to understand that sustainability is fundamentally a moral issue. That the nine planetary boundaries are *exceeded*, that Earth's resources are *overexploited*, and that strong forces in the economy and society lead to *inequality* are not statements of fact. They are normative statements. If climate change continues, the climate system will find a new equilibrium, which will not be favourable for humans to live in. That is highly problematic from a human, moral perspective. The same applies, for example, to the overexploitation of natural resources.

As said in the introduction to the book about the interpretivist legal theory applied in the book, what is meant here by 'moral issue' is not a universal morality existing as an independent metaphysical or religious phenomenon. What is meant is a political morality resting on the rights of all citizens to equality and freedom established in the treaties on human rights and protection of the environment referred to in section 4.1 above. These are obligations that people and organisations have towards each other by virtue of being part of the same political community.

Sustainability is thus a moral issue, and it is this morality that forms the basis of EU sustainability law. The rules of sustainable business are morally based. It is important to understand what this actually means. This chapter begins with a summary description of the European Court on Human Rights ruling in *Verein*

Klimaseniorinnen Schweiz and others v. Switzerland on 9 April 2024. Thereafter, sustainability is discussed from a more economic perspective, with a focus on so-called external effects. It then describes how, behind this perspective, lies a moral reality, which is, to a large extent, also reflected in the ruling by the European court. It is important not to equate all immoral actions with unsustainable ones, which is why the chapter then points out what, from a moral perspective, is specific to unsustainable actions. The chapter ends with a statement of what it means to conduct unsustainable versus sustainable business.

5.1 THE EUROPEAN COURT OF HUMAN RIGHTS ON HUMAN RIGHTS AND CLIMATE CHANGE

In a landmark ruling on 9 April 2024, the European Court of Human Rights established – in *Verein Klimaseniorinnen Schweiz and others v. Switzerland* – that the human right to protection of privacy and family life, as expressed in Article 8 of the European Convention of Human Rights, encompasses a right for individuals to effective protection by state authorities from serious adverse effects of climate change on their life, health, well-being and quality of life. While this ruling is dated later than all the EU laws covered in this book, it nevertheless is well suited to serve as an explanation of the moral character of sustainability.

5.1.1 Background

In the case, a Swiss association named *Verein Seniorinnen Schweiz* and four women lodged a complaint against the Swiss government, alleging that the government had violated their rights to life, fair trial, respect for privacy and family life and effective remedies under ECHR in the area of climate-change mitigation. The purpose of the association was to promote and implement effective climate protection on behalf of its members – older women in Switzerland.

The claimants basically held that the Swiss government had not done enough to prevent climate change, which violated their human rights. The individual applicants testified of having experienced difficulty during heatwaves, feeling pain, collapsing while exposed to the sun, having to stay indoors almost the entire day, having the need for medical attention, having to refrain from recreational activities and so on.

5.1.2 Important Questions in the Case

The case raised a number of formal questions regarding the applicant's legal standing in the case, but these can all be ignored for the purpose of this chapter. The key questions were 'questions of merit': What responsibility can a state reasonably have for, for example, an older woman having to stay inside during a heatwave, considering the multitude of combined causes leading to it? Climate change is the result of actions and failures to act by billions of people, governments, companies, other organisations and so on. Switzerland contributes to global greenhouse gas emissions to a very small extent, for example, so would it really have mattered to the applicants if the Swiss government had done more? Switzerland's contribution to the problem is a drop in the ocean. And even if that contribution could be properly established, the causality chain from Switzerland's failure to take action to an old woman having to stay inside during a heatwave is, to say the least, long and complex. Not least because the heatwaves are the result of not a failure to take a specific action but of actions and failures to take actions over a long period of time.

Another important but slightly different question concerned what the court was entitled to do. To say that a government has failed to take appropriate actions to mitigate climate change is very close to a political intervention in what, it can be argued, should be subject to democratic processes and not court decisions.

All these questions are relevant for companies - not only for companies' greenhouse gas emissions but also for all forms of negative environmental and social impact. As will be described below, when it comes to sustainability, it is not single acts and failures to act that are relevant but sustained and repetitive behaviour over time which, together with actions taken by others, lead to irreversible negative impact. Rarely are those negative effects only attributable to one company, and often, the causality chain between a specific company's actions and a negative effect will be hard to establish. This raises, as will be described, both moral and legal questions.

5.1.3 Is Protection Against Climate Change a Human Right?

It was thus by no means obvious that the Swiss government was responsible for what the applicants claimed it was responsible for. But the court held that that was the case. First of all, the court held, consistent with rulings in the past, that while there exists no human right to a healthy and quiet environment, climate change can have effects on the enjoyment of human rights, for example, the right to respect for privacy and family life in Article 8 and Article 2 regarding the right to life.[58] The court referred to IPCC reports and other evidence to establish the detrimental effects on human health and life quality due to climate change.

Therefore, there exists no human right in ECHR directly tied to the environment, but the court simply found that the environment - the climate - can affect peoples' possibility to live a life without external interference from others protected by Article 8.

5.1.4 The Scope of a State's Responsibility for Climate Change

As regards the question of one (small) state's responsibility for something which is caused by so many, the court held that a state cannot evade its responsibility for its own failures by pointing at others, saying that they also failed to take action.[59] The court referred to other cases on similar situations, saying that a state can be held responsible

58. Sections 431-436.
59. Section 442.

for its 'share of the responsibility'.[60] Anything else was, of course, out of the question since another view would immediately have led to a situation where a tragedy of the commons dilemma would relieve everyone of responsibility.[61] The fact that others violate peoples' human rights cannot relieve you from your own responsibility to respect those rights.

As regards the 'drop in the ocean' argument (referred to as such by the court),[62] the court *could have* said that since climate change would not have been improved just because Switzerland had done its part to mitigate it, Switzerland cannot be responsible for climate change. This argument would have implied, in the language of moral theory, a consequentialist moral reasoning, where you are not responsible for anything but for the bad consequences of your actions or failures to act.

The court took a more nuanced approach by not just looking at consequences. It referred to the duty, regardless of consequences, of states, according to the United Nations Framework Convention on Climate Change (UNFCCC), to take measures to anticipate, prevent or minimise the causes of climate change and mitigate its adverse effects. But consequences or likely consequences are, of course, also important, so the court said that for responsibility, it is enough that 'reasonable measures which the domestic authorities failed to take could have had a real prospect of altering the outcome or mitigating the harm'.

Failures to follow duties which make no difference should not be condemned. But failure to take actions within your control that could reasonably have positive consequences for others violates the rights of those whom you fail to help.

5.1.5 Time and Tipping Points

A characteristic of sustainability is that the focus is not so much on single actions or failures to act but on repetitive behaviour, which, over time, leads to sustained negative effects. While a single action, for example not adopting a law or emitting a number of tons of greenhouse gases into the atmosphere, may not be a problem due to its limited effects, this action can be highly problematic when seen as part of a larger pattern of behaviour.

This aspect was also clear in the court's reasoning. The court did not establish a direct obligation for Switzerland to reduce emissions, but instead, an obligation to put in place measures and regulations aimed at preventing an increase in green house gas concentrations in the Earth's atmosphere and a rise in global average temperature beyond levels capable of producing serious and irreversible adverse effects on human rights.[63] There are two important aspects to this statement. First of all, the obligation of the state is to *act by establishing rules for action* – or rules of the game with reference to the framework of this book. Second, those rules should be aimed at *preventing*

60. Section 443.
61. *See* section 2.3 of this book.
62. Section 444.
63. Section 546.

patterns of action that, over time, lead to the breaking of tipping points, for example, some of the nine planetary boundaries.[64]

5.1.6 Obligation to Act with Due Diligence

The court's focus on rules is highly relevant to this book. But, as stated, it is important to notice that this case concerned a state and its obligations and not a company. The state, at least its legislative arm, acts by establishing laws for acting for itself and those who are subject to those laws. Using the important distinction between primary and secondary rules made by legal positivt H.L.A. Hart, a state sets the primary rules relevant for mitigating, in this case, climate change by application of its secondary rules, i.e., the laws regarding the democratic process for adopting laws.[65]

The European court did not assess Switzerland's secondary rules, i.e., its legislative procedure. Instead, two things were assessed: (1) to what extent Switzerland, in *applying* its secondary rules, acted with *due diligence* when *adopting* its primary rules regarding climate change mitigation;[66] and (2) if and to what extent those adopted primary rules, were sufficient to safeguard the protection granted under Article 8 of ECHR. Both those perspectives are highly relevant for companies too.

As regards Switzerland's due diligence – which, of course, is of interest given the fundamental due diligence norm in EU sustainability law – the Swiss government argued before the court that a state, when choosing the best means to combat climate change, has to take into account many different and often competing interests.[67] Measures to combat climate change can be very costly, which means that fewer resources can be used for other things that are also important for a country. How should, for example, expenses on public childcare be weighed against expenses on climate change mitigation? The Swiss state basically argued that it is not for the European court to make such assessments since it is a matter of policy more than human rights. This is a relevant point also for businesses, which always will have to take a large number of aspects and interests into consideration when becoming more sustainable.

The court approached this matter as a question of a state's 'margin of appreciation', i.e., the degree of discretion that a state has in applying its secondary rules.[68] This margin of appreciation is not entirely set by the states themselves but is framed by the human rights set out in ECHR. Following the interpretivist legal theory used in this book, it can be said that human rights set out what it means to treat everyone as equals. The margin of appreciation for a state when applying its secondary rules is shaped by this requirement to treat everyone as equals.

The court thus recognised that a state must take *all* competing interests into consideration, which is natural considering any democratic state's duty to treat its

64. *See* section 1.3 of this book regarding the nine planetary boundaries.
65. *See* Hart, HLA., *ibid.*
66. Section 538(e).
67. Section 351.
68. Section 544.

citizens as equals.[69] But the court also stated clearly that, given the grave nature of climate change, this particular consideration should be given considerable weight in relation to other considerations.[70] This is also natural. Treating everyone as equals does not mean that everyone's interests deserve the same attention. The level of attention must be proportionate to the level of harm which can arise if actions are not taken. Even though, to use the same example, high-quality childcare is important not only for children and their parents but also, it could be argued, for society in general, combating climate change must perhaps be prioritised since it will affect more people, affect people more negatively than poor childcare and is also for that matter a condition for qualitative childcare.

It is important that the court also said that, in its assessment of this matter, it should take into account the extent to which the views of the citizens of the relevant state were taken into account during the decision-making (i.e., legislative) process.[71] This is directly corresponding to the obligation under the due diligence norm to take the views and interests of corporate stakeholders into account.

5.1.7 A State's Positive Obligations to Adopt Rules

Having found that a state's margin of appreciation in applying its secondary rules is restricted by human rights, the court went on to establish the state's positive obligations, i.e., obligations related to the primary rules.

The court now said that since there is a causal relationship between climate change and potential violations of human rights, the state must not primarily take mitigating actions but must instead put in place *rules* – the necessary regulations and measures to prevent an increase in greenhouse gas emissions.[72] A binding regulatory framework – rules of the game for combatting climate change – followed by adequate implementation, including targets and timelines, is what is required.[73]

This is where Switzerland had failed. Switzerland had adopted rules, but they were deemed insufficient given Switzerland's obligation to protect the human rights of its citizens.

5.1.8 Relevance for Business

It is not yet clear what the ruling in *Verein Klimaseniorinnen Schweiz and others v. Switzerland* means for business. Some preliminary conclusions can probably be drawn. As already stated, EU law shall be interpreted in light of the rulings of the European court on Human Rägths. The ECHR is, of course, law but can also be said to form the 'political morality' which shall inform the interpretation of EU sustainability laws addressed to companies. As said, those laws are largely an implementation of the

69. Section 538(e).
70. Section 542.
71. Section 539(b).
72. Section 545.
73. Sections 549 and 550.

OECD guidelines and the UNGPs, which can be said to be a 'translation' of what the treaties on human rights and environmental protection applicable to states mean for business. The ruling from the ECHR should shape how those documents are interpreted and, therefore, also the EU rules implementing them.

The ruling from ECHR forms, as said, an excellent basis for clarifying the moral aspects of sustainability underlying the EU legislation.

5.2 THE UNINTERNALISED EXTERNAL EFFECTS

What causes the catastrophic consequences of the Too Little Too Late scenario in the Earth4All model? There are, of course, several interlinked factors and causal relationships. In *Verein Klimaseniorinnen Schweiz and others v. Switzerland*, the focus was on a state's failure to act. What is clear, however, is that companies are also responsible for a large part of the problems.

When companies cause damage to the environment and people, it is often referred to as *externalities* or *external effects.* A negative external effect is *the company's negative impact on people or the environment that the company does not carry the costs for.*[74] These can be environmental effects, such as pollution, greenhouse gas emissions and social effects, such as the deterioration of living conditions, the creation of bad health and so on. If a company starts to pay to avoid the external effect, either through a tax from the government or internally by investing in equipment that avoids emissions, this is referred to as the company *internalising the external effect.* The external effect has been made internal.

In the case *Verein Klimaseniorinnen Schweiz and others v. Switzerland*, this terminology was not used, which is natural since the case was about a state and not a company. But the case was clearly about Switzerland's obligations to take the necessary actions, including the allocation of governmental resources, to prevent Switzerland's contributions to climate change. And other rulings from the ECHR have made clear that states can be obliged to adopt legal frameworks that force companies within their jurisdictions to internalise their external effects.[75]

In his book *The Profiteers – How Business Privatizes Profits and Socializes Costs*, finance professor Christopher Marquis offers a large number of examples of how companies generate external effects.[76] Carbon emissions are just the most obvious example. Marquis interestingly points out how it is easy to think that less business travel and more online meetings will decrease carbon emissions, while in fact, the enormous amounts of electricity needed to run the cloud service data centres enabling those meetings may just mean that the emissions are shifted from aeroplanes to data centres. Marquis further points to the damages to Earth and people caused by the dominant systems for agriculture and food production, how plastics and other waste

74. In the book, I use the concept of external effects and externalities interchangeable to refer to companies' negative impacts for which they do not carry the costs.
75. *See, e.g., Jugheli and Others v. Gerorgia*, 13 July 2017, section 75.
76. Marquis, C., The Profiteers - How Business Privatizes Profits and Socializes Costs, Public Affairs, 2024.

are dumped in nature, how most of the chocolate we eat is produced by the use of forced and child labour and so on.

Companies can be induced to internalise their external effect in different ways. A common way is through legislation, where carbon taxes are an oft-cited example. The tax means that the company must pay for its emissions, but it also gives the company an incentive to avoid the emissions.

A large part of the problems described in the Earth4All model are external effects. It is the damages to the environment, people and society that have been caused directly or indirectly by companies, but where companies do not carry the costs for these damages, nor do they carry the costs of avoiding them.

Admittedly, it can be difficult to accurately measure the size of a company's external effects in economic terms, which is a familiar phenomenon from, for example, tort law. How can one measure, for example, the harm caused by a violation of someone's right to freedom of expression in economic terms? Still, external effects can often be measured adequately. They can be measured from at least two perspectives: on the one hand *from the company's perspective* and on the other hand from the perspective of *the negatively affected* environment or humans.

From *the company's perspective,* the cost of the external effect can be measured as the company's cost of avoiding the external effect. For example, it is possible to measure what it would cost for a company to make investments that eliminate greenhouse gas emissions or to enter into and accept the consequences of a collective bargaining agreement with the employees.

From the perspective of the *affected environment or person*, the cost of the external effect can be measured in terms of the cost of remedying the *damage from the external effect*. For example, it is possible to measure what it would cost to clean up a polluted lake or to compensate people who may have lost their jobs because they were not protected by a collective bargaining agreement.

In economic terms, external effects are an example of market failure, which occurs when the market functions in a way that means that resources in society are not efficiently distributed. External effects mean that profits and costs end up in different hands – for example, profits go to the company that sells products, but the costs of producing these products are borne by someone else. This is, in economic terms, a suboptimal allocation of resources.

This becomes clear when comparing the cost of an external effect from the perspective of the company and the affected surroundings. *If the cost for the company to avoid the damage is lower than the harm for those who are negatively affected, it is, from a socio-economic perspective, inefficient for the company not to take the cost and avoid the harmful activity*. If the cost for a company to make investments to prevent pollution of a lake is lower than the cost of cleaning the lake, then the cost to society will be unnecessarily high if the company does not make the investment. If, for example, higher personnel costs for a company that signs a collective bargaining agreement are lower than the costs of restoring redundant employees to work, the social cost will be unnecessarily high if the collective bargaining agreement is not signed.

The economic analysis of companies' negative impact on their environment is important. But it doesn't say anything about sustainability. This is because it doesn't really say anything at all about how companies and people *should* act. The economic fact that an economy in which firms do not bear the costs of their negative external effects is inefficient does not mean that companies should bear those costs or that legislation should be introduced to make sure firms start bearing those costs. It is an old truth, best explained by the Scottish eighteenth-century philosopher David Hume, that it is not possible to infer how something should be from how something is.

However, the economic reality described above conceals a moral reality.[77] The uninternalised external effects can be viewed as economic descriptions of moral violations of people's right to equality and freedom.

5.3 MORAL THEORIES

It should, again, be emphasised that the claim that sustainability *is* a moral question is not intended to be a metaphysical statement about some sort of inner nature of sustainability. The claim is simply that all claims about what is sustainable or not are statements of value, of what is good and bad and, therefore, what *ought* to be done or avoided. These values derive, from a legal perspective, from the treaties of human rights and protection of the environment. It is from those documents that the *oughts* come from.

It is important to uncover this underlying morality for mainly two reasons: first because, it is important for interpreting the EU sustainability laws such as the CSRD or the EU taxonomy. Second, and equally important, because a shift to sustainable business is basically about systematically implementing a moral perspective on the business, which often will have significant practical consequences.

What kind of moral perspective are we talking about here? Moral theory is, of course, a vast subject. Traditionally, the area is divided into at least three areas, covering the utilitarian theory of, e.g., British philosopher John Stuart Mill,[78] the deontological theory of, e.g., Immanuel Kant,[79] and the virtuous theory of, e.g., Aristotle.[80] And, of course, there are those who claim that it is useless to discuss morality in the first place since all morality is relative and subjective.

The purpose of this book is mainly practical and not philosophical, even though philosophy can be very useful to draw practical conclusions. It is, therefore, not important to enter deeply into the philosophical debates of moral relativity or the merits of different moral perspectives. What is important is to uncover the morality underlying the norms of positive contribution and due diligence as they are expressed

77. The reader is asked to not take this claim too literally and think that I claim that there exists a parallel, moral universe.
78. Mill, J.S., Utilitarianism, Aeterna Classics, 2018.
79. Kant, I., Critique of Practical Reason, The Big Nest, 2016.
80. Aristotle, Nicomachean Ethics, Good Press, 2023.

in, for example, the UNGPs and OECD Guidelines and how these norms are further detailed in the EU sustainability regulations.

This is in line with the interpretivist legal theory described in the book's introduction, according to which the law should be interpreted in light of its underlying normative principles. As discussed, interpretivism discards utilitarianism and its expressions in law and economics. It is highly useful to adopt some thinking tools from economics when discussing law and morality, but ultimately, law and economics have unacceptable consequences, which would lead to recommendations violating basic human rights.

In what follows, therefore, I sketch what can be called a 'sustainability morality' based on the moral theory of Ronald Dworkin, a theory that lies close to the theories of Derek Parfit, Thomas Nagel and Thomas Scanlon.[81] In later chapters of the book, this sustainability morality is referred to and also further elaborated in the environmental, social and governance sustainability areas.[82]

5.4 A SKETCH FOR A SUSTAINABILITY MORALITY

5.4.1 Dignity

The due diligence norm in the UNGPs and OECD Guidelines is an elaboration of what it should mean for companies to conduct responsible business, not violating human rights or harming the environment. The starting point for the sustainability morality underlying the norms of due diligence and positive contribution is, therefore, human dignity.[83] Article 1 of the Universal Declaration of Human Rights states that 'all human beings are born free and equal in dignity and rights'. The Charter of Fundamental Rights of the European Union states that 'human dignity is inviolable. It must be respected and protected'. Those articles express a fundamental moral conception of human dignity linked to equality and freedom, which forms the basis of sustainability law. In fact, through a quite simple model of what human dignity is, it is possible to

81. For those interested in categorising this theory, it is perhaps best described as a combination of deontological and virtuous ethics – not that it matters much. Dworkin, Scanlon and others are, by law and economist scholar Richard Posner, referred to as 'academic moralists', against which Posner himself sets his 'pragmatic' approach. The rhetoric used by Posner is striking, clearly drawing on the popular view of academics sitting in the ivory towers out of touch with reality, where Posner the 'pragmatist' is living in the real world and, being a practicing judge, knows how things really work. Posner then makes the very 'academic move', saying that no universal morality exists but is all relative, which is so obviously a view of the world than only an academic can take as compared to people living in the real world, who often think that morality really matters and is not just a play of words, as Posner indicates. (Posner, R., The Problems of Jurisprudence, Harvard University Press, 1993.)

82. It deserves emphasising that the choice of Ronald Dworkin's moral theory is not arbitrary. It is chosen because, in the eyes of the author, it is the theory that makes best sense of EU's sustainability laws.

83. For a very good and rather simple elaboration of the perspective adopted here, with human dignity as the starting, moving on to equality and freedom, *see* Dworkin, R., Is Democracy Possible Here?: Principles for a New Political Debate, Princeton University Press, 2006, Chapter 1.

capture and demonstrate connections between a large number of phenomena in the field of sustainability and sustainability law.

5.4.2 Equality

As stated in the Universal Declaration of Human Rights, dignity is first and foremost about equality. No human is worth more than another. This means, first, that, in the words of Immanuel Kant, no human should be treated merely as a means to other ends but must be seen as an end in itself.[84] Equality means that every human should be respected as a human being.

Why should all people treat all people as equals? In a modern society, it is difficult to refer to religious or so-called natural law theories. Nor is it necessary. Most people agree that one's own life is important, that it should be taken seriously, and that it should not be wasted. Most people also agree that integrity, in the sense of adherence to principles, is an important quality. A person of high integrity consistently acts according to a set of values and ideals, although short-term gains may arise from acting contrary to those ideals. For most people, it's not just their own life that is important to take seriously; being a person with integrity is also important.[85]

But the person who holds these personal ideals is also compelled to respect these ideals in others. If I feel that it is important to take my life seriously, the ideal of integrity forces me to also consider that other people's lives are important and should be taken seriously too. My life is important, not because of me but because I am a human being, and since others are also human beings, their lives must be taken seriously too.

5.4.3 Freedom

The second dimension of human dignity is freedom. Every human must be allowed to live his/her life as he/she sees fit, in accordance with the goals and values he/she sets for himself/herself. It also follows that no one has the right to restrict other people's opportunities to live their lives according to their own goals and values.

The principle of freedom can be said to follow logically from the norm of equality and one's own duty to take one's life seriously. If my life is important to take seriously, it means I must also make something good out of it. I do this through the goals I set, the values I live by, and how I follow those goals and values. Again, my integrity requires me to acknowledge that all other people have the right to do the same.

5.4.4 Human Rights

As described in Chapter 3, the treaties on human rights are, together with the treaties on environmental protection, sustainability law's starting point. It is easy to see the

84. Kant, I., Fundamental Principles of the Metaphysics of Morals, The Big Nest, 2016, 56.
85. Anyone who doubts this can ask themselves how they perceive another human being who lacks integrity, who does not keep his word, who claims to be in favour of freedom but oppresses others, and so on.

connection between human rights and the fundamental principles of equality and freedom. This is obvious in the European court's ruling in *Verein Klimaseniorinnen Schweiz and others v. Switzerland*, in which the connection between climate change and the right to respect for private and family life was established.

The various international treaties on human rights show many similarities. The Charter of Fundamental Rights of the European Union can be taken as an example. Article 1 states that human dignity is inviolable. Article 2 establishes the right to life and the prohibition of the death penalty, which is a logical consequence of everyone having an equal right to their lives being taken seriously and considered important (equality). The same principle is expressed in the right to physical and mental integrity in Article 3 and the prohibitions against torture and slavery in Articles 4 and 5. Articles 20, 21 and 23 establish the rights of equality before the law, non-discrimination and equality between men and women.

Human rights that are linked to the norm of freedom are expressed in the right to liberty and security in Article 6, respect for private and family life in Article 7 and the right to the protection of personal data in Article 8. Articles 10, 11 and 12 establish the rights to freedom of thought, expression, information, assembly and association. All these rights are necessary to protect every human's opportunity to live a life where they live according to the goals and values they have set for themselves. Articles 27 to 32 set out the rights of workers, which are all concerned with respect for workers' freedom and not being subject to the will of another (the employer).

To strictly divide the rights of the EU Charter into rights linked to equality and freedom, respectively, is of course misleading. Many rights express both principles, which is not surprising since they are two sides of the same coin - human dignity. Citizens' right to vote in Article 39 is an example of a human right relying on both equality and freedom. The right to vote is a freedom that everyone over a certain age has; it is about respect for the equal value of every human.

Article 37 does not express a right but expresses a standard of a high level of environmental protection under the principle of sustainable development. Of course, this principle also expresses the principles of equality and freedom. A healthy environment for people is a prerequisite for exercising all other rights, for being able to live a life in which people take that life seriously, in accordance with the goals and values that are important to them, for equality and freedom.

5.4.5 To Help and Not to Harm Others

Morality is, of course, much more than human rights in a more formal, legal sense. It is present in every everyday situation - including in the operations of a company - and is then expressed in a duty to help others.

Suppose a person is standing on a dock and another person in the water is drowning. Is the person on the dock obliged to help the person in the water? It may seem obvious, but it still requires moral consideration. Not rescuing the person in the water violates his/her right to equal treatment and means that his/her life is not taken seriously. But let us say the person on the dock cannot swim and can only save the person in the water at the risk of his or her own life. Then, it is not as obvious. Instead, what is required is perhaps that the person on the dock calls for others who can help the person in the water. Still, it is a moral duty to help others under certain conditions.

This principle was clear in *Verein Klimaseniorinnen Schweiz and others v. Switzerland*, where the European court, in line with its previous practice, said that the protection of human rights does not only involve refraining from harmful actions but also *positive obligations*; in that case, positive obligations to adopt a legal framework to combat climate change. Here, we can see part of the origin of the norm of positive contribution in EU sustainability laws.

In the same way, people sometimes have a moral obligation not to harm each other. This also follows from the principles of equality and freedom. To physically harm someone means to violate their equality. If the physical injury restricts the injured person's ability to lead a full life, it is also a violation of his or her freedom. The same applies if, for example, a person poisons their neighbour's drinking water so it becomes undrinkable or, in other ways, destroys the neighbour's living environment.

But sometimes, it is not so obvious that an action someone else perceives as bad is morally wrong. Let's say a woman lives in a house with several apartments and her great passion is to sing opera. The problem is that when she sings, it disturbs the neighbours. Is she morally obligated not to sing so that it disturbs the neighbours? The answer may seem obvious in the affirmative – her singing restricts the freedom of others to live their lives undisturbed from the neighbours. But it is not self-evident because the problem is reciprocal. Neighbours' complaints about her singing mean that neighbours are restricting *her* life. So who has the moral duty to whom: is she morally obliged to the neighbours to stop singing, or are the neighbours morally obliged to tolerate her singing?

This is a question applying the principle of everyone's equal value. Suppose that the singing woman is an opera singer and thus sings at her work. Her neighbours, however, really dislike opera and don't want to hear opera singing through the walls of their homes. One could say here that the singing woman's sacrifice is less if she does not sing at home than the neighbours' sacrifice if she sings at home because she sings at work after all.

An example closer to this book may be a company establishing a plant by a lake where many people live. The company pollutes the lake, making it impossible to fish from or swim in. It is easy to blame the company for acting immorally, but again, the problem is reciprocal. The comparison made in section 5.2 between the costs of avoiding the damage and the cost of repairing the damage can now be used to make what is, in reality, a moral assessment. If the former costs are lower than the latter, the company should make the investments necessary to avoid the damages. Not for economic reasons – here money is only used as a tool for thinking of relative importance. The reason is moral since it is, in that case, only if the company carries the cost that everyone is treated with equal respect.

In this way, many moral judgments are made. When people cross paths and realise that their life plans are not compatible with each other, one must assess the relative importance of their life plans. If it costs one less to compromise on their plans than it costs the other if the compromise were to not happen, then there is a moral duty to make the compromise. Not singing opera at home. Not to pollute water sources on which society depends. And so on.

Again, this principle was in play in *Verein Klimaseniorinnen Schweiz and others v. Switzerland*, where the court said that a state is obliged to take all competing interests into account but should pay particular attention to climate change due to the gravity of the harm caused.

The moral duty not to harm anyone else if the cost of avoiding the harm is lower than the harm caused is the moral mirror image of the principle of internalising external effects discussed above. In fact, the duty to internalise one's external effects is a moral obligation not to violate the equality and freedom of other people. The inequality which, in economic terms, is an inefficient allocation of resources, is, in fact, a moral misstep, violating human dignity.

5.4.6 Time and the Tipping Points

So far, the focus has been on the link between the moral duty to help and not harm others and to internalise external effects. This indicates that sustainability is a moral issue. But there are two important parts of the concept of sustainability and the due diligence norm missing from the argument: tipping points and time.

Sustainability implies some *tipping point* at which something no longer holds and thus breaks. Sustainability and the due diligence norm also imply *time*. The due diligence norm is not a norm for a single action but focuses on systematic behaviour over time. The single immoral act, which takes place instantaneously, cannot be unsustainable. It is an action that, over time, leads to, or risks leading to, passing a tipping point that is unsustainable. If, on a single occasion, a company negligently discharges pollutants into a watercourse, it is unnatural to call it unsustainable. These two aspects of sustainability are dealt with separately below.

5.4.6.1 Tipping Points

For an action to be unsustainable, there must be something that does not hold, that is, that at some juncture breaks. This is clearly expressed in the nine planetary boundary framework described above. These boundaries are set with humans in mind. They are set from the perspective that there are certain boundaries that the planetary processes must stay within for humanity to have the opportunity to live the life that humanity has been accustomed to for the last 12,000 years, i.e., during the *Holocene*. Beyond these boundaries – beyond the tipping points – the planetary processes risk finding new equilibrium and continuing to function as self-sustaining systems, but they will not be human-friendly systems.

These tipping points are often expressed in environmental quality standards in environmental law, which precisely limit values that the legislator has said must be within.

The same perspective can be taken on an individual and their health. The body's health can deteriorate due to illnesses, injuries, and more, but it can recover. But there are tipping points beyond which the body cannot be restored, either not without medical help or even regardless of medical assistance. The body normally stays around 36.5 °C to 37.5 °C. In the case of a high fever, the body temperature can approach 40 °C, but above 43 °C, death usually occurs. The same goes for mental health and stress. Burnout is a stage beyond a person's stress tolerance tipping point. Burnout is a new state of equilibrium, but it is a state in which the individual feels very bad.

Tipping points are important for assessing the sustainability of an action. An action can be immoral without being unsustainable. Occasionally, exposing a person to severe stress may be immoral, but it is hardly unsustainable as long as there is good reason to assume that this person will recover and not burn out and be degraded to a 'lower equilibrium'.

As already mentioned, this aspect of sustainability was also in play in *Verein Klimaseniorinnen Schweiz and others v. Switzerland*. The European Court established the state's obligation to adopt a legal framework preventing increasing greenhouse gas emissions in the atmosphere *beyond the levels capable of producing serious and irreversible adverse effects on human rights*.[86]

It is not always clear where a tipping point lies. For example, researchers find it difficult to define where the tipping points for biodiversity lie. Different individuals also have different tipping points for their health. Does this mean that an action cannot be unsustainable as long as you do not know where the tipping point lies? That can hardly be the case. Quite the opposite. If you know where the tipping point lies, an action may be immoral but not necessarily unsustainable if you know that the negative effects of the action will be restored and that the rupture will not occur. If, instead, one only knows that a tipping point exists and there are also no mechanisms in place to reverse the negative effects of the harm, then there is a moral duty to refrain from that action. This is the essence of the precautionary principle in environmental law.

5.4.6.2 *Time and the Moral Character of Companies*

The tipping points and the crossing of them point to the temporal dimension of the concept of sustainability. That something is unsustainable means it does not stand the test of time. This is probably obvious to most people, but it has important consequences, not least for sustainability law, as we will see. In moral judgments, the focus is often on the act itself. But because sustainability is about tipping points that risk being exceeded over time, not every immoral act is an unsustainable act. One might then ask what it is that is actually being judged when one says that an action is unsustainable. It is important to look beyond the individual actions and to the common denominator behind these actions, i.e., the *person acting*.[87]

---

86. Section 546.
87. For the theoretically interested, there is thus a shift here from a combined deontological and consequential to a more virtuous ethics focus.

An analogy can be made with a person who many perceive as an immoral person. There is an important difference between this person and a person who commits an immoral act on a single occasion. The immoral man acts immorally, but what makes the man immoral is not those actions but the *underlying character*. When you say that a person is immoral, it is a statement about their personality, where the immoral actions express that personality. What is it about the personality that makes a person considered immoral? Most people would probably agree that it is largely a matter of the immoral person disregarding or violating the three values that are used here to discuss human dignity – equality, freedom and integrity. The immoral person violates the dignity of others by not treating others equally, by oppressing them in various ways, and so on. The immoral person also lacks integrity, which here is very much about considering one's own life, one's own goals and values, and so on, as important to take seriously, but without respecting the corresponding rights of others.

The moral man has integrity and other characteristics, which means he consistently fulfils his obligations not to harm others and his obligations, when necessary, to help others.

The temporal dimension of the idea of sustainability thus makes it necessary to look at the character or personality of the person who commits acts that violate the equality and freedom of others. This explains, as will be shown below, the central parts of the sustainability laws that require companies to report how their business models, strategies, policies, etc., take sustainability matters into account. It may seem unnatural to talk about the 'character of a company' in the same way that you talk about personal character. But the comparison can still be made, and must be made, as this is fundamental to sustainability law. A personal character combines qualities, values, points of view, etc., which together express themselves in certain habits and actions. The character can be said to be a person's more or less unconscious rulebook for action. In the same way, the business model, strategy, company organisation, governing documents, corporate culture, etc., are the company's formal and informal rulebook, a rulebook that is expressed in how the company actually behaves in the market. It is the rulebook – the formal and informal rules – that determines whether business activities are sustainable or unsustainable. This is what has already been described in section 3.2, with the illustration of a company as an iceberg, with revenues, costs, profits, as well as environmental and social impact, lying above the surface and explained by everything from corporate purpose to contracts beneath the surface.

In *Verein Klimaseniorinnen Schweiz and others v. Switzerland*, it would not be natural to say that the 'character of Switzerland' was under scrutiny. But still, the European Court clearly established the state's positive obligation to adopt a 'rulebook' to mitigate climate change. The temporal character of sustainability meant that the court focused not on Switzerland's emission levels but on the rules allowing for these emission levels. The court, it could be said, focused not on the iceberg above but beneath the surface.

The elements of the iceberg model for a company can, based on this, be a bit more elaborated. A key element of what's 'beneath the surface' is the business model. The business model is, according to a common description, the basic logic according to which a company creates value for others and, in sales, also captures a part of that value of itself as revenues. Most companies are based on a basic idea and logic of how certain needs of people, companies or organisations can be met – for example, as goods or services – and how goods or services can be produced with the help of inputs, labour, etc., at a cost that is lower than revenue, thus creating profit. The business model usually comes with some form of corporate strategy, which is the answer to how the business model can be used successfully in a market where many companies compete for the same customers. It is common here to make a fundamental distinction between low-cost strategies and differentiation strategies. The former are primarily about winning customers by keeping prices low; the latter is about meeting customer needs in unique ways.[88]

The business model and strategy are institutionalised in various ways, not least through how the company is organised. When the company is starting out and few people are involved, it is often easy to make sure the actions that bring the business model to life are repeated over and over again, with adjustments for what you learn over time. As the company grows and engages more individuals, so does the need to coordinate the actions of many individuals in other ways to reproduce the same behaviour on a larger scale. Policies and other governing documents begin to be adopted, manuals begin to be written, values are set and so on. The underlying business model and strategy are systematised and institutionalised.

The more formal institutional structure also includes the informal rules of the game, expressed in the corporate culture. As is well known, this can differ considerably between different companies, and there are also often subcultures within the same company. As will be seen later, corporate culture is important to a company's ability to run a sustainable business.

In this way, the results of a company's activities express the underlying institutional structure, just as a person's actions can be said to express his underlying character. The results produced by the company over time, for example, greenhouse gas emissions, can be considered unsustainable or sustainable. But what is to blame is not the emissions as such, but the underlying institutional structure – the character – that causes the continuity of emissions that makes them unsustainable.

5.5 WHAT ARE THE FEATURES OF SUSTAINABLE BUSINESS?

It is now possible to tie together several threads to describe, from both an economic and moral perspective, what an unsustainable business can be said to be. It is a business that:

- does not internalise their external effects, which in a moral sense is the same as violating the dignity of others in terms of their equality and/or freedom;
- does not act proactively to remedy the lack of equality and freedom of others when morally called for, which

88. Porter, M., Competitive Advantage, Free Press, 1985.

- is caused by an underlying formal and informal institutional structure expressed in the business model, strategies, policies, corporate culture, etc.;
- takes place over time; and which
- means or risks implying that, if the action does not stop, some tipping point will be reached, such as tipping points regarding the environment or human health.[89]

A company that acts in this way can be said to be conducting a morally unsustainable business activity. Conversely, of course, this means that a sustainable business is a business in which the company:

- continuously internalises its external effects, i.e., respects the equality and freedom of others;
- continuously act proactively to reduce others' deficits of equality and freedom when morally called for; and
- this happens as a result of the underlying formal and informal institutional structure (business model, strategies, corporate culture, etc.).

This is what a business implementing the norms of positive contribution and due diligence norm look like, according to the EU legislator. The details of how this is expressed in the various legal acts will become clearer throughout the book.

It is important to emphasise the limits of the moral commitments in sustainable business. Companies do not have these obligations to every individual in the world. In sustainability law, as discussed further below, the concept of *stakeholder* is central, which refers to the categories of people who are significantly affected by the company's business activities. The concept captures the fact that moral obligations rarely arise out of nothing, but people are confronted with each other in different ways when their paths cross, and their plans for how to live their lives are not fully compatible with each other (remember the example of the opera-singing woman and her neighbours). Trade-offs must then be made to find the solution that best respects the equality of both parties, which can be said to be the solution that gives both as much freedom as possible without infringing on each other's freedom. This means that companies need to act morally as described above in relation to the people who are or may be negatively affected by the company's activities.

This underlying moral perspective forms, it is argued here, the basis of the EU's ideal image for sustainable business. This is what is meant by conducting business according to the norms of due diligence and positive contribution. In the remaining parts of the book, there will be frequent references to this sustainability morality, since many rules of sustainability law become difficult to understand without understanding the normative basis.

89. For the sake of clarity, it should be emphasised that even a failure to act can, of course, also be untenable in this sense.

5.6 THE CHALLENGES FROM BEHAVIOURAL ETHICS

It should be obvious to many that transforming the entire business to follow the norms of due diligence and positive contribution poses an almost monumental challenge. There is reason here to point out a specific part of this challenge. Fundamentally, implementing these norms is about introducing moral considerations everywhere in economic activities. In this context, the insights from the research area known as *behavioural ethics* should be considered, not least the realisation that the use of economic language can easily cause people to ignore the moral aspects of decisions to be made.

Behavioural ethics does not study what ethical behaviour is but rather whether and to what extent people actually act as their own stated ethics dictate. It is a large field of research, and there is not enough space here to deal with it other than briefly.[90]

Behavioural ethics shows that people have a strong sense of justice, fairness and morality and act more morally than is predicted by, for example, economists who assume that people only look out for their own self-interest. At the same time, people act far less morally than their own stated morality dictates. When people are asked how they would act in a situation, they often predict that they will act more morally than they actually do later. Looking back, people can also justify their actions and deny that they acted immorally. An important factor that affects how people actually act is whether they even see that a particular decision has a moral dimension. An effective way, it has been shown, to exclude the moral dimension from the spotlight is to (unconsciously) formulate the decision as an economic decision or as a decision on a compliance issue. A fundamentally moral dilemma is instead reformulated as a so-called cost-benefit decision.

The practical implications of the conclusions of behavioural ethics are troubling. It seems that extensive training in, for example, ethics or compliance has no proven effect other than that they can actually *worsen* the situation.[91] This is something to remember for the companies that report how many of their employees have taken a course in anti-corruption in their sustainability reports. Such courses are of great value, but they should not be confused with the effective implementation of an anti-corruption culture.

What seems to matter most is *culture*, which is notoriously difficult to influence and change. There is a clear chicken-and-egg problem here. If you create an unsustainable business where the staff are not aware that they are acting contrary to their own moral ideals, how can the same staff change the corporate culture? The question will not be dealt with in this book, but it is difficult to see any other way out of this dilemma than what, for lack of better words, can be called *enlightened leadership*.

---

90. This is based on Bazerman, M. and Tenbrunsel, A., Blind Spots: Why We Fail to Do What's Right and What to Do about It, Princeton University Press, 2012.
91. *See, e.g.*, Langevoort, D., Cultures of Compliance, 54 American Criminal Law Review, 2017, 933-977.

CHAPTER 6

The Ground Rules of the Game: Corporate Purpose and Values

Having sketched the political morality underlying sustainability law, there is an immediate question that should be addressed: a question on which EU sustainability law is politely silent. That is the question of corporate purpose, i.e., what is the purpose of a business. According to many, the purpose of a business is to maximise shareholder value, while others hold that the purpose is instead to generate value for all stakeholders. Others still argue that the purpose should be to maximise shareholder welfare.

This is a question that should not be ignored. In fact, any business - both in the financial market and all other markets - with some ambitions to become more sustainable should start the entire discussion with this question: what is the purpose of our business?

As will be argued, the answer to a company asking if their purpose should be to maximise shareholder value, shareholder welfare, or stakeholder value is none of the above. Instead, companies should, first of all, make a distinction between their *purpose* and their *values*. The purpose is the company's most fundamental idea of what kind of value it brings to its customers. The values are the basic norms that the company commits to follow while pursuing its purpose. Viewed in light of the sustainability morality underlying EU laws, the purpose is tied to the positive contribution norm, while the values are tied to the due diligence norm.

This chapter will begin with a simple explanation of why it is so important to state corporate purpose and corporate values. Thereafter, important aspects of the corporate purpose debate will be presented. Having argued that corporate law does not really support any of the perspectives, it is argued that this is because all the sides of the debate are stuck within a thought paradigm ultimately based on the concept of utility, which seems hard to defend both from an empirical and normative point of view. To enable businesses to start Beto truly think about corporate purpose and values, it is therefore important to try to draw this 'utilitarian sting'.[92] To help companies do that, it is important to understand where this sting comes from, namely a power struggle, not least within academia, about the right to define the rules of the game for business.

Having been relieved from the utilitarian sting, it will be possible to look at the question of corporate purpose and value with fresh eyes.[93]

6.1 THE IMPORTANCE OF PURPOSE AND VALUES

The claim that the corporate purpose and values are the ground rules of the game is, first of all, empirical and not normative. It is based on the system theoretic view that is important to understand and discuss both empirical and normative questions about sustainability. In the iceberg metaphor of the company in section 3.2, the corporate purpose lies at the deepest level, affecting all elements above it. The corporate values lie at the level directly above. The purpose of *any* system is a ground rule of the system, which will shape everything else. For human systems, the values embraced by the people forming the system will do the same.

It is not hard to see that corporate purpose, if properly stated that is, will have quite profound effects on how the business is run. It should be sufficient to take a financial market participant as an example and ask what will happen if the purpose is either set to maximise return on invested capital or to, say, maximise value for society. If the aim is to maximise return on invested capital, at least short to mid-term, a good choice in today's market – written in the spring of 2024 – seems to be to invest in one of the major oil and gas companies, given their profit levels in 2023. If the aim is to maximise value for society, the perspective will change fundamentally. The point here is not to argue for or against either perspective; the point is that the stated purpose will have fundamental importance for how the business is run, from the board room to the factory floor. The purpose *is*, together with the values, in this sense the ground rule of the game. This is why it is so important to address the question when discussing sustainable business.

6.2 THE CONFUSING CORPORATE PURPOSE DEBATE

When starting to think about corporate purpose, it is easy to get lost in the long and complex debate that has been held by mainly academics since the 1930s. It is hard to avoid this debate, if not for other reasons than to – which is recommended here – discard it as missing the point.

92. In his book *Law's Empire*, Ronald Dworkin pointed to the necessity of drawing the 'semantic sting', which was his term for certain theories about laws claiming that the concept of law is a semantic and not a political question. *See* Dworkin, R., Law's Empire, Harvard University Press, 1986, Chapter 2. In a similar manner, it is here claimed that the utilitarian sting must be drawn to start to think about sustainable business in a more non-politicised way.

93. The author would like to thank professor and Nobel laureate Oliver Hart for very valuable critical comments to this chapter.

Below, three different lines of thought on the question of corporate purpose are described. The description is far from complete and each line of thought also comes with sub-themes. But hopefully, the description will be comprehensive enough for the purpose of this book. The purpose is to, eventually, show that the debate, while being very important, is largely irrelevant to setting the ground rules of the game for a sustainable business.[94]

6.2.1 Primacy of Shareholder Value

Around the 1970s, at least in the US, the broad consensus was that the managers should manage the company in the interest of the entire community. Since the 1930s, there had, primarily in the United States, been a discussion on how to respond to the fact that companies had gone from being largely run by the very people who owned them to large conglomerates with powerful corporate leaders and shareholders as a passive group.[95] Should the managers run the company in the interest of the shareholders or in the interest of the wider community? And was there not a risk that the managers mostly ran the companies in their own interests? However, the large consensus was that the company should be in the interest of all stakeholders, even though that was not the specific terminology used.[96]

But then things changed. Some thirty years later, in 2001, professors Reinier Kraakman and Henry Hansmann published an essay titled 'The End of History for Corporate Law',[97] in which they wrote: 'There is no longer any serious competitor to the view that corporate law should principally strive to increase long-term shareholder value.' What had happened? Two things: starting in economics, the idea that the purpose of a business is to maximise shareholder value started to dominate the scene. Thereafter, this idea passed over and started to influence law through the law and economics perspective of the corporation.

In 1970, the American economist Milton Friedman famously wrote in the *New York Times* that the social responsibility of business is to increase its profits.[98] His starting point was that a company cannot have responsibility, only people. 'A corporation is an artificial person and in this sense may have artificial responsibilities, but "business" as a whole cannot be said to have responsibilities, even in this vague sense.' Thus, the focus must be on the responsibilities of the company's representatives - board members and management. Friedman argued that the company's representatives should be regarded as employees of the shareholders and that they,

94. This does not mean, of course, that the debate can be important for other purposes, for example, as input to corporate law.
95. This discussion was largely shaped by the influential book *The Modern Corporation and Private Property*: *see* Berle, A. and Means, G. The Modern Corporation and Private Property, 2nd edn, Harcourt, Brace and World, 1967.
96. Stout, L., The Shareholder Value Myth, Berret-Koehler Publishers, 2012, 24.
97. Hansman, H. and Kraakman, R., The End of History for Corporate Law, 89 Georgetown Law Review, 2001, 439.
98. Friedman, M., The Social Responsibility of Business Is to Increase Its Profits, *New York Times*, 13 September 1970.

therefore, have a responsibility to this particular 'employer' and no one else. In other words, the company's representatives must act in the interest of the shareholders. What, then, is the interest of the shareholders? According to Friedman, it is 'to make as much money as possible while conforming to the basic rules of the society'. In other words, to maximise profits within the limits of the law.

With this in mind, Friedman asked a number of questions: What does it mean that a business leader (i.e., not the company) has a *social* responsibility? Surely this means he or she must act in a way *not* in the primary interest of the employer (shareholders). For example, the manager should refrain from a price increase for the social purpose of not contributing to inflation, even though this reduces the company's profits. Or make investments to reduce emissions to a greater extent than what is profitable for the company or what is required by law. Or employing the long-term unemployed instead of more qualified and profitable people to help reduce poverty in society. Friedman believed that such actions by business leaders would be tantamount to socialism, a political ideal that the free market-inclined Friedman famously did not like. No, a business can only have one purpose: to maximise the value for the shareholders.

Friedman's view was then further elaborated within economics. Most importantly, it was formalised by, among others, the economists Michael Jensen and William Meckling in terms of so-called *agency theory*, from where the step over to law via law and economics legal theory was short.[99] Since then, the shareholder-stakeholder debate has largely been held within the agency theory framework, and it is, therefore, important to understand the basics of this framework to then be able to leave it.

As discussed in section 3.2, economist Ronald Coase famously claimed that companies exist because sometimes it is cheaper to organise business activities within a firm instead of organising the same activities through contracts entered into on the market. Elaborating on the meaning of this idea, Jensen and Meckling adopted the view that there is, in reality, not much difference between a company and the market. A company is a 'nexus-of-contracts' entered into on competitive terms, i.e., contracts entered into between, for example, the company and shareholders, employees, creditors, suppliers and others, all of which are assumed to be rational utility maximisers. It is only if this contract view is adopted that it is relevant to analyse whether it is cheaper to let those contracts form a company or to let them only exist in the market; the contracting and transaction cost perspectives cannot be separated.

Based on the nexus-of-contracts perspective, transaction costs are then analysed in terms of conflicts of interest between the contracting parties because, to a large extent, it is those that generate transaction costs. As said, Jensen and Meckling analysed those conflicts based on agency theory. Under this theory, a principal, for example, a shareholder, hires an agent, for example, a manager, to act on behalf of the principal. But the agent is assumed to act in its own self-interest, wherefore a conflict of interest arises between the principal and agent. This will increase transaction costs, called 'agency costs'.

99. Jensen, M. and Meckling, W., Theory of the Firm: Managerial Behavior, Agency Costs and Ownership Structure, 3(4) Journal of Financial Economics, 1976, 305-360.

Now, Jensen and Meckling claimed that the best way to minimise agency costs is to have management work to maximise value for the shareholders, basically the share price of the company. Within the framework of this theory, this is a natural conclusion. In reality, the shareholders don't have a contract with the company, but the creditors, employees and other contractual stakeholders do. The latter are protected by contract law, and they can argue and fight for their own self-interests in negotiations with the company on a free market. The shareholders are, instead, unprotected and referred to as the 'residual claimants', having the right to what is left on the table of the company revenues when everyone else has been paid. Who will fight for them and represent their interests? Presumably, it must be those representing the company when negotiating contracts with all the other stakeholders, i.e., management.

This leads to the seemingly unavoidable conclusion that the purpose of a business should be to look out for the interests of the shareholders. If the company management does not represent the shareholders' assumed profit maximising interest, no one will, which first will lead to the shareholders not investing in the first place, and second, if they do invest, management and other stakeholders will take benefit of the shareholders, to the detriment of aggregate wealth in society.

This powerful theory fundamentally changed the view of corporate purpose in favour of shareholder value maximisation. Law and economics was developed in parallel with agency theory - both at the University of Chicago - and the step to incorporate the agency perspective in law and economics analysis of corporate law was natural. The shareholder value perspective on business found its way into law, for example, through the influential book *The Economic Structure of Corporate Law* by Easterbrook and Fishel.[100] By 2001, Kraakman and Hansmann could, in their article referred to above, argue that the fight was over, the shareholder primacy perspective had won. The perspective has been further reinforced by, not least, the influential book *The Anatomy of Corporate Law* by Kraakman et al.[101] A large number of articles and books have been written on this perspective.[102]

6.2.2 Primacy of Stakeholder Value

Friedman's and his followers' position has not gone unchallenged. Friedman took a limited shareholder and also monetary perspective when it comes to a company's purpose and responsibility. At the other end of the spectrum is the so-called stakeholder perspective, which, as we have seen above, was dominant in the 1970s. This perspective was put back on the agenda in the early 1980s by the American philosopher Edward Freeman[103] but has strong supporters also today.[104] From this perspective, shareholders are one among several stakeholders, along with, for example, employees,

100. Easterbrook, F.H. and Fishel, D.R., The Economic Structure of Corporate Law, Harvard University Press, 1991.
101. Kraakman, R., et al., The Anatomy of Corporate Law, 3rd edn, Oxford University Press, 2017.
102. *See, e.g.*, Bebchuk and Tallarita, The Illusory Promise of Stakeholder Governance (26 February 2020), 106 Cornell Law Review, 2020, 91-178. *See also* McLean, R.D., The Case for Shareholder Capitalism: How the Pursuit of Profit Benefits All, Cato Institute, 2023.
103. *See, e.g.*, Freeman, E. Strategic Management: A Stakeholder Approach, Pitman, 1984.

trade unions, government bodies, and society. The books *Prosperity* by Professor Colin Mayer and *Growing the Pie* by Professor Alex Edman have lately been highly influential.

It is easy to fall into the trap of viewing the entire discussion as a zero-sum game, for example, by saying that more profits to the shareholders must necessarily be bad for the stakeholders. In fact, the opposite is, of course, often true since profits can often be generated *by* creating value for stakeholders. Both Mayer and Edman give a number of concrete examples of companies which have generated substantial shareholder value *by* providing value to stakeholders and society in general.

6.2.3 Primacy of Shareholder Welfare

A third alternative, between the pure shareholder perspective and the stakeholder perspective, also exists. It has been presented by economists Oliver Hart and Luigi Zingales, among others.[105] The economist's perspective is typically which alternatives or solutions are most effective, i.e., create the most possible economic value, for society. Hart and Zingales agree with Friedman's view that the primary responsibility of corporations is to their shareholders. But they question a number of Friedman's basic assumptions. First, Friedman assumes that the only thing shareholders care about is getting as much money as possible, as illustrated in the quote above. This is a common assumption among traditional economists but has been proven to be wrong. Hart and Zingales, therefore, assume that shareholders may also have what they call pro-social preferences, that is, that they care about others and attach at least some importance to how their actions affect others.

Second, they question Friedman's basic assumption, not apparent in the *New York Times* article, that markets are perfectly efficient. Friedman's claim that corporate representatives maximise social welfare by maximising shareholder profits presupposes that corporations also bear all the costs of their impact on the outside world; in other words, corporations have – in the language of economics – internalised all externalities.[106] If, for example, a company does not bear all the costs that society is caused by the company's pollution, it is by no means certain that the social benefit will be maximised if the company maximises its profits. Thus, Hart and Zingales *do not* assume that all externalities have been internalised.

With these and other changing basic assumptions, Hart and Zingales seek to show that a company can best serve the interests of its shareholders by maximising their *welfare* instead of their wealth. They assume, quite realistically, that most shareholders won't feel responsible for the actions of the companies they own shares unless they can be blamed at least partly for those actions. Therefore, it will be

104. *See, e.g.*, Mayer, C., *Prosperity*: Better Business Makes the Greater Good, Oxford University Press, 2018, Edmans, A., Grow the Pie, Cambridge University Press, 2020, Schwab, K., Stakeholder Capitalism, World Economic Forum, 2021, Henderson, R., Reimagining Capitalism in a World on Fire, Penguin Books, 2020.
105. Hart, O. and Zingales, L., Companies Should Maximise Shareholder Welfare Not Market Value, 2 Journal of Law, Finance and Accounting, 2017, 247-274.
106. *See* Chapter 5.

important to maximise social welfare, to let shareholders have more influence and hence feel more responsibility for decisions with a negative impact on people or the environment. If such a decision – for example, on an investment – is made subject to shareholder decision, it will be important to look at three factors: the cost of the investment with the negative impact, the cost of the investment without the negative impact, and the degree of the shareholders' pro-social preferences. Let's assume that the investment without a negative impact costs EUR 2 million more than the investment with a negative impact. Those extra costs will, if the investment without negative impact is chosen, decrease the company profits by EUR 2 million. Each shareholder will 'suffer' from this cost increase in proportion to its share of the company. A shareholder owning 1% of the shares will thus suffer EUR 20,000. For a purely self-interested shareholder, this would settle the case: the cheaper and, thus, more profitable investment should be made. But for a shareholder with pro-social preferences, the situation will be different. As long as the strength of those pro-social preferences comes down to more than 1% of the extra cost, that shareholder will go for the investment without negative impact.

This has important implications. First of all, it means that companies should, in their investment decisions, internalise much more of the external effects of those decisions, which should be done under traditional assumptions of purely self-interested shareholders. But it also means that the larger the shareholder, the less inclined it will be to choose investment decisions without negative impact because the larger the share of stocks, the larger the share of the 'downside' of the more expensive investment decision. This conclusion naturally leads to the practical consequence that it is important to find methods to find out not only what the larger shareholder prefers but also what all the other shareholders prefer. As long as the latter group can be made to vote, there will be a higher chance that decisions will be adopted that not only take shareholder welfare into account but that also, by definition, are better for other stakeholders.

6.3 WHAT DOES THE LAW SAY?

There are thus a number of different and non-compatible answers to the question of what the purpose of a business is or should be. Some may think that it does not matter since corporate law, in fact, requires the business to be run based on the shareholder primacy perspective. This is, for the most part, incorrect. In fact, the economic view of the company does not fit well with the law in any legal system. In her book, *The Shareholder Value Myth,* Professor Lynn Stout showed, in a US context, what is true also in a European context.[107] In general (because exceptions can exist), there is no corporate legislation saying that the purpose of business is to maximise shareholder value.

There are a number of assumptions in the agency theory underlying the idea of shareholder value, and they don't fit into corporate law. The first assumption is

107. Stout, L., The Shareholder Value Myth, Berret-Koehler, 2012.

that the shareholders own the company. This is, of course, wrong under most conceptions of what ownership means legally. The shareholder owns *shares* in the company, which gives them certain rights: voting rights in general meetings, rights to dividends when such exist, rights to sell the shares to others and so on. This is not ownership of the company.

A second assumption is the idea of the shareholders as the residual claimants, i.e., the idea that the shareholders are paid last when the employees, customers, creditors, the government, etc., have been paid. This is true, but only when the company files for bankruptcy. When the company is running as it should, the shareholders have no *claim* for dividends. They have a right to dividends in proportion to their share ownership, but typically only if the general meeting adopts a decision to declare dividends, which typically requires a proposal from the board to do so.

The third assumption is that the shareholders are principals and the directors their agents. Friedman made an even stronger claim, i.e., that the directors are the *employees* of the shareholders. This is, of course, wrong. But it is also wrong that the directors are the agents. The directors and managers are not hired to promote the interests of the shareholders but to manage and promote the interests of *the company*. This is, of course, impossible if you look at the company as a nexus of contracts and, thus, as an entity which does not really exist. However, since the law does not view the company as a nexus of contract (a fourth wrong assumption) but as a legal entity with rights and obligations, it is perfectly possible under the law.

In some jurisdictions, the law says that the board of directors has a fiduciary duty to the shareholders as well as the company. In other jurisdictions, a similar principle exists as a principle of loyalty. But this is something else. While it makes sense to ensure that the board of directors or management don't dispose of the shareholders' investments without considering their interests in the value of the investment, this is not the same as saying that the purpose of the business as such is to maximise this value.

No corporate legislation in the European Union says that the purpose of business is to maximise shareholder value and none of the assumptions underlying this idea fits into what the law says.[108]

It should, however, be noted that the same is true for both the shareholder welfare perspective and the stakeholder value perspective. There are no laws saying that the purpose of a business is to or that company directors should maximise shareholder welfare, nor to maximise some kind of stakeholder value.[109]

108. Sjåfjell, Beate and Taylor, Mark B., Clash of Norms: Shareholder Primacy vs. Sustainable Corporate Purpose (28 August 2019). International and Comparative Corporate Law Journal, 13 (2019) 3.

109. The Companies Act in the United Kingdom now includes a duty of directors to promote the success of the company and, while doing that, have regard for the interests of employees, suppliers and so on. But this is not the same as saying that the purpose of the company is to have such regard. Actually, this does not say anything about the purpose of business (other than it should be successful, which basically means nothing).

6.4 BEYOND THE SHAREHOLDER-STAKEHOLDER DICHOTOMY

The debate about corporate purpose is thus already from the beginning comprehensive and confusing. The fact that the laws do not really support any of the shareholder value, shareholder welfare or stakeholder value perspectives just adds to the confusion. This confusion is, however, no coincidence. It is, it can be argued, to a large extent a theory-generated confusion lying at the heart of much of economics and definitely in law and economics, i.e., the theories from which the entire debate has sprung.

This has been pointed out by, among others, law professors Beate Sjåfjell and Jukka Mähönen at Oslo University.[110] They argue that the shareholder-stakeholder dichotomy is only relevant within a law and economics approach to law and ask lawyers to guard against the strong influence of this approach. They could be said to argue that those who debate within the shareholder-stakeholder dichotomy all suffer from theory induced blindness, i.e., that they only see those aspects of reality which are relevant given the underlying theory they implicitly or explicitly apply.

According to Sjåfjell and Mähönen, the law and economics approach leads to a dichotomy between shareholders and stakeholders where, within the law and economics framework, it is natural to give priority to shareholders, as described above. The main problem with this is not necessarily that the shareholders are given priority. The main problem is instead that the non-contractual stakeholders are excluded, which in practice means that external effects are of no concern to corporate law. There is nothing logical about this; it is only a result of the theoretical perspective adopted.[111]

This is a serious challenge to all the debating parties. The claim is, to simplify, that it is only within agency theory and its application in law and economics that the choice of corporate purpose looks like a choice between shareholder value, shareholder welfare or stakeholder value. If agency theory and, for that matter, law and economics are wrong, other options should present themselves. In the next section, a deeper analysis of those theories will therefore be made. To get rid of mental models which just restrict your thoughts, it is often important to dig deep.

6.5 THE DESCRIPTIVE AND NORMATIVE SIDE OF UTILITY

Law and economics is explicit in that it makes both descriptive and normative claims.[112] For example, in *The Anatomy of Corporate Law*, the authors mean that the adopted view on companies as mechanisms for reducing transaction costs is not only in fact correct but is also morally prescribed. Corporate law is, *in fact*, handling

110. Sjåfjell, B. and Mähönen, J., Corporate Purpose and the Misleading Shareholder v Stakeholder Dichotonomy, 34(2) Bond Law Review, 2024.
111. It should be noted that Hart and Zingales solution partly escapes from this criticism, since they assume that shareholders to some extent do take external effects into consideration into their utility function. But Hart and Zingales agree with Friedman that shareholder welfare is or at least should be the objective purpose of a company.
112. *See, e.g.*, Posner, R., *ibid.*, p 31.

conflicts of interest between principals and agents and *should* also be designed to deal with such conflicts in the most efficient way.

How is this possible? As already said, the Scottish philosopher David Hume famously showed that it is not possible to argue for how things *should be* (the normative side) based on how things *are* (the descriptive side) – Hume's law. Law and economics seem to be dangerously close to doing exactly this, doing what some refer to as a forbidden 'normative leap'. But it can be argued that this is, in fact, not so. Proponents of law and economics can both analyse the law and make recommendations on what ought to be based on the concept of *utility*. This is a Janus-faced concept, which, on the one side, looks at the world as it is and, on the other side, looks at the world as it should be.

Both perspectives are, however, seriously flawed and since the shareholder-stakeholder dichotomy is based on these persectives, a worldview shaped by those perspectives is also seriously flawed, as will be shown below.

6.5.1 Expected Utility Theory and Social Efficiency

To a large extent, economic theory relies on what is called expected utility theory.[113] While complex in its implications, the theory is simple in its core. It is a theory of how people make choices, primarily economic choices. According to the theory, humans face a large number of choices on how to act. They then assess the degree of utility of each of the choices as well as the probability that each course of action will give that utility. The theory then predicts that people choose the course of action which provides the greatest expected utility. It is, therefore, a theory that utility maximisation is the key motivator of human action.

Critical is also the notion that people experience what is called diminishing marginal utility. If we take drinking water as an example, the idea of diminishing marginal utility simply means that a person will experience less and less utility for each additional centilitre of water she is drinking.

Based on this theory, it is possible to build powerful, often mathematical, models on how different rules, incentive systems, etc., generate more or less total utility in the economy, where the economy is more or less 'efficient' depending on the total utility generated.

Economists have, of course, thought a lot about how to make the leap from one individual's utility to the total utility of society, which is comprised of many individuals. A theory of total utility is needed to be able to compare the efficiency of, for example, two alternative policy decisions on taxes or, for that matter, assess if corporate law should say that the purpose of business is to maximise shareholder value or some other purpose.

Several efficiency concepts have been proposed over the years. Interestingly, one possible conclusion from the idea of decreasing marginal utility is that only an

113. *See, e.g.*, Anand, P., Foundations of Rational Choice under Risk, Clarendon Press, 1993.

economy with equal distribution can be efficient. Since rich people have more than poor people, rich people will experience less utility with what they have. The best way to increase total utility in society is then to take from the rich and give to the poor.[114] This was, in fact, a conclusion that influential economists came to in the early twentieth century.[115]

Other economists don't agree.[116] They mean that this conclusion is wrong since it is based on the allegedly false premise that peoples' individual experiences of utility can be compared. Lisa has, they claim, a different feeling of pleasure from drinking water than John, and these two different experiences cannot be combined under the common notion of utility. It is, therefore, wrong to say that social efficiency improves when giving from the rich to the poor.[117]

Based on this, other economists developed what were to become the dominating efficiency concepts in economic theory, including agency theory and law and economics: Pareto efficiency and Kaldor-Hicks efficiency.

A policy is, to simplify, Pareto efficient if it increases the utility for some without decreasing it for others. Let us say the legislator is considering adopting a corporate law saying that boards of directors should maximise shareholder value. Let us say that it is made plausible that such law would generate the maximum utility for the entire society. If, however, such law also means that some, for example, employees or workers in the value chain, are made worse off, then this law is not Pareto improving. No one may lose just so others can win, even if the aggregate utility generated is positive.

Such law can, however, be Kaldor-Hicks efficient.[118] Let us say that the law under consideration will lead to increased utility for shareholders of EUR 1,000, for example, EUR 10 for one hundred imagined shareholders. Let us also say that employees and workers in the value chain would lose EUR 500, for example, through lower wages, longer working hours and so on. The one hundred shareholders *could*, however, in theory, compensate those people by each providing EUR 5 of their newly earned EUR 10. If the employees and workers in the value chain are thus compensated, nothing will have changed for them but the shareholders will have gained in total EUR 500. According to the Kaldor-Hicks efficiency criterion, such solution would be efficient. Note that it is not necessary that compensation is actually paid; what is important is that it *could* happen.

114. Pigou, A, The Economics of Welfare, 4th ed., Macmillan and Co., 1952, Chapter VII.
115. Cook, E., Efficiently Unequal: The Global Rise of Kaldor-Hicks Neoliberalism, 9(1-2) Global Intellectual History, 2024, 247-269.
116. Robbins, L., Interpersonal Comparisons of Utility: A Comment, 48(192) The Economic Journal, 1938, 635-641.
117. 'The Law of Diminishing Marginal Utility does not justify the inference that the transferences from the rich to the poor will increase total satisfaction.' (Robbins, L., An Essay on the Nature and Significance of Economic Science, Macmillan and Co., 1932, 125).
118. This criteria was developed in parallel by the economists John Hicks and Nicholas Kaldor. *See* Hicks, J., The Foundations of Welfare Economics, The Economic Journal, 1939, 49 (196): 696-712. N., Welfare Propositions in Economics and Interpersonal Comparisons of Utility, The Economic Journal, 1939, 49 (195): 549–552.

This may sound strange. The Pareto and Kaldor-Hicks efficiency criteria were both developed under the assumption that individual utility experiences cannot be compared. How is it then possible, under the Kaldor-Hicks criteria, to say that a winning party can compensate a losing party? Does this not imply that the utilities of both parties are commensurate?

Not according to the inventors of this criteria. The purpose of introducing the possibility for compensation was not to show that a certain solution is fair or equitable since that would indeed imply that individuals' utility can be compared. The purpose was to enable comparison between different solutions (for example, laws) on a societal level, comparing which alternative makes society richer in terms of money. Focus was shifted from individual utility to *social wealth*. Society has reached maximum wealth if goods are allocated to those who would pay the most for them.

Law and economics typically rely on the Kaldor-Hicks efficiency criterion to evaluate what decisions and laws are efficient.[119]

Expected utility theory is highly problematic, which is well known by now. The problem is twofold: First of all, when faced with empirical reality, people often don't act as predicted by the theory. Second, there are groups who act more as predicted by the theory than others, namely people trained in economics or law and economics, which undermines the theory even more.

In Chapter 2, I have already referred to the fact that even such a prominent economist as Douglass North recognised that it is not possible to understand the institutions of society based on expected utility theory. Studies in behavioural economics point to humans' bounded rationality,[120] the tendency to act much more altruistically than predicted and so on.[121] Other studies also show that people are sometimes willing to punish others if they feel treated unfairly, even though it means walking away from money.[122]

Another finding is that whether peoples' more egoistic or altruistic side will dominate largely depends on the economic environment, for example, the economic environment generated by laws.[123] This is, of course, also confirmed by behavioural ethics, described in section 5.5, which has shown that an efficient way of making people ignore moral dilemmas is to formulate the situation into a cost-benefit analysis.

119. Posner, R., *ibid.*, p. 14. Kraakman et al., *ibid.*, p. 63 note 87. Parisi, Francesco (ed.), The Oxford Handbook of Law and Economics: Volume 1: Methodology and Concepts (2017; online edn, Oxford Academic, section 2.3.
120. Another term for saying that people are rational, but only to a limited extent, which is better to say than that people are totally irrational.
121. Christine J., Behavioral Economics and the Law, 6(3) Foundations and Trends in Microeconomics, 2011, 173-263.
122. *See, e.g.*, Thaler, R., The Ultimatum Game, in The Winner's Curse, Princeton University Press, 1992.
123. Fehr, E., & Schmidt, K.M., A Theory of Fairness, Competition, and Cooperation, 114(3) The Quarterly Journal of Economics, 1999, 817-868.

Another well-known example in the same area is the Israeli daycare centres, where the staff wanted the parents to pick up their children on time instead of late.[124] When they introduced a small fine for late-comers, the result was that *more* parents came late, in fact, twice as many. Why? Because turning a basically ethical question into an economic choice, the incentive structure changed from what is called intrinsic to extrinsic motivation, which made the parents more egoistic.

Under agency theory, it is hard to come to another conclusion than that the best way to run a company is to maximise the utility of the shareholders. This is based on the idea that both the managers and shareholders act in accordance with expected utility theory. The fact that they do not, of course, means that it is hardly evident that the best way to maximise social value is to have the company run for the purpose of maximising value for shareholders.[125]

The problems of expected utility theory mean that it can be questioned how useful it is to analyse companies in terms of conflicts of interest among utility maximisers, which form a nexus of contracts. It also means that it is by no means obvious that companies should maximise shareholder value to maximise social value because if the expected utility theory is so problematic, all conclusions based on this theory are equally problematic.

In addition, those problems should empirically mean that data should show that recommendations based on agency theory (which is based on expected utility theory) do not work. This actually seems to be the case. A concrete recommendation based on agency theory is that share prices should increase if company CEOs have their payment tied to share value so as to align the CEO's interest with the shareholders' interest. A number of studies have, however, shown that there is little correlation between CEO payment and company performance.[126] Does this mean that agency theory is trying to deal with a problem that largely exists in theory and not in reality?[127]

---

124. *See, e.g.*: https://freakonomics.com/2013/10/what-makes-people-do-what-they-do/.
125. A simplistic question should be asked: *who* is really motivated to go to work on Monday morning and work hard for the rest of the week for the purpose of generating profits to shareholders that no one typically has met? For most people, this would sound like a 'motivation killer', not because they have conflicting interests with the shareholders but because typically people work for more than money, especially for more than making money for others. Agency theory seems to be an archetypical example of what French sociologist Pierre Bourdieu called the 'scholastic fallacy', which is when the social scientist projects his or her own model for understanding how people act (according to expected utility theory) on those very people. *See* Bourdieu, P., Pascalian Meditations, Polity Press, 2000, Chapter 2.
126. *See, e.g.*, Jensen, M. and Murphy, K., Performance Pay and Top-Management Incentives, 98 Journal of Political Economy, 1990, 225-264. Tosi, H., et al., How Much Does Performance Matter? A Meta-analysis of CEO Pay Studies, 26 Journal of Management, 2000, 301-339. Frydman, C. and Jenter, D., CEO Compensation, 2 Annual Review of Financial Economics, 2010, 75-102.
127. When Hart and Zingales recommend focusing on shareholder welfare instead of market value, they have to some extent taken these challenges to expected utility theory into account. They assume, correctly, that people to some extent take the welfare of others into account when they make their decisions. It is, however, not clear why they still mean that shareholder welfare should be considered to be the objective purpose of a company. If shareholders have pro-social preferences, everyone has. If the nexus-of-contract view of a company is kept but the contracting parties are assumed to have pro-social preferences, conflicts of interests may still

As if this was not serious enough to undermine the usefulness of expected utility theory and, therefore, agency theory, there comes a second serious problem. Research shows that people trained in economics, among other things, expected utility theory, act more like rational utility maximisers than others. For example, in an experiment carried out by the Israeli economist Ariel Rubinstein, students in economics, law, philosophy and mathematics were presented with a fictive problem for a company in financial trouble that could fire workers to increase its profit. First of all, the result showed clearly, against the expected utility theory, that a majority of the students did *not* go for the profit-maximising alternatives, which meant firing a lot of workers. However, the results also showed that the economics students were much more inclined to choose the profit-maximising alternative than the other students.[128]

The same effects have been shown in the legal profession. As already mentioned in the introduction to the book, judges having been trained in law and economics show a significantly increased inclination to apply law and economics in judging cases than other judges, not only in the language used but in the substance of the decisions.[129]

What do these results imply? The economic theory underlying agency theory and law and economics has no explanation for these results. Looking at the world with the descriptive face of utility, these results should not be there. According to the applied theory, people do, in fact, act in accordance with, e.g., expected utility theory, regardless of their training. The fact that the training makes people act more like the theory 'predicts' makes the theory almost self-defeating. Agency theory and law and economics fail to explain how the world works. Already, without looking at the normative side of things, the shareholder value perspective is in trouble.[130]

6.5.2 Utilitarianism

The normative side of the utility concept is equally or even more problematic. It is important to note that the corporate purpose debate is also a moral debate. To claim, as Friedman and his followers do, that: (i) corporations cannot have a social, i.e.,

arise, but to a lesser extent than assumed in traditional agency theory. If people, as has been proven, care about fairness and equity more than assumed under expected utility theory, a too strong focus among the 'contracting parties' in the nexus of contract may well lead to high friction rates directly detrimental to the efficiency of the company, and thereby to the shareholders.

128. Rubinstein, A., A Skeptic's Comment on the Studies of Economics, 116 The Economic Journal, March 2006, C1-C9.
129. Ash, E. Chen, D. and Naidu, S., Ideas Have Consequences: The Impact of Law and Economics on American Justice (February 2022). NBER Working Paper No. w29788.
130. On a side note, the fact that training in law and economics makes judges more inclined to apply law and economics in their work not only means that law and economics falls as a descriptive theory. It also means that legal positivism and its claim that judges strictly follow the wording of legal text adopted in the past falls. If positivism had been correct, training in law and economics should not make a difference. Almost ironically, but not surprisingly, it also means that legal interpretivism is confirmed as a descriptive theory. According to this theory, judges assess cases based not only on the legal texts of the past but based on their interpretation of the underlying principles and norms than can be 'extracted' from these texts. It then becomes relevant to look at these normative principles applied in law and economics.

moral, responsibility; and (ii) their responsibility should solely be concerned with maximising shareholder value is to make moral claims since these claims have consequences for how corporations and their representatives should and should not act. So are claims that a company should focus on all stakeholder or shareholder welfare. References to economic reasoning about social efficiency do not change this. On the contrary, the reference to social efficiency is typically based on utilitarian moral theory, where focus is on aggregate welfare generated by actions. The question is a moral one.

The problem here is that a legal theory based on utilitarianism will have a very hard time coming to legitimate conclusions about what the law ought to be. To be legitimate, the law must treat everyone as equals, and utilitarianism fails to do this.

Utilitarianism has been criticised since it was first introduced by philosophers Jeremy Bentham[131] and John Stuart Mill.[132] A major attack on the theory was launched in the 1970s by, among others, political philosopher John Rawls in his widely influential *A Theory of Justice*.[133]

The moral appeal of utilitarianism is that it, as a personal morality, is fundamentally based on the idea that all people are born as equals. Between two individuals, they should treat each other so that the net sum of their happiness is as large as possible. The problem arises when utilitarianism as a personal morality shifts to a political morality, saying that laws and policies should be adopted that generate the greatest utility for the largest number of people. Still, it is because everyone's happiness and pain are *equally valuable* that utilitarians can say that the net sum of everyone's pain and happiness should be calculated. But in the jump from individual to societal level, utilitarianism unavoidably runs into the challenge that its recommendations mean that some people may have to sacrifice themselves for the greater good, which in consequence means that not everyone is treated as equal. The problem arises because society is then viewed as a kind of separate entity, larger than the sum of its individual citizens.

Nowhere are the morally unacceptable consequences of utilitarianism as a political morality clearer than in the Kaldor-Hicks criteria typically applied within law and economics and its focus on societal wealth. When saying, as shown in the previous section, that people's utilities are *not* commensurable, the economists claiming this also claimed that they were making a value-free statement and that the claim that they *are* commensurable is a normative (and hence unscientific) statement.[134] This is highly questionable. Both are statements of value. Why is this so, and what are the consequences?

131. Benthman, J., An Introduction to the Principles of Morals and Legislation, Good Press, 2022.
132. Mill, J.S., Utilitarianism, Andrews UK Limited, 2011 (electronic version).
133. Rawls, J., A Theory of Justice, The Belknap Press, 2005.
134. *See, e.g.*, Robins: 'But I still think, when I make interpersonal comparisons (as, for instance, when I am deciding between claims affecting the satisfactions of two very spirited children), that my judgments are more like judgments of value than judgments of verifiable fact.' (Robbins, L., Interpersonal Comparisons of Utility: A Comment, 49(192) The Economic Journal, 1938, 635-641.)

Digging even deeper into economic theory, the Pareto and Kaldor-Hicks efficiency criteria are based on what is called 'methodological individualism'.[135] This simply means that economists in this branch of economics mean that all social phenomena must be explained with the individual and the individual's choices as a starting point. There are no objective factors independent of the individual – such as social class, for example – that influence peoples' actions. People are separate 'atoms' which only act based on their choices, which are affected by how other people choose and act. Society and the economy are the sum of all choices made.[136]

But it is not, so the argument goes, possible to look into the minds of people making choices. We can only *observe* that choices are being made, that tea is preferred over coffee, cheddar cheese over brie, wine over beer and so on. We can assume that Irene chooses tea over coffee and Alex cheddar over brie because they experience greater utility in tea and cheddar, respectively. But we can never tell *the relative degree of utility*, i.e., how much more utility Irene experiences from tea as compared to coffee and Alex from cheddar over brie. And – which is key – since we cannot tell the relative utility for Irene and Alex as individuals, we can certainly not compare Irene's utility relative to Alex's. To claim otherwise is to make a value judgment and not a scientific judgment.

This may sound convincing. But the problem is that the same argument also means that the opposite claim cannot be proven and is equally 'unscientific'. It is equally impossible to prove that peoples' utility levels are not commensurate as it is to prove that they are. A claim that they are not commensurate cannot be falsified.[137] So, if claiming that individual utilities *can* be compared is a value judgment, so is claiming that they *cannot* be compared. What does this mean? It means, it can be argued, that it is a matter not of science but of *choice* if you use an efficiency concept that views peoples' utilities as commensurable or not. Efficiency is not a value-free concept but, on the contrary, value-based.

What are the consequences of this choice? The early twentieth-century view, based on the choice that individual utilities can be compared, led to the conclusion that efficiency requires equal distribution of resources. The view that they cannot be compared led to the conclusion that distribution is irrelevant to efficiency. It is basically a choice of whether to view people as equals when assessing efficiency or not. Inequality is built into the Kaldor-Hicks criteria and thus largely into law and economics and thus runs into absurd moral consequences. Ronald Dworkin showed this in his book *A Matter of Principle* from 1986, with an example similar to the following.

---

135. *See, e.g.*, https://plato.stanford.edu/entries/methodological-individualism/.
136. This book is not the place to discuss the problems of this approach in social science. Influential sociologists, such as Anthony Giddens and Pierre Bourdieu, have not only questioned the approach but have also made significant contributions to overcoming the dualism within social science between this 'subjectivist' view and its opposite, objectivist view. (Giddens, A., The Constitution of Society, Polity Press, 1984, Bourdieu, P., The Logic of Practice, Stanford University Press, 1980.)
137. On the concept of falsification, *see* Popper, K., The Logic of Scientific Discovery, Routledge, 2002, pp. 17 ff.

Suppose a poor woman owns a vase which she would sell for EUR 100, and a rich man wants the vase and would pay EUR 1,000 for it. There is a potential here to increase social value by EUR 900. The poor woman and the rich man could start a negotiation about the sale of the vase, which would be about how the added value of EUR 900 should be divided between them. However, this negotiation takes time and, therefore, generates transaction costs. The most economically efficient result is achieved by simply taking the vase from the woman and giving it to the man.[138] Completely logical but also unreasonable and immoral.[139]

To make this even more clear. The Kaldor-Hicks criterion is based on the idea that the winners can compensate the losers with money. This means, for example, that a law allowing a company to pollute a lake, with the consequence that children swimming in the lake die, could be passed since the company could, in theory, pay the parents for what they suffer when losing their children. This is, of course, absurd: not all losses can be compensated, and not everything can be bought for money.

Why does this matter in the context of this book? The shareholder-stakeholder value discussion is framed by agency theory implemented into law and economics and applied to corporate law. Much of law and economics derives its prescriptive force from utilitarianism, expressed in the Kaldor-Hicks efficiency criterion, which is based on a choice that people shall not be treated as equals when assessing efficiency. An argument that a company *should* be run to maximise shareholder value is a statement of morality as much as a statement of fact. The argument basically says that as long as the shareholders earn more than, for example, affected third parties' lose, it is morally right to maximise shareholder value, even though those third parties are, in fact, not compensated for their losses (if they can be compensated).

That should not be the case since the theory is morally wrong. To adopt laws based on utilitarian grounds means violating everyone's right to be treated as equals. The 'external effects' discussed in Chapter 5 are, it can be argued, neither internal effects nor market failures. They are the inevitable consequences of the very logic of the theory applied, and such theory should not be allowed to influence the laws.

6.5.3 A Head with Two Flawed Pairs of Eyes

The corporate purpose debate described above is held within a thought paradigm with a descriptive and a normative face based on expected utility theory and utilitarianism. The eyes of both these faces are, it is argued, flawed and should, therefore, not serve

138. *See* Dworkin, R., A Matter of Principle, Harvard University Press, 1985, p. 242, and Law's Empire, Harvard University Press, 1986, pp. 286 et seq.

139. Someone could argue that it is wrong to call this utilitarianism. The economist Lionel Robins, who was important in the development of the Kaldor-Hicks criteria, in fact criticised his fellow economist in the 1930s for sticking to utilitarianism. (*See* Robins, L., An Essay on the Nature and Significance of Economic Science p. 125.) But Robins still thought that economists could legitimately come with policy recommendations and that can *only* be based on a reference to some kind of appeal to what is socially beneficial, if not for every individual. And that appeal is in Robins' case an implicit appeal to utilitarianism as a political morality, skipping the personal morality of it.

as a starting point when discussing corporate purpose. This is easier said than done, though. Why? Because it is not only many academic economists and law and economics scholars that look at the world with those two faces and pairs of eyes. Millions of people all over the world who, over the years, have been trained at business schools and universities also adopt this Janus-faced view of the world. Many corporate leaders who are considering what the purpose of their business is will have this worldview as their starting point, and they will communicate with each other based on this worldview. They will have been trained in economics, often with some of the effects shown in the Rubinstein study referred to above. They should, therefore, start by scrutinising their own assumption and taken-for-granted perspectives of the world, looking at where they come from and if they may even be dangerous to the planet. Ultimately, a large part of one's perspective of the world is a matter of choice, and since those perspectives affect how people act, it is a moral choice. In the next section, we will look at what may happen if the Janus-faced view of the world underlying the shareholder-stakeholder debate is adopted and applied in practice. This means going even deeper in order to get rid of the shareholder-stakeholder dichotomy. The reader who is already convinced can skip the next section.

6.6 A REALITY SHAPED BY A FLAWED THEORY

A policy recommendation based on an incorrect idea that people are and should only be utility maximisers may, when implemented in society, turn the same people into just this – utility maximisers – and, in addition, ignorant of the effects of their actions on, for example, the environment. The perceived problems, for example conflicts of interest, that the policy recommendation aims to tackle are instead generated. Ironically, this will also confirm the economist's view of how people behave, a behaviour that the economist has actually generated in the first place.

Let us see what this may look like in more detail. An economist analyses the activities of companies based on expected utility theory and comes to the conclusions already described in section 6.2, i.e., a company is a nexus of contracts between various stakeholders, where the shareholders should be given primacy. The same economist also comes to the conclusion that companies should, acting in accordance with expected utility theory, only make investments with what is called positive net present value.[140] This is the current value of all future benefits from an investment minus the costs of the investment. Note that we are looking at the world with the descriptive face – the economist believes that companies actually do maximise profits for their shareholders and make investment decisions based on net present value. Now, the economist starts to look at the world with the normative face and recommends that companies maximise shareholder value and only make investment decisions based on positive net present value.

Let us say that everyone listens and follows the recommendations, for example, corporate leaders who have studied what the economist has taught in business schools

140. Brealey, R.A., et al., Principles of Corporate Finance, 14th edn, McGraw Hill, 2023, pp. 74 ff.

or in the economics department at business schools.[141] What will happen? Laws and policies are implemented based on the assumption that everyone is a rational utility maximiser. Dealing with the supposed conflict between management and the shareholders, incentive schemes tied to the share price are introduced. The managers will then act like the Israeli parents picking up their kids; they start to act based on extrinsic motivations instead of out of, for example, old-fashioned loyalty and professionalism. When making investment decisions, the finance departments begin to calculate the net present value of their investments. This first of all means that many investments are not made, for example in gyms and other facilities that would be nice for the employees to have. Why? Because the future revenues from such investments cannot be calculated with any accuracy. What cannot be measured does not exist and can, therefore, not have value.

So only investments which can be clearly calculated are even considered. And only costs that can be calculated are included in the net present value calculations. Potential damages to the environment and to, e.g., indigenous people are not included. First of all, of course, because those damages are not costs of the business. Second, because even if those costs could be calculated, those costs are – we could say – lower than the aggregate value generated, and the investment is, therefore, Kaldor-Hicks efficient. So, the investment is socially beneficial, apart from the fact that it is not since no one is compensating the harmed third parties (if they can be compensated). Third, the calculating finance person does not even perceive a moral conflict luring here, being subject to the psychologic repressive mechanisms identified in behavioural ethics.

Due to the economic context thus created by the economist's policy recommendations, people and the companies they represent now begin to act more like utility maximisers, meaning that the conflicts of interests which first mainly existed in the economist's head now also appear in reality, confirming what the economist thought from the beginning and therefore also the validity of the tools for analysis. The scandals of Enron and WorldCom in the 2000s now come as no surprise – the cheating managers acted exactly as they were supposed to, just that they took it a bit too far.

The result will be an increasingly unstainable economy. What has happened is that the policies, based on agency theory, have generated more egoistic behaviour, leading to unsustainable results.

Some economists will now start to argue that the shareholder value focus is too limited and that focus should be on all stakeholders. But now, the economists supporting the shareholder primacy perspective will have good ammunition. As an example, in an article titled *The Illusory Promise of Stakeholder Governance*, law and economics scholars Lucian Bebchuk and Roberto Tallarita very elegantly dismantle the case for 'stakeholderism'.[142] No manager can deal with the 'Herculean task' of taking

141. Almost any book in corporate finance theory will begin with the claim that the purpose of business is to maximise shareholder value. Perhaps nowhere is this more clear than this: 'Corporate finance is *all about* maximizing shareholder value.' [Italics added]. (Brealey, R.A., et al., Principles of Corporate Finance, 14th edn, McGraw Hill, 2023, p. 48.)

142. Bebchuk, L. and Tallarita, R., The Illusory Promise of Stakeholder Governance (26 February 2020), 106 Cornell Law Review, 2020, 91-178.

all stakeholders' perspectives into consideration. Who are the stakeholders in the first place? And if we know who they are, how could the manager possibly deal with all the trade-offs between stakeholder interests that will arise? Even more problematic, it will be necessary to give management a lot of room for discretion to make decisions on those trade-offs, and of course, there are strong reasons to believe that they will act *in their own* interests more than in the stakeholders' interests.

Looking at the data, this actually seems to be the case. In 2019, the influential Business Round Table (BRT) – an influential 'club' for US CEOs – famously stated that the era of Milton Friedman was over and that they now had adopted the stakeholder perspective. Even though announced as a kind of revolution, it is not surprising a closer analysis shows that what the CEOs actually said was that there are no trade-offs between the shareholders and other stakeholders. Obviously, acting in their own best self-interest, the sudden adoption of the stakeholder perspective had rarely been anchored with the board of directors, that is, the presumed representatives of the shareholders. Furthermore, corporate guidelines promoting shareholder primacy did not change much. Basically, Bebchuk and Tallarita claimed that the signing CEOs were hypocrites.

But there is more ammunition. Almost all CEOs of the BRT have their pay tied to the stock price, aligning the interests of the CEOs with the shareholders and not the stakeholders. The career interests of the CEOs create the same alignment since they will want to prioritise the stock price to increase future job opportunities. Furthermore, studies of private equity acquisitions for the past twenty years show that the negotiating CEOs did not take stakeholder consideration but instead shareholder and self-serving considerations.

Furthermore, how could incentive schemes aligning the CEO incentives with the stakeholder interests possibly be constructed? In fact, is not the entire stakeholderism movement generated by self-interested CEOs who have everything to win when the chains of the shareholders are loosened and the room for discretion increases?

It should be noted that this criticism is written in a US context, where the shareholder primacy view is particularly strong. But the point would, of course, be valid also in Europe: *this criticism of the stakeholder perspective is only natural and convincing if you ignore the fact that the very rules and policies that have created these incentive systems for the CEOs to a large extent are the products of the very theory that recommended introduction of those incentive systems in the first place*. And for the same reason, the stakeholder perspective will have a difficult time arguing for its case.

This story is not fiction but, to a large extent, reality. Our imagined economist is very close to the already referred to Michael Jensen, the main creator of the agency perspective on companies. He was not a mere analyst of the market; his explicit aim was to change the market by applying his theories.[143] He was, of course, not acting alone but was part of a larger story of social struggles, many of them fought by economists and others being members of the Mont-Pelerin society founded by, among others, the free market economists Friedrich von Hayek and Milton Friedman.

143. Fourcade, M. and Khurana, R., The Social Trajectory of a Finance Professor and the Common Sense of Capital. 49(2) History of Political Economy, June 2017, 347-381.

This is not the place to tell this story, which is step-by-step being analysed, mainly in other fields than in economics.[144] To be clear, this is not a conspiracy theory about a group of (mostly) men acting deliberately to shape the world according to their heads. It is a story about what the French sociologist Pierre Bourdieu called 'symbolic struggles', where ideas and theories (for example, agency theory, the Kaldor-Hicks criterion and so forth) are not only ideas and theories but also symbolic weapons in a contest for symbolic capital within various social fields (for example, the field of economics) and where the prize to be won is, simply put prestige and recognition.[145,146] In the market, the company winning the most customers wins. In the scientific world, the winner is the party managing to impose its worldview on the other and making that the 'natural' worldview. 'If I manage to naturalize my vision of the world, I have won.'[147]

It is through struggles like these that science has advanced throughout history. The problem is that the outcome of this struggle among economists and legal theorists has had a significant effect on how the world actually works, not least it being highly unsustainable.

Much of economics suffer from the weakness of not having a theory about the economic or societal effects of economic theory. Any sociologist will know that sociological theory has effects on the very people and society which is the object of analysis,[148] but this theory is lacking within economics, perhaps with the exception of Douglass North's version of new institutional economics. This should make everyone very cautious in applying this theory to law.

6.7 SEPARATING PURPOSE FROM VALUES

We may seem far from the subject of this chapter, which is to define the ground rules of the game for a sustainable business. Hopefully, however, the preceding sections are

144. *See, e.g.*: Mirowski. P and Plehwe, D. (eds), The Road from Mont Pelerin: The Making of the Neo-liberal Thought Collective, 2nd edn, Harvard University Press, 2016. Fourcade, M. and Khurana, R., From Social Control to Financial Economics: The Linked Ecologies of Economics and Business in Twentieth-Century America, 42(2) Theory and Society, 2013, 121-159. MacKenzie, D., An Engine, Not a Camera: How Financial Models Shape Markets, The MIT Press, 2006. Cook, E., Efficiently Unequal: The Global Rise of Kaldor-Hicks Neoliberalism, 9(1-2) Global Intellectual History, 2024, 247-269. Gane, N., Neoliberalism and the Defence of the Corporation, 40(3) Theory Culture & Society, 2023.
145. *See, e.g.*, Bourdieu, P., Science of Science and Reflexivity, The University of Chicago Press, 2004. Bourdieu, P., An Invitation to Reflexive Sociology, Polity Press, 1992. Bourdieu, P., Homo Academicus, Stanford University Press, 1990. The conservative revolution in US economics shows clear similarities with the corresponding conservative revolution in philosophy in Germany, largely led by Martin Heidegger: *see* Bourdieu, P., The Political Ontology of Martin Heidegger, Polity Press, 1991.
146. This is very clear when it comes to the development of the Kaldor-Hicks criteria. When economists had started to claim that peoples' utilities were not comparable, economists found themselves in an awkward position of becoming completely irrelevant as advisers of the public. For if utilities are not comparable, it should be impossible to find a way to aggregate them and thus make analysis and recommendations on a societal level. It is quite clear in both Nicholas Kaldor's and John Hicks' papers establishing the criteria (referred to earlier) that they fight to stay relevant as advisors of public policy, while at the same time making their opponents irrelevant. This is not criticism as such, this is how science advances.
147. Bourdieu, P., Classification Struggles, General Sociology Volume 1, Polity Press, 2018, p. 55.
148. *See, e.g.*, Giddens, A., The Constitution of Society, University of California Press, 1992, p. xxxii.

sufficient to show that it is important *not* to address this very practical question based on inherited views of corporate purpose, which largely rests on both empirical and normative views – based on the utility concept – which is very hard if at all possible to defend.

So what to do then? As said, the common approach today is to apply some kind of utility-based thinking when looking at the world with the descriptive and the normative faces, respectively. Better models must be used for both faces, and it is unlikely that it will be possible to find a fictive common ground as the one provided by the utility concept.

We should start with morality. We should do this because defining the ground rules of business is ultimately a moral choice. The first step here is to make a distinction between corporate purpose and corporate values. In Jim Collin's and Jerry Porras's influential book *Built to Last*, the authors identify the 'core ideology' of a company as a critical explanation behind corporate success. The core ideology they define as a combination of a company's core values and its core purpose.[149] Whether Collins and Porras were right in saying that the most successful companies nail their core ideology is an empirical question which is not in focus here. But their distinction between purpose and values should be kept. It will be argued below that the question of corporate purpose is best viewed in light of the positive contribution norm described in the previous chapters. The moral duties to comply with when pursuing the purpose stem from the due diligence norm. They thus relate more to corporate culture and values than to corporate purpose.

6.7.1 A Separate Look at Purpose

When looking at purpose, it seems important to, again, not conflate questions that should be separated. As discussed above, law and economics are heavily influenced by Coase's view that companies exist since it is sometimes cheaper to run a business in corporate form than through contracts on the market. But that – creation of social welfare by reduction of transaction costs – is not the corporate purpose. The transaction cost reduction can, instead, be said to be the reason why the corporate form was chosen to run the business instead of another form, such as a partnership or through individual contracts. The purpose of a business is not the same as the purpose of running a business in the form of a corporation.

Also, the founders' purpose when establishing a corporation should not be mistaken for the purpose of that corporation. The founders may (or may not) have founded the company to become as rich as possible. Or they may, taking the Hart/Zingales perspective, have founded it to become rich and, at the same time, promote some socially positive impact. But that is not the purpose of the company as such.

It seems important to recall the wisdom of the management guru Peter Drucker, who said that to say that the idea that the purpose of a business is to make a profit is

149. Collins, J. and Porras, J., Built to Last, Harper Business, 1994, Chapter 3.

not only false, it is *irrelevant*.[150] Profit as such is not irrelevant, but for a corporate purpose it is. Profit is, instead, according to Drucker, a test of the validity of the purpose and the commercial decisions made when fulfilling that purpose.

According to Drucker, the purpose of a business is 'to create a customer'.[151] What he means is that a business is always run based on some kind of idea of what creates value for customers. This is obviously true. A founder of a business may, as said, do this to maximise his or her wealth of welfare. But he or she has always had an idea that this personal purpose can be fulfilled by: (1) satisfying a customer's need equally good or better than others, and (2) doing this in the form of a corporation instead of just contracting with individuals on the market.

The purpose of a company is thus always to provide some kind of customer value. Of course, many companies provide different kinds of value and can thus have several purposes.

The EU taxonomy, described in more detail in Chapter 9, can be used as an example here. According to Article 3 of the taxonomy, a commercial activity must, to be allowed to be called environmentally sustainable, first of all, contribute substantially to some of the environmental objectives stated in Article 9, for example, climate change mitigation or the transition to a circular economy. The Commission delegated regulation (EU) 2021/2139 sets out the kind of activities that, under law, can contribute substantially to climate change mitigation. Examples are the manufacturing of renewable energy technologies, manufacturing of batteries, renewal of wastewater collection and treatment and renovation of existing buildings. Those are examples of business which, in the words of Professor Alex Edmans, has the potential to 'grow the pie' since they are examples of businesses that may 'do well by doing good'.

The purpose of the business thus lies very close to the value proposition in the business model, which will be discussed further in Chapter 17. The value proposition is the basic idea of how the company satisfies customer needs. The purpose is thus operationalised in a business model, where the value proposition is the starting point in the business model.

Below is a list of (as of when this book is published) the announced corporate purposes of ten well-known companies:

- **Google**: To organise the world's information and make it universally accessible and useful.
- **Unilever**: To make sustainable living commonplace.
- **Apple**: To bring the best user experience to its customers through its innovative hardware, software, and services.
- **Siemens**: To pioneer solutions in electrification, automation, and digitalisation to benefit people and the planet.
- **Amazon**: To be Earth's most customer-centric company, where customers can find and discover anything they might want to buy online.

150. Drucker, P., The Purpose and Objectives of a Business, in The Essential Drucker, Harper, 2001, p. 18.
151. *Ibid.*, p. 20.

- **IKEA**: To create a better everyday life for many people by offering a wide range of well-designed, functional home furnishing products at prices so low that as many people as possible will be able to afford them.
- **Microsoft**: To empower every person and every organisation on the planet to achieve more.
- **Nestlé**: To enhance quality of life and contribute to a healthier future.
- **Tesla**: To accelerate the world's transition to sustainable energy.

These are all so-called mission statements, i.e., statements of why these companies exist. The purpose of a system will or should guide the activities and all other parts of the system. From this perspective, the Nestlé purpose is rather vague, at least compared to, for example, the IKEA mission statement, which is much more concrete. But the common denominator is that all these statements define, at various levels of concreteness, what value the company is aiming to contribute.

A sustainable business complying with the norms of positive contribution and due diligence must, of course, have a purpose that means a positive contribution to society, be it environmental or social. The starting point for any discussion about corporate purpose is: what kind of value do we bring to our customers that also makes the world a better place to live in?

6.7.2 A Separate Look at Values

The problem is that while a corporate purpose may be good, the company may do badly when fulfilling this purpose. An oil and gas company is an obvious example. However, unpopular those companies are today, it is still the case those companies have been extremely important for improving the lives of billions of people by providing rather cheap energy. The problem is that they, simultaneously, have undermined humanity's possibility to survive on the planet, by the greenhouse gases emitted through their products. It is not natural, however, to call those greenhouse gas emissions the purpose of those companies, even though it has been a logical consequence of their business. The problem here is not a problem of purpose but of values. While the purpose is good – providing energy to humanity – the values have been bad since the day those companies realised the negative effects on humanity they contributed to.

To be clear, I use the term 'values' to denote normative principles of a deontological kind, i.e., principles that say what is right and wrong. Right and wrong is, fundamentally, about respecting or disrespecting peoples' dignity, that is their rights to equality and freedom.

It is rather uninteresting to look at the corporate values of different companies. From a moral perspective, this should not be a difficult discussion. Any company, at least within the European Union, should ask itself: 'Are there *any* reasons why our values should be anything else than the due diligence norm?' As shown earlier,[152] this

152. *See* Chapter 5.

norm obliges companies to respect the equality and freedom of everyone affected by its operation by systematically identifying, eliminating, mitigating and remediating negative impacts and risks for such negative impacts on people and the environment.

6.8 THE CORE IDEOLOGY OF A SUSTAINABLE BUSINESS

In *Built to Last*, referred to above, Collins and Porras illustrated the core ideology of the companies they analysed with a yin and yang symbol. Based on the content of this chapter, the same can be done for a business aiming to be sustainable and planning to comply with EU sustainability laws:

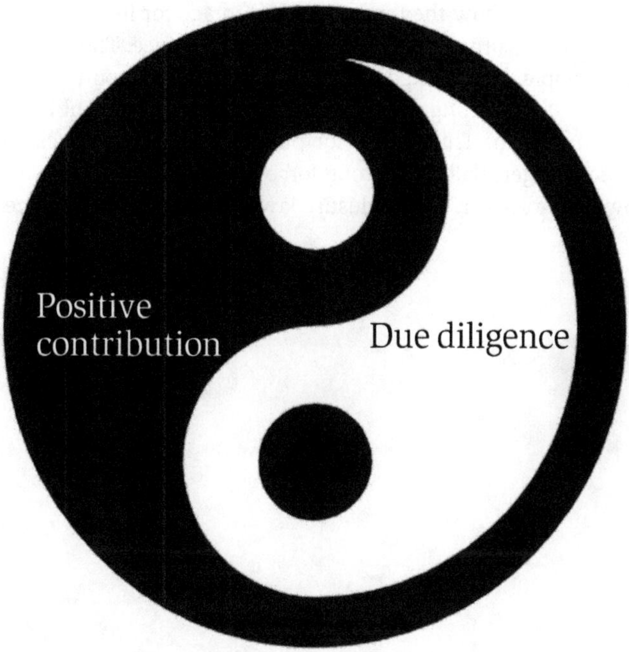

Readers still stuck in the shareholder-stakeholder dichotomy may now hesitate and perhaps ask questions like: But what shall the guiding light for management now be, if the company is not run to maximise shareholder value? How on earth shall the company be governed? Will this not give CEOs, being agents, too much discretion? There are two answers to this question.

First, the proponents of shareholder value focus are typically also quick to praise the creativity of entrepreneurs to innovate and find new ways to create value, typically with a follow-up that they shall not be restricted in their creative process by governmental intervention. The market under capitalism may have contributed to taking the world to an unsustainable state, but in the meantime, miracles have also been created. Not that it was the market in that specific case, but if humanity could land a man on the moon and bring him back again with the technology of 1969, it seems likely that humanity will solve this problem also, as long as they don't have to be restricted in the creative process by agency theory and other theories which are empirically and normatively weak.

Second, an attempt to answer is provided by the EU sustainability disclosure laws. As will be shown in the coming parts of the book, those laws require companies to transparently describe how they meet an ideal image for investors and businesses based on the norms of positive contribution and due diligence. The will to comply with norms that most people, when asked, would agree are more important than wallet size typically becomes quite strong when you have to show in public how you are complying with the norm. This search for public recognition, which the disclosure requirements may trigger, will be a strong force of change.

Let's now take a look at the disclosure laws for sustainable finance.

PART II Sustainable Finance

CHAPTER 7

Introduction to Sustainable Finance

7.1 A CONCEPT WITHOUT DEFINITION

As explained in Chapter 4, EU law on sustainability begins with the regulation of finance. For readers not active in the financial markets, it is still important to understand those rules because the requirements in, e.g., the SFDR and EU taxonomy on financial market actors have important implications for other businesses, not least because the requirements will shape the demands and expectations of investors and lenders on businesses. It will, for example, be hard to understand why the Corporate Sustainability Reporting Directive, described in Part III, is written as it is without having at least some understanding of what the laws regarding sustainable finance say.

As said, the European Commission's Action Plan on Financing Sustainable Growth aims to:

- reorient capital flows towards sustainable investment in order to achieve sustainable and inclusive growth;
- manage financial risks stemming from climate change, resource depletion, environmental degradation and social issues; and
- foster transparency and long-termism in financial and economic activity.

This second part of the book discusses the legal rules that have been followed as a result of this action plan. These are primarily the Regulations 2019/2088 on sustainability-related disclosures in the financial services sector (the SFDR), 2020/852 on the establishment of a framework to facilitate sustainable investments (the EU Taxonomy), 2023/2631 on European Green Bonds and the delegated acts adopted under these regulations. The important question of sustainable finance contracts will be dealt with in Part IV.

All these regulations use disclosure requirements as a mechanism to promote sustainable investments. By forcing the financial market participants to be transparent on which sustainability concerns they take in their business – simply put, how they meet the norms of positive contribution and due diligence in their investments – they shall be incentivised to make sustainable investments out of concern that the final investors with sustainability preferences will choose competing and more sustainable alternatives.

Financial market participants typically have in common that they do not generate profit through the production of goods or services sold for money. Instead, their purpose is to create increased returns by financing companies through equity or lending. The demarcation is not clear, as there are also a large number of financial advisers on the market who undeniably belong to the financial market but who do not themselves generate returns through investments. Important players in the financial markets include banks, insurance companies, private equity firms, pension funds, fund management companies and securities companies.

The figure below shows a possible breakdown of the different forms of financing:

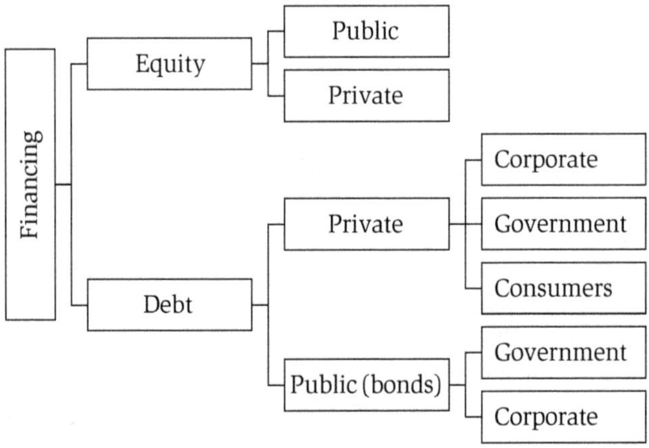

As said, companies are financed through equity or debt. Financing through equity can take place publicly, i.e., on a stock exchange or privately. Financing through debt can also be done publicly, through the issuance of bonds, or privately through bank loans. From the perspective of the financial actors, there are further divisions to be made. For example, a bank's lending activities can be divided into loans to companies, to governments and to consumers.

There is no accepted market definition of what is sustainable finance or a sustainable investment. In English, terms such as 'impact investing', 'responsible investing', 'ethical investing', 'sustainable investing', 'impact lending', 'sustainable lending' and 'green lending' are used to describe a number of different phenomena with a more or less strong connection to sustainability.

It is appropriate to look at sustainable finance as meaning that different types of financing and approaches to sustainability exist on a scale. At one end of the scale is traditional financing with the aim of maximising profits and without any consideration of sustainability matters. At the other end of the scale are various forms of so-called impact financing, where financing is done with equity or debt for the express purpose of achieving positive results for sustainability matters and where the profit requirement is subordinate to the sustainability goals:

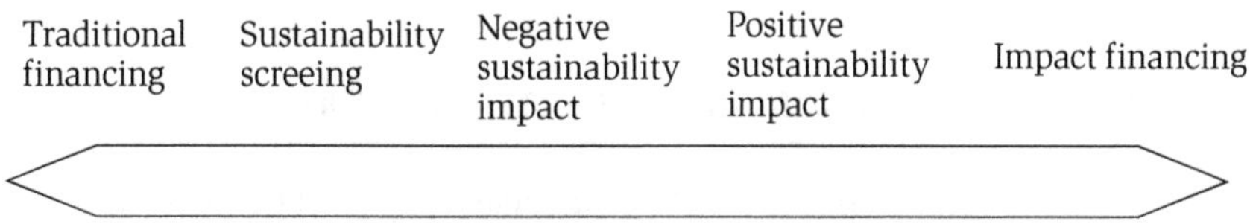

In a first step from traditional to more sustainable financing, financiers are refraining from financing activities deemed 'ugly', such as operations in oil and gas, controversial weapons and so on (sustainability screening). Apart from this, financing is carried out in accordance with standard methods and return-on-investment requirements. In the next step, the financier considers sustainability-related risks for the company, which can affect the company's ability to run a profitable business in the long term. This may involve analyses of the company's dependence on certain key assets, which may be threatened by climate change or biodiversity loss. Pricing and analysing such risks are major challenges. The aim is still profit maximisation but with a broader (and sensible) perspective on the business that also includes sustainability aspects.

In the next step, companies' negative impact on sustainability matters begins to be taken into account. This analysis becomes important, for example, as soon as it seems likely that the company will need to change its operations, for example, to meet the demands of customers and the outside community for increased sustainability. This change will usually affect both revenues and costs for the business and, thus, the valuation of the business.

So far, the focus has been on financial risks and negative sustainability impacts. As a next step, companies' potential positive impact on sustainability matters is instead beginning to be considered. A so-called sustainability-linked loan is a form of loan to a business where the loan may be used for the business in general but where the loan terms are linked to certain sustainability factors. For example, the borrower can get better loan terms if it achieves certain targets for greenhouse gas emissions set in the loan agreement. Thus, the purpose of the funding is not to reduce emissions, but such reductions may still result from the funding. In this step, the funding can also be explicitly tied to activities or projects that will achieve a positive impact on sustainability matters. So-called green loans are examples of this, where the loan is given to finance activities or projects that are environmentally friendly. For the same purpose, companies can also issue so-called green bonds. Various forms of green funds or sustainability funds, where the funds are invested as equity, have also become increasingly common. Here, economic, social and environmental value can be said to weigh equally in funding.

In the final stage, there is so-called impact funding or investing. The term lacks a definition. The aim is still to explicitly contribute positively to sustainability factors. Here, however, the environmental and/or social value takes a superior position in relation to the economic value, at least directly calculable financial value. Funding is still provided with the expected economic returns, but only as part of achieving environmental or social benefits.

The scale of different degrees of sustainable finance described here is good to keep in mind in the rest of the presentation.

7.2 FINANCIAL MARKETS IN THE EARTH4ALL MODEL

In the Earth4All model, described in section 1.3, financial market participants play the role that financial markets play in the economic system, i.e., as a channel between those with less money than they need at the moment and those with more money than they need at the moment.[153] The core of the economy is *companies* which produce goods and services for remuneration, and *people* who work for the companies for a salary and who consume the companies' goods and services. The *state* plays an important role in creating predictable rules of the game in the economy, including regulating property rights, contract enforcement, tax collection and so on. In addition, there are also *actors who make investments through debt or equity*, i.e., banks, private equity firms, pension funds, insurance companies, and so on. These actors make money from money - expressed in various forms of financial instruments - and not from the sale of goods and services.

The systemic role of financial market participants in the economy and society is well known. The concept of *too big to fail* says it all - some of these actors cannot fail without bringing the economy and society to a standstill. This simply means that financial market participants have enormous power over how the economy and society develop. It, therefore, goes without saying that it is crucial for the future of humanity whether these actors act according to the model of traditional finance or for one of the levels of sustainable finance.

With traditional financing, financing will always be provided through the most profitable option, without considering the externalities created by the companies in which the investments are made. Finance theory was the product of the same economic theory project as agency theory, described in Chapter 6, and it has been largely adopted by the market.[154]

On the contrary, it easily comes across as an excellent business idea to generate revenue while letting others pay for it. The expected rates of return and time horizons will be determined accordingly, which will severely limit the ability of the financed companies to conduct sustainable business operations. In addition, the forces that, as described in section 1.3, increase inequality in society will be given large room in self-reinforcing relationships. Short-term return requirements shape demands to keep wages down and to replace employees with technology where it is more productive in the short term. This lowers consumption levels and, thus, growth. Therefore, when the

153. However, it is now more widely accepted that banks do not fulfil their role as intermediaries between those who have too much and too little capital at the moment by simply intermediating capital. Banks create money through their lending.
154. *See* MacKenzie, D., An Engine, Not a Camera – How Financial Models Shape Markets, The MIT Press, 2006.

rate of return on capital exceeds the rate of growth, the incomes of the owners of capital increase faster than the incomes of the workers, which increases inequality. And so on.

If financial market participants were instead to act to make a positive contribution to sustainability matters, the consequences would, of course, be dramatic. Huge investments would be made to phase out fossil fuels and increase energy efficiency, support the shift to a circular economy based on recyclable products, and so on while requiring that people should not be harmed but, on the contrary, be well treated. This would counteract inequalities in society, thereby lowering social tensions and increasing trust, which would increase society's capacity for collective action to deal with the already extensive damage to nature and the consequences of climate change that inevitably occurs anyway due to historical emissions.

The above description suffices to state that financial markets play a key role in the Earth4All model.

7.3 SUSTAINABILITY MORALITY FOUNDATION

In section 5.3, a sketch for a sustainability morality underpinning the fundamental norms of positive contribution and due diligence was presented. In this section and other similar sections in the book, that sketch will now be used on a more specific topic, in this case, sustainable finance. The purpose is to uncover the norms underlying and legitimising the EU legislation to make the legal text easier to understand.

The moral framework used here distinguishes between the duty not to harm others and the duty to help others, where the cost of harm and costs to avoid harm or to help need to be weighed into moral decisions. These duties are expressed in the norms of due diligence and positive contribution to the EU sustainability laws. In the laws focusing on sustainable finance, these basic norms come into play both in the actual financing operations and decisions taken and in how the financial market actors communicate about their operations, where the latter is very much about what is typically referred to as greenwashing.

7.3.1 Investment Operations and Decisions

Any form of financing of an activity or project contributes to and enables the activity or project, which is why the actor providing the financing has a moral responsibility for it. The above description of different steps towards sustainable finance can be read as a question of increasing moral responsibility for financing decisions. In principle, no moral responsibility is taken for the investment in question in traditional finance, perhaps based on a perception that no such responsibility exists for the investor.

When sustainability screening takes place or the investor begins to consider sustainability risks, moral responsibility increases. However, it is not a question of morally consistent action. The profit motive is still the overarching purpose. If consideration is given to people and the environment, it is done for this profit motive. Treating humans as mere means to other ends is not compatible with the requirement of respect for human dignity.

In the next step – when funding is made to make a positive contribution to sustainability matters – moral responsibility increases radically. Compliance with the positive contribution norm begins.

In the final step, focus is not only on positive contributions but also on not harming people and the environment.

As will be described below, SFDR and the EU taxonomy set requirements for how companies – in this case, financial market participants and financial advisors – shall report on their operations from a sustainability perspective. The regulations establish what can be described as an ideal image of sustainable finance operations. As will be explained in more detail below, this ideal image means that investments are made with the aim of achieving social or environmental sustainability objectives without doing significant harm to people or the environment. This ideal, of course, reflects the combination of the norms of positive contribution and due diligence.

7.3.2 Communication about Finance Operations: Greenwashing

The above description refers to the financial actor's moral responsibility for its financing decisions. However, it should be underlined that the transparency requirements in, for example, the SFDR are very much about the responsibility of these actors in relation to the ultimate investors, such as those who buy the financial actor's products. The sustainability morality basis for this coincides with, for example, the requirements for marketing and information in marketing, consumer and personal data law.

The risk managed in this perspective is the risk of greenwashing. It is not an entirely appropriate term since it indicates that it is only environmental aspects which are important, which is, of course, not true since misleading communication about the social and governance aspects of sustainability have equal importance. Nevertheless, the term greenwashing will be used here.

What is greenwashing? There is no common definition, but it could be said to be a practice where an actor in the financial market or just any company tries to increase sales by communicating about its products or services, which makes them look more 'sustainable' than they really are. Favourite expressions to do this are 'green', 'sustainable', 'environmentally friendly' and the like. Why communicate in this way? The purpose is to make this information form part of the information base forming the consumers' purchase decisions. What happens, morally speaking, when the consumer buys the product or service based on this information while it, in fact, is untrue? This is basically a violation of the consumer's dignity since the company violates the consumer's moral right to make autonomous decisions based on the principle of freedom.

As will be shown below, the disclosure requirements in, for example, the SFDR and the EU taxonomy is very much about restricting greenwashing in the market by forcing actors in the financial market to transparently substantiate any claims about the sustainability of its operations or products.

CHAPTER 8

Sustainable Finance Disclosures

The Sustainable Finance Disclosure Regulation (SFDR) and the EU taxonomy are the most central sustainability regulatory frameworks for the financial markets. As seen below, those two regulations have complementary functions to achieve the same aim, i.e., to increase the volumes of capital flows into sustainable investments. In addition to the SFDR, the European Commission has also adopted the Delegated Regulation (EU) 2022/1288 on technical standards specifying how information under the SFDR should be provided.

8.1 APPLICABILITY

The SFDR applies to financial market participants and financial advisers, respectively. According to Article 2(1) of the SFDR, 'financial market participant' means any of the following:

- an insurance undertaking which makes available an insurance-based investment product (IBIP);
- an investment firm which provides portfolio management;
- an institution for occupational retirement provision (IORP);
- a manufacturer of a pension product;
- an alternative investment fund manager (AIFM);
- a pan-European personal pension product (PEPP) provider;
- a manager of a qualifying venture capital fund registered in accordance with Article 14 of Regulation (EU) No. 345/2013;
- a manager of a qualifying social entrepreneurship fund registered in accordance with Article 15 of Regulation (EU) No. 346/2013;
- a management company of an undertaking for collective investment in transferable securities (UCITS management company); or
- a credit institution which provides portfolio management.

The term 'financial advisor' refers to:

- an insurance intermediary which provides insurance advice with regard to IBIPs;
- an insurance undertaking which provides insurance advice with regard to IBIPs;
- a credit institution which provides investment advice;
- an investment firm which provides investment advice;
- an AIFM which provides investment advice in accordance with point (b)(i) of Article 6(4) of Directive 2011/61/EU; or
- a UCITS management company which provides investment advice in accordance with point (b)(i) of Article 6(3) of Directive 2009/65/EC.

The list is thus quite comprehensive for the participants in the financial system.

8.2 THE CONCEPT OF 'SUSTAINABLE INVESTMENT'

As said, the EU legislator can be viewed as setting forth an ideal image for financial sector players based on the norms of positive contribution and due diligence. Under the SFDR, financial market participants and advisors are obliged to report their operations in relation to this ideal image. The contours of this ideal image are expressed in the definition of 'sustainable investment' in Article 2.17 of the SFDR:

> An investment in an economic activity that contributes to an environmental objective, as measured, for example, by key resource efficiency indicators on the use of energy, renewable energy, raw materials, water and land, on the production of waste, and greenhouse gas emissions, or on its impact on biodiversity and the circular economy, or an investment in an economic activity that contributes to a social objective, in particular an investment that contributes to tackling inequality or that fosters social cohesion, social integration and labour relations, or an investment in human capital or economically or socially disadvantaged communities, provided that such investments do not significantly harm any of those objectives and that the investee companies follow good governance practices, in particular with respect to sound management structures, employee relations, remuneration of staff and tax compliance.

According to this definition, three key conditions must be met for an investment to be sustainable and, thus, for the ideal image of EU law to be met:

- The investment shall contribute to an environmental or social objective.
- The investment must not cause significant harm.
- The investee company must comply with good governance practices.

It is important, however, to understand what kind of concept the concept 'sustainable investment' as defined in the SFDR is, as well as the important concepts such as 'contribution to sustainability objectives', 'do no significant harm' and 'good governance practice'. For few concepts in the EU's sustainability law have caused more confusion than those, and this seems to be because of a lack of such understanding.

The confusion has, it seems, been increased due to the closeness of the SFDR definition of sustainable investment and the definition, dealt with in Chapter 9, in the EU taxonomy of what economic activities are *environmentally* sustainable.

Legal theorist Ronald Dworkin made, in discussing what kind of concept the concept of 'law' is, an important distinction between three kinds of concepts: criterial, natural kind and interpretive concepts.[155] The natural kind concepts can be set aside here, but the distinction between criterial and interpretive concepts helps shed light on the definition of sustainable investment. All concepts fulfil a function in human communication, and to serve this function, people must, at least to some extent, have a shared understanding of their meaning. Some concepts are then 'criterial' in the sense that people agree on a definition of the concept based on certain criteria. People can talk about bachelorhood because they have a shared understanding that a bachelor is an unmarried male, or they can talk about an equilateral triangle because they know that such triangle has sides of equal length.

Many legal concepts are criterial concepts. In such cases, the legislature provides a more or less precise definition of the concept. In fact, the definition of environmentally sustainable economic activities in the EU taxonomy is, as will be discussed further below, such a concept. However, the concepts 'sustainable investment', 'contribution to sustainability objectives', 'do no significant harm' and 'good governance practice' in Article 2.17 of the SFDR are *not* criterial concepts. Instead, they are what Dworkin calls interpretive concepts.

What kind of concept is that? Take the concept of 'courtesy', for example.[156] People can communicate based on this concept and argue whether courtesy requires that men open doors to women, that you bring a gift to a family who has invited you for dinner and so on. However, people do not share an understanding of a distinct set of criteria for what courtesy is. The same goes for concepts such as justice, equality, right, wrong, cruelty, etc. As with courtesy, those concepts are used to communicate about human practices and activities, and they serve the function of classifying such practices based on an understanding of what makes those practices valuable or important in some sense. Courtesy is not a neutral concept, like equilateral triangle. It is used to evaluate certain kinds of behaviour. Most people would agree that this value somehow relates to what it means to show people 'respect', which, of course, then is another interpretive concept.

This distinction between criterial and interpretive concepts is helpful to interpret the SFDR. With the definition of 'sustainable investment' in Article 2.17 of SFDR, the EU legislator has not laid down a definition of a criterial concept. The legislator has instead laid down a kind of structure for an interpretive concept, saying that just as 'respect' may constitute the core value of 'courtesy', so 'contribution to a sustainability objective', 'do no significant harm' and 'good governance practice' constitute the core values of a 'sustainable investment'. As will be seen below, the legislator then only asks the financial market participants to be transparent about *their own* definitions of these latter three concepts. In an attempt to clarify things, ESMA wrote in an

155. *See, e.g.*, Dworkin, R., Justice in Robes, Harvard University Press, 2006, pp. 9-12.
156. *See* Dworkin, R., Law's Empire, Harvard University Press, 1986, pp. 68 ff.

explanatory note that 'the SFDR does not set out minimum requirements [i.e., criteria] that qualify concepts such as contribution, DNSH, or good governance, i.e., the key parameters of a "sustainable investment". Financial market participants [...] must carry out *their own assessment* for each investment and disclose their underlying assumptions [italics added]'.[157]

8.3 FOUR LEVELS OF AMBITION TOWARDS SUSTAINABLE FINANCING

Even though, as shown in the previous section, the SFDR does not lay down a criterial definition of what a 'sustainable investment' is, this definition still serves a key function in the entire logic of the regulation. The aim of the regulation is to orient capital flows to sustainable investments. The mechanism to obtain this chosen by the legislature is rather unusual. The legislature can be said to have constructed four ambition levels towards sustainable investments and financing, with increasing degrees of disclosure requirements of information depending on which ambition level a particular financial market participant wants to claim they belong to. These four ambition levels and scopes of information are the following:

- Ambition level 1: Integration of *sustainability risks* into investment decisions and advice.
- Ambition level 2: Consideration of *principal adverse sustainability impacts* at entity level in investment decisions and advice, respectively.
- Ambition level 3: *Promotion of environmental or social characteristics* by a financial product.
- Ambition level 4: *Sustainable investment is the objective* of the financial product.

The four levels of ambition for financial products can be said to be four steps towards fulfilling the requisites for sustainable investments and, thus, the EU's ideal image for sustainable finance based on the norms of positive contribution and due diligence. As can be seen, the levels lie closely to the continuum of financing discussed in section 8.1.

On the market, SFDR is often described as having three categories of products and investments, falling within the scope of Articles 6, 8 and 9, respectively. It has become somewhat of a market practice to talk about, e.g., 'Article 8 products' or 'Article 9 funds'. This way of reading SFDR is basically incorrect, a seldom highlighted fact. First of all, Articles 8 and 9 deal with financial products, which is not the case with Article 6. When a financial product is classified as an 'Article 6 product', it basically means that it cannot be categorized under Articles 8 or 9. Second, which will be further elaborated below, it is incorrect to say that a certain financial product is, e.g., an 'Article 8 product', thereby indicating that it meets certain criteria set out in that article. This reading of the SFDR implies, referring to the previous section, that Articles 6, 8

157. ESMA, Concepts of sustainable investments and environmentally sustainable activities in the EU Sustainable Finance framework, 22 November 2023, p. 21.

and 9 work with criterial and not interpretive concepts. Neither Article 6 nor 8 nor 9 set out criteria to be met.

8.4 INTEGRATION OF SUSTAINABILITY RISKS

At the first level, financial market participants and financial advisers may disclose information on their websites about their policies on the integration of sustainability risks into their investment process and advice, respectively.[158] According to Article 2(22) of the SFDR, sustainability risk is defined as an environmental, social or governance event or condition which, if it occurs, would have an actual or potential material negative impact on the value of the investment. It is not a requirement, but if the actor does not consider sustainability risks to be relevant, the reasons for this must be stated. In this case, it refers to the equivalent of what is referred to in the European Sustainability Reporting Standards, described in Part III of the book, as 'financial impact'.

In section 15.3 below, the risk and opportunity analysis framework created by the Task Force on Climate-Related Financial Disclosures (TFCD) is presented. Even though that framework is designed specifically for climate change, it is suitable for gaining a basic understanding of all sustainability risks and how they may affect the value of the investment. It is, therefore, relevant to make the following basic distinction between different risk classes:

(i) **Transition Risks:** Risks related to the transition to a more sustainable economy.
  - Policy and legal risks: risks related to regulations of business related to sustainability and litigation risks.
  - Technology risks: risks for loss of competitiveness, increased costs and similar risks related to technology supporting transition to a more sustainable economy.
  - Market risks: risks for shifts in supply or demand for products and services related to the sustainability transition.
  - Reputational risks: risks for reputational damage due to changing customer and community perceptions related to sustainability.

(ii) **Physical Risks:** risks for damages to assets, supply chain disruption and similar risks resulting from climate change or similar sustainability-related factors.
  - Acute risks: event-driven risks, for example, weather-related.
  - Chronic: long-term risks, for example, rising sea levels or chronic heat waves.

Financial market participants and financial advisers shall further include information in their remuneration policies on how those policies are consistent with the

158. Article 3 SFDR.

integration of sustainability risks. That information shall also be published on the company's website.[159]

In addition, financial market participants and financial advisers shall disclose, before entering into a contract, how sustainability risks are integrated into investment decisions and the results of the assessment of the likely impact of risks on the returns of the financial products they make available.[160] Article 6(3) of the SFDR provides more detailed information on how different categories of financial market participants should present this information.

8.5 PRINCIPAL ADVERSE IMPACTS ON SUSTAINABILITY FACTORS

At the next level, financial market participants and financial advisers can disclose on their websites up-to-date information on the principal adverse impacts of investment decisions and advice on sustainability factors.[161] Sustainability factors are defined as environmental, social and employee matters, respect for human rights, anti-corruption and anti-bribery matters.[162] It is not a requirement to disclose how the adverse impacts are considered, but if they are not considered, the reasons for this shall be explained.

This is, therefore, the equivalent of 'material impact' in the double materiality analysis under the CSRD.[163] It should be noted, however, that the concepts differ. Reporting principal adverse impacts is, at least from a purely linguistic point of view, different from reporting material impacts. It is currently unclear whether there is any real difference between the concepts. The important thing here is that what is meant is the external impact of the investments.

A financial market participant that considers principal adverse impacts shall submit:

- information about their policies on the identification and prioritisation of principal adverse sustainability impacts and indicators;
- a description of the principal adverse sustainability impacts and of any actions in relation thereto taken or, where relevant, planned;
- brief summaries of incentive policies in accordance with Article 3g of Directive 2007/36/EC,[164] where applicable;
- a reference to their adherence to responsible business conduct codes and internationally recognised standards for due diligence and reporting and, where relevant, the degree of their alignment with the objectives of the Paris

159. Article 5 SFDR.
160. Article 6 SFDR.
161. Article 4 SFDR.
162. Article 2.24 SFDR.
163. *See* section 16.2.
164. Directive 2007/36/EC of the European Parliament and of the Council of 11 July 2007 on the exercise of certain rights of shareholders in listed companies.

> Agreement, information on their policies for identifying priority for principal adverse impacts and indicators for sustainable development.[165,166]

The template set out in Table 1 of Annex I and also possibly Annex I to Delegated Regulation (EU) 2022/1288 on technical standards shall be used to present this information.[167] The template shows that there is a wide range of factors to be considered, including

- greenhouse gas emissions;
- biodiversity;
- water;
- waste; and
- social and human resources issues.

These are what are commonly referred to as the PAI indicators (primary adverse impact indicators). There is an important connection here between the SFDR and the CSRD and, in particular, the ESRS since the ESRS partly can be said to ensure that companies report on data that financial market participants need to report on the PAI indicators.[168] Further details on what information is to be presented and how are set out in Chapter II of Delegated Regulation (EU) 2022/1288.

8.6 PRODUCTS PROMOTING ENVIRONMENTAL OR SOCIAL CHARACTERISTICS (ARTICLE 8 PRODUCTS)

At the next ambition level, financial market participants and financial advisors can say publicly that a financial product also promotes, among other things, environmental and social characteristics. The actor may only do this if it also shows how the investment targets follow good governance practices. But first, the actor shall provide information on how the environmental or social characteristics are promoted and, where an index has been designated as a benchmark, whether and how that index is consistent with the promoted characteristics.[169] This is what is usually referred to as Article 8 products, even though this description is somewhat misleading, as said in section 8.2 above. Those products thus meet two of the three key elements of sustainable investment – promotion of sustainability characteristics and good governance. What is missing is the do no significant harm element.

8.6.1 Environmental and Social Characteristics

A financial product can promote environmental or social characteristics in a variety of ways. The definition of sustainable investment Article 2.17 of the SFDR provides

165. It is unclear why the term 'sustainable development' is used here instead of 'sustainability factors' and whether any difference is actually meant here.
166. Article 4(2) SFDR.
167. Article 4(2) of Delegated Regulation (EU) 2022/1288.
168. *See* section 8.4.
169. Article 8 SFDR.

several examples. As for environmental objectives or environmental characteristics, resource efficiency is referred to in terms of the use of energy, renewable energy, raw materials, water and land, the generation of waste and greenhouse gas emissions, or in terms of effects on biodiversity and the circular economy. Regarding social objectives or characteristics, they refer to investments that contribute to combating inequalities or that promote social cohesion, social inclusion and good industrial relations, or investments in human capital or in favour of economically or socially disadvantaged groups. Of course, the Sustainable Development Goals (SDGs) also provide an appropriate list of possible environmental or social characteristics and goals.

However, it is necessary when interpreting Article 8 to keep in mind the analysis of the concept of 'sustainable investment' in section 8.2, where it was shown that this concept, as well as its key elements – 'contribution to sustainability objectives', 'do no significant harm' and 'good governance practices' – are not criterial but interpretive concepts. When it comes to the concept of promotion of environmental and social characteristics, it would therefore be a mistake to ask questions like what criteria must be fulfilled for a financial product to promote such characteristics, or is it necessary for a product to promote those characteristics set out in Article 2.17?

As already stated, the SFDR does not provide criteria to respond to the first question, and the second question is not relevant for the same reason. What Article 8 says is that if the financial actor in some way indicates publicly that the financial product promotes such characteristics, whether it is true or not that it actually does, then it must explain how the actor means that those characteristics are promoted. It will then be up to the potential buyer of the financial product to judge whether he/she thinks that the explanation is good enough for the buyer.

In a somewhat confusing statement, the EU Commission has actually stated that the concept 'promote' refers more to how the financial market actor communicates about and thus promotes *the product* than to how the product promotes sustainability characteristics. A broad range of activities can be said to fit into this concept, including 'direct or indirect claims, information, reporting, disclosures as well as an impression that investments pursued by the given financial product also consider environmental or social characteristics in terms of investment policies, goals, targets or objectives or a general ambition in, but not limited to, pre-contractual and periodic documents or marketing communications, advertisements, product categorisation, description of investment strategies or asset allocation, information on the adherence to sustainability-related financial product standards and labels, use of product names or designations, memoranda or issuing documents, factsheets, specifications about conditions for automatic enrolment or compliance with sectoral exclusions or statutory requirements regardless of the form used, such as on paper, durable media, by means of websites, or electronic data rooms'.[170] This is, of course, rather confusing, but it still makes sense – the Commission simply says that the examples given are ways in which financial market actors can publicly say that their product promotes sustainability

170. EU Commission, 14 July 2021, Question related to Regulation (EU) 2019/2088 of the European Parliament and of the Council of 27 November 2019 on sustainability-related disclosures in the financial services sector (Sustainable Finance Disclosure Regulation 2019/2088).

characteristics, which will have as a consequence that Article 8 of SFDR and its disclosure requirements will be applicable.

8.6.2 Good Governance Practices

Article 8 is not ideally written. It says that where the product promotes environmental or social characteristics, as discussed in the previous section, certain information about the product shall be disclosed, *provided that the companies in which the investments are made follow good governance practices.* Before even going into the discussion of what the concept of 'good governance practices' means, it must be pointed out that a possible interpretation is that a financial market participant can easily escape the information requirements of Article 8, even though it says that the product promotes sustainability characteristics if the investee companies do *not* follow good governance practices.

This would, however, be an incorrect reading of the article. The EU Commission has, in response to an explicit question, said that where a financial product referred to in Article 8 fails to invest in companies following good governance practices, the product is in breach of Article 8.[171] What Article 8, therefore, says is that financial market participants may only say publicly that the product promotes environmental or social characteristics, provided that the investee companies follow good governance practices.

Again, it is important to keep in mind that the 'good governance practices' concept is interpretive and not criterial. The only requirement on the financial market participant is to disclose how, *in its view,* the investee companies follow good marketing practices.

Does this mean that the part of the sustainable investment definition in Article 2.17 SFDR, focusing on good marketing practices ('in particular with respect to sound management structures, employee relations, remuneration of staff and tax compliance'), has no real legal relevance? Could a financial market participant say that, in its view, good governance practices do not entail tax compliance or sound management structures. Even though it is not crystal clear, the most plausible answer is that the concepts of 'sound management structures', 'employee relations', 'remuneration of staff' and 'tax compliance' are *also* interpretive, just as good governance practice. This would then mean that when the financial market participants explain how the investee companies follow good governance practices, they must do so by usage of at least those four concepts.

8.6.3 Information to Be Disclosed

Annex II to Delegated Regulation (EU) 2022/1288 sets out a template to be used by undertakings to disclose information under Article 8 of the SFDR before contracting for

171. EU Commission, 17 May 2022, Questions related to Regulation (EU) 2019/2088 of the European Parliament and of the Council of 27 November 2019 on sustainability-related disclosures in the financial services sector (SFDR).

an investment.[172] The template is structured as a questionnaire, which includes the following questions:

(i) What environmental and/or social characteristics are promoted by this financial product?
  - What sustainability indicators are used to measure the attainment of each of the environmental or social characteristics promoted by this product?
  - What are the objectives of the sustainable investments that the financial product partially intends to make, and how does the sustainable investment contribute to these objectives?[173]

(ii) How do the sustainable investments that the financial product partially intends to make not cause significant harm to any environmental or social sustainable investment objectives?[174]
  - How have the indicators for adverse impacts on sustainability factors been taken into account?
  - How are sustainable investments aligned with the OECD Guidelines for Multinational Enterprises and the UN Guiding Principles on Business and Human Rights?

(iii) Does this financial product consider principal adverse impacts on sustainability factors?

(iv) What investment strategy does this financial product follow?
  - What are the binding elements of the investment strategy used to select the investments that attain each of the environmental or social characteristics promoted by this financial product?
  - What is the minimum rate to reduce the scope of investments considered prior to the application of the investment strategy?
  - What is the policy to assess good governance practices in investee companies?

(v) What is the asset allocation planned for this financial product?
  - How does the use of derivatives attain environmental or social characteristics promoted by the financial product?

(vi) To what minimum extent are sustainable investments with an environmental objective aligned with the EU Taxonomy?[175]
  - What is the minimum share of investments in transitional and enabling activities?

(vii) What is the minimum share of sustainable investments with an environmental objective that is not aligned with the EU Taxonomy?

(viii) What is the minimum share of socially sustainable investments?

(ix) Which investments are included in '#2 Other', what is their purpose, and are there any minimum environmental or social safeguards?

172. Article 14(1) of Delegated Regulation (EU) 2022/1288.
173. Only relevant if the financial product partially makes sustainable investments.
174. *See* previous note.
175. Relevant if it is environmental characteristics that are promoted by the financial product.

(x) Is a specific index designated as a reference benchmark to determine whether this financial product is aligned with the environmental and/or social characteristics that it promotes?
- How is the reference benchmark continuously aligned with each of the environmental or social characteristics promoted by the financial product?
- How is the alignment of the investment strategy with the methodology of the index's calculation ensured on a continuous basis?
- How does the designated index differ from a relevant broad market index?
- Where can the methodology for the calculation of the designated index be found?

(xi) Where can I find more product-specific information online?

If the characteristics promoted by the financial product are environment-related characteristics, the company must also, as stated in the list of questions above, provide certain information according to the Taxonomy Regulation.[176]

In addition, companies shall provide, on their websites, information for each financial product describing the environmental or social characteristics and the methods used to assess, measure and monitor those characteristics.[177] Information shall also be provided in regular reports.[178]

8.7 PRODUCTS WITH SUSTAINABLE INVESTMENT AS THEIR OBJECTIVE (ARTICLE 9 PRODUCTS)

The fourth and final ambition level includes financial products that have sustainable investment as their objective. These are what are usually referred to as Article 9 products. This ambition level can be expressed in four different variants, as explained below. The table below illustrates the main differences between Article 8 and Article 9:

Sustainable Investment Requirements under SFDR	*Article 8*	*Article 9*
Promotion of environmental or social characteristic	X	X
Adherence to good governance practices	X	X
Sustainable investment as objective		X
Do no significant harm		X

176. Article 6 of Regulation (EU) 2020/852 and Articles 15 to 17 of Delegated Regulation (EU) 2022/1288.
177. Article 10(1) SFDR.
178. Article 11 SFDR.

8.7.1 Sustainable Investment as Objective

Financial products referred to in Article 9 shall have sustainable investment as their objective. This can be interpreted in different ways, and the legislation is somewhat unclear.

The concept of sustainable investment, as defined in Article 2.17 of the SFDR, means that the investment is made in a specific economic activity. Under Article 9 of the SFDR, the objective of a financial product, such as a fund, must be sustainable investments. This reasonably means that the financial product shall have the objective of investing in activities that are sustainable, as defined in Article 2.17.[179]

The important difference between Article 8 and Article 9 products is that Article 9 products, in addition to contributing to social or environmental objectives and following good governance practices, must also comply with the DNSH. The question arises as to what this term means.

8.7.2 Do No Significant Harm

Like the idea of good governance practices, there is no definition of 'do no significant harm'. The reason for this is, of course, that this concept too is an interpretive and not criterial concept. Article 9 requires only that the financial market participant presents how the investee companies, *in its view,* do no significant harm.

However, the financial market participant is not granted full discretion. Delegated Regulation (EU) 2022/1288 requires that the actor explains its interpretation of no significant harm by elaborating upon:

(1) how the indicators of adverse impacts in Table 1 of Annex I to the Delegated Regulation – i.e., the PAI indicators – as well as the relevant indicators in Tables 2 and 3, have been taken into account; and
(2) whether sustainable investments are in line with the OECD Guidelines for Multinational Enterprises and the UN Guiding Principles on Business and Human Rights.

Based on the provision of this information, it will be up to the end investors to judge whether the financial market participant's interpretation of what 'do no significant harm' means is good enough.

179. This interpretation is also supported by an interpretative communication from the Commission (Commission decision C(2023) 2281, dated 5 April 2023). The Commission points out that investments in an activity that meets the requirements of the EU Taxonomy shall be considered to meet the definition of sustainable investment in the SFDR. However, the Commission also points out that if the financing relates to equity or a general loan, i.e., the financing is not tied to the specific taxonomy-aligned business, an assessment of the other activities must be made to analyse whether the entire investment is to be considered a sustainable one under the SFDR. This kind of interpretation would have been meaningless if it *were not* for the fact that Article 9 products need to invest in activities that meet the definition of sustainable investment.

8.7.3 Indices and Benchmarks

Article 9.3 of SFDR refers to the concepts of the EU Climate Transition Benchmark or EU Paris-aligned Benchmark. A proper understanding of Article 9 in general requires some understanding of these concepts, which are defined in EU regulation (EU) 2016/1011 on indices used as benchmarks in financial instruments and financial contracts or to measure the performance of investment funds, as amended through regulation (EU) 2019/2089 – the Benchmark Regulation (BMR).

The purpose of BMR is, according to Article 1, to ensure the accuracy and integrity of indices used as benchmarks in financial instruments and financial contracts or to measure the performance of investment funds in the EU. BMR is intended to contribute to the proper functioning of the internal market while achieving a high level of consumer and investor protection. The regulation is widely applicable to everyone from central banks to media referring to benchmarks.

Title II of BMR focuses on the integrity and reliability of benchmarks in general. Chapter 1 focuses on governance, transparency and avoidance of conflicts of interest for administrators of benchmarks, including their employees. Chapter 2 regulates the input data and methodologies to calculate benchmarks, not least that the methodologies used shall be transparent. Chapter 3 regulates the code of conduct and other requirements for contributors to benchmarks.

Title III of BMR regulates various types of benchmarks, for example regulated data benchmarks, interest rate benchmarks, and commodity benchmarks. Through regulation (EU) 2019/2089, two additional categories of benchmarks were introduced: EU Climate Transition Benchmarks and EU Paris-aligned Benchmarks, commonly referred to as CTB and PAB. BMR sets out that benchmarks may only be referred to as CTB or PAB if they meet the criteria set out in the definitions of those concepts.

An *EU Climate Transition Benchmark* (CTB) is defined as a benchmark which is labelled as an EU Climate Transition Benchmark, where the underlying assets are selected, weighted or excluded in such a manner that the resulting benchmark portfolio is on a decarbonisation trajectory and which also fulfils certain minimum criteria adopted by the EU Commission in delegated acts.[180] 'Decarbonisation trajectory' means a measurable, science-based and time-bound trajectory towards alignment with the objectives of the Paris Agreement by reducing Scope 1, 2 and 3 carbon emissions.[181]

An EU Paris-aligned Benchmark (PAB) means a benchmark which is labelled as an EU Paris-aligned Benchmark, where the underlying assets are selected, weighted or excluded in such a manner that the resulting benchmark portfolio's carbon emissions are aligned with the objectives of the Paris Agreement, is constructed in accordance with certain minimum criteria adopted by the EU Commission and where the activities relating to its underlying assets do not significantly harm other environmental, social and governance objectives.

180. Article 3(1).23 a of BMR.
181. Article 3(1).23 c of BMR.

8.7.4 The Variants of Ambition Level in Article 9

While the general ambition level in Article 9 is that the financial product has sustainable investments as its objectives, there are a number of variants set out in the article, with different transparency requirements set out, depending on the variant opted for.

	Index Used as Benchmark (Article 9.1)	*Index Not Used as Benchmark (Article 9.2)*
Reduction in carbon emission as objective (art 9.3)	Variant 1	Variant 2
Other sustainability objectives	Variant 3	Variant 4

Variant 1: In some cases, the financial market actor uses a benchmark to compare the financial product's sustainability performance. Not seldom, the sustainability objective is a reduction in carbon emissions. This combination is herein referred to as variant 1. According to Article 9.1, the financial market actor must first of all explain how the chosen index is tied to the CO_2 emissions reduction objective. Here, the CTB and PAB referred to in the previous sections can come into play. The financial market actor can choose a CTB or PAB provided by an administrator to substantiate its claim of alignment with the reduction objective and the chosen index. Still, the actor must provide an explanation as to why and how the designated index aligned with that objective differs from a broad market index. Again, this should be easier if a CTB or PAB is chosen.

Variant 2: The financial product can have CO_2 emission reductions as its objective but not refer to a published index as a benchmark – here referred to as variant 2. In such case, information must, in accordance with Article 9.2, be provided on how the objective shall be attained. Here, Article 9 is a bit unclear. Paragraph 2 of Article 9.3 provides for a scenario where Article 9.2 is applicable (no benchmark is chosen), but a CTB or PAB is still used. This should probably understood as a variant where the CTB or PAB is used to explain how the CO_2 emission reduction objective shall be attained, even though they are not used as benchmarks. If, however, a CTB or PAB are not used, Article 9.3 second paragraph stipulates that the information about the financial product shall include a detailed explanation of how the continued effort of attaining the objective of reducing carbon emissions is ensured in view of achieving the long-term global warming objectives of the Paris Agreement.

Variant 3: Variant 3 is the same as variant 1, but the sustainability objective is another objective than CO_2 emission reductions, for example, objectives related to biodiversity, poverty, etc. On the market, there are a number of more general ESG indices that can be used as benchmarks and Article 9.1, again, requires the financial market actor to use such benchmarks to explain how the index is aligned with the chosen objective and how that index differs from a broad market index.

Variant 4: Variant 4, finally, is the situation where the financial market actor has another sustainability objective than CO_2 emission reductions, and no index is used. In such case, information must, in accordance with Article 9.2, be provided on how the objective shall be attained.

8.7.5 Information to Be Disclosed

Annex III to Delegated Regulation (EU) 2022/1288 sets out a template to be used by undertakings to disclose pre-contractual information under Article 9.[182] Again, it is a list of questions:

(i) What is the sustainable investment objective of this financial product?
(ii) What sustainability indicators are used to measure the attainment of the sustainable investment objective of this financial product?
(iii) How do sustainable investments not cause significant harm to any environmental or social sustainability objective?
  - How have the indicators of adverse impacts on sustainability factors been taken into account?
  - How are sustainable investments aligned with the OECD Guidelines for Multinational Enterprises and the UN Guiding Principles on Business and Human Rights?

(iv) Does this financial product consider principal adverse impacts on sustainability factors?
(v) What investment strategy does this product follow?
  - What are the binding elements of the investment strategy used to select investments to attain the sustainable investment objective?
  - What is the policy to assess good governance practices of the investee companies?

(vi) What is the asset allocation and the minimum share of sustainable investments?
  - How does the use of derivatives attain the sustainable investment objective?

(vii) To what maximum extent are sustainable investments with an environmental objective aligned with the EU Taxonomy?[183]
  - What is the minimum share of investments in transitional and enabling activities?
  - What is the minimum share of sustainable investments with an environmental objective that is not aligned with the EU Taxonomy?
  - What is the minimum share of sustainable investments with a social objective?

182. Article 18(1) of Delegated Regulation (EU) 2022/1288.
183. Relevant if it is environmental characteristics that are promoted by the financial product.

  - Which investments are included in '#2 Not sustainable', what is their purpose, and are there any minimum environmental or social safeguards?

(viii) Is a specific index designated as a reference benchmark to meet the sustainable investment objective?
  - How does the reference benchmark take into account sustainability factors in a way that is continuously aligned with the sustainable investment objective?
  - How is the alignment of the investment strategy with the methodology of the index ensured on a continuous basis?
  - How does the designated index differ from a relevant broad market index?
  - Where can the methodology used for the calculation of the designated index be found?

(ix) Where can I find more product-specific information online?

As in the case of financial products that promote environmental or social characteristics, the company shall also disclose information on the relevant financial products on its website and in periodic reports.[184]

184. Articles 10 and 11 SFDR.

CHAPTER 9

The EU Taxonomy

The previous chapter described the definition of sustainable investment according to the SFDR, a definition that focuses on contribution to social or environmental objectives, do no significant harm, and good governance practices. As explained, those concepts are not based on clear criteria set down by the legislator but are instead interpretive concepts where the only real requirement on the financial market participant is to explain how it interprets those concepts. The downsides to this approach are obvious. The possibility of claiming that a wide range of activities and practices are sustainable risks leading to a lack of fulfilment of the EU's goals of transitioning to a sustainable economy by channelling financial flows towards sustainable investments. The risk of greenwashing is obvious, but the risk that investments are not made where it is scientifically most justified to do so is perhaps even more important.

These and related factors are the reason for the adoption of EU Regulation 2020/852 on the establishment of a framework to facilitate sustainable investment – often referred to as the EU taxonomy or simply the taxonomy. Although the EU Taxonomy contains several obligations that companies must comply with, this is secondary. In principle, the EU Taxonomy is one long legal definition of what is considered *environmentally sustainable economic activities*. And *this* concept is criterial, i.e., a concept with criteria laid down by the legislature.

The EU taxonomy does not actually consist of one regulation, although it is referred to as a single entity. The main document is Regulation 2020/852. However, based on this regulation, the European Commission has adopted a number of delegated regulations in which the screening criteria and the criteria for non-significant harm for each environmental objective are specified. When the term 'EU taxonomy' is used here, it refers to Regulation 2020/852.

9.1 ENVIRONMENTALLY SUSTAINABLE ECONOMIC ACTIVITIES

According to Article 3 of the EU taxonomy, an economic activity is considered to be environmentally sustainable if it:

- contributes substantially to one or more of the environmental objectives set out in Article 9 in accordance with Articles 10 to 16;
- does not significantly harm any of the environmental objectives set out in Article 9 in accordance with Article 17;
- is carried out in compliance with the minimum safeguards laid down in Article 18; and
- complies with technical screening criteria that have been established by the Commission in accordance with Article 10.[185]

The six environmental objectives listed in Article 9 of the EU Taxonomy are:

(1) climate change mitigation;
(2) climate change adaptation;
(3) the sustainable use and protection of water and marine resources;
(4) the transition to a circular economy;
(5) pollution prevention and control; and
(6) the protection and restoration of biodiversity and ecosystems.

As has already been pointed out, ESRS E1 covers the objectives of climate change mitigation and adaptation, while there is then one ESRS standard for the respective environmental objectives in the EU Taxonomy. In the following, each of the six environmental objectives and their implications will instead be described.

9.2 ENVIRONMENTAL OBJECTIVES IN THE EU TAXONOMY

Articles 10-15 of the EU Taxonomy specify the precise meaning of the environmental objectives listed in Article 9. Below is a description of each of the environmental objectives, where the text is largely taken from the articles themselves.

9.2.1 Climate Change Mitigation

An economic activity shall qualify as contributing substantially to climate change mitigation where that activity contributes substantially to the stabilisation of greenhouse gas concentrations in the atmosphere at a level which prevents dangerous anthropogenic interference with the climate system consistent with the long-term temperature goal of the Paris Agreement through the avoidance or reduction of

185. Article 3 EU Taxonomy.

greenhouse gas emissions or the increase of greenhouse gas removals, including through process innovations or product innovations, by:

- generating, transmitting, storing, distributing or using renewable energy, including through using innovative technology with a potential for significant future savings or through necessary reinforcement or extension of the grid;
- improving energy efficiency;
- increasing clean or climate-neutral mobility;
- switching to the use of sustainably sourced renewable materials;
- increasing the use of environmentally safe carbon capture and utilisation (CCU) and carbon capture and storage (CCS) technologies that deliver a net reduction in greenhouse gas emissions;
- strengthening land carbon sinks, including through avoiding deforestation and forest degradation, restoration of forests, sustainable management and restoration of croplands, grasslands and wetlands, afforestation, and regenerative agriculture;
- establishing energy infrastructure required for enabling the decarbonisation of energy systems;
- producing clean and efficient fuels from renewable or carbon-neutral sources; or
- enabling any of the above activities.

An activity shall be considered to cause significant harm to climate change mitigation if it results in significant greenhouse gas emissions.[186]

Annex 2 of the book lists the activities that the European Commission has identified as activities relevant to assess whether the requirements for substantial contribution are met for this environmental objective.

9.2.2 Adaptation to Climate Change

An economic activity shall qualify as contributing substantially to climate change adaptation where that activity:

- includes adaptation solutions that either substantially reduce the risk of the adverse impact of the current climate and the expected future climate on that economic activity or substantially reduce that adverse impact without increasing the risk of an adverse impact on people, nature or assets; or
- provides adaptation solutions that contribute substantially to preventing or reducing the risk of the adverse impact of the current climate and the expected future climate on people, nature or assets without increasing the risk of an adverse impact on other people, nature or assets.[187]

186. Article 17(1)(a) EU Taxonomy.
187. Article 11(1) EU Taxonomy.

An activity shall be considered to cause significant harm to climate change adaptation where that activity leads to an increased adverse impact of the current climate and the expected future climate on the activity itself or on people, nature or assets.[188]

Annex 3 lists the activities that the European Commission has identified as activities relevant to assess whether the requirements for substantial contribution are met for this environmental objective.

9.2.3 Sustainable Use and Protection of Water and Marine Resources

An economic activity shall qualify as contributing substantially to the sustainable use and protection of water and marine resources where that activity either contributes substantially to achieving the good status of bodies of water, including bodies of surface water and groundwater, or preventing the deterioration of bodies of water that already have good status, or contributing substantially to achieving the good environmental status of marine waters or preventing the deterioration of marine waters that are already in good environmental status, by:

- protecting the environment from the adverse effects of urban and industrial wastewater discharges, including from contaminants of emerging concern such as pharmaceuticals and microplastics, for example, by ensuring the adequate collection, treatment and discharge of urban and industrial wastewater;
- protecting human health from the adverse impact of any contamination of water intended for human consumption by ensuring that it is free from any micro-organisms, parasites and substances that constitute a potential danger to human health, as well as increasing people's access to clean drinking water;
- improving water management and efficiency, including by protecting and enhancing the status of aquatic ecosystems, promoting the sustainable use of water through the long-term protection of available water resources, *inter alia*, through measures such as water reuse, ensuring the progressive reduction of pollutant emissions into surface water and groundwater, by contributing to mitigating the effects of floods and droughts, or through any other activity that protects or improves the qualitative and quantitative status of water bodies;
- ensuring the sustainable use of marine ecosystem services or contributing to the good environmental status of marine waters, including by protecting, preserving or restoring the marine environment and by preventing or reducing inputs in the marine environment;
- enabling any of the activities listed above.[189]

An activity shall be considered to cause significant harm to the sustainable use and protection of water and marine resources where that activity is detrimental to the

188. Article 17(1)(b) EU Taxonomy.
189. Article 12(1) EU Taxonomy.

good status or the good ecological potential of bodies of water, including surface water and groundwater or to the good environmental status of marine waters.[190]

Annex 4 lists the activities that the European Commission has identified as activities relevant to assess whether the requirements for substantial contribution are met for this environmental objective.

9.2.4 Transition to a Circular Economy

An economic activity shall qualify as contributing substantially to the transition to a circular economy, including waste prevention, reuse and recycling, where that activity:

- uses natural resources, including sustainably sourced bio-based and other raw materials, in production more efficiently;
- increases the durability, reparability, upgradability or reusability of products, in particular in designing and manufacturing activities;
- increases the recyclability of products, including the recyclability of individual materials contained in those products, *inter alia*, by substitution or reduced use of products and materials that are not recyclable, in particular in designing and manufacturing activities;
- substantially reduces the content of hazardous substances and substitutes substances of very high concern in materials and products throughout their life cycle, in line with the objectives set out in Union law, including replacing such substances with safer alternatives and ensuring traceability;
- prolongs the use of products, including through reuse, design for longevity, repurposing, disassembly, remanufacturing, upgrades and repair, and sharing products;
- increases the use of secondary raw materials and their quality, including by high-quality recycling of waste;
- prevents or reduces waste generation, including the generation of waste from the extraction of minerals and waste from the construction and demolition of buildings;
- increases preparing for the reuse and recycling of waste;
- increases the development of the waste management infrastructure needed for prevention, preparing for reuse and recycling while ensuring that the recovered materials are recycled as high-quality secondary raw material input in production, thereby avoiding down cycling;
- minimises the incineration of waste and avoids the disposal of waste, including landfilling, in accordance with the principles of the waste hierarchy;
- avoids and reduces litter;
- enables any of the activities listed above.[191]

190. Article 17(1)(c) EU Taxonomy; The text of the law uses the term 'marine waters', which must be a typographical error.
191. Article 13(1) EU Taxonomy.

An activity shall be considered to cause significant harm to the circular economy if:

- that activity leads to significant inefficiencies in the use of materials or in the direct or indirect use of natural resources such as non-renewable energy sources, raw materials, water and land at one or more stages of the life cycle of products, including in terms of durability, reparability, upgradability, reusability or recyclability of products;
- that activity leads to a significant increase in the generation, incineration or disposal of waste, with the exception of the incineration of non-recyclable hazardous waste; or
- the long-term disposal of waste may cause significant and long-term harm to the environment.[192]

Annex 5 lists the activities that the European Commission has identified as activities relevant to assess whether the requirements for substantial contribution are met for this environmental objective.

9.2.5 Pollution Prevention and Control

An economic activity shall qualify as contributing substantially to pollution prevention and control where that activity contributes substantially to environmental protection from pollution by:

- preventing or, where that is not practicable, reducing pollutant emissions into air, water or land other than greenhouse gases;
- improving levels of air, water or soil quality in the areas in which the economic activity takes place while minimising any adverse impact on human health and the environment or the risk thereof;
- preventing or minimising any adverse impact on human health and the environment of the production, use or disposal of chemicals;
- cleaning up litter and other pollution, or
- enabling any of the activities listed above.[193]

An economic activity shall be considered to cause significant harm to pollution prevention and control where that activity leads to a significant increase in the emissions of pollutants into air, water or land, as compared with the situation before the activity started.

Annex 6 lists the activities that the European Commission has identified as activities relevant to assess whether the requirements for substantial contribution are met for this environmental objective.

192. Article 17(1)(d) EU Taxonomy.
193. Article 17(1)(e) EU Taxonomy.

9.2.6 Protection and Restoration of Biodiversity and Ecosystems

An economic activity shall qualify as contributing substantially to the protection and restoration of biodiversity and ecosystems where that activity contributes substantially to protecting, conserving or restoring biodiversity or to achieving the good condition of ecosystems or to protecting ecosystems that are already in good condition, through:

- nature and biodiversity conservation, including achieving favourable conservation status of natural and semi-natural habitats and species, or preventing their deterioration where they already have favourable conservation status, and protecting and restoring terrestrial, marine and other aquatic ecosystems in order to improve their condition and enhance their capacity to provide ecosystem services;
- sustainable land use and management, including adequate protection of soil biodiversity, land degradation neutrality and the remediation of contaminated sites;
- sustainable agricultural practices, including those that contribute to enhancing biodiversity or to halting or preventing the degradation of soils and other ecosystems, deforestation and habitat loss;
- sustainable forest management, including practices and uses of forests and forest land that contribute to enhancing biodiversity or to halting or preventing degradation of ecosystems, deforestation and habitat loss; or
- enabling any of the activities listed above.

An economic activity shall be considered to cause significant harm to the protection and restoration of biodiversity and ecosystems where that activity is significantly detrimental to the good condition and resilience of ecosystems or detrimental to the conservation status of habitats and species, including those of Union interest.

Annex 7 lists the activities that the European Commission has identified as activities relevant to assess whether the requirements for substantial contribution are met for this environmental objective.

9.2.7 Enabling Activities

As stated above, an activity can be considered to contribute significantly to one of the environmental objectives by enabling other activities to contribute significantly to the objectives. This happens if the activity directly enables other activities to contribute substantially to any of the environmental objectives, provided that the activity does not lead to the lock-in of assets that undermine long-term environmental objectives and have a material positive environmental impact based on life cycle considerations.[194]

194. Article 16 EU Taxonomy.

9.3 MINIMUM SAFEGUARDS

Under the EU Taxonomy, environmentally sustainable investments must also comply with a number of minimum safeguards, which basically means the implementation of the due diligence norm into the business. Article 18(1) requires these measures to be procedures to ensure that the company complies with the OECD Guidelines for Multinational Enterprises and the UN Guiding Principles on Business and Human Rights, including the eight core conventions of the ILO. Article 18(2) requires the undertaking to comply with the principle of non-significant harm in the SFDR when following these procedures. It is worth noting, however, that the division in Article 18(1) and (2) is confusing. The OECD Guidelines and the UN Guiding Principles are not only procedures but also sets due diligence requirements. The classification of the conduct of the proceedings in Article 18(2) therefore, seems to be unnecessary.

9.4 COMPANIES' REPORTING OBLIGATIONS UNDER THE EU TAXONOMY

Part III of the book describes companies' sustainability reporting obligations under CSRD. However, the EU taxonomy also includes reporting requirements for non-financial undertakings. Article 8 of the EU Taxonomy states that companies covered by the CSRD must also include in their financial statements information on how and to what extent the company's activities are associated with economic activities to be considered environmentally sustainable under Articles 3 and 9 of the EU Taxonomy.

In particular, non-financial undertakings shall disclose:

- the proportion of their turnover derived from products or services associated with economic activities that qualify as environmentally sustainable under Articles 3 and 9;
- the proportion of their capital expenditure and the proportion of their operating expenditure related to assets or processes associated with economic activities that qualify as environmentally sustainable under Articles 3 and 9.

The detailed requirements for this reporting can be found in the European Commission's Delegated Regulation 2021/2178. The requirements apply to both non-financial and financial companies. As with the reporting requirements under the SFDR, these are detailed requirements, which will not be dealt with here. At its core, however, the logic is simple. A distinction is made between activities eligible for the EU Taxonomy and activities that are not. Article 1(5) of the Delegated Regulation states that an activity is to be considered to be taxonomy-eligible if it is an activity described in the screening delegated acts that the European Commission has adopted or will adopt under Articles 10 to 15 of the EU Taxonomy. Annexes 3–8 list the activities in the European Commission's delegated regulations at the time of publication of the book.

Once the company has divided its activities into those that are and those that are not covered by the EU Taxonomy, a calculation must be made of the proportion of turnover that comes from activities that are also *aligned* with the EU Taxonomy. The activity is aligned with the EU Taxonomy if it meets the requirements of Article 3 of the EU Taxonomy. The screening criteria set out in the delegated acts must be met, the minimum safeguards set out in Article 18 must be followed, and the undertaking must not cause significant harm to the other environmental objectives.

For example, an undertaking may carry out activities relating to the construction and operation of electricity generation installations that produce electricity using photovoltaic technology as set out in point 4.1 of Annex I to Regulation (EU) 2021/2139. Here, the activities are covered by the EU Taxonomy. The activity meets the minimum requirements set out in Article 18 of the EU Taxonomy. However, the business has not carried out an environmental impact assessment. In that case, the undertaking has not fulfilled the requirement of not causing significant harm set out in Appendix D to Annex I.

In this way, the company must analyse activity by activity, assess whether it is eligible, assess alignment with the EU Taxonomy, and then report according to the templates provided.

CHAPTER 10
European Green Bonds Regulation

As of 21 December 2024, EU Regulation 2023/2631 on European Green Bonds and optional disclosures for bonds marketed as environmentally sustainable and for sustainability-linked bonds apply. So far, no official standards for so-called green bonds have existed, which has led to a number of private, voluntary standards having been established. The rather confusing landscape is problematic. Unclarity on what is a sustainable investment leads to risks of greenwashing. Unclarity on what is really green about a green bond leads to the same risk. According to Recital 5 of the regulation, confusion impleads the ability of investors to identify, trust and compare environmentally sustainable bonds and the ability of issuers to use environmentally sustainable bonds to transition their activities towards more environmentally sustainable business models. Therefore, clarity is needed. This is done through the establishment of a voluntary standard – the 'European Green Bond' or 'EuGB'. According to Article 1 of the regulation, it lays down uniform requirements for issuers of bonds who wish to use these designations for their bonds, establishes a system to register external reviewers of European Green Bonds, and also provides optional disclosure templates for bonds marketed as environmentally sustainable and for sustainability-linked bonds in the EU.

10.1 REQUIREMENTS TO USE 'EUROPEAN GREEN BOND' OR 'EuGB'

According to Article 3, a bond may only be designated as a European Green Bond or EuGB if it fulfils the requirements of the regulation. The main rule is that the proceeds from the bond shall, before its maturity, be allocated fully in accordance with the requirements of the EU Taxonomy, including the screening criteria set out in the delegated acts of the taxonomy.

The issuer can then follow one of two approaches. According to the 'gradual approach' set out in Article 4.1, the proceeds must be fully allocated to fixed assets, certain categories of capital expenditure (CapEx), certain categories of operating expenditures (OpEx), financial assets or assets and expenditures of households. According to the 'portfolio approach' set out in Article 4.2, issuers may instead allocate proceeds from one or more European Green Bonds to a portfolio of fixed assets or financial assets in accordance with the requirements of the EU Taxonomy. If the proceeds are allocated to financial assets, the proceeds from those assets shall, according to Article 6.1, only be allocated to taxonomy-aligned activities. If the proceeds are allocated to capital expenditures, Article 7 sets out obligations to publish a CapEx plan.

Article 5 provides certain flexibility for issuers as a derogation from the main rule in Article 4.1 in cases where the issuers want to allocate proceeds that are taxonomy-aligned but where no delegated act with screening criteria has yet been adopted. Issuers may allocate up to 15% of the proceeds from the European Green Bond to such activities, provided that the issuer also describes the activities concerned in a EuGB factsheet included in Annex I to the regulation.

10.2 TRANSPARENCY, EXTERNAL REVIEW AND REPORTING

Before a EuGB is issued, the issuer shall, according to Article 10, complete a European Green Bond factsheet set out in Annex I or the regulation and ensure that the factsheet has been subject to a pre-issuance review with a positive opinion by an external reviewer. The issuer shall furthermore, according to Article 11.1, draw up a European Green Bond allocation report according to Annex II of the regulation for every twelve-month period until the full allocation of the proceeds for the bond.

The issuer shall also, when proceeds have been fully allocated and at least once during the lifetime of the bond, publish a European Green Bond impact report on the environmental impact of the use of the proceeds, using the template in Annex III of the regulation.

Title IV of the regulation contains a comprehensive regulation regarding external reviewers, which shall be registered with ESMA. The articles include requirements on organisation, documentation and governance processes, including the establishment of a permanent compliance function (Article 29).

10.3 SUPERVISION AND SANCTIONS

Title V of the regulation sets out the rules for supervision of compliance with the regulation. The competent authority of the home Member State of the issuer shall supervise issuers, while ESMA shall supervise external reviewers. Article 45 lays down a number of powers that the Member States shall ensure that the national authorities have, including rights to require issuers to publish European Green Bond factsheets, annual reports and impact reports. The national authorities shall furthermore, according to Article 49, be granted powers to impose administrative penalties and take other administrative measures against non-compliant issuers.

CHAPTER 11

Regulation of ESG Ratings

The rules for the financial markets described in the previous chapters have been and are being complemented by rules that regulate tools that the financial market actors use in their operations to set prices for and communicate about their products. Benchmarks are, for example, used to compare a financial product's performance against portfolios of similar products. Ratings are used to make a quality assessment of a financial product against set evaluation criteria.

Obviously, both benchmarks and ratings can be important tools to attract customers to financial products. That makes these tools vulnerable to manipulation. As an example, the London Interbank Offered Rate (LIBOR) was a classic benchmark tool, indicating the interest rates that major global banks lent to one another in the international interbank market for short-term loans. It is now replaced by Secured Overnight Financing Rate (SOFR) since a number of major financial institutions colluded to manipulate LIBOR, which had an effect on everything from home mortgage interest rates to option pricing.

As regards rating, it became apparent in the aftermath of the 2008 financial crisis that credit ratings institutions such as Standard & Poor and Moodys had severe conflicts of interests since they were financed by the very customers whose financial products they were set to rate. This was a contributing reason why the risks related to subprime loans were not discovered earlier.[195]

As a result of the manipulations of LIBOR and similar scandals, the European Union adopted regulation (EU) 2016/1011 on indices used as benchmarks in financial instruments and financial contracts or to measure the performance of investment funds – the Benchmark Regulation (BMR), already described briefly in Chapter 8. The purpose of the regulation is to not least ensure the integrity and impartiality of the providers of benchmarks.

195. Tooze, A., Crashed. How a Decade of Financial Crisis Changed the World, Penguin Books, 2019, pp. 49 ff.

Benchmarks and ratings related to sustainability have grown in importance over the years, and, of course, such benchmarks and ratings are subject to the same vulnerabilities as benchmarks such as LIBOR. As a result, regulation 2016/1011 was amended on the same day as the SFDR was adopted to cover also certain sustainability-related benchmarks. Moreover, in February 2024, a political agreement was reached within the EU regarding ESG rating activities in the regulation of the transparency and integrity of ESG rating activities (referred to here as the 'ESG Rating Regulation' or 'ERR'). The BMR rules on CTB and PAB have already been described in Chapter 8. This chapter focuses instead on the coming rules regarding ESG ratings.

11.1 PURPOSE AND APPLICABILITY

According to Article 3.1 of the ESG Rating Regulation, an ESG rating means an opinion, a score or a combination of both regarding a rated item's profile or characteristics with regard to environmental, social and human rights, or governance factors or exposure to risks or the impact on environmental, social and human rights, or governance factors, that are based on both an established methodology and a defined ranking system of rating categories, irrespective of whether such ESG rating is explicitly labelled as 'ESG rating', 'ESG opinion' or 'ESG score'. The regulation should thus cover most of the communication intended to evaluate companies, governmental bodies and financial products from a sustainability perspective.

The purpose of the regulation is, according to Article 1, to enhance the integrity, transparency, comparability where possible, responsibility, reliability, good governance, and independence of ESG rating activities. This is intended, in turn, to contribute to the transparency and quality of ESG ratings and to the sustainable finance agenda of the EU.

As with many EU regulations, the overall purpose is, of course, to ensure the smooth functioning of the internal market. But the main purpose is to protect consumers and investors from greenwashing and what is referred to as 'social-washing'.

The ERR is, according to Article 2, applicable to ESG rating providers, both those who are established in the EU and those who are established outside the EU, which, simply provide their ratings to actors in the EU.

11.2 REQUIREMENTS ON ESG RATING PROVIDERS

To provide ESG ratings, ESG rating providers must, according to Articles 5 and 9 of ERR, be authorised by ESMA to do so. ESMA shall, according to Article 13, establish and maintain a register about all authorised ESG rating providers.

ERR is similar to the Benchmark Regulation (BMR) in that it focuses much on the integrity and reliability of the ESG rating activities. Article 14 of ERR thus sets out a number of general principles. To take some examples, the ESG rating providers shall ensure the independence of their rating activities, including from all political and economic influences or constraints. They shall adopt and implement internal due diligence policies and procedures that ensure that their business interests do not impair the independence or accuracy of the assessment activities. They shall furthermore use rating methodologies for the ESG ratings they provide that are rigorous, systematic, independent and capable of justification and shall apply those rating methodologies continuously and in a transparent manner.

ESG rating providers must furthermore, under Article 15, refrain from carrying out a number of activities which could generate conflicts of interest, for example, consulting activities to investors or undertakings, credit ratings, CTBs or PABs. The rules to avoid conflicts of interest also apply to employees, who, under Article 16, shall be appropriately trained and must not enter into fee negotiations with entities whose products are ESG-rated.

Of course, the ERR contains a number of provisions regarding transparency requirements for ESG rating providers, set out in Chapter 2 of Title III of the regulation. Article 21 sets out public disclosure requirements, which shall comply with technical standards to be adopted by ESMA. Article 22 sets out disclosure requirements towards users of ESG ratings and the rated entities themselves.

11.3 SUPERVISION AND FINES

ESMA supervises the provision of ESG ratings and is granted broad powers to investigate and take actions against violations of ERR. But each Member State shall also, according to Article 28, designate their own competent authorities for the purpose of the regulation. ESMA may collect information, conduct investigations and carry out on-site inspections. It may, furthermore, according to Article 33, withdraw ESG rating authorisations, temporarily prohibit publications of ESG ratings and also impose fines on ESG rating providers. The fines can, according to Article 34, at maximum be 10% of the total annual net turnover of the ESG rating provider.

PART III Sustainable Business

CHAPTER 12

Should-Haves and Must-Haves in Sustainable Business

Part II dealt with the EU rules regarding sustainable finance, forming the third level of sustainability law as per the framework set out in Chapter 4. In the EU legislator's view, only regulating the financial market participants would be insufficient for the transition to a sustainable economy. Those actors need data from the investment objects to be able to report according to the SFDR and the EU taxonomy. In addition, large corporations often have a significant impact on sustainability matters regardless of financing.

Therefore, the fourth level of sustainability law – the subject of Part III of the book – contains rules for sustainable business operations and reporting on those operations. This part has three primary purposes:

(1) to describe how, according to the EU ideal image, companies should work with sustainability to meet the norms of positive contribution and due diligence;
(2) to describe the requirements under the CSDDD that companies to which the directive applies must meet regarding the sustainability of their operational activities; and
(3) to describe CSRD's rules for how companies should report their work with sustainability.

These are not three separable areas. CSRD requires companies to publicly describe how their operations relate to the set ideal image. Area 2 focuses on the legal requirements where the set, more moral ideal image in area 1 is also translated into legal obligations.

CHAPTER 13

The EU Ideal Image for Sustainable Business

In Chapter 5, the foundations of a sustainability morality underlying EU law were sketched. A sustainable business is, on a general level, a business that incorporates the two norms of positive contribution and due diligence. In Chapter 6, it was recommended to apply those two norms to define the 'core ideology' of the business.

This is still quite vague, and the question is what it means in practice, both from a business and legal point of view. The EU legislator has established what can be called an 'ideal image for sustainable business', which can be said to be a detailing of what the norms of positive contribution and due diligence mean in practice. It is important to understand what this ideal image looks like and what implications it has. An understanding of the ideal image is important to be able to interpret the different directives and regulations. Current and future directives and regulations must be interpreted in light of these norms and principles.[196]

As described in the previous chapter, sustainability *finance* places almost equal importance on the norms of positive contribution and due diligence. When it comes to the ideal image of sustainable *business*, a stronger emphasis is on the due diligence norm, but, as we shall see, the positive contribution norm plays an important role, however, in a more indirect way.

---

196. The view that the legal provisions should be interpreted in the light of the ideal image of EU law expresses the interpretivist legal theory on which the book is based (*see* the introduction of the book for a more detailed description). Anyone looking for an explicit statement from the legislator that CSRD expresses an ideal image of sustainability morality will have to look in vain. The view is instead based on an interpretation of the regulations, through which I have tried to make the logic and meaning of the legislation comprehensible with the support of the underlying norms and principles that can be extracted from the legal text, so to speak, and without which the legal text becomes difficult to understand. The legal rights and obligations expressed in the CSRD and other regulatory frameworks express broader political rights and obligations, which are expressed, for example, in the Charter of Fundamental Rights of the European Union.

The importance of the due diligence norm for sustainable business is most obvious in the CSDDD (the Corporate Sustainable *Due Diligence* Directive), where the intention to implement the due diligence norm from the UNGPs and OECD guidelines is explicit.[197] The ideal image of a sustainable business following the due diligence norm is a business which carries out the following actions consistently:

- integrating due diligence into their policies;
- identifying actual or potential adverse impacts;
- preventing and mitigating potential adverse impacts, bringing actual adverse impacts to an end and minimising their extent;
- establishing and maintaining a complaints procedure;
- monitoring the effectiveness of their due diligence policy and measures; and
- publicly communicating on due diligence.

CSDDD was adopted in June 2024, i.e., later than disclosure frameworks such as SFDR and CSRD. Nevertheless, it is quite obvious that these frameworks are based on the same ideal image as CSDDD, however with additions from the norm of positive contribution. When it comes to sustainable business operations, Article 19a of the CSRD sets out the overall ideal in more detail. The article describes what the sustainability report for companies covered by the legislation must contain:

(a) a brief description of the undertaking's business model and strategy, including:
   (i) the resilience of the undertaking's business model and strategy in relation to risks related to sustainability matters;
   (ii) the opportunities for the undertaking related to sustainability matters;
   (iii) the plans of the undertaking, including implementing actions and related financial and investment plans, to ensure that its business model and strategy are compatible with the transition to a sustainable economy and with the limiting of global warming to 1.5°C in line with the Paris Agreement under the United Nations Framework Convention on Climate Change adopted on 12 December 2015 (the 'Paris Agreement') and the objective of achieving climate neutrality by 2050 as established in Regulation (EU) 2021/1119 of the European Parliament and of the Council, and, where relevant, the exposure of the undertaking to coal-, oil- and gas-related activities;
   (iv) how the undertaking's business model and strategy take account of the interests of the undertaking's stakeholders and of the impacts of the undertaking on sustainability matters;
   (v) how the undertaking's strategy has been implemented with regard to sustainability matters;

(b) a description of the time-bound targets related to sustainability matters set by the undertaking, including, where appropriate, absolute greenhouse gas

197. *See*, *e.g.*, sections 5 and 6 of the preamble to the directive.

emission reduction targets at least for 2030 and 2050, a description of the progress the undertaking has made towards achieving those targets, and a statement of whether the undertaking's targets related to environmental factors are based on conclusive scientific evidence;

(c) a description of the role of the administrative, management and supervisory bodies with regard to sustainability matters and of their expertise and skills in relation to fulfilling that role or the access such bodies have to such expertise and skills;

(d) a description of the undertaking's policies in relation to sustainability matters;

(e) information about the existence of incentive schemes linked to sustainability matters which are offered to members of the administrative, management and supervisory bodies;

(f) a description of:

   (i) the due diligence process implemented by the undertaking with regard to sustainability matters and, where applicable, in line with Union requirements on undertakings to conduct a due diligence process;

   (ii) the principal actual or potential adverse impacts connected with the undertaking's own operations and with its value chain, including its products and services, its business relationships and its supply chain, actions taken to identify and monitor those impacts, and other adverse impacts which the undertaking is required to identify pursuant to other Union requirements on undertakings to conduct a due diligence process;

   (iii) any actions taken by the undertaking to prevent, mitigate, remediate or bring an end to actual or potential adverse impacts and the result of such actions;

(g) a description of the principal risks to the undertaking related to sustainability matters, including a description of the undertaking's principal dependencies on those matters and how the undertaking manages those risks;

(h) indicators relevant to the disclosures referred to in points (a) to (g).

The term 'sustainability matters' is defined in the directive as environmental, social and human rights and governance factors, including sustainability factors as defined in point (24) of Article 2 of Regulation (EU) 2019/2088. That article defines 'sustainability factors' as environmental, social and employee matters, respect for human rights, anti-corruption and anti-bribery.

Read as an ideal of how to conduct sustainable business, the following picture emerges:

(i) The company has, through governing documents and through its corporate culture, implemented processes and procedures to always act with *due diligence*. This means, among other things, that the company, in all its operations:

- *identifies* its (i) potential and actual negative impacts and (ii) opportunities to create positive impacts on the environment, people and society;
- *takes steps* to address both negative and positive impacts. In the case of adverse impacts, this means that the company prevents, mitigates, remediates or puts an end to adverse impacts;
- *monitors and follows up* to make sure the measures taken have the intended effect.

(ii) The company's due diligence processes referred to in the previous paragraph cover not only the company itself but its entire *value chain*, including its suppliers and distributors.[198]

(iii) As part of exercising due diligence, the company has established a *business model* and a *strategy* that:
- take the interests of not only the company and its shareholders but *all stakeholders* affected by the company's operations from a sustainability perspective into account;
- consider the risks to the company's operations arising from factors such as climate change, corruption in society, poverty, inequality and gender inequality;
- consider the business opportunities created by sustainability factors;
- include how the company's operations are or will become sustainable, including how they will be financed and what investments are planned, including contributing to limiting global warming to 1.5°C.

(iv) The company implements the strategy according *to a clear plan* (here called a sustainability plan) *with time-bound targets* for the factors – for example, regarding environmental impact, human health, corruption and so on – where the company's impact is material.[199] As for the environmental objectives, they must be based on unambiguous scientific evidence.

(v) The company's *administrative, management and supervisory bodies* – board of directors, management team, audit committees, etc. – are responsible for the strategy and sustainability plan and its implementation. These bodies have the knowledge and competence needed to set and implement the strategy.

(vi) The company has a *policy* and other governing documents that govern the company's operations, so the established strategy and sustainability plan are put into practice and achieved.

(vii) The company has implemented *incentive systems* that do not conflict with, but instead create the conditions for, implementing the strategy and sustainability plan.

The details of this overall ideal for sustainable business can be found in the sustainability reporting standards described in this part of the book. As is clear, the

198. In CSDDD, the term 'chain of activities' is used.
199. On the concept of materiality, *see* section 16.2.

emphasis is put on the due diligence norm. But the norm of positive contribution also shows, for example, in the requirements to report how the company has dealt with *opportunities* to make positive contributions to sustainability matters. Not taking advantage of such an opportunity when the possibility exists is to violate the norm of positive contribution.

Below is a brief illustration of the expressed ideal image for sustainable business. In this illustration, the iceberg illustrated in section 3.2 has been transformed into a kind of wheel, where the intention is to show that business is *repetitive* and dynamic and not static, which the iceberg may be interpreted to indicate:

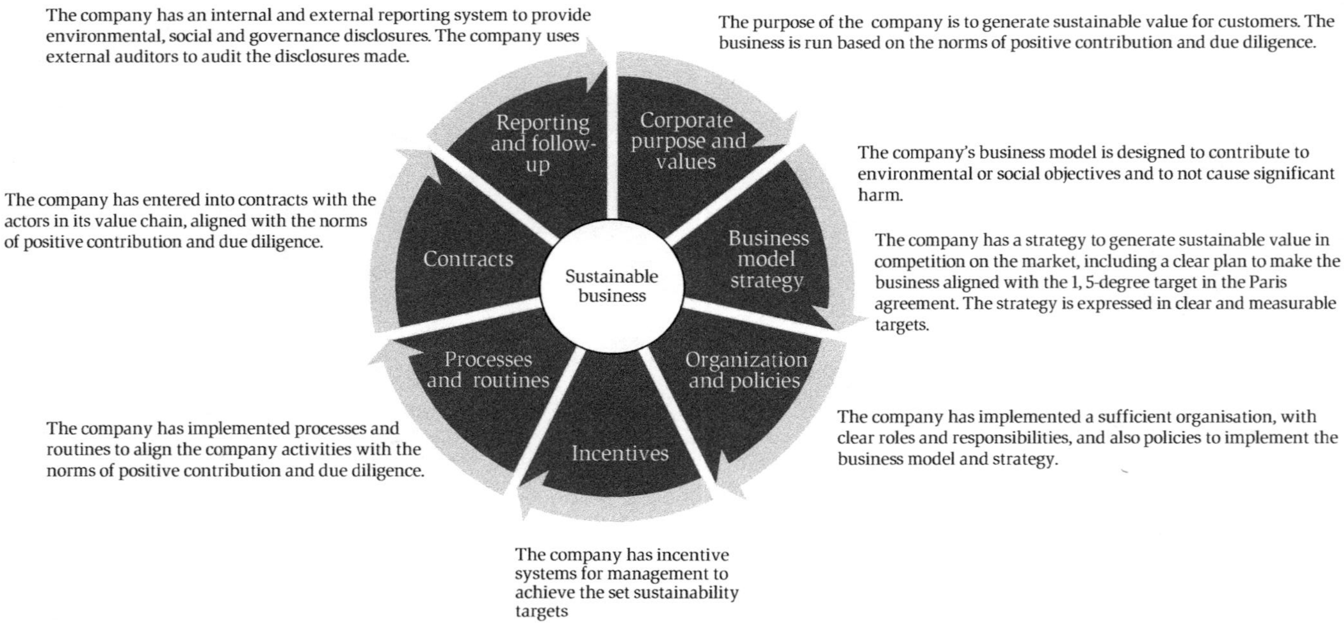
The company has an internal and external reporting system to provide environmental, social and governance disclosures. The company uses external auditors to audit the disclosures made.
The purpose of the company is to generate sustainable value for customers. The business is run based on the norms of positive contribution and due diligence.
Reporting and follow-up
Corporate purpose and values
The company's business model is designed to contribute to environmental or social objectives and to not cause significant harm.
The company has entered into contracts with the actors in its value chain, aligned with the norms of positive contribution and due diligence.
Business model strategy
The company has a strategy to generate sustainable value in competition on the market, including a clear plan to make the business aligned with the 1, 5-degree target in the Paris agreement. The strategy is expressed in clear and measurable targets.
Contracts
Sustainable business
Processes and routines
Organization and policies
The company has implemented processes and routines to align the company activities with the norms of positive contribution and due diligence.
Incentives
The company has implemented a sufficient organisation, with clear roles and responsibilities, and also policies to implement the business model and strategy.
The company has incentive systems for management to achieve the set sustainability targets

These are several components that follow a logical thread but are not static, which is why the illustration describes a continuous process. The starting point, at the top right, is in *Company Purpose and Values*. This topic has been dealt with in detail in Chapter 6.

In the next step, the institutionalisation of sustainable business operations is initiated through the company's business model, which needs to be designed to contribute positively to humans and the environment and not cause significant harm. Institutionalisation continues through the company's *strategy, goals and measurement criteria* to measure goal achievement. Of course, the strategy must be based on the purpose, values and business model.

The business model and strategy are further put into practice *in governing documents* and in the company's *organisation and policies*. In the next stage, *an incentive structure* is established that aims to align everyone's actions with the company's strategy and goals in accordance with the values. In the next step, we have the companies' processes and routines. This is where true institutionalisation begins, where purpose business models, etc., are transformed into daily, repeated activities throughout the organisation. Institutionalisation in the company's market relationships comes in the next steps through *contracts*. As we will see, this is an area which is underdeveloped in the EU sustainability framework but is still critical since all the companies' revenues and most of their costs run through contractual relationships. Finally, a structure for *follow-up and reporting* is established.

Each of the different components of this picture will be covered in different places in this book, including in the description of ESRS 2. These are critical parts of the rules of the game for sustainable business.

Chapter 14
Corporate Sustainability Due Diligence

When this book was published, the Directive 2024/1760/EU on corporate sustainability due diligence – the CSDDD – was published in the Official Journal but not yet implemented into the national laws of any EU Member State. The obligations of the directive form a natural starting point for describing what it means to conduct sustainable business operations. Only large companies, as described below, are obliged to follow the directive's obligations, but since they shall be applied across the value chain, indirectly, a very large number of companies will be affected by the directive when implemented.

As already stated above, the directive explicitly transforms the non-binding UNGPs and OECD guidelines into binding legal obligations. Those texts, already described in section 4.2 above as constituting the second level of sustainability law, are referred to already in sections 5 and 6 in the preamble to the directive, along with Agenda 2030, the EU Climate Law and a number of other documents and legal instruments in the following sections. Thereafter, in section 16, the aim of the directive is stated to be 'to ensure that companies active in the internal market contribute to sustainable development and the sustainability transition of economies and societies through the identification, and where necessary, prioritisation, prevention and mitigation, bringing to an end, minimisation and remediation of potential or actual adverse human rights and environmental impacts connected with companies' own operations, operations of their subsidiaries and their business partners on the companies' chain of activities, and ensuring that those affected by a failure to respect this duty have access to justice and legal remedies'.

The CSDDD is not the first EU legal act addressing due diligence in business operations and supply chains. Regulation (EU) No 995/2010 regarding obligations of operators who place timber and timber products on the market imposes due diligence requirements related to timber (the EU Timber Regulation). It will be replaced by (EU) 2023/1115 regarding the making available on the Union market and the export from the Union of certain commodities and products associated with deforestation and forest degradation (the Deforestation Regulation). Regulation (EU) 2017/821 sets requirements on supply chain due diligence obligations for Union importers of tin, tantalum and tungsten, their ores, and gold originating from conflict-affected and high-risk areas (the Conflict Mineral Regulation). Regulation (EU) 2023/1542 concerning batteries and waste batteries furthermore imposes due diligence obligations related to batteries. This chapter will, however, only focus on the CSDDD.

14.1 APPLICABILITY

The CSDDD is applicable to two categories of companies: large companies and certain companies in sectors identified as high-impact sectors. According to Article 2 of the directive, it shall apply to companies formed in accordance with the legislation of a Member State and which fulfil one of the following conditions for two consecutive financial years:

(i) The company had more than 1,000 employees[200] on average and a net worldwide turnover of more than EUR 450 million in the last financial year, from which annual statements have been or should have been adopted.
(ii) The company did not reach the thresholds above but is the ultimate parent company of a group that reaches the thresholds.

There is also a threshold for franchise and licensing agreement organisations. The directive is also applicable to companies formed under the laws of non-EU countries but where the net turnover in the EU meets the EUR 450 million threshold.

It is important to note that parent companies in groups shall be entitled to fulfil many of their subsidiaries' obligations on behalf of those subsidiaries.

14.2 ADVERSE ENVIRONMENTAL AND HUMAN RIGHTS IMPACT

The CSDDD applies to 'adverse environmental impacts' and 'human rights impact', which makes a proper understanding of these concepts important. As set out in Chapter 4, sustainability law is built on different levels, with the international treaties on human rights and environmental protection in the base. The European Court of Justice has, as mentioned, explicitly said that those international treaties form a part of EU law.[201] They, therefore, form the 'political morality', which is gradually converted into laws at the higher levels, for example, the CSDDD. The European Court of Human Rights ruling in *Verein Klimaseniorinnen Schweiz and others v. Switzerland*, described in section 5.1, now forms an important part of this political morality.

Annex I to CSDDD lists all the EU rules and international treaties, which include prohibitions related to human rights and the environment for which CSDDD is relevant. Each of those prohibitions provides rights of protection for individuals, which

200. According to Article 3, part time employees shall be viewed as full-time employees.
201. C-366/10, Air Transport Association America and others, section 101 and C-308/06, Intertanko, section 42.

can be abused, in this case, by companies. As already set out in Chapter 5, human rights are expressions of the general principles of equality and freedom, which in combination establish each human's right to dignity.

14.2.1 Adverse Environmental Impact

Adverse environmental impact is, in Article 3.1 (b) defined as an adverse impact on the environment resulting from a breach of prohibitions specified in Annex I to the directive. The list of prohibitions is extensive and here, only an overview will be provided. The prohibitions are listed in points 18 and 19 in Part I and Part II of Annex 1.

Article 6 of the International Covenant on Civil and Political Rights states that every human being has the inherent right to life, a right that shall be protected by law. No one shall be arbitrarily deprived of his life. Article 11 of the International Covenant on Economic, Social and Cultural Rights recognises, with an interesting choice of gender form, the right of everyone to an adequate standard of living for himself and his family, including adequate food, clothing and housing, and to the continuous improvement of living conditions. Article 12 of the same covenant recognises the right of everyone to the enjoyment of the highest attainable standard of physical and mental health.

These three articles are referred to in points 18 and 19 of Part I in Annex 1 of CSDDD. Point 18 refers to, with reference to these three articles, the prohibition of causing any measurable environmental degradation, such as harmful soil change, water or air pollution, harmful emissions, excessive water consumption, degradation of land, or their impact on natural resources, such as deforestation, that:

- substantially impairs the natural bases for the prevention and production of food;
- denies a person access to safe and clean drinking water;
- makes it difficult for a person to access sanity facilities or destroys them;
- harms the health, safety and normal use of land or lawfully acquired possessions of a person; or
- substantially adversely affects ecosystem services through which an ecosystem contributes directly to human well-being.

Harming the environment often means harm to people and their opportunity to live a life in dignity, as expressed above. This was, of course, firmly established in *Verein Klimaseniorinnen Schweiz and others v. Switzerland*, where the focus was on respect for private and family life as well as life and health.

This technique of listing prohibitions or obligations with reference to international treaties continues in point 19 and furthermore in Part II of Annex I. Prohibitions and obligations listed are, for example, obligations to avoid or minimise adverse impacts on biodiversity and prohibitions regarding:

- export endangered species;
- manufacturing, import, export and use of mercury, mercury compounds and mercury waste;
- production and use of chemicals being 'persistent organic pollutants';
- collection, storage and disposal of waste;
- export of certain chemicals;

and so on.

14.2.2 Adverse Human Rights Impact

Article 3.1 (c) of CSDDD defines 'adverse human rights impact' as abuses in one of two categories of human rights. In the first category are human rights explicitly listed in section 1 of Part I of Annex I. In this category falls, for example:

- right to life;
- prohibition of torture, cruel, inhumane or degrading treatment;
- right to liberty and security;
- protection of privacy, family, home, correspondence, honour or reputation;
- freedom of thought, conscience and religion; and
- just and favourable working conditions.

The international instruments in which those human rights are established are, however, not necessarily clear in all aspects. It is possible that they will, in the future, be interpreted as establishing additional human rights in addition to those explicit rights listed above (and others). In the second category fall, therefore, human rights that follow from international treaties listed in section 2 of Part I in Annex I, not listed in section 1, provided that those human rights can be abused by a company or legal entity, an abuse directly impairs the legal interests expressed in those human rights instruments and, finally, that the company could reasonably have foreseen the risk that such human right may be affected.

14.3 THE OVERALL DUE DILIGENCE NORM

The CSDDD thus lays down more detailed requirements under the overarching due diligence norm, focusing on the adverse environmental and human rights impacts described in the previous section. The overall sustainability obligation is set out in Article 5 of the directive, according to which companies to which the directive applies shall conduct risk-based human rights and environmental due diligence by carrying out the following actions:

- integrating due diligence into their policies and risk management systems;
- identifying and assessing actual or potential adverse impacts and, where necessary, prioritising potential and actual adverse impacts;

- preventing and mitigating potential adverse impacts, and bringing actual adverse impacts to an end and minimising their extent;
- providing remediation to actual adverse impacts;
- carrying out meaningful engagement with stakeholders;
- establish and maintain a notification mechanism and complaint procedure;
- monitoring the effectiveness of their due diligence policy and measures; and finally
- publicly communicating on due diligence.

Each of those activities is further described in the following sections.

14.3.1 Engagement with Stakeholders

In the debate about corporate purpose, described in Chapter 6, a common criticism against what is referred to as 'stakeholder capitalism' is that it would be an almost impossible task for company management to take into consideration all relevant stakeholders. This concern is politely ignored in CSDDD, where engagement with stakeholders is a critical element. Before taking stakeholders' interests into consideration according to the corporate values, it is necessary to communicate with them in order to find out about their views and interests.

This stakeholder engagement obligation comes first into play when the company shall, according to the next, develop and adopt a due diligence policy. This policy shall be developed in prior consultation with the company employees and their representatives.[202] But then there is a more general obligation for the company to carry out meaningful engagements with stakeholders. Stakeholders are then defined as the company's employees, the employees of its subsidiaries, trade unions and workers' representatives, consumers, other individuals or groups, communities or entities whose rights or interests are or could be affected by the products, services and operations of the company. Employees, trade unions and workers' representatives of business partners are included, as well as national human rights and environmental institutions and civil society organisations.[203]

The stakeholder engagement shall basically cover all the activities carried out when complying with the due diligence norm, including the below described assessment of potential and actual negative impact, development of prevention and correction plans, decisions to terminate business relationships and so on.[204]

14.3.2 Integration of Due Diligence into Companies' Policies and Risk Management Systems

Under Article 7 of the directive, companies shall adopt a separate corporate policy for risk-based due diligence and also integrate due diligence into all their relevant corporate policies and risk management systems.

202. Article 7.2.
203. Article 3.1(n).
204. Article 13.3.

The article is silent about what is meant by company policies, but it should be quite obvious that what is referred to is documented corporate guidelines to be followed by management, the staff and possibly also entities with which the company does business. It is common for companies to have policies, e.g., for working conditions, environment, human rights, anti-bribery, personal data and so on. All such policies must be updated to reflect the due diligence norm, which often means that the policy now should state the systematic, repetitive approach taken to the relevant matter.

The due diligence policy, which shall be updated annually, shall contain all of the following:

- a description of the company's approach, including in the long term, to due diligence;
- a code of conduct describing rules and principles to be followed by the company's employees and subsidiaries;
- a description of the processes put in place to implement due diligence, including the measures taken to verify compliance with the code of conduct and to extend its application to established business relationships.

The obligations are thus vague, but the context of the directive provides further input on what a due diligence policy should probably include, namely rules regarding the other actions set out in Article 5 of the CSDDD. Thus, the due diligence should most likely include a description of the processes to be followed regarding the identification of actual and potential negative impact, prevention and bringing to an end such impact, complaints procedures, monitoring and communication.

It is interesting to note the similarity of this obligation and the positive obligations of states to adopt a regulatory framework to combat climate change established by the European Court of Human Rights in *Verein Klimaseniorinnen Schweiz and others v. Switzerland*. The first obligation under CSDDD is for the company to adopt the rules – the policy – to prevent violations of adverse human and environmental impact.

14.3.3 Identification of Actual and Potential Adverse Impacts

Under Article 8 of the CSDDD, companies shall take appropriate measures to identify actual and potential adverse human rights impacts and adverse environmental impacts arising from their own operations or those of their subsidiaries. The identification process should also cover the company's 'chain of activities', which is an important concept in CSDDD. This concept, commonly referred to as the value chain, comprises:

- activities of the company's *upstream* business patterns related to the production of *goods* or the provision of *services* to the company, and

- activities of the company's *downstream* business partners related to the distribution, transport and storage of the *products*.[205]

It is important to note that disposal of the product is thus not covered,[206] nor is the provision of services downstream.[207] Furthermore, no downstream activities of regulated financial undertakings are covered.[208]

A 'business partner' comprises both direct and indirect business partners. A direct business partner is a legal entity which whom the company has a commercial agreement related to the operations, products or services of the company or to whom the company provides services. An indirect business partner is a company which is not a direct business partner but which performs business operations related to the operations, products or services of the company.[209]

The scope of the identification exercise is thus very broad. This does not mean, as will be explained below, that the obligations to mitigate or end negative impact are equally broad.

The process of identifying actual and potential adverse impacts under the CSDDD is best carried out as part of the double materiality assessment made under the CSRD, as described below. The assessment made under the CSDDD is more limited than the assessment made under the CSRD, but the latter will definitely encompass the former. For this reason, the actual process of identifying adverse impacts will only be briefly described here since a deeper description is provided in Chapter 16.2.

As set out in that chapter, it is practical to begin the analysis by using the table of potential sustainability matters for the company set out in Annex III to the reporting standard ESRS 1, included in Annex I in this book. But the analysis cannot stop there. Since any identified potential or actual adverse impact must be prevented or ended, it is important to further analyse *why* the adverse impact potentially or actually exists. Not seldom, it is because such risks or actual impacts are built into the company's business model or strategy, which is further discussed in Chapter 17. Other forms of adverse impact may not be part of the business model or strategy but a result of, e.g., heavily cost-focused procurement methods used when finding new suppliers in the market. The point here is that the adverse impact analysis should be accompanied by a root cause analysis of how the adverse impacts actually or potentially arise.

According to CSDDD, the identification process should be carried out in two steps. First, the company shall identify *general areas* where adverse impacts are most likely to occur and to be most severe. In a second step, the company shall carry out an in-depth analysis of the areas where adverse impacts are most likely to occur and are most severe.[210]

205. Article 3.1(g) CSDDD. Distribution, transport and storage of products subject to export control regulations are excluded from downstream chain of activities.
206. *See* section 25 of the preamble.
207. *See* section 26 of the preamble.
208. *See* section 26, of the preamble.
209. Article 3.1(f).
210. Article 8.2.

The impact assessment under Article 8 can lead to the identification of two forms of adverse impact: potential and actual. As regards potential adverse impacts, Article 10 sets out that companies shall take appropriate measures to prevent, or where prevention is not possible or not immediately possible, adequately mitigate potential adverse human rights impacts and adverse environmental impacts that have been, or should have been, identified pursuant to Article 8. Actual impacts shall instead, according to Article 11, be brought to an end. Companies are, however, entitled to prioritise between actions taken if it is not feasible to prevent, mitigate, bring to an end or minimise all identified adverse impacts at the same time to their full extent.[211] The prioritisation shall, of course, be based on the severity and likelihood of adverse impacts, and when more serious impacts have been handled, the less severe ones shall be dealt with.

14.3.4 Preventing Potential Adverse Impacts

Article 10 sets out a number of actions that companies are required to take if potentially adverse impacts are identified. Some identified potential adverse impacts may be simple to prevent, but others are more complex, involving different steps and actors. In such cases, the company is obliged to, together with relevant stakeholders, develop and implement a prevention action plan with timelines and qualitative and quantitative indicators against which progress can be measured.

If the potential adverse effect is identified not in the company's direct operations but in the chain of activities, the company should enter into a contract with the relevant entity, ensuring compliance with the company's code of conduct. Also, for such entity, it may be a complex project to prevent a potential negative impact, so it may be necessary to adopt a prevention action plan with such entity. In Chapter 26, I discuss the weakness of a too strong contractual focus on compliance with a code of conduct and the need to often also take a broader view of business model and contract model in the contract.

In some cases, the potential adverse impact can only be definitely prevented if the company makes certain investments, for example, in machinery or software systems.

Many suppliers are small or medium-sized companies, which may have challenges with complying with the company's code of conduct or an action plan. If that is the case, the company shall provide 'targeted and proportionate support' to such SMEs to help them prevent the potentially adverse impact. Article 7 finally sets out an obligation for companies to, within the framework of competition law, collaborate with others to ensure the prevention of the potentially negative impact.

Article 10.5 sets out further details if the company uses a contract as a mechanism to prevent a potentially adverse impact. The contract shall then include clauses entitling the company to verify compliance. As regards contracts with small and medium-sized companies, the terms of the contract shall be 'fair, reasonable and non-discriminatory', and any costs incurred as a result of third-party verification shall be borne by the company.

---

211. *See* Article 9.

Sometimes, it is not possible to influence a contracting party to prevent an adverse human rights or environmental impact. In such case, the company shall refrain from entering into new or extending the existing relations with such contracting party. The company shall also, within the limits of the law, temporarily suspend the commercial relationship or end terminate the relationship if the potential adverse impact is severe.

The CSDDD is based on a much too simplified view of contracts and how they can and should be used to conduct sustainable business. The matter is discussed in detail in Part IV of the book and also in Part V as regards contracts in the value chain.

14.3.5 Bringing Actual Adverse Impacts to an End

While Article 10 of the CSDDD deals with the prevention of potential impact, Article 11 instead deals with *actual* adverse impacts. The obligations are, however, almost identical to the obligations in Article 10 and will therefore not be repeated here.

14.3.6 Other Obligations

Articles 12–16 of the CSDDD contain further obligations on companies, forming a part of the overall due diligence norm. According to Article 14, companies shall provide the possibility to submit complaints to them where they have legitimate concerns regarding actual or potential adverse human rights or environmental impacts, covering both the company's own operations and value chain.

According to Article 15, companies shall carry out periodic assessments to monitor the effectiveness of the actions taken according to the directive, based on appropriate qualitative and quantitative indicators, every twelve months or more often if necessary.

According to Article 16, finally, companies to which the CSRD is not applicable shall disclose information annually about their compliance with the CSDDD.

14.4 CLIMATE CHANGE TRANSITION PLAN

In addition to the general measures adopted according to Articles 7-16, companies shall adopt and put into effect a transition plan, ensuring that the business model and strategy are compatible with the limiting of global warming to 1.5°C in line with the Paris Agreement. The plan shall identify the extent to which climate change is a risk for or an impact on the company's operations. If that is the case, the company shall include emission reduction objectives in its plan.

Companies shall also take into account the fulfilment of the obligations regarding the transition plan and emission reduction objectives when setting variable remuneration if variable remuneration is linked to the contribution of a director to the company's business strategy and long-term interests and sustainability.

14.5 CIVIL LIABILITY

What happens if a company fails to prevent a potential adverse impact or end an actual impact? Article 29 of the CSDDD lays down rules regarding civil liability in such cases. A company can be liable for damages if a failure to take such actions leads to the adverse impact occurring.

There are two basic conditions that must be fulfilled for liability for damages:

(i) The company must intentionally or negligently have failed to comply with the obligations to prevent potential impact or bring actual impact to an end.
(ii) As a result of the above failure, damage must have been caused to the natural or legal person's legal interests protected under national laws.[212]

The company cannot be held liable if the damage was caused only but its business patterns in its chain of activities.

Interestingly, CSDDD requires Member States to adopt laws making it possible for trade unions, human rights and environmental NGOs to bring actions to enforce the rights of the alleged injured party.

Any civil liability case brought under CSDDD will largely be a matter of what can be proven. If the claimants present reasoned justification for their claim, containing reasonably available facts and evidence and have indicated that additional evidence is controlled by the company, the courts shall be able to order such additional evidence to be disclosed.

The ECHR's reasoning in *Verein Klimaseniorinnen Schweiz and others v. Switzerland* will probably be applied when interpreting Article 29. Referring to the description of the case in section 5.1, it will probably be a challenge for a company to successfully claim that it should not be liable just because other companies have not done their part or have also caused the harm relevant in a case under Article 29. In the case, the court found that the individual applicants did not have so-called victim status under the convention since it could not be proven that, to simplify, their health problem was related to climate change. But the association which they all were a member of was also an applicant, and that association was given victim status due to the interest in combatting the negative human effects of climate change it was established to protect. This may become highly relevant in future court cases under Article 29 of the CSDDD. It could mean that while individuals may have trouble proving a relevant causality between their harm and the acts or failures to act by a company, an NGO may be able to prove that those acts or failures to act harm the interests which the NGO is established to protect. The future will show how Article 29 will be interpreted in this respect.

212. Article 22.1 CSDDD.

14.6 SANCTIONS

In addition to civil liability, a company failing to fulfil the obligations under the CSDDD can be sanctioned by the competent authority. The maximum penalties to be imposed are 5% of the worldwide turnover.[213]

14.7 TRANSPOSITION

The CSDDD shall be implemented within two years from its entry into force. The obligations shall then be gradually imposed on companies. Three years after the entry into force of the directive, companies to which the directive is applicable with more than 5,000 employees and a turnover of more than EUR 1,500 million. The CSDDD shall be applicable for the full scope of companies five years after its entry into force.

213. Article 27,4.

CHAPTER 15

Corporate Sustainability Reporting

The previous chapter described the sustainable due diligence obligations under the CSDDD. That directive and its direct sustainability obligations are only applicable to a limited number of companies. The core of the EU legislation coming from the EU Green Deal instead consists of sustainability reporting obligations.

Transparency is a key principle of the European Green Deal and the ideal image for sustainable business. The legislation on sustainability reporting is largely about companies being incentivised to conduct their business sustainably by requiring them to be transparent about how their operations are conducted. The idea behind this can only be understood against the background of the normative, moral foundation of sustainability law. Although many people act immorally every day, very few can bear to openly show and admit it. Anyone who is forced to act publicly has a strong incentive to act morally correctly.

CSRD – Directive 2022/2464 on corporate sustainability reporting – has been briefly described in Chapter 4. It is an important part of the transformation to a more sustainable business sector by increasing investments in companies that conduct sustainable business activities.

The central importance of transparency is already evident in the preamble to the directive. There, the problem of *information asymmetry* is an important theme, i.e., the difference between users' information needs and sustainability information provided by companies. Recital 13 of the CSRD points out that the Commission's reviews had found that many companies do not disclose material information on all significant sustainability-related issues. Absent policy measures, information asymmetry is likely to increase to the detriment of both investors and civil society actors.[214]

Transparency in relation to whom? Recital 9 of the directive emphasises that sustainability reporting has two main groups of users: on the one hand, investors who want to better understand the risks and opportunities that sustainability matters pose to their investments and the impact of investments on people and the environment,

214. Recital 14.

and on the other hand, civil society actors, such as NGOs and social actors, who want to better hold companies accountable for their impacts on people and the environment. The principle of double materiality, which is discussed below, is expressed here.

The basis of the CSRD is thus about transparency in relation to investors and civil society, towards whom companies should be forced to be transparent about whether and to what extent they conduct their business in accordance with the ideal image of EU law.

15.1 APPLICABILITY

The CSRD will be introduced gradually for a growing number of companies in the EU. Article 5 of the CSRD sets out the following schedule for when the CSRD comes into force for different companies:

(i) 1 January 2024: The CSRD is applied to large public-interest undertakings[215] with an average of over 500 employees in the relevant financial year.

(ii) 1 January 2025: The CSRD becomes applicable to
- large undertakings other than large enterprises covered by the paragraph above, and
- parent undertakings of large groups;[216]

(iii) 1 January 2026: The CSRD becomes applicable for
- small and medium-sized undertakings (SMEs) of general interest;[217]
- small and non-complex credit institutions and captive insurance companies if they are large undertakings or small and medium-sized undertakings of general interest

Large, medium, and small undertakings are categorised in the CSRD as follows:[218]

Category	*Number of Employees*	*Turnover*	*Balance Sheet Total*
Large	More than 250	Over EUR 50 million	Over EUR 25 million
Medium	50–249	Below EUR 50 million	Below EUR 25 million

215. An enterprise of public interest is defined in Article 2.1 in directive 2013/14/EU as entities (a) governed by the law of a Member State and whose transferable securities are admitted to trading on a regulated market of any Member State (b) certain credit institutions and (c) certain insurance undertakings or (d) designated by Member States as public-interest entities.
216. The term large group is defined in Article 3.7 in directive 2013/34/EU as groups consisting of parent and subsidiary undertakings to be included in a consolidation and which, on a consolidated basis, exceed the limits of at least two of the three following criteria on the balance sheet date of the parent undertaking: (a) balance sheet total: EUR 20,000,000, (b) net turnover: EUR 40,000,000 and (c) average number of employees during the financial year: 250.
217. The directive is not applicable to so-called micro-undertakings.
218. Article 3 in directive 2013/34/EU.

Category	*Number of Employees*	*Turnover*	*Balance Sheet Total*
Small	Less than 50	Below EUR 10 million	Below EUR 5 million

Companies that are subsidiaries need not meet the requirements for sustainability reporting as long as the company and its subsidiaries are included in the parent company's sustainability report. This applies even if the parent company is established outside the EU. However, the new Article 19a(9) sets out certain conditions for the exemptions to apply.

15.2 GENERAL REQUIREMENTS

The overall requirements for the sustainability report have been described in Chapter 13 and will not be repeated here. Similar requirements apply to groups of companies, with the difference that reporting must take place at group level.[219]

However, it follows from the new Article 19a(6) of the CSRD that small and medium-sized undertakings need not comply with the same requirements as large undertakings. For these companies, the sustainability report must instead include:

- a brief description of the undertaking's business model and strategy;
- a description of the undertaking's policies in relation to sustainability matters;
- the principal actual or potential adverse impacts of the undertaking on sustainability matters and any actions taken to identify, monitor, prevent, mitigate or remediate such actual or potential adverse impacts;
- the principal risks to the undertaking related to sustainability matters and how the undertaking manages those risks; and
- key indicators necessary for the disclosures referred to in the points above.

The fourth subparagraph of Article 19a(3) of the CSRD provides for an important exception to the general transparency requirement. Member States may allow information relating to impending developments or matters in the course of negotiation to be omitted in exceptional cases where, in the duly justified opinion of the members of the administrative, management and supervisory bodies, acting within the competences assigned to them by national law and having collective responsibility for that opinion, the disclosure of such information would be seriously prejudicial to the commercial position of the undertaking, provided that such omission does not prevent a fair and balanced understanding of the undertaking's development, performance and position, and the impact of its activity.

219. Article 29a CSRD.

15.3 SUSTAINABILITY REPORTING STANDARDS AND RECOMMENDATIONS

The CSRD gives the Commission a mandate and duty to adopt sustainability reporting standards, which should specify in more detail the information that the sustainability reports must contain. Those standards shall ensure the quality of the information to be reported by requiring it to be understandable, relevant, verifiable, comparable and accurately produced. As stated above, lower reporting requirements apply to medium-sized and small companies.

The standards – ESRS – that have been adopted at the time of writing this book are described in this part of the book. They have been prepared, on behalf of the European Commission, by the European Financial Reporting Advisory Group (EFRAG), which was established in 2001 on the initiative of the European Commission. The standards have been developed considering several existing standards and frameworks. Three organisations whose standards and frameworks should be specifically mentioned to create an understanding of the structure and content of the ESRS are the Global Reporting Initiative (GRI), the Task Force on Climate-Related Financial Disclosures (TCFD) and the Task Force on Nature-related Financial Disclosures (TNFD).

15.3.1 Global Reporting Initiative

Global Reporting Initiative (GRI) is an independent, international organisation based in Amsterdam that works to help companies and other organisations take responsibility for their impact on the environment and other sustainability factors by helping them communicate about these impacts in a consistent language. Under GRI, impact means the impact that the organisation has on the economy, the environment and people as a result of the company's own operations or business relationships.[220] Over the years, GRI has published a large number of standards that companies can use to report their sustainability impact. There are three categories of GRI standards:

General Standards. The GRI 1-3 standards contain general requirements that apply to all companies. GRI 1 contains overarching principles, definitions of key concepts, and so on. GRI 2 contains general disclosure requirements regarding the reporting organisation, its value chain, its employees, the company's governance, strategy, policies and processes for managing material impacts. GRI 3 describes how companies should go about identifying their material impact areas.

Sector-specific standards. Several GRI standards have been developed for specific industries and sectors: oil and gas (GRI 11), coal (GRI 12) and the agriculture and fisheries sectors (GRI 13).

Subject-specific standards. Several GRI standards apply regardless of sector but focus on certain specific topics, divided into the overarching areas of environmental, social and governance (ESG). Examples of such standards are standards for accounting

220. GRI 1, point 2.1. This is an important difference from the ESRS, which also focus on the financial impact of sustainability factors on the organisation, which therefore requires a so-called double materiality analysis.

for anti-corruption (GRI 205), materials (GRI 301), energy (GRI 302), employment (GRI 401) and diversity and equal opportunity (GRI 405). A substance-specific standard shall be used if the company, in its due diligence process, has identified that the company has a material impact on that substance.

15.3.2 Task Force on Climate-Related Financial Disclosures

Task Force on Climate-Related Financial Disclosures (TCFD) is a body established by the Financial Stability Board, an international organisation that monitors and issues recommendations on the global financial system. TCFD was established to develop recommendations on what information companies should disclose to support investors, lenders and insurers in accurately assessing and pricing risks linked to climate change. The result of TCFD's work is not standards but recommendations. Several elements from these recommendations are important for understanding the ESRS standards.

TCFD recommends that companies disclose information from four perspectives:

(i) **Governance**. The organisation's governance regarding climate-related risks and opportunities.
(ii) **Strategy**. The impact of actual and potential climate-related risks and opportunities on the company's operations, strategy and financial planning.
(iii) **Risk management**. The process that the company uses to identify, assess and manage climate-related risks.
(iv) **Metrics and targets**. The metrics and targets that the company uses to assess and manage relevant climate-related risks and opportunities.

This structure is directly implemented in the ESRS standards, not only in terms of climate but in all areas. TCFD also provides a framework for risk analysis. It is specifically designed for climate-related risks but has general applicability, and the framework is implicated in several places in the ESRS.[221] The framework is described in the illustration below:

221. TCFD (2017), Recommendations of the Task Force on Climate-related Financial Disclosures, p. 8.

First, TCFD makes a fundamental distinction between two types of risks: transition risks and physical risks. Transition risks are defined as risks related to the transition to a low-carbon economy, as this transition may involve major changes in the legal environment, technologies used, market environment, and so on. Instead, physical risks refer to risks that result directly from climate change, such as damage to property or indirect impact through supply chain disruptions. Some of these are acute, that is, caused by specific events. Others are chronic and thus long-lasting.

However, climate change also presents opportunities for companies, for example, increased efficiency in using resources, the transition to fossil-free energy sources, the development of low-emission products and services, the opening of new markets or market segments, and increased resilience to disruptions of various kinds.

Climate-related risks and opportunities can have different types of financial impacts on companies, both related to the income statement and balance sheet. TCFD provides several examples:[222]

- **Revenue**: Transition risks and physical risks can affect demand for a company's products and services.
- **Costs**: Businesses can be vulnerable to climate change differently depending on their cost structure. For example, companies and suppliers with already low costs may be more resilient to cost increases that climate change may bring.
- **Assets and liabilities**: Both transition risks and physical risks can affect the valuation of companies' assets.
- **Capital and financing**: Climate-related risks and opportunities can affect the company's equity and debt financing, for example, through increased indebtedness to compensate for reduced cash flows or investments in research and development.

222. TCFD (2017), Recommendations of the Task Force on Climate-related Financial Disclosures, p. 9.

This analytical framework regarding financial risks and opportunities is important in several respects. It should be used to carry out risk analyses and to report on the matter according to the ESRS and also according to the SFDR.

15.3.3 Taskforce on Nature-Related Financial Disclosures

In the wake of TCFD's work, the Taskforce on Nature-related Financial Disclosures (TNFD) has issued recommendations. TNFD is also an international organisation and has a mission to develop and provide risk management and disclosure frameworks to report on and respond to *nature-related* risks. The ultimate aim is to support a shift in global financial flows from negative to positive outcomes for nature.[223]

The background to the framework is the insight that both society and companies are highly dependent on services provided by nature, such as water, air, biodiversity and so on. The ongoing environmental crisis, therefore, creates risks for both companies and financial actors. The framework is designed to be consistent with TCFD's climate change framework and follows, for example, the structure of governance, strategy, risk management, and metrics and targets. The framework has eleven recommended disclosures related to nature that companies should disclose. These are not reported here because EU actors covered by the CSRD will need to comply with the ESRS.

However, several of the ESRS in the environmental area refer to the process for identifying, evaluating, prioritising and managing environment-related risks and opportunities that is part of the TNFD framework. The process is called LEAP, which stands for Locate, Evaluate, Assess, Prepare. It is schematically set up below:

223. TNFD, Recommendations of the Taskforce on Nature-related Financial Disclosures, September 2023.

An important starting point in the LEAP method is that the mutual impact between companies and the environment takes place in specific locations and that the evaluation and management of risks and opportunities linked to both assets and activities must, therefore, be assessed locally. That's why the first step – Localise – is so important.

To support the risk assessment stage, TNFD is also developing risk management methods. There are three different methods, which can be said to be about different levels of ambition for assessments of risks and opportunities.

15.3.4 European Sustainability Reporting Standards

On 31 July 2023, the European Commission adopted a delegated regulation 2023/2772, which adopted twelve accounting standards to be used for reporting under the CSRD.

The standards – ESRS – that have been and will be developed by EFRAG – derive a lot of structure and content from GRI and TCFD. The environmental standards also refer to the TNFD LEAP process in several places.

The division into general, sector-specific and subject-specific standards is taken directly from the GRI standards. At the time of writing, no industry-specific ESRS has yet been developed. The structure of governance, strategy, risk management, metrics and targets is taken from TCFD and directly implemented in the general ESRS 2 standard as well as in the subject-specific standards.

At the time of writing this book, the following ESRS have been published and adopted:

- ESRS 1: General requirements
- ESRS 2: General disclosures
- ESRS E1: Climate Change
- ESRS E2: Pollution
- ESRS E3: Water and marine resources
- ESRS E4: Biodiversity and ecosystems
- ESRS E5: Resource use and circular economy
- ESRS S1: Own workforce
- ESRS S2: Workers in the value chain
- ESRS S3: Affected communities
- ESRS S4: Consumers and end users
- ESRS G1: Business conduct

Each of these standards is covered below. Each standard has a similar structure, in addition to following the outline of governance, strategy, impact, risks, and opportunities management:

- Disclosure Requirements: This describes the general requirement for how the company must disclose information.
- Data points: This section describes more detailed information on how the information under the relevant disclosure requirement should be presented.
- Application Requirements. In the appendix to each standard, there are even more detailed requirements on how information, according to the disclosure requirement, is to be reported.

The disclosure requirements follow a certain numbering standard. The general ESRS 2 standard uses acronyms and numbers linked to the overall structure, such as:

(i) Basis for preparation (BP)
- Disclosure Requirement (BP-1)
- Disclosure Requirement (BP-2)

(ii) Governance (GOV)
- Disclosure Requirement GOV-1
- Disclosure Requirement (GOV-2)
- Etc.

(iii) Strategy (SBM)
- Disclosure Requirement SBM-1
- Etc.

(iv) Impact, Risk and Opportunity management (IRO)
- Disclosure Requirement IRO-1
- Etc.

(v) Minimum Disclosure Requirement – Policies MDR-P

(vi) Minimum Disclosure Requirement – Actions MDR-A

(vii) Metrics and targets (MDR-M and MDR-T, respectively)
- Minimum disclosure requirement – MDR-M
- Minimum disclosure requirement – MDR-T.

In the subject-specific standards, there are references back to ESRS 2, where subject-specific information must sometimes be given linked to, for example, disclosure requirements SBM-1 or IRO-2. The specific disclosure requirements are then numbered:

[Sustainability area (E, S, G)] + [number of standard within the area] + number of the disclosure requirement]

Disclosure requirement E1-4 then stands for the fourth disclosure requirement (4) within the first standard (1) in the environmental field (E). Disclosure requirement S2-2 stands instead of the second disclosure requirement (2) within the second standard (2) in the social area (S).

CHAPTER 16

General Requirements for the Sustainability Report (ESRS 1)

ESRS 1 sets out general requirements for the sustainability report. The most important of these are dealt with in this chapter.

16.1 QUALITY REQUIREMENTS FOR THE SUSTAINABILITY REPORT

ESRS 1 describes several basic quality requirements for companies' sustainability reports according to CSRD. There are five basic requirements, which are described in more detail in Appendix B of ESRS 1:

- relevance;
- faithful representation;
- comparability;
- verifiability; and
- understandability.

According to QC 1, information is *relevant* if it can influence the decisions of persons intended to use the information in the sustainability report, which refers to both employees of the company and people affected by the company's operations.

The information in the sustainability report has not only to be relevant. It should also give a *faithful representation* of the phenomena it seeks to describe. Faithful representation requires, according to QC5, information to be (i) complete, (ii) neutral and (iii) accurate. A complete description includes all the information needed for the user to understand, for example, the risks and opportunities associated with various sustainability matters. A neutral description is without bias. Both positive and negative aspects shall be described, including descriptions of challenges in achieving results on the sustainability matters described. Risks and opportunities must neither be underestimated nor overestimated. The accuracy of the information does not mean it needs to be precise in all dimensions. The accuracy of the information implies that the company has internal controls in place to avoid mistakes and false claims. If estimates are provided, this shall be clearly stated.[224]

That the information in the sustainability report must be *comparable* means it can be compared with corresponding information from the company in earlier periods and with information from other companies, in particular those with similar activities or operating within the same industry.[225] Furthermore, the fact that it must be *verifiable* means that various knowledgeable and independent observers could reach a consensus, although not necessarily complete agreement, that a particular depiction is a faithful representation.[226] Verifiability creates important confidence that the information given in the report is correct.

Finally, the *understandability* of the information means it must be clear and concise.[227] Information that is not specific to the company in question should be avoided. Clear and simple language must be used. The information should be presented in a coherent way so you can understand how different parts of the report are connected.

The five requirements should be understood in the context of the ideal image of sustainable business, described in Chapter 13. The sustainability report, according to CSRD, is intended to help the users of the report assess if and to what extent companies live up to this ideal image. The report should help readers decide on how they want to act in relation to the company, such as whether they want to own shares in the company, work or stop working for the company, criticise or praise the company, and so on. To enable this, companies must live up to this ideal image in how the company presents its own business. A company that provides misleading information does not respect the dignity of its readers. This may seem pompous, but that is what it is all about. To respect the right of others to dignity, companies must take other people's lives seriously – respect them – and allow them to decide for themselves how they want to live their lives, set their goals and values and live by them. Lying to a person is like undermining the information base on which people try to live a free life. That is the primary reason lying is morally reprehensible.[228] Of course, the five requirements for the quality of the sustainability report go further than not lying, but it is basically the same moral foundation on which the requirements stand. Companies must not present themselves as either better or worse than they actually are because anything else violates the reader's dignity.

This is a point where the corporate values discussed in Chapter 6 may become relevant. Many companies are struggling with how transparent they should be and want to look at what their competitors do. The worry is, presumably, that no company wants to look worse than its competitors for fear of negative stakeholder reactions. These are important questions, of course, but companies having those concerns should

224. *See*, e.g., QC 9.
225. *See*, e.g., QC 10.
226. *See*, e.g., QC 14.
227. *See*, e.g., QC 16.
228. Dworkin, Justice for the Hedgehogs, Harvard University Press, 2011, p. 305.

also ask themselves what they should report if they would stay 100% true to their corporate values. Sometimes, being totally honest is perceived as a sign of integrity, which may improve the company's image.

16.2 DOUBLE MATERIALITY AS THE BASIS OF THE SUSTAINABILITY REPORT

Section 3 of ESRS 1 sets out the basic perspectives and methodologies to be used to assess the information to be disclosed by the company in the sustainability report. It is about which stakeholders the information should be aimed at, that the information must be material, and that materiality must be assessed from two perspectives.

16.2.1 Stakeholders in the Sustainability Report

Through the sustainability report, companies show how and to what extent they act with due diligence in relation to the stakeholders significantly affected by the company's activities. There are two primary categories of stakeholders:

(1) persons and organisations whose interests are affected, positively or negatively, by the company's activities; and
(2) users of the sustainability report, such as investors, lenders, creditors, as well as societal actors such as trade unions, NGOs, governments and academics.[229]

Investors have an interest in assessing the company's profitability, for example, future cash flows and more. Sustainability matters such as climate change, inequality, and more can affect a company's financial performance. Investors, therefore, have an interest in understanding how sustainability factors affect the company. In addition, investors may have an interest in understanding how the company affects sustainability matters, not least if the investors want to make sustainable investments. But other actors also have an interest in this latter information. It can be not only employees considering whether they want to take a job with the company but also non-governmental organisations, the media and others considering whether they want to hold the company accountable for its impact or because it does not take advantage of opportunities in sustainability matters. These latter actors can then be assumed to act on behalf of those who are adversely affected by the company's activities.

Of course, there are many kinds of investors, consumers, employees, etc., which may have different levels of understanding, concern for sustainability matters, etc. This challenge is discussed below as part of the legal interpretation of the concept of materiality in section 16.2.6.

229. *See* data point 22 in ESRS 1.

16.2.2 Double Materiality

The two main categories of stakeholders for the sustainability report shape the perspectives to be applied in the sustainability report, namely both how the company affects its business environment and how the outside world affects the company from a sustainability perspective.

The ESRS specify what information the company must disclose about its material impacts, risks and opportunities. 'Impact' refers to the positive and negative sustainability-related impacts that are connected with the company's business. Instead, 'risks and opportunities' refers to the company's sustainability-related financial risks and opportunities. It is, therefore, always a question of a description of materiality in this dual perspective, and therefore, the concept of 'double materiality' is fundamental.[230]

The requirement for reporting double materiality is based on the same normative basis as the quality requirements in the sustainability report, described in the previous section. Companies must provide information that allows people to assess how they want to act in relation to the company. Information about the financial impact of sustainability factors is important for anyone with a financial interest in the company or who is considering investments in the company. The impacting factors are important for all those who are otherwise affected by the company's operations from a sustainability perspective.

16.2.3 Materiality Analysis

Through the ESRS, the European Commission has sought to strike a balance between, on the one hand, obtaining complete information from companies and, on the other hand, not overburdening companies in terms of resources. This balance is first expressed in the requirement that only information deemed *material* should be disclosed in the sustainability report. The materiality assessment must then be made both from the perspective of impact and from the perspective of opportunities and risks. It is possible for a sustainability matter to be considered non-material from one perspective but material from the other.

Accordingly, companies shall disclose information in the sustainability report under the ESRS based on an analysis of the materiality of the company's impacts, risks and opportunities in relation to sustainability matters, except for information under ESRS 2, where all information must be disclosed.[231] Appendix A to ESRS 1 lists the areas and sub-areas into which sustainability matters in the different ESRS are divided, which can be found in Annex 1 in this book. The list is only a support and does not replace the company's responsibility to make its own analysis.

Section 3.2 of ESRS 1 describes a step-by-step decision-making approach to assessing which information to include in the sustainability report:

230. *See* data point 14 in ESRS 1.
231. Data point 29 in ESRS 1.

(1) Assess whether a sustainability matter in a particular subject-specific standard or any of the subtopics described in Appendix A to ESRS 1[232] is material:
   (a) If no sustainability matter is deemed material in the standard, no information under this standard needs to be disclosed. However, the company may voluntarily disclose the conclusion of its materiality analysis.[233]
   (b) If there is a sustainability matter deemed to be material in the standard, information under the disclosure requirements of the relevant standard shall be provided, with possible exceptions under the continued process below.[234]
(2) Assess what information about policies, activities and goals in the current sustainability standard should be provided:
   (a) If the company has adopted a policy, carried out activities or has set targets, information under the disclosure requirements must be disclosed in the financial statements.
   (b) If the company has not adopted a policy, has not carried out activities or has not set targets, information need not be provided, but then the company must provide information that this is the case. The company may then voluntarily provide information on when policies, activities and goals are deemed in place.[235]
(3) Assess what information on metrics in the relevant sustainability standard should be provided:
   (a) If the information in a disclosure requirement regarding metrics is deemed material, information about metrics must be provided.
   (b) If, however, information in a specific data point within a disclosure requirement is not deemed material and if the entity determines that the information need not be disclosed to fulfil the purpose of the disclosure requirement, information under that specific data point need not be disclosed.[236]
(4) Assess what information should be disclosed according to the disclosure requirements that the company will apply according to the process above. The applicable information in the disclosure requirement shall be disclosed if the entity considers it relevant depending on:
   (a) the significance of the information in relation to the issue that the information is intended to highlight or explain, or
   (b) the ability of information to meet the needs of stakeholders to make decisions.[237]

In this way, some flexibility is created for companies, depending on where they are in their sustainability work. The company only needs to disclose information about

232. *See* annex 2 of this book.
233. Data point 32 in ESRS 1.
234. Data point 30 in ESRS 1.
235. Data point 33 in ESRS 1.
236. Data point 34 in ESRS 1.
237. Data point 31 in ESRS 1.

impacts, risks and opportunities linked to the sustainability matters that are material. For the sustainability matters that are material, the companies that have not implemented measures to address the sustainability matter need not report any measures either. However, information needs to be provided that no measures have been taken, which, of course, means that the company reports it does not meet the ideal image for sustainable business as expressed in the CSRD and ESRS.

16.2.4 Impact Materiality

A sustainability matter is material from an impact perspective if it pertains to the company's material, actual or potential, positive or negative impacts on people or the environment over the short, medium or long term.[238] A distinction must be made between actual and potential material adverse effects. An *actual* adverse impact shall be assessed based on its severity. A *potential* adverse impact shall be assessed based on its severity and likelihood of the adverse impact occurring. The severity is assessed based on scale, scope, and whether the negative impact is remediable or not.[239] In the case of a potential negative human rights impact, the severity of the impact takes precedence over its likelihood.[240]

Examples of impacts that can be material are greenhouse gas emissions, increased inequality, contributions to societal instability through corruption, and so on. Companies shall also report the material impact that the company can inflict on its surroundings by dealing with sustainability matters. If a company discontinues production based on fossil fuels, it can harm social sustainability factors, for example, through redundancies. In that case, this must be stated in the information.[241]

It is easy to focus too strictly on negative impact but it should not be forgotten that the company is also obliged to report potential positive impacts on sustainability matters. This clearly shows how both the due diligence norm and the norm of positive contribution are in play in the disclosure requirements. The obligation to report on negative material impact obviously follows from the due diligence norm. The obligation to report on actual and potential material *positive* impact follows from the norm of positive contribution.

This is perhaps most clear when it comes to *potential* positive impact. Why report that? Why not report only on the *actual* positive impact? Well, if a company has an opportunity to generate a positive impact on the environment, for example, but does not take advantage of this opportunity, that would often be a violation of the norm of positive contribution. This is why it should also be reported.

16.2.5 Financial Materiality

The information regarding financial materiality is primarily aimed at investors, lenders and others with financial interests in the company, for whom the information is

238. Data point 43 in ESRS 1.
239. Data point 45 in ESRS 1.
240. Data point 45 in ESRS 1.
241. *See* section 3.6 in ESRS 1.

relevant in addition to the information stated in the financial reporting.[242] The information shall be viewed as material if omitting, misstating or obscuring that information could reasonably be expected to influence decisions that primary users of general-purpose financial reports make on the basis of the company's sustainability report.

Financial materiality refers to the impact of sustainability matters on the company's development, financial position, financial performance, cash flows, access to finance or cost of capital over the short, medium or long term. Financially material factors may also be those that affect the company indirectly, for example, by affecting the company's subcontractors or other business partners.[243]

Examples of issues that could be financially material are the lack of access to raw materials or other inputs due to climate change or environmental degradation, a shortage of a skilled workforce, production or supply uncertainties linked to countries with high levels of corruption, and so on. In this context, the TCFD framework for risk analysis can be used.[244]

16.2.6 The Concept of Materiality

When conducting the double materiality analysis, it is easy to fall into one of two traps. Falling into the first trap means landing in an analysis where most factors in the ESRS are deemed material. Falling into the other trap means deciding, for practical purposes, that the company should focus and report on the areas which *the company* thinks are material. Both approaches are wrong, and to understand why, it is necessary to interpret the concept of materiality.

Although the ESRS 1 standard provides some guidance on how the concept of materiality should be interpreted, it is not a complete guide. In fact, it could be argued that the legislator has done a poor job in this area. In Chapter 8 on SFDR, reference was made to the important distinction between *criterial* and *interpretive* concepts; a distinction important to interpret the concepts of sustainable investments in SFDR and the EU taxonomy. People can communicate based on criterial concepts because they agree on the criteria underlying the concept. Concepts such as 'chair', 'tree', 'sky' and 'car' are examples of such concepts. When we say that a glass is 'full' of water, that it is a 'long' road to the city or that a box is 'heavy', we are also using criterial concepts, even though what is heavy may differ between a strong and a weak person. When using criterial concepts, we typically imply some reference to the empirical reality.

People can also communicate based on interpretive concepts, but now in a different way. In Chapter 8, the concept of 'courtesy' was used as an example. When people discuss whether a decision was 'just', if a piece of music is 'beautiful' or if a book is 'bad literature', interpretive concepts are used. Interpretive concepts are typically concepts implying some sort of values. Legal concepts such as 'misleading marketing' and 'unfair business practices' are obviously in this category.

242. Data point 48 in ESRS 1.
243. Data point 49 in ESRS 1.
244. *See* Chapter 15.

What about the concept of 'materiality' in the ESRS? It would be easy to interpret this as a criterial concept, but that would be a mistake. The concept is clearly interpretive and must, therefore, be interpreted on the basis of the moral principles that underpin sustainability law in general.[245]

A good way to approach the materiality concept is to think about promises. Why is it (often) morally bad to break a promise? In Chapter 5, a distinction was made between the moral obligation to help and not to harm others. I can harm others by treating my own interests as more important than others. When I make a promise, I provide the promisee with information based on which she can exercise the responsibility for her own life. If I lie and therefore break the promise, I have corrupted the base of information through which the promisee exercises her right to live a life of equality and freedom. Promise breaking is a form of harming others.[246]

A sustainability matter should be considered to be material if *not* disclosing this information would be tantamount to lying in this way. This is the case when *not* disclosing the information can be assumed to make the stakeholders act in a way in which though would not have done had the information been disclosed. Not disclosing information can be as bad as lying.

These moral considerations are, to make a comparison, clearly expressed in the (interpretive) concept of *misleading commercial practices* under directive 2005/28/EC concerning unfair business-to-consumer practices (UCPD). According to Article 5 of the directive, unfair commercial business practices shall be prohibited. A commercial practice shall, according to Article 5.2, be unfair if it is contrary to the requirements of professional diligence and it materially distorts or is likely to materially distort the economic behaviour of the receiver of marketing with regard to the product. Behind the concept, 'economic behaviour' is nothing fancier than the purchase of the marketed product. An example of an unfair commercial business practice is *misleading* marketing communication. According to Article 7, *omitting* information can also make marketing misleading. Article 7.1 states that a commercial practice shall be regarded as misleading if it *omits material information* that the average consumer needs to make an informed transactional decision and thereby *causes or is likely to cause* the average *consumer to take a transactional decision that he would not have taken otherwise.*

I will return to the concept of 'average consumer' below since that concept too is useful in this context. Here, the clear parallel between this way of describing a misleading market practice and the criterion set out in data point 48 of ESRS 1 for assessing financial materiality should be pointed out. According to that data point, the information is financially material if its disclosure is likely to *influence the decision of the people acting based on the financial information*. In other words, the information is material if the person reading the sustainability report can be assumed to act in a different way if information about the sustainability matter is provided compared to if

245. *See* the introduction on the interpretivist theory of law on which the book is based. A legal positivist or representative of law and economics would, in principle, regard the concept of materiality not as an interpretive concept, but as an criterial one. An interpretation of the concept would then be about finding a point on a scale in the empirical reality where an impact should be considered significant. It is claimed here that this would be a futile undertaking.

246. Dworkin, R., Justice for the Hedgehogs, Harvard University Press, 2011, p. 305.

the information is not provided. Note that the information should not be disclosed because it is material. It is because, applying the moral reasoning above, the information *should* be disclosed that it is material. It should be disclosed because disclosure is the option that best respects the investor's dignity.

The example relates to financial materiality. However, the same reasoning should be applied to the assessment of impact materiality. It is then, again, a question of assessing whether a reader of the sustainability report would act differently if information about a certain sustainability matter is disclosed compared to if it is not disclosed. The alternative action can be a variety of actions, such as:

- A consumer who chooses to buy a certain item from another company instead.
- A person in a recruitment process who chooses not to take a job with the company.
- A nearby resident who chooses to sue the company linked to environmental degradation.
- An NGO that campaigns for the company to stop certain harmful activities.

If different actions can be assumed to be taken in the examples above, depending on whether sustainability information is disclosed or not, that information should be viewed as material.

An obvious challenge here is that consumers are different in their preferences, understanding of sustainability, etc. So are potential employees, residents and NGOs. When, for example, assessing whether information about greenhouse gas emissions is material from a consumer perspective, which consumer are we talking about? Are we talking about a climate activist with in-depth knowledge about climate change or a much less informed consumer? The ESRS provide no answer or guidance, which is a clear weakness. But here is where the reference to the concept of 'average consumer' in the UCPD becomes relevant. This concept was first developed by the European Court of Justice and later implemented in UCPD. The concept is further explained in section 18 of the preamble to UCPD. The average consumer is a consumer 'who is reasonably well-informed and reasonably observant and circumspect, taking into account social, cultural and linguistic'. This approach should, arguably, be applied when assessing materiality from the perspective of various stakeholders, where the concept of 'average consumer' is expanded to 'average stakeholder'. The assessment would then have to be made, considering, for example, the 'average investor', the 'average consumer', the 'average employee' and so on. Hopefully, further guidance will be provided in the future, but it would be surprising if the approach suggested here is not adopted.

Summing up the above, a sustainability matter is thus material if omitting information about the matter would likely affect the decision-making of the average stakeholder, where consideration needs to be taken, of course, of the different categories of stakeholders. Based on this, a good way to carry out the materiality assessment would be to follow the following four steps:

(1) Identify the categories of stakeholder(s) to whom the information could be material, in that their actions could change if the information were disclosed compared to if it were not.
(2) Assess, in relation to each stakeholder category, the actions or decisions that the disclosure of the information could affect.
(3) Assess, for each stakeholder category and for each action, if disclosing the information would be likely to make the average stakeholder in the category choose another course of action than if it is not disclosed.
(4) If the assessment under (3) is, for any relevant stakeholder category, that the disclosure of the information would change the average stakeholder's course of action in relation to the company, the information should be viewed as material.

Of course, it will always be a question of an overall assessment where the different steps above overlap. However, for the sake of analysis and clarity, it may be a good idea to use the process above or a similar one to make the materiality assessment.

16.3 VALUE CHAIN INFORMATION

In many companies, significant parts of value creation do not take place directly by the company or its group companies but in the so-called value chain, i.e., by suppliers, subcontractors and distributors of the company's goods and services as well as customers. When companies report on material risks, opportunities and their impact on sustainability matters, the information must include information related to the value chain.[247] Gathering this information is part of the due diligence process that companies are expected to implement and follow.

Information need not be provided on every actor in the value chain. Instead, only the essential information needs to be included.[248] Information shall be disclosed if necessary to enable stakeholders in the sustainability report to understand the entity's material impacts, risks and opportunities or to provide information that meets the general quality requirements.[249] This means, referring to the analysis of the materality concept above, that information should be provided if it can be assumed that disclosing the information could alter the stakeholders' actions in relation to the company compared to if the information is not disclosed.

16.4 TIME HORIZONS

The reporting period for the company's sustainability report shall be consistent with that of its financial statements.[250] But the report should take the form of a story that

247. Data point 63 in ESRS 1.
248. Data point 64 in ESRS 1.
249. Data point 65 in ESRS 1.
250. Data point 73 in ESRS 1.

describes the company's past, present and future from a sustainability perspective in an understandable whole. The company must have a clear base year, with which data and other parameter comparisons can be made in later years.[251] Furthermore, reporting must be based on short, medium and long term. *Short term* refers to the same period as in the financial report. *Medium term* refers to the period from the end of the short period and four years thereafter (i.e., a five-year perspective). *Long term* refers to a period longer than five years.[252] However, the company may deviate from the medium- and long-term definitions if those definitions result in non-relevant information being disclosed because the company uses different time horizons to identify and manage material impacts, risks and opportunities or to set targets.[253] In that case, the company shall specify which time horizons are applied and why.[254]

There are probably several reasons why reporting should take place with different time horizons. One of the most important is to avoid what is sometimes called *the tragedy of the horizon*, which is a variant of the tragedy of the commons. The tragedy of the horizon stems from the fact that when taking measures to increase sustainability, the costs are borne now in the short term, while the effects will come in the long term.[255] Many companies, executives and investors take a short-term perspective, exemplified by quarterly financial reporting and compensation systems based on annual performance.

This discourages the incentives to plan and operate in the long term, which is often necessary to improve sustainability factors such as climate change and inequality. It also creates a risk of what can be called a lack of integrity, namely, if the company claims to have long-term plans for improved sustainability but runs the company with a short-term perspective, thus making it impossible to meet the long-term goals. The purpose of the sustainability report is, to a large extent, to give users a picture of the 'character' of the company, which includes consistency in decision-making and in words and deeds.[256] Requiring companies to describe in their sustainability reports their short-, medium- and long-term plans and actions that make it possible to assess precisely this character and, thus, the extent to which, from this perspective, the company engages in sustainable activities in accordance with the due diligence norm.

16.5 STRUCTURE OF THE SUSTAINABILITY REPORT AND RELATION TO OTHER INFORMATION

The sustainability report shall be included in the company's management report but may also be published as a separate document. The report shall follow the structure set out in Appendix D of ESRS 1:

251. Section 6.3 in ESRS 1.
252. Data point 77 in ESRS 1.
253. Data point 80 in ESRS 1.
254. Data point 9 in ESRS 2.
255. Schoenmaker, D., and Schramade, W., Principles of Sustainable Finance, Oxford University Press, 2019, section 90.
256. *See* section 5.5.

Part of Sustainability Reporting	*Relevant Accounting Standard*	*Title of the Standard*
1. General information	ESRS 2	General disclosures
2. Environmental information	ESRS E1	Climate change
	ESRS E2	Pollution
	ESRS E3	Water and marine resources
	ESRS E4	Biodiversity and ecosystems
	ESRS E5	Resource use and circular economy
3. Social information	ESRS S1	Own workforce
	ESRS S2	Workers in the value chain
	ESRS S3	Affected communities
	ESRS S4	Consumers and end-users
4. Governance information	ESRS G1	Business conduct

Appendix F to ESRS 1 provides an example of how the sustainability report can be structured. The company may include disclosures and information required by local legislation and other accounting standards – such as GRI standards – in the sustainability report as long as the quality requirements described in section 16.1 are met.[257]

To avoid having to report information about the same thing in several places, the company may make references in the sustainability report to, for example, other parts of the report, to the financial report, and to separate management reports, as long as the information referred to is published at the same time and meets the same quality requirements as the sustainability report.[258]

Each part of the sustainability report is part of a larger whole, where the whole must describe how the company meets the norms of positive contribution and due diligence and thus whether and to what extent a sustainable business is conducted. The sustainability report, in turn, is part of a whole, which also includes other reporting from the company, primarily the financial report. Section 9.2 of ESRS 1, therefore, requires putting information in the sustainability report into context and helping the reader understand how the information presented is related to other parts of the sustainability report and to the financial information. For example, the company may need to explain what effects a presented sustainability strategy will have on the company's financial performance, how the use of natural resources or changes in the supply chain will change the company's impacts, risks and opportunities, production costs, and so on.[259] Basically, it is about meeting the quality requirements presented in section 16.1, so it is possible for the reader to decide on the basis of clear and understandable information what activities or measures should be taken because of the information.

257. Data point 113 in ESRS 1.
258. *See* section 9.1 in ESRS 1.
259. Data point 122 in ESRS 1.

16.6 TRANSITIONAL PROVISIONS

Over time, the European Commission will adopt several ESRS standards, which means that companies may initially have to rely on company-specific disclosures instead of ESRS standards. For example, companies can then use GRI standards. Section 10.1 of ESRS 1 states that companies, in their first three CSRD sustainability reports, may use such other standards.

Furthermore, it can be challenging for companies to access all the information on actors in the supply chain required to meet the different accounting standards. Companies may, therefore, in the first three sustainability reports according to CSRD, waive the requirements, provided that the company also explains what efforts have been made to gain access to relevant information, the reasons why relevant information has not been obtained, and the company's plans to access relevant information in the future.[260] During the first year, the company need not present comparable information.[261] Appendix C of ESRS 1 sets out further possibilities for companies to only gradually comply with certain disclosure requirements.

260. Data point 132 in ESRS 1.
261. Data point 136 in ESRS 1.

CHAPTER 17

Business Model, Strategy and Governance in Sustainable Business (ESRS 2)

In Chapter 6, the importance of setting the 'ground rules of the game' - the corporate purpose and values - was discussed. An important part of the exercise is to free oneself from the misleading shareholder-stakeholder discussion and instead start to focus on what, along with Jim Collins and Jimmy Porras, was called the 'core ideology' of the company. The purpose of the business answers, on a quite general level, what fundamental customer value is, which creates the company's *raison d'être*. The values are the basic norms and principles to be followed when pursuing this purpose.

The next building blocks of a sustainable business - referring to the illustration in Chapter 13 about the EU's ideal image - are the company's business model, strategy and governance structure. Those building blocks are also, along with the company's identification and management of its material impact, risk and opportunities, the subject of the ESRS 2 standard. This standard sets out a number of disclosure requirements common to all entities, no matter the outcome of their materiality analyses. To begin with, companies must provide information on the basics of preparing the sustainability report and on some specific issues such as time horizons.[262] But the rest is, to return to the framework of the book, about a continued description of the most fundamental features of the company's 'character', i.e., its institutional structure and processes. It is about how the company is organised to meet the norms of positive contribution and due diligence norm.

17.1 THE COMPANY'S BUSINESS MODEL AND STRATEGY

The ESRS 2 standard is structured to follow the TCFD structure described in section 15.3: Governance, Strategy, Risk Management, Metric and Targets. While it is good to have this alignment, it still neither makes sense to begin with governance nor with

262. *See* Disclosure Requirement BP-1 and BP-2 in ESRS 2.

strategy. Every business starts with a business model. Based on the business model, the company can build a strategy on how to win customers in competition on the market. How the company is governed should be based on business model and strategy. Strategy cannot come first. Therefore, even though the ESRS 2 standard starts with governance, this book starts with the business model.

17.1.1 Business Model

The company's business model and strategy determine the formal and informal rules of the game that govern the actions and results of companies. Therefore, these must be described in the sustainability report.

The concept of a business model is in ESRS 2 defined as a system of transforming inputs through its activities into outputs and outcomes that aim to fulfil the company's strategic objectives and create value over the short, medium and long term. The requirements for how the business model should be described are brief.[263] The description shall include:

- the company's inputs and its approach to gathering, developing and securing those inputs;
- the company's outputs and outcomes in terms of current and expected benefits for customers, investors and other stakeholders; and
- the main features of its upstream and downstream value chain and the undertaking's position in its value chain, including a description of the main business actors (such as key suppliers, customers, distribution channels and end-users) and their relationship to the undertaking.

The application requirements in Appendix A of ESRS 2 provide more detailed requirements. The description of the business model shall also consider:

- the company's key activities, resources, distribution channels and customer segments;
- the company's key business relationships and their key characteristics, including relationships with customers and suppliers;
- the cost structure and revenue of its business segments, in line with IFRS 8 disclosure requirements in the financial statement, where applicable; and
- the potential impacts, risks and opportunities in its significant sectors.[264]

A company or group of companies can have several business models.

One of the most common tools for developing or describing business models is the so-called business model canvas.[265] The use of this tool will capture most of the

263. Data point 42 in ESRS 2.
264. AR 14 in Appendix B to ESRS 2.
265. Osterwalder, A. and Pigneur, Y., Business Model Generation: A Handbook for Visionaries, Game Changers and Challengers, John Wiley & Sons, 2010.

business model description requirements under ESRS 2. The image below gives an overview of the different parts of the tool:

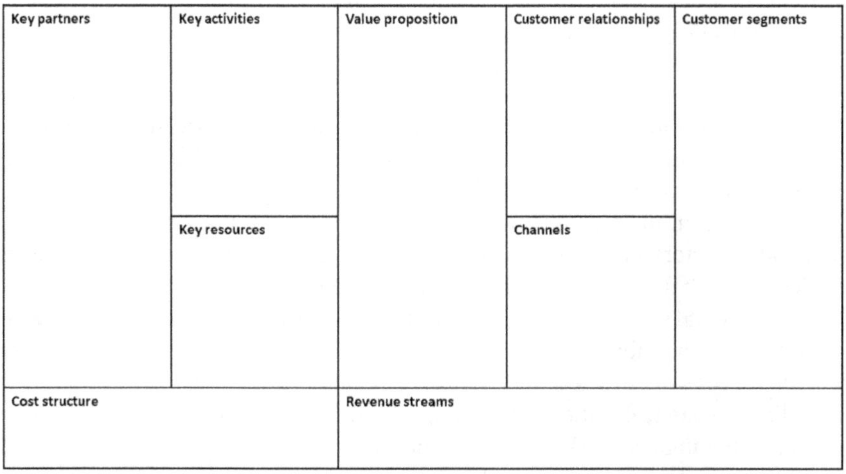

The starting point of the canvas – in the middle – is the *value proposition*. For a customer to want to pay for what the company offers, it must create value for the customer. The value proposition describes what that value is. Referring to the discussion about corporate purpose in Chapter 6, the value proposition could be described as the first high-level answer to how the corporate purpose is fulfilled.

For a company that sells mobile phones, the phones are not the value proposition, but it is the ability to communicate, obtain information, etc. For a company that sells fossil-free steel, the steel is not the value proposition but the opportunity steel gives companies in, for example, the automotive sector, to build vehicles with lower carbon dioxide emissions. For a consulting company in the IT industry, it is the opportunity that the customer gets, for example, to develop software that supports the company's own customer offerings, which is the value proposition. For a social media company, there are often two value propositions, as such companies often operate in two markets – on the one hand, the value for end users to create and share content with each other and the value for advertisers to market their goods and services to end users. For a bank, the value proposition is not, for example, mortgages, but enabling consumers to live their lives in the places where they want to live.

It is important to clarify what the value proposition is because it is often this that largely, together with the purpose and values, establishes the core of the company as an institution, as a set of formal and informal rules that generate results that can be more or less sustainable from a moral perspective. Here, the company shows in more detail how it meets the norm of positive contribution. Furthermore, it is often in the formulation of the value proposition that the opportunity to transition from an unsustainable to a sustainable business lies, as the example of the transition to fossil-free steel shows.

The left-hand side of the tool describes the company's input side. The value proposition is created through several key activities, which include several key resources. Many of these key resources are provided by key providers. It is useful to start from the key resources, often described as different forms of capital – financial capital, physical capital (machines, factories, computers, premises, etc.), intellectual capital (knowledge, intellectual property, skills, etc.), human capital (employees and consultants). In the context of sustainability, it has become more common to also include natural capital, i.e., 'services' provided by nature, and social capital, such as stable social institutions.[266] These key resources are then used to create the value proposition through several key activities.

A large part of a company's material impact and the financial impact of sustainability factors on the company is precisely about the key resources and the activities in which they are used. This is largely where the decoupling between growth and environmental impacts, described in section 1.5, needs to take place. This is where carbon dioxide emissions are generated, people develop or get burned out, water resources are consumed or regenerated, gender equality is increased or decreased, and so on. Climate change or other factors can, in turn, affect the company's access to key assets, affecting financial risks and performance.

Often, important parts of the value proposition are not produced by the company itself but by its suppliers on one or more levels. This is the upstream value chain. From a sustainability perspective, there is no difference here. A climate threat to a supplier's access to critical resources equals a threat to the purchasing company. Using forced labour to produce what is supplied is the same as the use of forced labour since the value proposition is partly produced through forced labour.

The right-hand side of the tool focuses on the company's output side and the downstream value chain. Customer relationships refer to the nature of the company's customer relationships, whether it involves many contracts with more or less anonymous consumers, a few contracts in long-term customer relationships or some other variant. The channels are about how the value proposition is distributed to customers. An e-retailer is likely to use some type of distribution solution. A company that delivers streamed music distributes through an app. A consulting firm often delivers through verbal or written communication.

The company's customers can often be divided into different segments. Examples of such segments can be consumers and enterprises, consumers in different age categories, enterprises in different industries, and so on. Segmentation is typically closely related to the value proposition, which can be varied to adapt to the needs of different customer groups.

A company's impact on sustainability factors, as well as their financial impact on the company, is, of course, also largely on the company's output side. Different forms of distribution can have different environmental impacts. The company may or may not respect the privacy of its customers depending on how their personal data is

266. *See, e.g.*, IIRC (International Integrated Reporting Council) (2013), The International <IR> framework.

processed, how the company's services are marketed, what rights consumers get, and so on.

The bottom part of the tool is an economical reflection of the upper part. The key suppliers, key assets and activities are represented by the cost side of the income statement. Customers and customer relationships are represented by the revenue side.

The description above also illustrates how the tool makes it possible to identify many of the company's key stakeholders. These are typically closely associated with the business model as such. In addition to the fact that the description of the business model enables the dialogue with relevant stakeholders that the sustainable company is expected to have, it is often possible to discern with that description whether the company conducts a sustainable business or not. A company that bases its profitability (the share of costs in revenue) on the use of fossil fuels, precarious workers, etc., will, once the analysis is complete, rarely be considered a sustainable company. This can, of course, create an interest for the company not to be overly clear in the description of its business model. However, it follows from the quality requirements of the report, described in section 16.1, that embellishments or vague descriptions are not allowed.

17.1.2 Corporate Strategy

As already said, a company's strategy cannot be described without first describing its business model. The business model describes how companies create and capture value. However, the business model does not describe how the company will succeed, especially in a market where other companies compete for the same customers. This is instead done in the strategy.

According to ESRS 2, the description of the company's strategy should include several elements. The requirements are limited to those parts of the strategy that relate to or affect sustainability matters.[267] However, it seems difficult to draw a line here as, in most cases, there are probably very few parts of the strategy that are not relevant to sustainability matters. The description of the strategy shall include:

(i) a description of the:
   - significant groups of products and/or services supplied;
   - significant markets and/or customer segments to which the company supplies;
   - the number of employees in different geographical regions; and
   - products and/or services that, where applicable, are banned in various markets;

(ii) a breakdown of the company's total revenues, as in the financial statements, linked to the sectors identified in various ESRS standards. Here, the IFRS 8 standard must be followed;

(iii) a list of the other ESRS sectors in which the company engages in significant activities in addition to those set out above;

267. Data point 38 in ESRS 2.

(iv) a statement, where relevant and, if so, including revenue data, if the company is engaged in:
- the fossil fuel sector;
- production of chemicals;
- controversial weapons; and/or
- cultivation and production of tobacco;

(v) the company's sustainability-related goals related to the company's products and services, customer categories, geographies and stakeholder relations;

(vi) an assessment of its current significant products and/or services, and significant markets and customer groups, in relation to its sustainability-related goals; and

(vii) the elements of the company's strategy that relate to or impact sustainability matters, including the main challenges ahead and critical solutions or projects to be put in place when relevant for sustainability reporting.[268]

As seen, the reporting requirements are considerably more extensive than the requirements for the business model, and it is difficult to get an overview of what is actually to be reported. It is important to see the requirements in context and what they are ultimately aimed at. To understand this, it is appropriate to briefly address the area of business strategy.

17.1.2.1 Bad and Good Strategies

The field of business strategy is flooded with models, tools, and good advice. It is, to say the least, unclear what the Commission actually means by corporate strategy. From the perspective of the information to be provided under ESRS 2, it seems as if the Commission equates strategy with a set of sustainability-related goals tied to the company's products and services. This, it must be said, is a very weak definition and invites the creation of strategies, which one of the leading academics in the field – Richard Rumelt – has characterised as the template for creating *bad* strategies.[269] The template follows the pattern:

- **Vision**. A description of what the company's bright future looks like.
- **Mission**. A politically correct statement about the company's ultimate purpose, for example in terms of innovation, human development or sustainability are popular examples.
- **The values**. A description of the company's so-called core values, where concepts such as integrity and respect are common.
- **Strategies**. A number of ambitious goals, which are, however, called strategies.

268. Data point 40 in ESRS 2.
269. Rumelt, R., Good Strategy, Bad Strategy, Profile Books Ltd, 2013.

Rumelt argues that bad strategies are characterised by the fact that they often fail to describe the challenges that the company faces and that the strategy is intended to solve. Furthermore, goals are often confused with strategy. Goals are important, but strategy is about the plan for how to meet the goals, considering the challenges that the company faces. A bad strategy is also characterised by the goals being too loosely written and often far too many. Finally, bad strategies are characterised by too much 'fluff' - often quite meaningless concepts such as customer focus, quality focus, etc., which become meaningless because they are so obvious that they are hardly good enough to base strategies on.

A good strategy, Rumelt says, is characterised by three things:

(i) **A diagnosis**. A description of the main challenges that the company faces in meeting its set goals. It can be about too high costs, too poor presence in certain markets, competitors, etc.
(ii) **A guiding policy**. A comprehensive approach to managing and preferably overcoming the identified challenges.
(iii) **Coordinated activities**. Steps, activities, etc., that coherently implement the guiding policy.

Another of the leading thinkers in business strategy is Michael Porter, who is not least known for his description of how a company needs to analyse its market position based on five market forces: customers' bargaining power, suppliers' bargaining power, substitutes for the product or service, competition from new entrants and competition between existing players.[270]

In his book *Competitive Strategy*, Porter distinguished between three basic strategies:

(i) **Low-cost strategies**. The company creates more value for its customers than its competitors by maintaining lower costs and, thus, prices.
(ii) **Differentiation strategies**. The company creates more value for customers through unique value propositions.
(iii) **Focus strategies**. The company uses a differentiation strategy that is focused on, for example, certain customer segments.

In a number of articles and books, Porter has further developed these ideas, not least in a classic article in the *Harvard Business Review* from 1996 entitled 'What is strategy?' In the article, Porter provides three answers to that question. The essence of a strategy is to *do something different from the competition*, which customers consider more valuable. Strategy is also about *making trade-offs*. For example, it is typically difficult to have a low-cost and differentiation strategy at the same time. What often makes a strategy difficult for competitors to imitate is that the company has made tough choices which others shy away from making. Finally, a strategy is about *establishing a system of mutually supportive activities*. IKEA's combination of do-it-yourself products,

270. Porter, M., Competitive Strategy, Free Press 1980.

large stores in areas with not very high rents, free parking and so on are often cited as examples of this.

17.1.2.2 Business Strategy and Sustainability Strategy

Rumelt and Porter are just two of a plethora of business strategy thinkers, but their theories are arguably more influential than most others. Both point to the importance of an analysis of the current situation, of the company's position and challenges. Both point to the importance of choosing a path and opting out of other paths based on actual position and actual challenges. Both point to the importance of setting up a system of activities that reinforce each other, not least because this makes a strategy difficult to imitate for others. None point to the importance of vision, mission and core values for the strategy.

The extensive list of requirements for how the strategy should be described should be interpreted according to its purpose. The purpose is indirectly stated in the SBM-3 disclosure requirement, where the company must report its significant impact, risks and opportunities linked to sustainability matters and how these originate in and trigger adjustments to the company's business model and strategy.[271] Although sustainability matters have received growing focus in many companies, they have not traditionally been the focus of business strategy. Companies are expected to change this according to the ideal image of sustainable business. In the presentation of the strategy, companies are required to provide information to readers on a number of key issues:

- If the company has a strategy, how is it affected by sustainability matters, and what does it mean for the company's impact on sustainability matters (double materiality)?
- Has the company adapted its strategy based on the double materiality analysis of sustainability matters?
- Does it seem likely, given the company's market position, that the company will succeed in its sustainability-adapted strategy?

This is about showing the 'character' of the company in a moral sense. Not setting sustainability-related targets at all in a business with a clear external impact is not in line with the EU's ideal image, nor is setting fluffy goals.

With Rumelt, a diagnosis should be made where the challenges posed by sustainability matters are identified and analysed. A suitable starting point is the company's existing business strategy.

A simple example would be a company with an explicit low-cost strategy. Such a strategy can be implemented in different ways, but there is, of course, a risk that such a company, for example, makes purchases based on price without considering, for

271. Data points 46 and 47 in ESRS 2.

example, sustainability matters, which means that the company generates externalities. In addition, the company may be more vulnerable to cost shocks caused by sustainability matters than other companies. Thus, in order to achieve certain sustainability goals, the company may need to adapt its strategy. Depending on the company's position, the general competitive pressure, and so on, this can be a major challenge that the company needs to face. For example, the challenge could be met by buying more expensive but fewer products, which would be part of a transition to a circular business model.

Another example is companies with an explicit differentiation strategy. Perhaps the company's uniqueness is based on a strong customer service function, which may not be sustainable from a social sustainability perspective. Perhaps uniqueness is instead based on access to materials, raw materials or other things which may not be used in a sustainable way.

In this way, companies should follow Rumelt's recommendation to make the right diagnosis and identify the challenges that sustainability matters pose to the company.

Here, Porter's five-force model is, of course, highly relevant. For example, are there new players who are trying to gain market share by offering more sustainable products or services? Are there many suppliers who can support the company in the transition to sustainable business, or are there only a few which thus have a lot of bargaining power? These and similar questions are important to ask.

Once the correct diagnosis of the company's sustainability challenges has been made, the company can then move on to – again with Rumelt – establishing a guiding policy to address the challenges and identify the consistent activities that need to be taken to follow the policy. In this way, companies can let corporate strategy and sustainability strategy coincide.

17.1.3 Interests and Views of Stakeholders

When disclosing the business model and strategy, the company must also disclose how the company considers the interests and perspectives of relevant stakeholders.[272] The report shall describe:

- relevant stakeholders, whether the company interacts with them, why it does so and the outcome of the interaction;
- the company's understanding of stakeholders' interests and perspectives insofar as they relate to the company's business model and strategy;
- how the company, if applicable, has adjusted or intends to adjust the business model or strategy to address the interests and perspectives of stakeholders; and
- whether the company's governing bodies have been informed of the interests and perspectives of its stakeholders.[273]

272. Disclosure Requirement SBM-2 in ESRS 2.
273. Data point 45 in ESRS 2.

Those requirements should, of course, be interpreted in light of the norms of positive contribution and due diligence. These norms are not abstract but apply in relation to someone. These 'someones' are the company's stakeholders – the categories of people who are actually affected or at risk of being negatively affected by the company's activities. These are the ones in relation to which the company must exercise due diligence and possibly contribute positively through the principles of equality and freedom. A sustainable business, according to the ideal image, requires that this consideration is built into the business model and strategy itself, and what should be reported is the extent to which this has happened. It does not mean that the purpose of the company is to provide stakeholder value. It means that the values of the company should be such that the dignity of the stakeholders is not violated.

17.2 CORPORATE GOVERNANCE

The business model and strategy described above are cornerstones of the company's institutional structure. However, they cannot be implemented in the business without clear structures and processes for the governance of the company. Therefore, this must also be reported in the sustainability report. ESRS 2 contains four parts to be described:

(1) decision-making bodies;
(2) incentive schemes;
(3) due diligence processes; and
(4) risk management processes.

The purpose of the requirements to report governance is, of course, to describe how the responsibilities for ensuring that the company acts in accordance with norms of positive contribution and due diligence norm are allocated.

In a standard textbook in corporate finance, the chapter about governance will say that the company should be governed to maximise shareholder value. As described in Chapter 6, that could hardly be the corporate purpose nor its values – at least not when conducting sustainable business respecting everyone's equality and freedom. The recommendation, according to agency theory, is to align management and shareholders' interests by tying management compensation to company performance and/or share prices. This approach may have merits but can hardly be a standard solution when the corporate purpose is no longer tied to shareholder value maximisation but to the creation of value for customers while complying with the corporate values. In fact, incentives can only form one part of a larger governance system, and companies with sustainability ambitions must be creative in answering the question of how this larger system should be structured to succeed with the corporate strategy based on the business model. Shareholders and other investors will no doubt and rightly have questions about how their interests are considered in this system, without that meaning that meeting their interests is the purpose of the company. Other stakeholders, such as employees, affected communities and others, will have equally legitimate questions about the same thing. All these stakeholders will or should at least ask: how has the company set up its governance system to ensure that our interests are somehow considered when the company fulfils its corporate purpose?

Let us look at the disclosure requirements in ESRS 2.

17.2.1 Corporate Governance Reporting in the Sustainability Report

According to disclosure requirement GOV-1 of ESRS 2, the company shall describe the composition of administrative, management and supervisory bodies. To that end, the company must declare regarding all three types of bodies:

- the number of executive and non-executive members;
- representation of employees and other workers;
- experience relevant to the sectors, products and geographic locations of the company;
- percentage by gender and other aspects of diversity that the company considers; and
- the percentage of independent board members.[274]

In addition, the sustainability report shall describe the responsibilities of the governing bodies regarding sustainability matters. The role of the management must be described, including whether this role is delegated to a specific management-level position - such as a sustainability manager or sustainability officer - and how this person is followed up. In addition, the description shall include how the different governing bodies oversee the setting of targets related to material impacts, risks and opportunities, and how they monitor progress towards them.[275] In addition, the description shall describe the sustainability-related expertise that the management bodies have or have access to and how this expertise relates to the company's impacts, risks and opportunities.[276]

The sustainability report shall also provide information on whether and to what extent the company's management bodies are informed of sustainability matters and how these matters were addressed during the reporting period. These are detailed requirements, including that the company must report on:

- whether, by whom and how frequently the company's governing bodies are informed of material impacts, risks and opportunities, the implementation of the due diligence process, and the results and effectiveness of adopted policies;
- how the governing bodies consider impacts, risks and opportunities when overseeing the company's strategy, deciding on major transactions, and so on;
- a list of material impacts, risks and opportunities that have been addressed by the management bodies during the reporting period.[277]

274. Data point 21 in ESRS 2.
275. Data point 22 in ESRS 2.
276. Data point 23 in ESRS 2.
277. Data point 26 in ESRS 2.

In the requirements for what companies must report regarding the governance of sustainability matters, further details of the EU's ideal image for sustainable business emerge. The requirements for companies that want to live up to the ideal image are quite tough:

- Organisational responsibility for sustainability matters should lie with the highest management bodies.
- The responsible bodies need to have or have access to the necessary expertise to follow the due diligence norm, which includes considering material impacts, risks and opportunities where relevant.
- The responsible bodies shall be frequently informed about the relevant sustainability matters and are expected to make decisions and act where necessary to comply with the due diligence norm.
- Responsibility may be delegated to, for example, a sustainability officer, but he or she must then report directly to the responsible decision-making bodies, and it must also be clear who monitors how this role fulfils its mission.

17.2.2 Incentive Schemes

The institutional structure of the company includes not only how the company is organised. The financial incentives of management and staff are also important to the company's actions and results. The incentive structure has an important impact on how companies can follow the due diligence norm. Disclosure requirement GOV-3 in ESRS 2, therefore, requires the company to disclose information on how it has integrated sustainability matters into its incentive programs.

According to data point 29 of ESRS 2, the company shall also disclose whether the performance of senior executives is assessed in relation to sustainability-related targets, and if so, which targets, a description of the main characteristics of incentive programmes, including the weighting of sustainability matters, and who is responsible for approving and updating the incentive programmes.

On a detailed level, it is not very clear what the EU, according to the ideal image, believes that companies' incentive systems regarding sustainability should look like. In order not to lack character or integrity, companies must, of course, avoid building goal conflicts in their incentive systems. One such conflict of goals could be, for example, that a CEO is given financial incentives to maximise corporate value and to take comprehensive measures to avoid harming people and the environment.

17.2.3 The Due Diligence Process

Chapter 13 describes the process that companies are expected to follow to demonstrate compliance with the due diligence norm according to the set ideal for sustainable business. The requirement to disclose this process is set out in disclosure requirement GOV-4 in ESRS 2. The different steps in the process recur in different places in the disclosure requirements, so the reporting requirement must be met by mapping out in which parts of the sustainability report it is possible to find information about how each process step is met.

17.2.4 Risk Management Systems

As a final step in describing the entity's governance of sustainability, the sustainability report shall, under disclosure requirement GOV-5 in ESRS 2, also describe the entity's system for internal risk management and control regarding sustainability matters. The information shall include:

- the scope, main features and components of the risk management and internal control processes and systems in relation to sustainability reporting;
- the risk assessment approach followed, including the risk prioritisation methodology;
- the main risks identified and their mitigation strategies, including related controls;
- a description of how the company integrates the findings of its risk assessment and internal controls as regards the sustainability reporting process into relevant internal functions and processes; and
- a description of the periodic reporting of the findings referred to above to the administrative, management and supervisory bodies.

17.3 THE COMPANY'S MATERIAL IMPACTS, RISKS AND OPPORTUNITIES

One of the most important requirements for the sustainability report is that the company must report whether and to what extent the company's business model and strategy generate material impacts, risks and opportunities, referred to as IRO.[278] ESRS 2, therefore, sets out extensive requirements for the disclosure of these factors. The information should include:

- how the entity's material adverse or positive impacts affect people or the environment, the time horizons within which those impacts are likely to occur, whether the company directly or indirectly (through contractual partners) causes those impacts, and whether and how those impacts are caused by or related to the company's strategy or business model;
- how material risks and opportunities will affect the company's financial performance, business model and strategy;
- the effects of the company's material impacts, risks and opportunities on the company's strategy and decision-making and, where relevant, changes to strategy and business model;
- financial effects of material risk and impact;

278. Disclosure Requirement SBM-3 in ESRS 2.

- information on the resilience of the company's strategy and business model in terms of ability to manage its material impact, risk and opportunities;
- changes in material impacts, risks and opportunities in relation to the previous reporting period; and
- the material impacts, risks and opportunities covered by disclosure requirements in ESRS and by firm-specific disclosures, respectively.[279]

It goes without saying that the disclosure requirements regarding strategy, stakeholders, risks and opportunities are part of a whole where the purpose is to give the reader a good understanding of how the company's business model and strategy generate risks and opportunities regarding sustainability matters, which stakeholders are affected, how changes have been made or are expected to be made to the business model and strategy, and so on. The concept of 'materiality' has been discussed in some detail in section 16.2.6.

17.4 MANAGEMENT OF IMPACTS, RISKS AND OPPORTUNITIES

According to the previous section, the company had to disclose the material impacts, risks and opportunities generated by the company's business model and strategy. To gain a full understanding of these, it is also important to understand how the company has arrived at the current list of impacts, risks and opportunities and further how the company subsequently manages the impacts, risks and opportunities that have been identified. Such information must also be disclosed in the sustainability report.

17.4.1 The Process for Assessing Materiality

When investors and other users of the sustainability report read it, it is easy to focus on what is written in the report itself. It is often more difficult to see what is *not* in the report, for example, why certain types of impacts or risks are not reported. To gain a complete understanding of the company's actions in accordance with the norms of positive contribution and due diligence, it is therefore important to get an overall picture of both what is and is not in the report. The company must, therefore, report its processes to identify its impacts, risks and opportunities and then assess which ones are material.[280] The concept of materiality as such has been discussed in more detail in section 16.2.

Again, it is a question of detailed expectations, including requirements for the disclosure of information on:

- the methods used and assumptions made;
- the process of identifying, assessing and prioritising potential and actual impacts on people and the environment;

279. Data point 48 in ESRS 2.
280. Disclosure Requirement IRO-1 in ESRS 2.

- the process for identifying, assessing and prioritising sustainability-related risks and opportunities that have or may have a financial impact on the company; as well as
- how he company has carried out the actual materiality assessment.[281]

17.4.2 Disclosure of Covered Disclosure Requirements

Companies must only comply with disclosure requirements where material impacts or material risks or opportunities related to sustainability matters have been identified. Based on the materiality assessment process, the entity needs to assess which disclosure requirements of the ESRS standards it must follow. However, the company must clearly disclose which ESRS standards are being followed and which are not.[282]

17.4.3 Minimum Policy Requirements

As set out in Chapter 4, corporate policy documents constitute the sixth level of sustainability law. This is natural since those policies obviously form part of the 'rules of the game' for business. Within the ideal image of sustainable business, the policies form part of the governance of the business. In this role, it is only natural that ESRS 2 sets out minimum requirements for policy reporting.

Companies only need to report information about policies linked to the sustainability matters deemed to be material, provided that a policy has been adopted. If information about policies is to be provided, certain minimum requirements are set out in the disclosure requirement MDR-P in ESRS 2.

Policy is defined as a set or framework of general objectives and management principles that the company applies to its decision-making. A policy implements the company's strategy or management decisions related to a material sustainability matter. Each policy is under the responsibility of defined person(s), specifies its perimeter of application, and includes one or more objectives (linked when applicable to measurable targets). A policy is validated and reviewed following the undertakings' applicable governance rules. For each relevant policy, the company is expected to describe:

- the key content of the policy;
- the scope of the policy, for example, in terms of activities, relevant stakeholders, etc.;
- where the responsibility lies in the organisation for implementing the policy;
- a reference to any third-party standards to which the company commits;

281. Data point 53 in ESRS 2.
282. Disclosure Requirement IRO-2 in ESRS 2.

- the extent to which the company has taken relevant stakeholders into account when deciding on the policy; and
- whether and how the policy is made available to relevant stakeholders.[283]

17.4.4 Minimum Requirements for Activities and Resources

As with policies, companies must disclose information about activities and resources related to material sustainability matters, but only if such activities have been undertaken. Here, too, minimum requirements are specified, in this case, in the disclosure requirement MDR-A of ESRS 2. The information shall then include:

- the key actions taken in the reporting year and planned for the future, including information on how the activities contribute to the achievement of the policy objectives and targets set;
- the scope of the key actions, such as geographical scope;
- the timetable for each activity;
- significant actions taken to compensate people who have been harmed by actual adverse effects of the company;
- qualitative and quantitative reporting of progress in established activity plans; and
- other relevant information to understand the activities.[284]

The disclosure requirements regarding activities and resources are some of the weaker ones in the ESRS. As repeated throughout this book, sustainable business is about repetitive corporate actions, month after month, year after year. When implementing a sustainable business model and strategy, this will not, or should at least not, be done through 'activities' but through *processes and routines*. This is why, in the illustration of the EU's ideal image for a sustainable business in Chapter 13, processes and routines were used instead of activities. To implement or upgrade a process could be an activity, but it seems odd to refer to the following process as an activity as such.

17.4.5 Minimum Requirements for Metrics and Targets

For metrics and targets, information should also only be given if it is considered material.[285] If information is to be provided, certain specified minimum requirements must be met. For metrics, the MDR-M disclosure requirement applies. Metrics shall be reported in relation to material impacts, risks and opportunities.[286] The subject-specific

283. Data point 65 in ESRS 2.
284. Data point 68 in ESRS 2.
285. *See* section 12.4.
286. Data point 75 in ESRS 2.

ESRS standards contain metrics, which is why they must be reported.[287] In addition, for each metric, the company must:

- disclose the methodologies and significant assumptions behind the metric, including the limitations of the methodologies used;
- disclose whether the measurement of the metric is validated by an external body other than the assurance provider and, if so, which body;
- label and define the metric using meaningful, clear and precise names and descriptions;
- when currency is specified as the unit of measure, use the presentation currency of its financial statements.

The company must also, under disclosure requirement MDR-T, report its targets linked to material sustainability matters. For each such target, the company shall disclose:

- a description of the relationship of the target to the policy objectives;
- the defined target level to be achieved;
- the scope of the target, including the company's activities and/or its upstream and/or downstream value chain where applicable and geographical boundaries;
- the baseline value and base year from which progress is measured;
- the period to which the target applies and, if applicable, any milestones or interim targets;
- the methodologies and significant assumptions used to define targets;
- whether the company's targets related to environmental matters are based on conclusive scientific evidence;
- whether and how stakeholders have been involved in target setting for each material sustainability matters;
- any changes in targets and corresponding metrics or underlying measurement methodologies, significant assumptions, limitations, sources and processes to collect data adopted within the defined time horizons; and
- the performance against its disclosed targets.[288]

287. Data point 76 in ESRS 2.
288. Data point 80 in ESRS 2.

CHAPTER 18
Environmental Sustainability (E)

In the acronym ESG, the E - Environmental - comes first. That makes sense. Sustainability is about people, and a healthy environment is, of course, a prerequisite for human well-being, equality and freedom. In this chapter, sustainable business from an environmental perspective will be discussed. An attempt is made to combine both the practicalities of running an environmentally sustainable business and to report on this business according to the ESRS E-standards. Five environmental sustainability standards have been published so far:

- ESRS E1 Climate Change
- ESRS E2 Pollution
- ESRS E3 Water and marine resources
- ESRS E4 Biodiversity and ecosystems
- ESRS E5 Resource use and circular economy.

This chapter will deal with each of these standards. Before that, the place of environmental sustainability in the Earth4All model and the sustainability moral basis for environmental sustainability will be addressed.

18.1 RELATIONSHIP TO THE EARTH4ALL MODEL

How often do companies' unsustainable activities relate to the ongoing environmental crisis on Earth? It is easy to feel that there is a long distance between one's own activities and what is happening on the planet. The Earth4All model, described in Chapter 1, is used here to try to reduce this perceived distance. As already described, the model is partly based on research on the nine planetary processes and boundaries. These nine processes make it possible to understand a company's environmental impact at a more detailed level. Not all of the nine planetary processes are included in the Earth4All model, but several are. Climate change, measured in terms of average temperature, is an element of the well-being index used.

The Earth4All model can also put the ESRS described below into context. As explained in more detail in Chapter 9 of the EU Taxonomy, it is based on six environmental objectives listed in Article 9. The ESRS E-standards are mapped towards these environmental goals, with one common standard for the first two goals.

The following table can serve as a description of how the nine planetary boundaries, the environmental objectives of the EU taxonomy and the five ESRS on the environment relate to each other. The table is not exhaustive but only shows the main correlations:

Environmental Objectives	*ESRS Standard*	*Planetary Processes*
Climate change mitigation	ESRS E1 – Climate change	The climate system Oceans Freshwater Biodiversity
Climate change adaptions	ESRS E1 – Climate change	None (it's about adapting to impact, not counteracting impact)
Sustainable use and protection of water and marine resources	ESRS E3 – Water and Marine Resources	Oceans Freshwater The climate system
Transition to a circular economy	ESRS E5 – Resource Use and Circular Economy	Land use The climate system
Pollution prevention and control	ESRS E2 – Pollution	All
Protection and restoration of biodiversity and ecosystems	ESRS E4 – Biodiversity and ecosystem	Biodiversity The climate system Terrestrial environment Sea

The nine planetary processes are: (1) the climate system, (2) the ozone layer, (3) the ocean, (4) biodiversity, (5) the land system change, (6) fresh water, (7) biochemical flow, (8) novel entities and (9) airesols.

Of course, the nine planetary processes do not exist independently of each other. On the contrary, they interact and influence each other. The climate system, the ozone layer and the ocean are three major processes that affect all life and systems on Earth. Increased emissions into the climate system cause, among other things, ocean acidification and rising average temperatures which cause biodiversity loss. Since both oceans and forests are important for the uptake of carbon dioxide, a negative spiral arises, where changes in the climate system risk affecting, for example, the ocean's absorption capacity, which changes the climate system even more, and so on. The ozone layer's protective layer directly affects, for example, biodiversity, the sea and the terrestrial environment.

These interconnections mean that corporations affect the nine planetary systems in complex, both direct and indirect ways. Below are some examples of this.

The climate system. Companies' greenhouse gas emissions, for example, through the use of fossil fuels or through agriculture, have a known negative impact on the climate system, whose average temperature rises. Such emissions are dealt with in ESRS E1. But corporate pollution – treated in ESRS E2 – also contributes to climate change, for example, emissions of sulphur oxides. Due to the central importance of the climate system, companies' impact on the climate also has an indirect impact on, for example, the sea and the terrestrial environment.

Ozone layer. Companies can contribute to the depletion of the ozone layer through emissions of so-called ozone-depleting substances, which are covered by ESRS E2 on pollution. Companies can emit ozone-depleting substances by using chemicals such as chlorofluorocarbons, halons and methyl bromide in the production of products, such as refrigerators, air conditioning units, aerosols and firefighting systems. These chemicals can be transported up to the stratosphere and deplete ozone molecules, which can cause ozone holes and lead to increased exposure to harmful UV radiation. This, in turn, affects biodiversity, the terrestrial environment, the ocean and so on.

Sea and freshwater. Companies affect oceans and fresh water in a number of different ways. Unsustainable fishing is an obvious example, as is the extensive use of freshwater by many companies in their production processes. Such activities are covered in ESRS E3 on water and marine resources. Companies also affect oceans and freshwater through pollutant emissions, for example, by releasing various chemicals into watercourses and other water sources. Pollution can come from industries that use chemicals in their production, farms that use pesticides and fertilisers, wastewater treatment plants, and oil refineries that discharge wastewater. Examples of chemicals and pollutants that can contaminate water and affect the environment are oil-based substances, heavy metals, pesticides and fertilisers.

Biodiversity. Businesses can affect biodiversity in a variety of ways. Some examples of direct impacts are unsustainable logging of forests and the use of water resources. Companies' greenhouse gas emissions raise the average temperature, which increases the loss of biodiversity. Other types of emissions have the same effect, often more directly. This issue is covered by ESRS E4 on Biodiversity and Ecosystems.

Land. The terrestrial environment can also be affected by companies' activities in a variety of ways. Unsustainable agriculture, emissions of pollutants, emissions of greenhouse gases, mining of minerals and more are examples of this. Land erosion further leads to a reduced capacity to absorb greenhouse gases, which amplifies climate change and negatively affects biodiversity.

Biochemical flows. Through emissions, companies can affect the system of biochemical flows on Earth, for example, by influencing the nitrogen cycle. The nitrogen cycle is a natural process in which nitrogen is converted from one form to another with various uses, and nitrogen is an important constituent of both organic and inorganic compounds essential for life on Earth. However, increased nitrogen loads in ecosystems can disrupt this cycle and cause negative environmental effects such as eutrophication and acidification. For example, companies can disrupt the nitrogen cycle through emissions of nitrogen oxides through industrial processes and transport, using artificial fertilisers and through waste management.

As shown in Chapter 1, it is not only the case that the nine planetary processes are interconnected and that companies can influence several processes through the same actions but also that nature and the environment exist in a reciprocal relationship with society. Emissions have negative health effects that directly affect mortality in society. Through their use of land and other natural resources, businesses affect access to food, which also affects mortality. Climate change does not strike blindly but risks reinforcing already existing inequalities in society, leading to an erosion of trust and a deterioration in the ability to make collective decisions.

18.2 SUSTAINABILITY MORAL FOUNDATION

Why should the environment be protected? This question and the answers to it open up a multitude of dimensions in the sustainability morality outlined in this book.[289] EU environmental legislation is based on the concept of 'sustainable development' as first defined in the Brundtland Report 1987 and later in the Rio Conference Conventions 1992.[290] The focus is on people, more specifically on making sure present and future generations are assured of a healthy and good environment. But the environment is sometimes also considered to have its own protection value. However, it is difficult to understand what this would mean in practice. If the environment has its own protective value, in addition to the protection of human dignity, this should reasonably mean that the protection of human dignity - such as health and equality - should, under certain conditions, stand back in favour of the protection of the environment. However, this seems difficult to accept in a democratic society based on human rights. It also requires finding one or more overarching principles based on which such a balance between humans and the environment can be made. This may be possible to do, for example, by arguing that all life - humans, animals, plants - have the same status and thus protection value. However, it seems difficult to find acceptance for any principle that, for example, would mean sacrificing human life for the benefit of animals or plants.

Instead, it seems more appropriate, from a moral point of view, to regard the protection of the environment as resting on the same basis as other areas of sustainability - respect for human equality and freedom.[291] A healthy environment is a prerequisite for the ability to live well. Destroying the environment - the climate, lakes, forests, seas, soil, air and so on - is tantamount to undermining people's ability to live a dignified life. This means, on the one hand, not taking the lives of others seriously and, on the other hand, undermining the opportunities to live a life according to self-chosen values and plans.

289. *See* the introduction on the interpretivist theory of law on which the book is based. As pointed out there, sustainability morality refers to the political morality expressed in the rules of sustainability law.

290. *See* section 3.2.

291. The author is, of course, well aware of the anthropocentric perspective that is thus taken and that this particular perspective has been subjected to criticism.

This perspective does not mean that the environment must always take a back seat to humans in the event of conflict. However, since the environment is important for the protection of human dignity, the question will be which options are overall best respectful of human dignity, which could imply, for example, that a long-term interest in protecting the environment (and thus human dignity) takes precedence over a short-term interest in protecting humans.

Such an assessment involves a moral weighing up of the relative interests of the various parties involved. It is not only the interests and costs of those who can actually or potentially be harmed by, for example, emissions that must be weighed in but the interest and costs for those responsible for avoiding the emissions are also important – a different system would be contrary to the requirement of equal respect for all.

In addition, it is necessary to consider the potential harm that could be caused by the cessation of an activity that is not harmful to the environment. It is conceivable that rapid changes from an environmentally harmful to harmless activity could affect jobs and employment rates.

Protecting the environment is, therefore, not the only factor; the perpetrator of the damage and other people, such as employees, must also be considered in the moral assessments.

Another, often very complicated, issue is how different types of environmental considerations should be set against each other. Permits for offshore wind power are an example. The transition to a society based on renewable energy sources is key to mitigating the effects of the climate crisis. But other environmental considerations also weigh in, such as the protection of animals and biodiversity. In the type of moral considerations that are relevant here, it must also be considered that although climate and ecosystems are different planetary systems, they do not exist independently of each other. On the contrary, climate change is accelerating biodiversity loss. Biodiversity loss, in turn, restricts Earth's natural capacity to absorb greenhouse gases. From a moral perspective, the course of action must then be chosen that causes the least total harm, where harm is to be interpreted as a violation of human dignity in terms of equality and freedom. An assessment that is, of course, very difficult to make, partly because of the complicated causal relationships that need to be clarified to answer the question and the difficulty of choosing the right time perspective. There is no room here to dig into this trade-off.

18.3 CLIMATE CHANGE (ESRS E1)

The ESRS E1 standard describes how companies should report their operations related to climate change. The purpose of the standard is for the reader to understand:

- how the company affects climate change, in terms of material positive and negative actual and potential impacts;
- the company's past, current, and future mitigation efforts in line with the Paris Agreement (or an updated international agreement on climate change) and compatible with limiting global warming to 1.5°C;

- the plans and capacity of the company to adapt its strategy and business model in line with the transition to a sustainable economy and to contribute to limiting global warming to 1.5°C;
- any other actions taken by the company and the result of such actions to prevent, mitigate or remediate actual or potential negative impacts and to address risks and opportunities;
- the nature, type and extent of the company's material risks and opportunities arising from the company's impacts and dependencies on climate change and how the undertaking manages them; and
- the financial effects on the undertaking over the short-, medium- and long-term risks and opportunities arising from the undertaking's impacts and dependencies on climate change.[292]

The standard focuses primarily on emissions of the seven greenhouse gases: carbon dioxide, methane, nitrogen oxide, hydrofluorocarbons, perfluorocarbons, sulphur hexafluoride and nitrogen trifluoride.[293] Substances harmful to the ozone layer are dealt with in ESRS E2.[294]

18.3.1 Greenhouse Gas Protocol

ESRS E1 relies heavily on the Greenhouse Gas Protocol standards, developed by the World Business Council for Sustainable Development and World Resources Institute, in collaboration with a large number of companies and organisations. The purpose of the standards is to help companies and other organisations create a uniform inventory of their greenhouse gas emissions and then to inform strategies and initiatives related to these emissions. For the purposes of this book, only the corporate standard will be described.

The purpose of the GHG standards is, first and foremost, to create as accurate a list of the company's greenhouse gas emissions as possible. To make this possible, two demarcation matters must first be resolved: the first of which concerns organisational boundaries and the second concerns operational boundaries.

Organisational boundaries. Organisational boundaries are primarily relevant to company groups. In a group with a parent company and only wholly-owned subsidiaries, the issue is straightforward – the aggregated emissions from all companies are included in the list. However, the question arises as to how partly owned subsidiaries or other companies are to be treated in the list. Two options are offered. In the first option, the list is based on the equity share approach. In the second option, the list is based only on activities that the company controls, which means, for example, that the company reports all emissions from majority-owned subsidiaries (control approach). There are pros and cons to both options and the reporting company must decide on which option is the best fit for it.

292. Data point 1 in ESRS E1.
293. Data point 4 in ESRS E1.
294. Data point 8 in ESRS E1.

Operational boundaries. Once the organisational demarcation has been made, the next step will be to make an activity-related delimitation, divided into direct and indirect emissions.

GHG assumes that a company generates greenhouse gas emissions, where indirect emissions fall into two categories. The term 'scope' is central to GHG:

- **Scope 1**: Direct emissions generated from sources owned or controlled by the company. These include sources linked to the generation of electricity, equipment for the production of materials or chemicals, the transport of materials, products, waste and employees, as well as so-called fugitive emissions.
- **Scope 2**: Indirect emissions generated from the company's purchase of electricity. These emissions are listed separately to enable the company to make considered decisions about both energy efficiency improvements and the transition to renewable energy.
- **Scope 3**: Indirect emissions generated due to the company's operations, but from sources that are not owned or controlled by the company. These are emissions generated in the company's value chain as a result of the company's activities. Examples include extraction and production of purchased materials, transportation-related activities, electricity-related activities that do not fall within scope 2, lease assets and outsourced activities, and waste management.

It should be noted here that which emissions fall within scope 1 and 3 partly depends on how the organisational delimitation is made. If the equity method is used, a partially owned subsidiary's greenhouse gas generation will be included in scope 1 at a proportion equal to the ownership. Other emissions will be in scope 3.

Identification and calculation of emissions. Once the organisational and operational boundaries have been made, the next step will be to identify and calculate the company's greenhouse gas emissions within these boundaries. This is done through a five-step process: (i) the emission sources are identified; (ii) the calculation method is chosen; (iii) data is collected, and emission factors are selected; (iv) calculation tools are used; and (v) data is aggregated up to company or group level. Appendix D of the Corporate standard summarises the different types of emission sources. The most common way to calculate emissions is to use so-called emission factors, which are used to convert different emissions into tonnes of carbon dioxide or carbon dioxide equivalents, where emissions of methane and other greenhouse gases in addition to carbon dioxide are converted into the corresponding emissions in carbon dioxide emissions.

Follow-up of emissions over time. A list of greenhouse gas emissions is rarely a one-off event but is drawn up to serve as a basis for managing emissions over time. To make this possible, a so-called base year must be chosen, against which all emission levels in later years are compared. The base year can be chosen based on emissions in that particular year but can also be set based on a representative average of several years' emissions, for example, if the selected year would be affected by one-off events. When corresponding lists are drawn up in later years, it will be important to carry out recalculations, for example, due to mergers or divestments, to make the data for later years comparable with the data of the base year.

18.3.2 Science-Based Targets Initiative

ESRS E1 also requires companies to report whether their targets for reducing greenhouse gas emissions are science-based and consistent with the global 1.5°C target in the Paris Agreement. The most common way for companies to report science-based emission targets is by reference to the Science Based Targets Initiative (SBTi). In the same way as the Greenhouse Gas Protocol, the SBTi is the result of a collaboration between public and private actors. The purpose of this standard is to enable companies and organisations to set targets for greenhouse gas emissions based on up-to-date science.

The SBTi sets up a five-step process: (i) commit to setting science-based targets, (ii) develop the target, (iii) submit the targets to the SBTi, (iv) announce the targets, and (v) disclose progress towards the targets.[295] In the second step, the company must make sure the set goals meet a number of criteria. The SBTi relies heavily on the GHG standard, and a prerequisite is, therefore, to produce a list of greenhouse gas emissions according to that standard. Based on the list drawn up, the goals can be set. For scope 1 and 2 emissions, targets must cover 95% of emissions. For scope 3 emissions, 67% of emissions must be covered, provided that scope 3 emissions account for over 40% of the company's total greenhouse gas emissions.[296] The targets must be set for five or ten years after the base year, but the SBTi also recommends long-term targets for 2040 or 2050, for example. Since April 2023, there is also a standard for scientific targets for net-zero emissions.[297]

18.3.3 Reporting Requirements

The following is a general description of the reporting requirements of ESRS E1.

18.3.3.1 General Disclosure Requirements and Governance

The requirements of ESRS 2 also need to be met in the context of climate change.[298] The disclosure requirements of all the topic-specific ESRS shall be read and applied in conjunction with the disclosure requirements for governance, strategy and management of impacts, risks and opportunities in ESRS 2. This includes that the company must report whether people in management roles have incentive systems linked to the reduction of greenhouse gas emissions.[299]

295. SBTi Corporate Manual, section 8.
296. *Ibid.*, section 23.
297. SBTi Corporate Net-Zero Standard.
298. Data point 12 in ESRS E1.
299. Data point 13 in ESRS E1.

18.3.3.2 Business Model and Strategy

Disclosure requirement E1-1 requires the company to disclose its transition plan for climate change mitigation. This is defined as an aspect of a company's overall strategy that lays out the company's targets, actions and resources for its transition towards a lower-carbon economy, including actions such as reducing its greenhouse gas emissions with regard to the objective of limiting global warming to 1.5°C and climate neutrality.

If the company does not have such a plan, it shall indicate whether and, if so, when such a plan will be adopted.[300] The presentation of the plan should include:

- an explanation of how the company's targets are compatible with the limiting of global warming to 1.5°C in line with the Paris Agreement;
- an explanation of the decarbonisation levers identified and key actions planned, including changes in the company's product and service portfolio and the adoption of new technologies in its own operations or the upstream and/or downstream value chain;
- an explanation and quantification of the company's investments and funding supporting the implementation of its transition plan;
- a qualitative assessment of the potential locked-in greenhouse gas emissions from the company's key assets and products;
- for companies with economic activities that are covered by delegated regulations on climate adaptation or mitigation under the Taxonomy Regulation, an explanation of any objective or plans that the company has for making its economic activities taxonomy aligned;
- if applicable, disclosure of significant CapEx amounts invested during the reporting period related to coal, oil and gas-related economic activities;
- a disclosure on whether or not the company is excluded from the EU Paris-aligned benchmarks;
- an explanation of how the transition plan is embedded in and aligned with the company's overall business strategy and financial planning;
- whether the transition plan is approved by the administrative, management and supervisory bodies; and
- an explanation of the company's progress in implementing the transition plan.[301]

As part of disclosing information on impacts, risks and opportunities in accordance with disclosure requirements SBM-3 in ESRS 2, the company shall further disclose whether it assesses the respective climate-related risk to be a physical risk or a transition risk.[302] These concepts are taken from the TCFD framework, which is described in section 15.3.

300. Data point 17 in ESRS E1.
301. Data point 16 in ESRS E1.
302. Data point 18 in ESRS E1.

The company must report the results of an analysis of how resilient the company's business model and strategy are in relation to climate change.[303] Here, the double materiality analysis must be considered, i.e., both the company's impact on climate change and the impact of climate change on the company. Companies whose business model is based, for example, on assets that require the use of non-renewable energy and thus greenhouse gas emissions will, of course, be greatly affected by a transition to a low- or zero-GHG activity. Furthermore, it is probable that companies with low-cost strategies will need to make changes if it can be assumed that climate change will lead to higher production costs, for example, due to higher supplier prices.

18.3.3.3 Management of Impacts, Risks and Opportunities

The company must report on its process for identifying and assessing its climate-related impacts, risks and opportunities.[304] The description should include:

- impacts on climate change, including the company's greenhouse gas emissions;
- climate-related physical risks in its own operations and in the value chain; and
- climate-related transition risks in its own operations and in the value chain.[305]

Policies. The company shall also disclose which policies have been adopted related to climate change if such policies exist.[306] In such case, the report must meet the minimum requirements set out in ESRS 2.[307] The report shall include whether and how the policy addresses climate change mitigation, climate change adaptation, energy efficiency and the use of renewable energy.[308]

Actions. The company must also report which actions have been taken related to climate change mitigation and adaptation.[309] The minimum requirements for disclosure requirements MDR-A in ESRS 2 shall then be met. In addition, the company shall:

- present their activities for the decarbonisation of the business;
- describe reductions in greenhouse gas emissions; and
- relate important financial information related to CapEx and OpEx required to implement the activities.[310]

18.3.3.4 Metrics and Targets

ESRS E1 has a comprehensive list of requirements for companies to disclose their material greenhouse gas emission targets and results. These metrics and targets shall

303. Data point 19 in ESRS E1.
304. Data point 20 in ESRS E1.
305. Data point 20 in ESRS E1.
306. Disclosure Requirement E1-2 in ESRS E1.
307. Data point 24 in ESRS E1.
308. Data point 25 in ESRS E1.
309. Disclosure Requirement E1-3 in ESRS E1.
310. Data point 30 in ESRS E1.

form the basis for the presentation of the strategy in accordance with disclosure requirement E1-1.

Climate-related targets. Companies must report which climate-related targets have been set.[311] The company shall report under the minimum requirements of the MDR-T of ESRS 2. The company must then disclose its emission reduction targets and other targets to address material climate-related impacts, risks and opportunities, such as the use of renewable energy sources, energy efficiency, adaptation to climate change, and physical and transition risks. If the company has adopted such emission reduction targets, the company shall, among other things, report these targets in absolute terms for scopes 1, 2 and 3, emission levels during the base year and the current year, and whether the targets are set on a scientific basis.[312]

Energy consumption and energy mix. The company must also report its energy consumption and energy mix.[313] The report shall describe the energy consumption in MWh broken down into energy from fossil sources, nuclear power and renewable sources,[314] and the energy intensity related to the company's net revenues in sectors with a high climate impact.[315]

Gross emissions. The company must also report its gross emissions, broken down into scopes 1, 2 and 3.[316] Here, data points 45 to 55 have accounting requirements that detail the requirements that apply under the Greenhouse Gas Protocol.

Carbon capture and storage. The company must report whether it, in tonnes of carbon dioxide equivalents, has captured and stored carbon dioxide in its own operations or in the value chain and through any purchases of carbon credits.[317] If the company reports a net-zero greenhouse gas target, the company must report how it intends to neutralise (after approximately 90%-95% gross reductions) the remaining greenhouse gas emissions by being removed from its own operations or value chain.[318] If the company has made public climate-neutrality statements that include the use of carbon credits, the company shall explain the credibility and integrity of the carbon credits used.[319]

Carbon transfer pricing. Companies must also report whether they apply transfer pricing to carbon dioxide.[320]

Financial impact. Finally, the company must also report potential financial effects on the company linked to climate change, both from the perspective of risk and opportunities.[321] In doing so, the risks shall be accounted for from the perspective of physical risks and transition risks.[322] This is a detailed statement which must include

311. Disclosure Requirement E1-4 in ESRS E1.
312. Data point 34 in ESRS E1.
313. ESRS E1-5 in ESRS E1.
314. Data point 37 in ESRS E1.
315. Data point 40 in ESRS E1.
316. Disclosure Requirement E1-6 in ESRS E1.
317. Disclosure Requirement E1-7 in ESRS E1.
318. Data point 60 in ESRS E1.
319. Data point 61 in ESRS E1.
320. Disclosure Requirement E1-8 in ESRS E1.
321. Disclosure Requirement E1-9.
322. Data point 64 in ESRS E1.

the proportion of the assets at risk, the location of those assets and the net income at risk.[323]

18.4 POLLUTION (ESRS E2)

The ESRS E2 accounting standard describes how companies should report their activities related to pollution. The purpose of the standard is for the reader to understand:

- how the company affects pollution of air, water and soil, in terms of material positive and negative actual or potential impacts;
- any actions taken, and the result of such actions, to prevent or mitigate actual or potential negative impacts, and to address risks and opportunities;
- the plans and capacity of the company to adapt its strategy and business model in line with the transition to a sustainable economy and with the need to prevent, control and eliminate pollution;
- the nature, type and extent of the company's material risks and opportunities related to the company's pollution-related impacts and dependencies, as well as the prevention, control, elimination or reduction of pollution;
- the financial effects on the company over the short, medium and long term of material risks and opportunities arising from the company's pollution-related impacts and dependencies.[324]

The list of definitions defines pollution as a direct or indirect introduction, as a result of human activity, of pollutants into air, water or soil which may be harmful to human health and/or the environment, which may result in damage to material property, or which may impair or interfere with amenities and other legitimate uses of the environment.[325]

18.4.1 EU Action Plan 'Towards Zero Pollution for Air, Water and Soil'

One aim of the ESRS E2 standard is to contribute to implementing the EU Action Plan towards Zero Pollution of Air, Water and Soil.[326] There are several factors behind the action plan. Pollution causes many deaths each year; in the EU, one in eight deaths yearly.[327] Combating pollution is also fighting inequality, as the most vulnerable groups in society are typically those most affected by pollution. Pollution also threatens biodiversity. Finally, the costs of pollution to society are higher than the costs of remedying it.

323. Data points 65-70 in ESRS E1.
324. Data point 1 in ESRS E2.
325. The definition is taken from Article 3.2 of Directive 2010/75/EU.
326. COM(2021) 400.
327. EEA Report No. 21/2019: Healthy environment, healthy lives.

Because of these and other factors, the action plan sets out a zero-pollution vision for 2050: 'Air, water and soil pollution is reduced to levels no longer considered harmful to health and natural ecosystems and that respect the boundaries our planet can cope with, thus creating a toxic-free environment.' For 2030, a set of zero-pollution targets are set, according to which the EU should reduce:

- by more than 55% the health impacts (premature deaths) of air pollution;
- by 30% the share of people chronically disturbed by transport noise;
- by 25% the EU ecosystems where air pollution threatens biodiversity;
- by 50% nutrient losses, the use and risk of chemical pesticides, the use of the more hazardous ones, and the sale of antimicrobials for farmed animals and in aquaculture;
- by 50% plastic litter at sea and by 30% microplastics released into the environment;
- significantly total waste generation and by 50% residual municipal waste.

In addition, the Action Plan sets out a wide range of legislative and non-legislative measures that the Commission is planning to meet these goals and the zero-pollution ambition.

18.4.2 Reporting Requirements

18.4.2.1 General Disclosure Requirements

Process. ESRS 2 IRO-1 requires companies to disclose the process used to identify and assess material impacts, risks and opportunities. This also applies to pollution.[328] The company must then apply the method LEAP proposed by TNFD – Locate, Evaluate, Assess, Prepare.[329] The method is described in section 15.3. The first three steps of the method are the relevant ones, namely, to locate where one's own operations and value chain come into contact with nature, to evaluate pollution-related dependencies and impacts, and to assess significant risks and opportunities.

18.4.2.2 Management of Impacts, Risks and Opportunities

Policies. The company must disclose its policies regarding how the company manages significant impacts, risks and opportunities related to pollution prevention and control.[330] The report shall then follow the minimum requirements of the MDR-P of ESRS 2.[331] The report shall describe whether policies address, in the company's own operations and in the value chain, mitigations of adverse impacts related to pollution

328. Data point 11 in ESRS E2.
329. *See* AR1 i Appendix A till ESRS E2.
330. Disclosure Requirement E2-1 in ESRS E2.
331. Data point 14 in ESRS E2.

of air, water and soil, minimisation and substitution of substances of concern and avoidance of incidents and emergency situations.[332]

Actions. The company must also report what actions it undertakes related to pollution and what resources are allocated to implement them.[333] The minimum requirements of the MDR-A in ESRS 2 shall then be met. The activities may be allocated to one of the following links in a hierarchy to which they belong:

- avoid pollution, including any phase-out of materials or compounds that have a negative impact (prevention of pollution at source);
- reduce pollution; and
- restore, regenerate and transform ecosystems where pollution has occurred (control of the impacts both from regular activities and incidents).[334]

18.4.2.3 Metrics and Targets

Target. The company must report its adopted targets related to pollution.[335] The minimum requirements of the MDR-T in ESRS 2 must then be met. The statement shall include air pollutants and respective specific loads, emissions to water and respective specific loads, pollution to soil and respective specific loads and substances of concern and substances of very high concern.[336] The company may also report whether local ecological thresholds were considered when setting the targets.[337]

Metrics. The company shall disclose the pollutants that it emits through its own operations, as well as the microplastics it generates or uses.[338] The production, use, distribution, commercialisation and import/export of substances of concern and substances of very high concern, on their own, in mixtures or in articles must also be declared.[339]

Financial impact. Finally, potential financial effects on the company related to pollution must also be reported.[340]

18.5 WATER AND MARINE RESOURCES (ESRS E3)

The ESRS E3 accounting standard describes how companies should report their activities related to the use of water and marine resources. The purpose of the standard is for the reader to understand:

332. Data point 15 in ESRS E2.
333. Disclosure Requirement E2-2 in ESRS E2.
334. Data point 19 in ESRS E2.
335. Disclosure Requirement E2-3 in ESRS E2.
336. Data point 23 in ESRS E2.
337. Data point 24 in ESRS E2.
338. Disclosure Requirement E2-4 in ESRS E2.
339. Disclosure Requirement E2-5 in ESRS E2.
340. Disclosure Requirement E2-6 in ESRS E2.

- how the company affects water and marine resources, in terms of material positive and negative actual or potential impacts;
- any actions taken and the result of such actions to prevent or mitigate material actual or potential negative impacts to protect water and marine resources;
- whether, how and to what extent the undertaking contributes to the European Green Deal's ambitions for fresh air, clean water, healthy soil and biodiversity, as well as to the sustainability of the blue economy and fisheries sectors;
- the plans and capacity of the company to adapt its strategy and business model in line with the promotion of sustainable water use based on long-term protection of available water resources, protection of aquatic ecosystems and restoration of freshwater and marine habitats;
- the nature, type and extent of the company's material risks and opportunities arising from the company's impacts and dependencies on water and marine resources, and how the undertaking manages them; and
- the financial effects on the company over the short, medium and long term of material risks and opportunities arising from the company's impacts and dependencies on water and marine resources.[341]

As far as 'water' is concerned, the standard covers surface water and groundwater. As far as 'marine resources' are concerned, the standard covers the extraction and use of such resources.[342]

18.5.1 Reporting Requirements

18.5.1.1 General Disclosure Requirements

Process. ESRS 2 IRO-1 requires companies to disclose the process used to identify and assess material impacts, risks and opportunities. This also applies to water and marine resources.[343] As with ESRS E2 reporting on pollutants, the LEAP method shall be used.[344]

18.5.1.2 Management of Impacts, Risks and Opportunities

Policies. The company must disclose its policies regarding how the company manages significant impacts, risks and opportunities related to water and marine resources.[345] The minimum requirements of the MDR-P of ESRS 2 shall be met.

Actions. The company's actions related to water and marine resources must also be reported.[346] The minimum requirements of the MDR-A of ESRS 2 shall be met. The

341. Data point 1 in ESRS E3.
342. Data points 2 and 3 in ESRS E3.
343. Data point 8 in ESRS E3.
344. *See* section 15.3 above regarding this method.
345. Disclosure Requirement E3-1 in ESRS E3.
346. Disclosure Requirement E3-2 in ESRS E3.

activities may be allocated to one of the following links in a hierarchy to which they belong:

- avoid the use of water and marine resources;
- reduce the use of water and marine resources such as through efficiency measures;
- reclaiming and reusing water; or
- restoration and regeneration of aquatic ecosystems and water bodies.[347]

18.5.1.3 Metrics and Targets

Target. The company shall disclose adopted targets related to water and marine resources,[348] including whether and how the targets relate to the management of significant impacts, risks or opportunities related to water and marine resources and the reduction of water consumption.[349] The company may also report whether ecological thresholds were considered when setting the targets.[350] The minimum requirements of the MDR-T shall be met.[351]

Metrics. The company shall disclose its actual water consumption in relation to its material impacts, risks and opportunities,[352] including information on total water consumption in cubic metres, consumption in cubic metres in risk areas and necessary contextual information.[353]

Financial impact. The company must also report the financial effects of significant risks and opportunities related to impacts from water and marine resources.[354]

18.6 BIODIVERSITY AND ECOSYSTEMS (ESRS E4)

The ESRS E4 accounting standard describes how companies should report their activities linked to biodiversity and ecosystems. The purpose of the standard is for the reader to understand:

- how the company affects biodiversity and ecosystems, in terms of material positive and negative, actual and potential impacts, including the extent to which it contributes to the drivers of biodiversity and ecosystem loss and degradation;
- any actions taken, and the result of such actions, to prevent or mitigate material negative actual or potential impacts and to protect and restore biodiversity and ecosystems, and to address risks and opportunities;

347. Data point 18 in ESRS E3.
348. Disclosure Requirement E3-3 in ESRS E3.
349. Data point 23 in ESRS E3.
350. Data point 24 in ESRS E3.
351. Data point 22 in ESRS E3.
352. Disclosure Requirement E3-4 in ESRS E3.
353. Data point 28 in ESRS E3.
354. Disclosure Requirement E3-5 in ESRS E3.

- the plans and capacity of the company to adapt its strategy and business model in line with respecting planetary boundaries related to biosphere integrity and land system change, the vision of the Kunming-Montreal Global Biodiversity Framework and its relevant goals and targets, etc.;
- the nature, type and extent of the company's material risks, dependencies and opportunities related to biodiversity and ecosystems and how the company manages them; and
- the financial effects on the company over the short, medium and long term of material risks and opportunities arising from the company's impacts and dependencies on biodiversity and ecosystems.[355]

The definition of biodiversity is based on the definition in Article 2 of the Convention on Biological Diversity.[356] The standard recognises that biodiversity and ecosystems are closely linked to other environmental factors, with changes primarily driven by climate change, pollution, changes in land and sea, direct exploitation of organisms and invasive species.[357]

18.6.1 EU Biodiversity Strategy for 2030

One aim of the ESRS E4 standard is to make the reader understand how the company's business model and strategy are aligned with the EU Biodiversity Strategy for 2030.[358] This EU strategy was adopted during the COVID-19 pandemic, which raised awareness of the links between human health and the state of ecosystems. The strategy is based on several underlying factors. The economic benefits of preserving biodiversity are clear. The strategy refers to a report by the World Economic Forum, according to which more than half of the world's GDP depends on nature and the services it provides. Three sectors – construction, agriculture and food – are highly dependent on nature. The loss of biodiversity threatens not least food security. The strategy states that biodiversity loss and ecosystem collapse is one of the greatest threats facing humanity.

A key milestone of the strategy is for Europe's biodiversity to be on the path to recovery for the benefit of people, planet and climate by 2030, in line with the 2030 Agenda and the Paris Agreement. The strategy aims to address the five main drivers of biodiversity loss: land- and sea-use change, overexploitation, climate change and invasive alien species.

For 2030, key commitments and targets are set to protect and restore nature and ecosystems. The goals are ambitious and extensive:

- To legally protect at least 30% of the EU's land area and 30% of its seas and to integrate ecological corridors as part of the Trans-European Nature Network.
- To strictly protect at least one-third of the EU's protected areas, including all remaining primary and old-growth forests in the EU.

355. Data point 1 in ESRS E4.
356. *See* section 3.2.
357. Data point 4 in ESRS E4.
358. COM(2020) 380.

- To effectively manage all protected areas by defining clear conservation goals and measures and tracking them appropriately.
- Legally binding EU nature restoration targets proposed in 2021 following an impact assessment. By 2030, significant areas of degraded and carbon-rich ecosystems must be restored, habitats and species must show no deterioration in conservation trends and status, and at least 30% must reach favourable conservation status or at least show a positive trend.
- The decline of pollinators must be reversed.
- The risk and use of chemical pesticides are reduced by 50%, and the use of more hazardous pesticides is reduced by 50%.
- At least 10% of the agricultural area is under high-diversity landscape features.
- At least 25% of agricultural land is under organic farming management, and the uptake of agroecological practices has significantly increased.
- Three billion new trees are planted in the EU, in full respect of ecological principles.
- Significant progress has been made in the remediation of contaminated soil sites.
- At least 25,000 km of free-flowing rivers are restored.
- There is a 50% reduction in the number of Red List species threatened by invasive alien species.
- The losses of nutrients from fertilisers are reduced by 50%, resulting in the reduction of the use of fertilisers by at least 20%.
- Cities with at least 20,000 inhabitants have an ambitious Urban Greening Plan.
- No chemical pesticides are used in sensitive areas such as EU urban green areas.
- The negative impacts on sensitive species and habitats, including on the seabed through fishing and extraction activities, are substantially reduced to achieve good environmental status.
- The by-catch of species is eliminated or reduced to a level that allows species recovery and conservation.

18.6.2 Reporting Requirements

18.6.2.1 Business Model and Strategy

The company must disclose how it impacts biodiversity and ecosystem and from where dependencies, risks and opportunities originate and trigger the adaptation of its strategy and business model.[359] In doing so, the company shall describe the resilience of its strategy and business model in relation to biodiversity and ecosystems. The description should include:

359. Disclosure Requirement E4-1 in ESRS E4.

- an assessment of the resilience of the current business model and strategy to biodiversity and ecosystems-related physical, transition and systemic risks;
- the scope of the resilience analysis in relation to the company's own operations and its upstream and downstream value chain and in relation to the risks considered in that analysis;
- the key assumptions made;
- the time horizons used;
- the results of the resilience analysis; and
- the involvement of stakeholders.[360]

The company may describe its transition plan to improve and ultimately align between the business model, strategy and vision of the Kunming-Montreal Biodiversity Framework.

18.6.2.2 Management of Impacts, Risks and Opportunities

Process. The company shall describe its process for identifying material impacts, risks and opportunities.[361] The application requirements set out how companies can do this by using the LEAP method.[362] The description is relatively detailed, which can be assumed to be due to the lack of generally accepted standards in the field. The description of the process should include information about whether and how the company has:

- identified and assessed actual and potential impacts on biodiversity and ecosystems at their sites and in the value chain;
- identified and assessed their dependencies on biodiversity and ecosystems at their own sites and in the value chain;
- identified and assessed transition risks and physical risks and opportunities related to biodiversity and ecosystems;
- assessed systemic risks;
- consultations made with affected communities.[363]

Policies. The company must also report on the policies that have been put into practice to manage material impacts, risks and opportunities regarding biodiversity and ecosystems.[364] The minimum requirements of the MDR-P of ESRS 2 shall then be met. In addition, the report shall describe whether and to what extent these policies:

- relate to issues of climate change, land-use change, direct exploitation, invasive species and pollution;
- relate to significant impacts on biodiversity and ecosystems;

360. Data point 13 in ESRS E4.
361. Data point 17 in ESRS E4.
362. Application requirements 6-9 in ESRS E4.
363. Data point 17 in ESRS E4.
364. Disclosure Requirement E4-2 in ESRS E4.

- supports the traceability of products, components and raw materials to actual and potential impacts on biodiversity and ecosystems along the value chain;
- address production, sourcing or consumption from ecosystems that are managed to maintain or enhance conditions for biodiversity, as demonstrated by regular monitoring and reporting of biodiversity status and gains or losses, and
- address social consequences of biodiversity and ecosystem-related impacts.[365]

Actions. In addition, the company must report what actions are taken related to biodiversity and ecosystems and what resources have been given to implement these.[366] The minimum requirements of the MDR-A of ESRS 2 must then be met. In addition, the company must describe how the action has been given to their place in a hierarchy: avoidance, reduction and minimisation, recovery and rehabilitation.[367]

18.6.2.3 Metrics and Targets

Targets. The company must disclose the biodiversity and ecosystem targets it has adopted.[368] The minimum requirements of the MDR-T in ESRS 2 shall then be followed. The report shall include information on whether ecological thresholds and the allocation of impacts on the company were applied when the targets were set. If it did, the company shall specify whether the targets are informed by and consistent with the Kunming-Montreal Global Diversity Framework and relevant EU frameworks, how the targets relate to the company's operations and value chain, and the geographical scope of the targets.[369]

Metrics. In addition, the company must report metrics that describe the company's material impact on changes in biodiversity and ecosystems.[370]

Financial impact. Finally, potential financial impacts caused by significant risks and opportunities related to biodiversity and ecosystems must also be reported.[371]

18.7 RESOURCE USE AND CIRCULAR ECONOMY (ESRS E5)

The ESRS E5 accounting standard describes how companies should report their operations linked to resource use and circular economy. The purpose of the standard is for the reader to understand:

- how the company affects resource use, including resource efficiency, avoiding the depletion of resources and sustainable sourcing and use of renewable in terms of material positive and negative actual or potential impacts;

365. Data point 23 in ESRS E4.
366. Disclosure Requirement E4-3 in ESRS E4.
367. Data point 28(a) in ESRS E4.
368. Disclosure Requirement E4-4 in ESRS E4.
369. Data point 32 in ESRS E4.
370. Disclosure Requirement E4-5 in ESRS E4.
371. Disclosure Requirement E4-6 in ESRS E4.

- any actions taken, and the result of such actions, to prevent or mitigate actual or potential negative impacts arising from resource use, including its measures to help decouple its economic growth from the use of materials, and to address risks and opportunities;
- the plans and capacity of the company to adapt its strategy and business model in line with circular economy principles including but not limited to minimising waste, maintaining the value of products, materials and other resources at their highest value and enhancing their efficient use in production and consumption;
- the nature, type and extent of the company's material risks and opportunities related to the company's impacts and dependencies arising from resource use and circular economy and how the company manages them; and
- the financial effects on the company over the short, medium and long term of material risks and opportunities arising from the company's impacts and dependencies on resource use and circular economy.[372]

The focus of the standard is on inflows and outflows of resources as well as waste.[373] The concept of 'circular economy' is defined in the definitions list as an economic system in which the value of products, materials and other resources in the economy is maintained for as long as possible, enhancing their efficient use in production and consumption, thereby reducing the environmental impact of their use, minimising waste and the release of hazardous substances at all stages of their life cycle, including through the application of the waste hierarchy.

18.7.1 EU Circular Economy Action Plan

Like several of the other standards in the environmental area, ESRS E5 should be read in the context of established strategies within the EU, in this case, the EU's action plan for the circular economy.[374] There are several factors behind the action plan, the most fundamental of which is that the world is consuming resources that greatly exceed Earth's capacity. The extraction of resources causes more than half of total greenhouse gas emissions and over 90% of biodiversity loss, so a circular economy is considered necessary to achieve climate neutrality by 2050. The transition to a circular economy is also expected to create new jobs and lead to better and safer products and services for end users.

The action plan does not consist of a set of objectives but instead consists primarily of a list of legislative initiatives that the Commission will pursue, with several initiatives already taken since the adoption of the strategy. These include initiatives relating to:

372. Data point 1 in ESRS E5.
373. Data point 2 in ESRS E5.
374. COM(2020) 98.

- sustainable product design, which is important because 80% of the environmental impact of products is determined during the design phase;
- empowering consumers and public buyers, including through enhanced consumer legislation; and
- circularity in production processes.

The strategy identifies seven so-called key product value chains which are relevant in ESRS E5, namely:

- electronics and ICT;
- batteries and vehicles;
- packaging;
- plastic;
- textiles;
- construction and buildings; and
- food, water and nutrients.

18.7.2 Reporting Requirements

18.7.2.1 Management of Impacts, Risks and Opportunities

Process. ESRS 2 IRO-1 requires companies to disclose the process used to identify and assess material impacts, risks and opportunities. This also applies to resource use and the circular economy.[375] As with reporting according to, for example, ESRS E2 on pollution, the LEAP method must be used.[376] Appendix A of the standard sets out a wider range of application requirements for this process.[377]

Policies. The company must also disclose its policies for managing its material impacts, risks and opportunities related to resource use and circular economy.[378] The minimum requirements of the MDR-P of ESRS 2 shall then be followed. The report shall describe whether and how these policies address the transition away from the use of virgin resources and the sustainable sourcing and use of renewable resources.[379]

Actions. The company must also report what circular economy actions are being carried out and what resources are being used for this.[380] The minimum requirements of the MDR-A of ESRS 2 shall then be followed.

18.7.2.2 Targets and Metrics

Target. The company must report set targets regarding resource use and circular economy.[381] The minimum requirements of the MDR-T of ESRS 2 shall then be

375. Data point 11 in ESRS E5.
376. *See* section 9.3 regarding this method.
377. Disclosure Requirements 1-10 in Appendix B to ESRS E5.
378. Disclosure Requirement E5-1 in ESRS E5.
379. Data point 15 in ESRS E5.
380. Disclosure Requirement E5-2 in ESRS E5.
381. Disclosure Requirement E5-3 in ESRS E5.

followed. The report shall include a description of whether and how the targets are linked to the inflow or outflow of resources, the increase in circular design, the increased use of circular materials and the minimisation of non-renewable raw materials.[382] The company must also state whether ecological thresholds affected the set targets.[383]

Metrics. In addition, the company must report information on its material inflow.[384] The report shall describe the inflow of products (including packaging) and materials, property, plant and equipment used in the company's own operations and the value chain.[385] Companies that have assessed material inflow as material shall disclose more information on:

- the total weight of products and materials;
- proportion of biological material used to manufacture the company's products and services that are sustainably sourced; and
- the weight in absolute and % of reused and recycled components, materials, etc., used to manufacture the company's products and services.[386]

The company must also disclose information about its material output, including waste.[387] The report shall describe the company's key products and materials from the company's production process designed according to circular principles, including the circular principles of durability, reusability, reparability, disassembly, remanufacturing, refurbishment, recycling, recirculation by the biological cycle, or optimisation of the use of the product or material through other circular business models.[388] In addition, companies whose material outputs are significant shall provide information on the expected durability of products placed on the market, the reparability of products and the rates of recycled content of products and their packaging.[389] In addition, the company must disclose information about its waste, including the total waste generated and the extent to which different types of waste are or are not recovered.[390]

Financial impact. Finally, companies must reveal potential financial effects from significant risks and opportunities related to the impact of resource use and the circular economy.[391]

18.8 REPORTING REQUIREMENTS UNDER THE EU TAXONOMY

As has already been explained in more detail in Chapter 9, the EU taxonomy contains definitions of what are considered environmentally sustainable activities. According to

382. Data point 24 in ESRS E5.
383. Data point 26 in ESRS E5.
384. Disclosure Requirement E5-4 in ESRS E5.
385. Data point 30 in ESRS E5.
386. Data point 31 in ESRS E5.
387. Disclosure Requirement E5-5 in ESRS E5.
388. Data point 35 in ESRS E5.
389. Data point 36 in ESRS E5.
390. Data point 37 in ESRS E5.
391. Disclosure Requirement E5-6 in ESRS E5.

Article 8 of the EU Taxonomy, companies subject to the sustainability reporting requirement shall include information on how and to what extent the undertaking's activities are associated with economic activities to be considered environmentally sustainable under the EU Taxonomy.[392] Chapter 9 describes in more detail how this reporting should be done.

392. Article 8 EU Taxonomy.

CHAPTER 19
Social Sustainability (S)

In the scenarios made using the Earth4All model, described in Chapter 1, what is likely to happen first in the Too Little Too Late scenario is not an environmental collapse but instead a societal collapse, largely caused by the social tensions resulting from excessive levels of inequality. Businesses have a large potential and actual positive and negative impact on people and society. In this chapter, the focus has therefore shifted to social sustainability.

Four standards for social sustainability published so far: ESRS S1–S4:

(i) ESRS S1 - Own workforce
(ii) ESRS S2 - Workers in the value chain
(iii) ESRS S3 - Affected communities
(iv) ESRS S4 - Consumers and end-users

This chapter will deal with each of these standards. As in the previous chapter, relevant areas of law linked to each standard will be addressed, including labour law and marketing law. Before that, the place of social sustainability in the Earth4All model and the sustainable moral basis of social sustainability are discussed.

19.1 CONNECTION TO THE EARTH4ALL MODEL

The activities covered by the four ESRS-S standards are included in a variety of ways in Earth4All-Model. The first variable of the well-being index is dignity, measured in disposable income. Income often comes from businesses. The variable connection is measured in terms of government spending, where companies contribute to financing by paying taxes and undermine financing by avoiding paying taxes in the country. Whether companies contribute significantly to increasing or decreasing equality in society is measured in the fairness variable of the well-being index. Finally, firms influence the variable participation, as firms influence how well-being changes over time.

Section 1.3 presented the report on the impact of firms on inequality published by the BCTI. The report includes a list of ten activities that companies can influence to promote greater equality, mapped to the four stakeholder categories covered by the ESRS-S:[393]

	Own Workforce	*Workers in the Value Chain*	*Affected Communities*	*Consumers and End-Users*
Non-compliance with the UN Guiding Principles	X	X	X	X
Manufacturing expensive products that are not accessible to everyone			X	X
Lack of diversity, equity and inclusion	X	X	X	X
Failure to contribute to the transition to the future of work	X	X		X
Unsafe working conditions	X	X		
Low wages and incomes	X	X		
Discourage employee representation	X	X		
Discouraging effective public policy			X	
Avoiding tax			X	
Avoiding just transition to a net-zero economy	X	X	X	X

As shown in several places in the book, social sustainability is also closely linked to environmental sustainability, where inequality accelerates climate change and undermines trust in society, which leads to difficulties in adopting and making environmental reforms, and so on.

19.2 SUSTAINABILITY MORAL FOUNDATION

There are four categories of people affected by ESRS S1-4: the company's own workforce, workers in the value chain, people in affected communities, and consumers and end-users. For each category, it is a matter of respect for equality and freedom. However, the perspective will be slightly different depending on the category in

393. BCTi, Tackling inequality: An agenda for business action, 2023, section 29. The list is here rewritten as a list of activities that companies can take to increase inequality, and thus contribute to the reinforcing relationships described in the Earth4All model in the Too Little Too Late scenario.

question. The redesigned list from the BCTI report in the previous section is a list of examples of possible violations of the equality and freedom of individuals.

The company's own workforce. The moral foundation here is the same as the foundation for EU labour law. The basis of EU labour law is the strong dependence of employees on their employers. In a typical employment relationship, the employer accounts for the majority of the employees' income and has the right to decide what the employees should do for the majority of their waking hours during the week. This state of affairs creates powerful opportunities for employers to violate the equality and freedom of their employees, and labour law is aimed at creating a more balanced situation.

Workers in the value chain. Companies should also respect the equality and freedom of the workers in their value chain. Admittedly, there is an important difference here since these workers do not have the same dependence on the company as employees of the company. However, this does not prevent the company from having a moral responsibility. As seen in Part V of the book, companies can create clear negative social impacts through how they contract with actors in the value chain. This may involve price pressure and high delivery requirements from the customer, which are easily passed on as external effects from the supplier to its workers or to companies and workers at subcontractors. The company can, therefore, either respect or violate the equality and freedom of value-chain workers.

Affected communities. Companies also have an indirect impact on people in surrounding communities affected by the company's operations. Such people are affected in an even more indirect way by the company's operations than workers in the value chain. This does not prevent companies, from a moral perspective, from being required to respect their right to equality and freedom as well. Furthermore, companies have a general impact on society, for example, by paying or avoiding paying taxes. State funding is crucial for the state to provide the community-supporting institutions essential for a life of equality and freedom.

Consumers and end-users. The relationship between consumers and end-users with companies is not characterised by the same degree of dependence as employees' relationship with the employer. Still, it is about a relationship of subordination, where companies typically have a strong information advantage and have the opportunity to affect and even manipulate individuals through various activities to make decisions favourable to the company but not to the individual. Of course, the degree of possible impact depends on the size of the company and the goods or services involved.

Businesses can violate the dignity of consumers and end-users from both the perspective of equality and freedom. The perspective of freedom is perhaps the most obvious. It is about the individual's right and opportunity to set up and live according to their own goals and values without being limited by dependence on others. This includes the right to decide independently which goods and services one wants to consume. Such decisions require a basis of information, for example, about the options available, the advantages and disadvantages of different options from the individual's perspective, and so on. A company that manipulates this information base by giving the impression that a product has, for example, certain characteristics it does not have violates the individual's right to live an authentic, unmanipulated life. This is the basis for the marketing law's prohibition of unfair marketing. If the company also does this by, without the individual's knowledge, using information about their buying behaviours, tastes, preferences, etc., the moral offence increases. This is part of the basis for the personal data law's obligations regarding transparency, legal basis, etc. Of course, many rules of consumer law also fall into this moral category. But in consumer law, it can also be a matter of lack of respect for the individual's equality, for example, through the sale of products harmful to health.

19.3 OWN WORKFORCE (ESRS S1)

According to the ESRS S1 standard, companies must report their activities in relation to their own workforce. The purpose is for the reader to understand the company's material impact on its own workforce as well as risks and opportunities, including:

- how the company affects its own workforce in terms of material positive and negative actual or potential impacts;
- any actions taken, and the result of such actions, to prevent, mitigate or remediate actual or potential negative impacts, and to address risks and opportunities;
- the nature, type and extent of the company's material risks and opportunities related to its impacts and dependencies on its own workforce, and how the company manages them; and
- the financial effects on the company over the short, medium and long term of material risks and opportunities arising from the undertaking's impacts and dependencies on its own workforce.[394]

The report covers three main areas:

(1) working conditions;
(2) equal treatment and opportunities; and
(3) other work-related rights.[395]

19.3.1 General Disclosure Requirements

The requirements of ESRS 2 also need to be met regarding the company's own workforce. The company must disclose how the interests, opinions, rights and expectations of workers who are significantly affected by the company's operations have been considered.[396] Furthermore, the link between the company's business

394. Data point 1 in ESRS S1.
395. Data point 2 in ESRS S1.
396. Data point 12 of ESRS S1.

model and strategy and the impact on the company's own workers must be described.[397] This includes the impact caused by the company's operations, products or services. To create a nuanced understanding of these impacts, companies should include information on:

- a brief description of the types of employees and non-employees in its own workforce subject to material impacts by its operations, and specify whether they are employees, self-employed people, or people provided by third-party undertakings primarily engaged in employment activities;
- in the case of material negative impacts, whether they are either widespread or systemic in contexts where the company operates or related to individual incidents;
- in the case of material positive impacts, a brief description of the activities that result in the positive impacts, the types of employees and non-employees in its own workforce that are positively affected or could be positively affected;
- any material risks and opportunities for the company arising from impacts and dependencies on its own workforce;
- any material impacts on its own workforce that may arise from transition plans for reducing negative impacts on the environment and achieving greener and climate-neutral operations;
- operations at significant risk of incidents of forced labour or compulsory labour; and
- operations at significant risk of incidents of child labour.[398]

19.3.2 Management of Impacts, Risks and Opportunities

Policies. The company shall disclose its policies and procedures for managing its material impact on employees, including a summary of these documents.[399] The minimum requirements of the MDR-P in ESRS 2 shall then be met. This includes a description of any human rights commitments, including the UN Guiding Principles and the OECD Guidelines for Multinational Enterprises.[400]

Process. The company must also disclose its processes for interacting with its own employees and their representatives on issues of actual and potential material impact.[401] This requirement includes describing the scope of the interaction, how early in the process the workers are involved, and which function with the highest position within the company is responsible for the interaction.[402]

397. Data point 13 of ESRS S1.
398. Data point 14 of ESRS S1.
399. Disclosure requirement S1-1.
400. Data point 20 of ESRS S1.
401. ESRS S1-2 disclosure requirement S1.
402. Data point 27 of ESRS S1.

Companies must also report on their processes for remedying negative impacts on staff and which channels staff can use to make complaints, etc.[403] The process shall cover all fourteen domains described in data point 2 of ESRS S1 and presented in the table below.

Actions. In addition, the company must report the actions it undertakes to manage material adverse and positive impacts on its own workforce.[404] The minimum requirements of the MDR-A of ESRS 2 shall then be followed.

19.3.3 *Metrics and Targets*

Disclosure requirements S1-5 to S1-17 contain extensive requirements for reporting data and target figures linked to the fourteen areas of own workers specified in data point 2 of ESRS S1. The table below, which is a summary of appendices A.1 to A.4 of ESRS S1, lists the factors that can be considered in materiality assessments, which policies could be relevant in each area, possible activities to manage material impacts and possible target figures in each area.

The following table below should primarily be read as a description of the ideal image of EU law, which companies must relate to when they report their work with their own workforce.

Area	*Examples of Factors to Consider in Materiality Assessment*	*Examples of Policies*	*Examples of Activities*	*Examples of Goals*
Secure employment	Percentage of temporary contract employees, ratio of non-employee workers to employees, social protection	Restrictions on temporary employment, job security schemes	Offer permanent contracts and implement job security programmes when the government does not offer them	Increase the share of workers with employment contracts, in particular fixed-term contracts
Working time	Percentage of part-time employees in the workforce, satisfaction with working time	Restrictions on overtime, night work, weekend work, etc.	Job rotation, reduce too much overtime	Increase the share of workers with flexible working hours

403. ESRS S1-3 disclosure requirement S1.
404. ESRS S1-4 disclosure requirement S1.

Area	*Examples of Factors to Consider in Materiality Assessment*	*Examples of Policies*	*Examples of Activities*	*Examples of Goals*
Adequate wages	Legal definitions of fair and minimum wages	Adequate pay for all	Negotiate adequate wages in collective agreements	Pay adequate wages to all
Social dialogue	Extent of employee representation	Encouragement of social dialogue, information and consultation of workers' representatives	Increase discussion on sustainability issues in social dialogue	Increase social dialogue in places of establishment and countries
Freedom of association, collective bargaining	Percentage of own workforce with collective bargaining agreements	Affirm freedom of association and do not discourage it	Increase the scope of sustainability issues in collective bargaining	Increase the proportion of employees covered by collective bargaining agreements
Work-life balance	Family-related leaves, flexible working hours	Opportunities for parental leave, flexible working hours, etc.	Increase opportunities for parental leave and flexible working hours	Increase the proportion of employees covered by measures
Health and safety	Fatal accidents, accidents, work-related ill-health	Include all employees in your company's health and safety programme	Increase health and safety training, invest in safer equipment	Reduce the number of injuries and lost working time due to injuries
Gender equality and equal pay for work of equal value	Percentage of women in management team, pay gap between males and females	Gender equality and equal treatment in pay	Recruitment and promotion of women, reducing the pay gap	Increase the percentage of women in the workforce and top management

Area	*Examples of Factors to Consider in Materiality Assessment*	*Examples of Policies*	*Examples of Activities*	*Examples of Goals*
Training and skills development	Scope of training and education, regular performance and development meetings	Increase skills and career opportunities for employees	Increasing training to close skills gaps	Increase the percentage of employees who receive training and education
Employment and inclusion of people with disabilities	Percentage of employees with disabilities	Workplace accessible for disabled people	Take more steps to increase availability	Increase the proportion of employees with disabilities
Measures against violence and harassment in the workplace	Prevalence of violence and harassment	Zero tolerance for violence and harassment	Improve complaint mechanism, increase sanctions for violence and harassment	Include all locations in the scope of action.
Diversity	Representativeness in the workforce of women and ethnic minorities. Age distribution	Inclusion and positive action	Diversity and Inclusion Training, Targeted Recruitment	Increase the share of underrepresented groups in the workforce
Child labour	Businesses and geographies at risk of child labour	Identification and mitigation of risks	Measures to verify age, partnerships with NGOs, etc.	Increase the scope of operations to more than the percentage of the business
Forced labour	Activities and geographies at risk of forced labour	Identification and mitigation of risks	Measures to increase voluntary consent to employment	Increase the scope of operations to more than the percentage of the business

19.4 WORKERS IN THE VALUE CHAIN (ESRS S2)

According to the ESRS S2 standard, companies must report their activities in relation to workers in the value chain. A worker in the value chain is defined as an individual performing work in the value chain of the company, regardless of the existence or nature of any contractual relationship with the undertaking. In the ESRS, the scope of workers in the value chain includes all workers in the company's upstream and downstream value chain who are or can be materially impacted by the company.

The standard is in many respects similar to ESRS S1, which was discussed in the previous chapter. The aim is for the reader to understand:

- how the company affects workers in its value chain, in terms of material positive and negative actual or potential impacts;
- any actions taken, and the result of such actions, to prevent, mitigate or remediate actual or potential negative impacts, and to address risks and opportunities;
- the nature, type and extent of the company's material risks and opportunities, including those related to its impacts and dependencies on workers in the value chain, and how the company manages them; and
- the financial effects on the company over the short, medium and long term of material risks and opportunities, including those arising from the company's impacts and dependencies on workers in the value chain.[405]

The requirements cover three main areas:

(i) working conditions;
(ii) equal treatment and opportunities; and
(iii) other work-related rights.[406]

19.4.1 General Disclosure Requirements

The requirements of ESRS 2 also need to be met with regard to workers in the value chain. The company must, therefore, disclose how the interests, opinions, rights and expectations of workers in the value chain who are significantly affected by the company's operations have been considered.[407] Furthermore, the link between the company's business model and strategy and the impact on the value chain workers are described.[408] To create a nuanced understanding of these impacts, companies should include information on:

- the types of value chain workers who could be materially impacted by the company;
- any geographies or types of goods where there is a significant risk of child or forced labour;
- whether material adverse impacts are widespread or systematic in the environments in which the company operates;
- activities that result in positive impact; and

405. Data point 1 in ESRS S2.
406. ESRS S2 data point 2.
407. Data point 9 of ESRS S2.
408. Data point 10 of ESRS S2.

- significant risks and opportunities for the company due to the impact of or dependence on workers in the value chain.[409]

19.4.2 Management of Impacts, Risks and Opportunities

Policies. The company shall disclose its policies and procedures for managing its material impact on workers in the value chain, including a summary of these documents.[410] The minimum requirements of the MDR-P of ESRS 2 shall be followed. This includes a description of any human rights commitments, including the UN Guiding Principles and the OECD Guidelines for Multinational Enterprises.[411]

Process. The company must also disclose its processes for interacting with workers in the value chain and their representatives on issues of actual and potential material impact.[412] This requirement includes describing the scope of the interaction, how early in the process the workers in the value chain are involved and which function with the highest position within the company is responsible for the interaction.[413]

Companies must also report on their processes for remedying negative impacts on workers in the value chain and which channels workers in the value chain can use to make complaints, etc.[414]

Actions. In addition, the company must disclose the actions it undertakes to manage material negative and positive impacts on workers in the value chain.[415] The minimum requirements of the MDR-A of ESRS 2 shall be met. This includes reporting plans, resources used to implement the plans and individual activities.[416]

19.4.3 Metrics and Targets

Finally, companies must disclose time-bound and result-oriented targets for:

- reducing negative impacts on workers in the value chain; and/or
- advance the positive impact on workers in the value chain; and/or
- managing material risks and opportunities for people in the value chain.[417]

409. Data point 11 of ESRS S2.
410. Disclosure requirement S2-1.
411. Data point 17 of ESRS S2-1.
412. Disclosure requirement S2-2.
413. Data point 22 of ESRS S2.
414. Disclosure requirement S2-3.
415. Disclosure requirement S2-4.
416. Data point 32 of ESRS S2.
417. ESRS S2-5 disclosure requirement S2.

19.5 AFFECTED COMMUNITIES (ESRS S3)

According to the ESRS S3 standard, companies must report their work in relation to affected communities. Affected communities are defined as people or group(s) living or working in the same area that have been or may be affected by a reporting company's operations or through its upstream and downstream value chain, including indigenous peoples.

The standard is in many respects similar to both ESRS S1 and S2. The aim is for the reader to understand:

- how the company affects communities, in areas where impacts are most likely to be present and severe, in terms of material positive and negative actual or potential impacts;
- any actions taken, and the result of such actions, to prevent, mitigate or remediate actual or potential negative impacts, and to address risks and opportunities;
- the nature, type and extent of the company's material risks and opportunities related to its impacts and dependencies on affected communities, and how the undertaking manages them; and
- the financial effects on the company's over the short, medium and long term of material risks and opportunities arising from the company's impacts and dependencies on affected communities.[418]

The company shall describe its general approach to identifying and managing actual and potential material impacts on communities related to:

- the economic, social and cultural rights of communities (e.g., adequate housing, food and water);
- civil and political rights (e.g., freedom of expression and association); and
- particular rights of indigenous peoples.[419]

19.5.1 General Disclosure Requirements

The requirements of ESRS 2 also need to be met for affected communities. The company must, therefore, disclose how the views, interests, and rights of affected communities, including respect for their human rights (and their rights as indigenous peoples, where applicable), inform its strategy and business model.[420] To create a nuanced understanding of these impacts, companies should include information on:

- the types of communities that are materially affected by the company's own operations or value chain;

418. Data point 1 of ESRS S3.
419. ESRS S3 data point 2.
420. Data point 7 of ESRS S3.

- whether any material adverse impacts are widespread or systematic in the context in which the company operates;
- activities that result in a positive impact; and
- material risks and opportunities for the company due to impacts from or dependence on affected communities.[421]

19.5.2 Management of Impacts, Risks and Opportunities

Policies. The company shall describe its policies adopted to manage its material impacts on affected communities, as well as associated material risks and opportunities.[422] The minimum requirements of the MDR-P of ESRS 2 shall be followed. This includes a description of any human rights commitments, including the UN Guiding Principles and the OECD Guidelines for Multinational Enterprises.[423]

Process. The company shall further disclose its processes for interacting with affected communities and their representatives on issues of actual and potential material impact.[424] This requirement includes describing the scope of the interaction, how early in processes the affected communities are involved, and which person with the highest position within the company is responsible for the interaction.[425]

Companies must also report on their processes for remedying negative impacts on communities and the channels that affected communities can use to make complaints, etc.[426]

Actions. In addition, the company must report the actions it undertakes to manage material negative and positive impacts on affected communities.[427] The minimum requirements of the MDR-A of ESRS 2 must then be followed. This includes reporting plans, resources used to implement the plans and individual actions.[428]

19.5.3 Metrics and Targets

Finally, companies must disclose any time-bound and result-oriented targets for:

- reduction of negative impacts on communities; and/or
- advancing in positive impacts on communities; and/or
- management of material risks and opportunities affected communities.[429]

421. Data point 9 of ESRS S3.
422. Disclosure requirement S3-1.
423. Data point 16 of ESRS S1.
424. Disclosure requirement S3-2.
425. Data point 20 of ESRS S3.
426. Disclosure requirement S3-3.
427. Disclosure requirement S3-4.
428. Data point 31 of ESRS S3.
429. ESRS S3-5 disclosure requirement S3.

19.6 PROTECTION OF CONSUMERS AND END-USERS (ESRS S4)

According to the ESRS S4 standard, companies must report their work in relation to consumers and end-users. Consumers are defined as individuals who acquire, consume or use goods and services for personal use, either for themselves or for others, and not for resale, commercial or trade, business, craft or professional purposes. End users are defined as individuals who ultimately use or intend to ultimately use a particular product or service. As end-users are included, sales of goods and services by companies to other companies also need to be considered insofar as they are intended to be used by end-users. For example, it could be the other company's employees or customers.

The standard is similar to the other standards regarding social sustainability. The aim is for the reader to understand:

- how the company affects the consumers and/or end-users of its products and/or services in terms of material positive and negative actual or potential impacts;
- any actions taken, and the result of such actions, to prevent, mitigate or remediate actual or potential negative impacts and to address risks and opportunities;
- the nature, type and extent of the company's material risks and opportunities related to its impacts and dependencies on consumers and end-users, and how the company manages such risks and opportunities; and
- the financial effects on the company over the short, medium and long term of material risks and opportunities arising from the company's impacts and dependencies on consumers and/or end-users.[430]

The company shall describe its general approach to identifying and addressing actual and potential material impacts on consumers and end-users related to:

- information-related impact on consumers and end-users (e.g., privacy and freedom of expression);
- personal safety of consumers and end-users (e.g., health and safety);
- social inclusion of consumers and end-users (e.g., non-discrimination and responsible marketing).[431]

19.6.1 General Disclosure Requirements

The requirements of ESRS 2 also need to be met with regard to consumers and end-users. The company must, therefore, disclose how the interests, views and rights of its consumers and/or end-users, including respect for their human rights, inform its strategy and business model.[432] To create a nuanced understanding of these impacts, companies should include information on:

430. ESRS S4 data point 1.
431. Data point 2 of ESRS S4.
432. Data point 8 of ESRS S4.

- the types of consumers and end-users who are materially affected by the company's operations or value chain, including consumers and end-users: (i) by products that are inherently harmful to people or that increase the risk of chronic diseases; (ii) by services with a potentially negative impact on privacy, freedom of expression and non-discrimination; (iii) that rely on accurate product or service descriptions; and (iv) that are vulnerable to sales or marketing and sales strategies (e.g., children);
- whether any material adverse impacts are widespread or systematic in the environments in which the company operates;
- activities that result in positive impact;
- material risks and opportunities for the company due to the impact of or dependence on consumers and end-users.[433]

19.6.2 Management of Impacts, Risks and Opportunities

Policies. The company shall disclose its policies adopted to manage the material impacts of its products and/or services on consumers and end-users, as well as associated material risks and opportunities.[434] The minimum requirements of the MDR-P in ESRS 2 shall then be followed. This includes a description of any human rights commitments, including the UN Guiding Principles and the OECD Guidelines for Multinational Enterprises.[435]

Process. The company shall further disclose its general processes for engaging with consumers and end-users and their representatives about actual and potential impacts on them.[436] This requirement includes describing the interaction, how early in the process consumers and end users are involved, and which function with the highest position within the company is responsible for the interaction.[437]

Companies must also report on their processes for remedying negative impacts on consumers and end-users, as well as the channels that consumers and end-users can use to make complaints, etc.[438]

Actions. In addition, the company shall disclose the actions it undertakes to address material adverse and positive impacts on consumers and end-users.[439] This includes reporting plans, resources used to implement the plans and individual activities.

433. Data point 10 of ESRS S4.
434. Disclosure requirement S4-1.
435. Data point 16 of ESRS S4.
436. ESRS S4 disclosure requirement S3-2.
437. Data point 20 of ESRS S4.
438. ESRS S4-3 disclosure requirement S4.
439. ESRS S4-4 disclosure requirement S4.

19.6.3 Metrics and Targets

Finally, companies must disclose any time-bound and result-oriented targets for:

- reduction of negative impacts on consumers and end-users; and/or
- advancing positive impact on consumers and end-users; and/or
- addressing material risks and opportunities for consumers and end-users.[440]

440. ESRS S4-5 disclosure requirement S4.

CHAPTER 20

Governance (G)

Chapter 17 dealt with the general requirements for sustainability reports business in ESRS 2. Requirements regarding governance, strategies, business models and more were also described. The ESRS G1 standard deals with more specific requirements linked to companies' business conduct. This concept includes the following areas:

- business ethics and corporate culture, including anti-corruption and anti-bribery, the protection of whistleblowers, and animal welfare;
- the management of relationships with suppliers, including payment practices; and
- activities and commitments of the undertaking related to exerting its political influence, including its lobbying activities.[441]

This chapter covers a number of these areas, namely corporate culture, anti-corruption, supplier relationship management and lobbying. In the treatment of environmental and social sustainability, the links to the Earth4All model were described, as well as the sustainability moral basis for all relevant standards. However, ESRS G1 deals with disparate areas, so the connections to the Earth4All model and sustainability moral aspects are dealt with in the context of each area instead.

20.1 CORPORATE CULTURE

According to disclosure requirement G1-1, companies must disclose their policies regarding business conduct and how they foster their corporate culture. The purpose is for the reader to understand the extent to which the company has policies that address the identification, assessment, management and/or remediation of its material impacts, risks and opportunities regarding the company's conduct. The aim is also to create an understanding of the company's approach to corporate culture.[442]

441. Data point 2 of ESRS G1.
442. Data point 8 of ESRS G1.

20.1.1 Connection to Earth4All-Model

Chapter 2 dealt with Douglass North's description of institutions as a set of formal and informal rules of the game. His perspective is applied here to companies, where laws, adopted policies and procedures, employment contracts with incentive systems, and more constitute the formal rules of the game. But of course, there are also informal rules of the game within companies. These informal rules of the game are often referred to as *corporate culture* and often have a strong impact on the company's actions and results. In Chapter 6, it was recommended that the company adopt its core values as part of its core ideology, which is more or less the same as saying that a non-harming corporate culture should be created.

The corporate culture has an indirect, yet very important, connection to the Earth4All model. In principle, the corporate culture affects all actions in the company. Therefore, it is impossible to point out any specific areas within the Earth4All model that are particularly affected by corporate culture. Since the corporate culture permeates most of the company's activities, it is instead about influencing all of the company's actions that in some way are connected to the mechanisms of the Earth4All model. Some companies have a distinct low-cost culture, which can have advantages but also can mean that unsustainable alternatives are chosen. Other companies have an unequal corporate culture, which reinforces gender inequality and, thus, inequality in society. And so on.

20.1.2 Sustainability Moral Foundation

The requirement for a description of the corporate culture rests directly on the moral foundation on which sustainability law, in general, rests. Corporate culture is the informal values, principles and habits that guide the company's actions and, ultimately, the results of the company's operations. It is a well-known expression that corporate culture eats corporate strategy for breakfast. A company may have a business model, strategy, governing documents, processes, etc., that aim to follow the due diligence norm. However, if the informal corporate culture is not aligned with the formal rules of the game, the latter will play a minor role, or at least their effect will be severely limited. Having formal rules for due diligence but informal rules that do not support this is, from a moral perspective, tantamount to lacking integrity and showing a lack of 'character'. This is the reason the corporate culture should be accounted for.

20.1.3 Reporting Requirements

The requirement to disclose corporate culture is one of the most poorly described in the ESRS standards. *Every* company has a corporate culture. The important thing should be what behaviour this corporate culture generates, not least whether it generates behaviour that favours sustainable business or not. However, this is not how the requirement is formulated, but the requirement is only linked to corporate culture in the abstract sense: 'The undertaking shall disclose its policies with respect to business conduct matters and how it fosters its corporate culture.'

More specific reporting requirements are available in terms of company policies. The information shall include:

- a description of the mechanisms for identifying, reporting and investigating concerns about unlawful behaviour or behaviour in contradiction of the company's code of conduct or similar internal rules and whether it accommodates reporting from internal and/or external stakeholders;
- where the company has no policies on anti-corruption or anti-bribery consistent with the United Nations Convention against Corruption, it shall state this and whether it has plans to implement them and the timetable for implementation;
- how the undertaking protects whistleblowers;
- where the undertaking has no policies on the protection of whistleblowers, it shall state this and whether it has plans to implement them and the timetable for implementation;
- beyond the procedures to follow up on reports by whistleblowers in accordance with the applicable law transposing Directive (EU) 2019/1937, whether the company has procedures to investigate business conduct incidents, including incidents of corruption and bribery, promptly, independently and objectively;
- where applicable, whether the company has in place policies with respect to animal welfare;
- the company's policy for training within the organisation on business conduct, including target audience, frequency and depth of coverage; and
- the functions within the undertaking that are most at risk in respect of corruption and bribery.[443]

20.2 SUPPLIER RELATIONSHIP MANAGEMENT

Disclosure requirement G1-2 of ESRS G1 requires companies to describe how they manage their relationships with suppliers and their impact on their supply chain. The purpose is for the reader to gain an understanding of the company's management and of its procurement process, including fair behaviour with suppliers.[444]

20.2.1 Connection to the Earth4All Model

Through their impact on the supply chain, companies can have a significant indirect impact on all elements of the Earth4All model that companies in the supply chain influence, for example, in terms of greenhouse gas emissions, working conditions and

443. Data point 10 of ESRS G1.
444. Data point 13 of ESRS G1.

equality. It is, therefore, not possible to single out a specific area. Companies can create positive effects by setting requirements for and primarily choosing suppliers with low greenhouse gas emissions. They can also create negative effects by using unfair behaviour to squeeze suppliers' margins, to the detriment of their ability to invest in, for example, a good working environment for their staff. These are effects that, in turn, affect the suppliers' impact in the Earth4All model.

The question of how companies can influence environmental and social factors through their supplier relationships is discussed in more detail in Part IV on contracts and Part V on the value chain.

20.2.2 Sustainability Moral Foundation

The sustainability moral foundation for the requirements for reporting information about suppliers has both an indirect and a direct dimension. In the direct dimension, it is about the moral requirements of the company's direct relationship with the suppliers. A few examples will be enough to show this.

As stated above, companies are expected to report their routines for payment of supplier invoices. It is not uncommon for companies to apply a 60 or 90-day payment period for their supplier invoices, while the company expects payment of its customer invoices within 30 days. Sometimes, objective reasons for this inconsistency can be demonstrated, but in many cases, it is simply a matter of using power in relation to suppliers to improve their so-called working capital. Working capital is calculated by subtracting the current liabilities from the current assets and shows how the company finances its operations in the short term. Of course, the company's ability to finance increases if it is paid faster by its customers than it needs to pay its suppliers. The problem is that the supplier also needs good working capital to finance *its* operations in the short term. Treating a supplier less favourably than the company expects to be treated by its customers is, from a moral perspective, a violation of the principle of equality.

Using one's power to impair a supplier's working capital further limits the supplier's ability to act. This is where the more indirect sustainability moral dimension lies. With impaired working capital, the supplier's ability to choose sustainable materials, working methods, terms of employment and so on is easily limited, which risks the supplier contributing negatively to several aspects of the Earth4All model, for example, through its wages, carbon dioxide emissions and so on.

20.2.3 Reporting Requirements

CSRD's most comprehensive requirements are aimed at large companies. They often have a great deal of power in relation to suppliers as purchasers of goods and services. Companies should disclose how they manage their supplier relationships and their impact on the supply chain.[445] In doing so, the company shall include information

445. Disclosure requirement G1-2 of ESRS G1.

about the company's approach to its supplier relationships, taking account of risks to the company related to its supply chain and of impacts on sustainability matters and whether and how it takes into account social and environmental criteria for the selection of its suppliers. The company shall also provide a description of its policy to prevent late payments, specifically to small- and medium-sized enterprises.[446]

20.3 BRIBERY AND CORRUPTION

Disclosure requirement G1-3 requires companies to disclose their system for preventing, detecting, investigating and responding to allegations of or incidents related to corruption and bribery, including related training. The purpose of the requirement is, of course, to create transparency around these issues for the reader.[447]

20.3.1 Connection to the Earth4All Model

The link between corruption and, for example, the climate crisis is not obvious to everyone. However, the Earth4All model provides an opportunity to highlight the important connections between corruption and a socially and environmentally sustainable future. A distinction needs to be made between corruption in the public and private sectors. Corruption in the public sector is primarily harmful because it undermines trust in society – as citizens begin to doubt the state's impartiality – and can lead to an unequal distribution of resources that should be distributed equally. It can also make it unattractive for companies to invest in the country due to the uncertainty surrounding the return on investment. Corruption in the private sector is harmful because it undermines the efficiency of the market when resources are allocated on the basis of economically irrelevant considerations.

The link between social trust and the Earth4All model has already been described in Chapter 1. In the model, social trust primarily plays a role linked to society's ability to adopt reforms required to limit the climate crisis and its effects. However, studies show that corruption harms most aspects of human welfare, from public health to softer aspects such as life satisfaction, support for democracy, and perceptions of political legitimacy.[448] This means that corruption and bribery actually affect all factors in the well-being index of the Earth4All model.

20.3.2 Sustainability Moral Foundation

The legislation on bribery and corruption rests on the same moral foundation as sustainability law in general. It is about respect for human dignity, expressed in the two principles of equality and freedom. This connection is not necessarily clear to everyone. This is probably partly due to the difficulty of defining what actually constitutes

446. Data point 14 of ESRS G1. *See also* disclosure requirements G1-G in ESRS G1.
447. Data point 17 of ESRS G1.
448. Rothstein, B., Controlling Corruption, Oxford University Press, 2021, 11.

corruption. The political scientists Jan Teorell and Bo Rothstein have, to deal with this problem, pointed out that it is better to start from the opposite of corrupt behaviour. Uncorrupt actions, what is it? Teorell and Rothstein argue, rightly in my view, that this is an act of *impartiality*.[449] Impartial behaviour is characterised by the fact that the person deciding by a public authority or a commercial decision, for example, acts *independently of the* interests of those affected by the decision.

Teorell and Rothstein have only public sector employees in mind when they describe uncorrupt behaviour as impartiality. In the case of civil servants, it is clear what is meant: the state's power cannot maintain its legitimacy unless the state treats all its citizens equally, under the principles of equality and freedom. This means that civil servants must be impartial in the exercise of their authority and make decisions on the basis of objective criteria independent of those affected by the decision.

However, a company does not have a monopoly of power over all members of society. Its employees have, first and foremost, a duty of loyalty to their employer. Exactly what this duty of loyalty means is debatable, not least given the discussion in Chapter 6 about what the company's purpose really is. Regardless of whether the company's purpose is shareholder value maximisation or to consider the interests of relevant stakeholders, the private employee's duty is to promote the company's interests to make impartial decisions, and otherwise act impartially in relation to those affected by the decisions or actions to promote these purposes.

Whose equality and freedom are violated by bribery? It can be argued that the bribery is actually violating the bribed because the person bribing is trying to undermine the bribed person's independence, in violation of the principle of freedom. This only applies if the latter actually does not want to or will not allow himself to be bribed. However, it is mainly those who lose benefits or other value due to the bribe who are violated, such as the supplier who would have won a tender if the winning company had not bribed the customer.

20.3.3 Reporting Requirements

Companies must disclose information about their systems to prevent and detect, investigate, and respond to allegations or incidents relating to corruption and bribery, including related training.[450] The information shall include:

- a description of the procedures in place to prevent, detect, and address allegations or incidents of corruption and bribery;
- whether the investigators or investigating committee are separate from the chain of management involved in the matter; and

449. Teorell, J. and Rothstein, B., What Is Quality of Government: A Theory of Impartial Institutions (January 16, 2009), 21(2) Governance: An International Journal of Policy, Administration and Institutions, April 2008, 165-190.
450. Disclosure requirement G1-3 of ESRS G1.

- the process, if any, to report outcomes to the administrative, management and supervisory bodies.[451]

If the company does not have such procedures in place, this must also be reported and any plans to implement them.[452]

Finally, the company must disclose information on the number of cases in which the company has been convicted of violations of anti-corruption legislation and confirmed corruption or bribery incidents.[453]

20.4 POLITICAL INFLUENCE ACTIVITIES AND LOBBYING

Companies must, in accordance with disclosure requirement G1-5, disclose information on the activities and commitments related to exerting their political influence, including their lobbying activities related to their material impacts, risks and opportunities. The purpose is to create an understanding of the types of activities that are undertaken, as well as their purpose and costs.[454]

20.4.1 Connection to the Earth4All Model

It is not hard to see how lobbying activities tie into the Earth4All model, both in a positive and negative direction. It is well known that many companies try to create positive conditions for their business by trying to influence politicians and legislators. If the rules that companies lobby for reinforce negative correlations or weaken positive ones in the Earth4All model, it will defeat the goal of increased human well-being. This could, for example, involve influencing legislation to delay the transition to fossil-free energy sources, counteracting measures that lead to increased equality and gender equality, and so on.

20.4.2 Sustainability Moral Foundation

Lobbying and other political influencing activities are not necessarily morally reprehensible from a sustainability perspective. But to the extent that lobbying takes place with the aim of, for example, counteracting legislation that would be positive from a sustainability perspective, it needs to be assessed whether it is compatible with the requirement to treat everyone with equal respect. Of course, it is not possible, morally speaking, to say that any attempt to influence such legislation is wrong. An assessment must be made case by case.

What would be morally wrong, however, is for a company to say in its public communication that it has a certain attitude, for example, that fossil fuels should be

451. Data point 18 of ESRS G1.
452. Data point 19 of ESRS G1.
453. Data points 24 and 25 of ESRS G1.
454. Data point 28 of ESRS G1.

phased out, and at the same time lobby in the opposite direction. This kind of self-contradiction would then be an example of 'bad character' of the company.

20.4.3 Reporting Requirements

According to disclosure requirement G1-5, companies must, therefore, provide information about their activities and commitments regarding political influence, i.e., lobbying. This information shall include information about lobbying activities related to the company's material impact. The information shall include:

- if applicable, the representative(s) responsible in the administrative, management and supervisory bodies for the oversight of these activities;
- for financial or in-kind political contributions: (i) the total monetary value of financial and in-kind political contributions made directly and indirectly by the undertaking aggregated by country or geographical area where relevant, as well as type of recipient/beneficiary; and (ii) where appropriate, how the monetary value of in-kind contributions is estimated;
- the main topics covered by its lobbying activities and the undertaking's main positions on these in brief; and
- if the undertaking is registered in the EU Transparency Register or in an equivalent transparency register in a Member State, the name of any such register and its identification number in the register.[455]

In addition, the information shall describe whether the company has employed someone in an administrative, managerial or supervisory position in public administration in the past two years for employment in a similar role within the company.[456]

455. Data point 29 of ESRS G1.
456. Data point 30 of ESRS G1.

Part IV Sustainability and Contracts

CHAPTER 21

The Contract as a Bridge Between Morality and Economics

To a perhaps surprisingly large extent, sustainable finance and business is about contracts. As described in Chapter 2, economic and social outcomes are shaped by the institutional structure, a structure consisting of informal and formal rules of the game. The formal rules of the game can be divided into laws and contracts. In principle, all exchanges of goods, services and labour on the market take place within the framework of various forms of contract, some of which are governed by mandatory legislation but where there is still a great deal of freedom of contract.

How contracts are written and what processes are used to enter into contracts have a major impact on the rules of the game in the market. Not least, contracts have a major impact on whether business relationships lead to increased, decreased or maintained sustainability. Therefore, it is a natural part of the norms of positive contribution and due diligence to ensure that the company's contracts are designed so they minimise negative impact while taking advantage of opportunities for increased sustainability.

In previous chapters of the book, the EU ideal image for a sustainable business has been described in both economic, moral and legal terms. From an economic point of view, sustainable business is an activity that carries the costs of its negative external effects. The moral equivalent of this is that the company conducts its business without violating the dignity of any human, expressed in the principles of equality and freedom. The legal rules in, for example, environmental law, labour law, marketing law and anti-corruption can be said to constitute the bridge between morality and economics. The rules are based on a normative foundation that deals with people's equality and freedom and aims to make companies bear the costs of their external impact.

However, mandatory legislation has the disadvantage that it is general and thus not adapted to a specific situation. Most of what happens in the market takes place within the boundaries of freedom of contract and is only governed to a limited extent by legislation. In this sphere, it is contracts that largely govern the behaviour of market participants. Contracts set the rules of the game. In sustainable business, the contract must often take over the role of the bridge between morality and economics at the point when the rules of law no longer govern. As will be seen in this part as well as in Part V of the book, companies with ambitions to transition to a sustainable business need to review the processes they use to enter into contracts and the content of the contracts.

Some types of contracts of great importance are:

- employment contracts with staff and managers with incentives linked to sustainability matters;
- incentive programs for entrepreneurs in companies in connection with investments;
- customer-supplier agreements relating to goods or services, where sustainability matters are raised (as they are, in principle, always are);
- loan agreements where social and environmental factors are built into the terms and conditions of the loan;
- shareholders' agreements regarding investments in companies carrying out sustainable business operations.

How these contracts are written will directly affect the parties' incentives to act and, thus, whether the results of the business relationships contribute to or counteract sustainability. In this part of the book, general questions about contracts and sustainability will therefore be addressed.

It should be emphasised that this fourth part of the book is likely to be perceived as heavier for the reader than some of the other parts. It should, therefore, perhaps be emphasised that the subject discussed here appears to be one of the most important but least treated in the sustainability literature, which justifies a reasonably thorough review also from a theoretical perspective.

Chapter 22
Due Diligence, Positive Contribution and Contracts

The overarching moral standards of sustainability are, as often stated in the book, the norms of positive contribution and due diligence, both being expressions of the more general norms of equality and freedom. These norms permeate, or at least should permeate, the entire business and must, therefore, also affect companies' processes for entering into contracts. This applies both to companies' buying and sales processes and to investment processes.

The ESRS standards follow the structure of governance, strategy, management of impacts, risks and opportunities, as well as metrics and goals. This structure is appropriate to consider when exercising contribution and due diligence in relation to the company's contractual relationships. However, contract processes follow a different sequence, which is why adaptation should be made. The figure below describes a possible process for following the norms of positive contribution and due diligence regarding the company's contract, here focusing on the contract in a specific commercial relationship:

As a preparatory step 1, the company should adopt and put policies and other governing documents regarding sustainability into practice in contracts and contract processes. For example, Chapter 20 stated that according to CSRD, companies must report their strategy for supplier relationships related to sustainability.

In step 2, the company analyses the sustainability-related impacts, risks and opportunities that exist or will exist in the business relationship. This analysis is, of course, only an extension of the analysis that the company is supposed to report on anyway according to CSRD or, for some companies, should carry out according to CSDDD. At this stage, it is appropriate to carry out the economic analyses usually carried out in connection with the conclusion of contracts.

In step 3, the company makes a contract strategy based on the previous analysis, which means that the most important goals of the contract are set, preferably with identified metrics and goals.

In step 4, the parties negotiate, sign and enter into the contract. In step 5, the contract is finally followed up against the set goals. The process then starts again – at least in longer-term contracts – whereby changes should be made when the analysis reveals new forms of sustainability-related impacts, risks and opportunities, or financial risks.

These steps are discussed in more detail below. Before that, however, it is important to create a basic understanding of contracts and how contracts and sustainability matters are connected. As part of the transition to sustainable business operations, it is also necessary to take an updated view of the contract, which is one of the most important tools for every company conducting its business.

Chapter 23
Three Perspectives on Contracts

In economics, contracts are usually treated in the field of contract theory. It is a subject that often becomes technical and is filled with mathematical models that can easily be perceived as lacking contact with practical reality. However, a basic understanding of some essential elements of contract theory is central to sustainability law, given the important role of the contract in shaping the behaviour of companies, organisations and people.

The premise of contract theory is that *people and companies have much greater opportunities to create value by cooperating than by each working separately.*[457] Adam Smith, the leading founder of modern economics, pointed out how the division of labour – that is, the division of tasks carried out in collaboration – is one of the most important sources of increased productivity and growth. If nails are to be produced, using Smith's famous example, it is better that one person snips steel wire, another grinds, a third hardens, and so on. By dividing up the work in this way, productivity increases substantially compared to if each worker had produced whole nails individually, primarily because each worker improves and can work faster if they specialise than if they must work on several things at the same time. Division of labour can and does not only take place within companies but also between companies. Either way, the division of labour will take place based on contracts. If the work is organised within a company, it is a matter of contracts between employers and employees, often governed by collective bargaining agreements. If the work is organised between companies, it is about other types of contracts: supplier agreements, loan agreements, and so on. But the starting point is always the same: more value can be created if people cooperate than if they work separately.

This economic perspective on the value of human interaction can be extended to sustainability matters. When the environmental and social factors are weighed in, a

457. The presentation here is largely based on the Royal Swedish Academy of Sciences, Oliver Hart and Bengt Holmström: Contract Theory, Scientific Background on the Sveriges Riksbank Prize in Economic Sciences in Memory of Alfred Nobel 2016.

broader perspective on what value is must be taken. But the same basic principle applies – more environmental and social value can be created through effective human cooperation compared to if everyone acted alone.

From this point of view, it will be necessary to look at the conditions for effective collaboration. This is best achieved if the parties to the contract have aligned interests and expectations. At the same time, it is obvious that conflicts of interest and friction due to broken expectations arise all the time in business. A company buys the shares of another company and feels that it has been provided with incorrect information to make a correct valuation of the target company. A dispute arises between the buyer and the seller. A buyer and a contractor in a large construction project have different perceptions of whose fault it is that the project has been affected by long delays and increased costs. An employee and employer get into a fight about whether the employee's conduct of a side business is disloyal to the employer or not. And so on. There are endless examples to give.

The contract is one of the most important tools on the market to counteract and manage the effects of conflicts of interest and broken expectations. Both economic and sustainability efficiency are greatly affected by how the contracts that are written succeed or fail to create aligned interests.

Economic contract theory analyses how two or more parties can achieve effective cooperation through contracts, primarily by creating aligned interests. Three important themes in contract theory should be highlighted here, not least because they are all of great importance for contracts and sustainability. These themes or perspectives are:

- business model perspective;
- fairness and irrationality perspectives; and
- governance model perspective.

The business model perspective is about the model that the parties use to calculate how the value created in the deal should be allocated between them and how, for example, a supplier should be paid. The perspective of fairness and irrationality is about the fact that people's sense of fairness and often lack of rationality must be considered when contracts are written. The governance model perspective is about how the parties manage their relationship through the allocation of decision-making rights and how the ownership of assets that are important in the contract is allocated.

These three perspectives are dealt with separately below, taking sustainability into account. In the end, the question is: how should contracts be designed to avoid creation of an external negative impact on people and the environment?

23.1 THE BUSINESS MODEL PERSPECTIVE

It is common for CEOs and other senior executives to have parts of their remuneration linked not only to the company's financial performance but also to sustainability factors such as carbon emissions. This practice is largely the result of the agency theory developed and implemented on the markets during the 1980s, as described in Chapter

6. As described in that chapter, agency theory should be used with caution since it is largely based on incorrect assumptions about utility maximisation. But this does not mean that it is without value, and it is a good approach to use for understanding the more strict economic aspect of contracts.[458]

Tying payment to performance is also common in other areas. In so-called impact investing, it is common that the terms of the loan are linked to the borrower meeting certain social or environmental targets. In supplier contracts, it is fairly common for the supplier's payment to be tied to the achievement of certain environmental or social goals. The remuneration model, or rather the business model, between two or more parties affects the actions of companies and people related to issues of environmental, social and governance sustainability. A business model refers to how two parties in their relationship create value for each other and for others and how this value is allocated between the contracting parties.

Most contracts involve exchange of goods or services for money. This may include salary in exchange for work, compensation to a supplier for services rendered, payment of interest in exchange for loans, and so on. How can the compensation model create what all contracts are ultimately aimed at, i.e., aligned interests and expectations? This is a difficult issue, even when it comes to creating an alignment of *economic* interests. It is just as difficult, or more difficult, when it comes to creating interests linked to sustainability matters. What should a company do to give a CEO, for example, an incentive to reduce the company's carbon dioxide emissions, preferably without affecting the company's profitability too much? How should a lender create incentives for a borrower to work for a social goal, such as reduced poverty or increased biodiversity? What should a customer do to give a supplier an incentive to treat its staff well and ensure there is no corruption in the supply chain? How should shareholders create incentives for the management and employees of a company in which they invest to work towards set sustainability targets? The business model applied in the contractual relationship answers or should answer such questions.

There are two basic business models here, which need to be described separately:

(i) Transactional business model.
(ii) Outcome-based business model.

In some areas, it can also be important to make a further distinction between performance or output-based models on the one hand and outcome-based models on the other.

23.1.1 Transactional Business Model

In its purest form, the transactional business model means that, for example, a seller or a worker is remunerated for his or her effort, no matter the outcome of the effort. An employee or entrepreneur in a company in which an investment is made may receive

458. The following sections are primarily based on principal-agent theory. *See*, e.g., Eisenhart, K., Agency Theory: An Assessment and Review, 14(1) The Academy of Management Review, January 1989, 57-74 for a good, if incomplete, review of this theory.

a fixed monthly salary in exchange for a month's work; a supplier receives compensation for their production costs plus a margin for goods delivered, and a borrower receives its loan. Of course, a quid pro quo – work, products, services, interest and amortisation, and so on – is expected, but in the basic model, there are no requirements linked to this quid pro quo that affect the level of compensation if the requirements are not met. Compensation for the work is paid even if the employee does a poor job. Compensation for products is paid even if the supplier's products are of poor quality. The interest rate and amortisation rate do not change depending on the performance of the borrower's business. Thus, in this simple model, in principle, all the risk lies with the party paying (in the first case, the employer; in the second case, the customer; in the third case, the lender).

There are variants of this business model where, for example, the supplier still takes some risk. For example, it is unusual for a product supplier not to take any risk linked to the quality or delivery time of the products.

The model is called transactional because the effort of the in-kind performer is often divided into individual transactions, which are exchanged for money. This may involve compensation per hour or month for a supplier or an employee or compensation per case handled in customer service. In the case of loan agreements, for example, it is more difficult to say that a division into transactions takes place other than regular interest payments. However, the same term should be used because the core of the business model is the same, namely that remuneration is paid for activities no matter the outcome of those activities.

The business model has clear advantages, not least because it is simple. It also makes it relatively easy to compare, for example, the prices of different suppliers for the same goods. The problem is that it is rarely enough to create sufficient alignment of interests between the parties. On the contrary, it often creates directly conflicting interests between the parties, at least if these interests are isolated to the purely economic ones. A manager who receives a fixed monthly salary regardless of performance has, in a strictly economic sense, an interest in making a little effort, which is not in the employer's interest. A contractor in a construction contract who receives compensation for materials and labour no matter the outcome of the work instead has an interest in using a lot of materials and working many hours, which is often in conflict with a buyer's interest in, for example, cost control.

These challenges with the transactional model need to be addressed through the contract's governance model. In principle, it is a question of using the contract to limit the ability of the performing party to act freely and of giving the paying party the right to decide on certain matters. In the area of sustainability, the common market practice of obliging a supplier to comply with the customer's code of conduct is an example of this solution. These issues are discussed in more detail in section 23.3 on governance models.

23.1.2 Outcome-Based Business Model

Thus, the transactional business model has advantages but also clear disadvantages. For the paying party to be sure of getting the value for money it expects, it is necessary, in principle, with such a business model, to monitor and follow up all the actions and actions of the other party. As a rule, this is prohibitively expensive. An employer cannot, for example, constantly monitor every employee and control what they are working on in every single detail.

An important step towards creating more aligned interests between the parties through the business model is, therefore, to use an outcome-based business model. In such a model, the remuneration is linked to performance according to certain specified outcome parameters that the buyer can observe. Some examples of an outcome-based business model are:

- An employment contract in which a CEO's remuneration is tied to the company's share price or perhaps certain parameters regarding carbon emissions.
- A maintenance contract in which a supplier of maintenance of, for example, trains or aircraft receives compensation for kilometres driven or flown without interruptions.
- A loan agreement in which the terms of the loan are tied to the borrower's compliance with certain financial or sustainability targets.
- An outsourcing agreement where the supplier's remuneration depends on how satisfied the end users are with the outsourcing provider's services.

As mentioned above, in some contexts, it is appropriate to divide the outcome-based business model into two subcategories, namely the output-based and the outcome-based business model. It is a matter of degree, which is nevertheless important, and is about the extent to which the provider is able to control the outcome. In the output-based model, payment is linked to measured output that is largely within the control of the non-wage earner. For example, it is common for the remuneration of cloud service providers to depend on the availability of the services provided, a factor that they can typically control to a high degree. Another example is in an impact investment where the number of individuals who have completed a certain training is measured.

The remuneration is, therefore, linked to the direct service of the service provider (or employee, borrower, etc.). The disadvantage is that the compensation is not tied to the end result. For example, that several individuals undergo training does not mean that the ultimate purpose of the training, such as social inclusion, is achieved. So, in the outcome-based model, this direct performance is only an input for the ultimate result, which is also affected by other factors. A service contract where remuneration is linked to customer satisfaction is an example, as the satisfaction of the end-users of a service is often linked to factors other than just the service provider's performance. An employment contract in which a CEO's remuneration is tied to the company's share price is another example, as the share price is naturally influenced by a variety of factors other than the CEO's work.

The outcome-based business model is used in many variants on the market, both in employment contracts, supplier agreements and various types of financing agreements. It is basically intended to create more aligned interests between the parties. But it is not without its problems. The fundamental problem is that outcomes are never merely the result of the actions of, e.g., a seller, service provider or worker but of a host of other factors. There is always a 'noise' in the data that reports the outcome of the performance. There is, therefore, a risk that the performing party (CEO, supplier, borrower, etc.) will either be rewarded or penalised for factors beyond its control.

There is an important balance here between incentives and risk-sharing. Suppose that a bus company providing public transport for a municipality receives its compensation depending on the degree to which the company is punctual in traffic. For simplicity, it is assumed that the entire remuneration is linked only to punctuality. At 100% punctuality, EUR 10 million is paid in compensation, and the remuneration is otherwise linear (EUR 100,000 per percentage point punctuality is paid). Because punctuality depends on several factors beyond the control of the bus operator, it may be estimated there is only a 70% probability of reaching 100% punctuality. The bus operator then (at least in theory) adapts its efforts and costs to that level of probability, with the result that 100% punctuality is not achieved since it does not, therefore, put in the necessary effort. There is thus a misalignment between the bus company's interest in not incurring higher costs than what it is reimbursed for and the customer's (the public transport authority's) interest in having 100% punctuality.

One way to solve this problem is to reduce the risk for the bus operator, for example, by switching to a transactional business model, where compensation is paid no matter the outcome. If, however, the bus operator were to have all its costs covered, i.e., not bear any risk, the purely economic incentives to achieve high punctuality would disappear. Even too low a risk for the bus operator leads to a conflict of interest.

The same problem arises in employment contracts with incentives linked to outcomes. A CEO who receives his or her entire remuneration based on the development of the share price is taking a big risk since the share price is based on such a large number of uncertain factors. The CEO has a low incentive to put in a lot of effort, in the same way as the bus operator in the example above. However, with only a fixed monthly salary, the CEO, in a strictly financial sense, is also incentivised to make little effort to maximise the difference between salary and effort.

The challenge is thus to find the optimal point in the balance between risk and incentive. Both too much and too little risk, e.g., for a service provider or an employee, weakens his or her interest in achieving the money provider's goals.

In addition, for example, a customer, lender or other paying parties wants the seller, borrower or similar actors not just to achieve one goal but several. A board of directors may want a CEO to achieve a certain share price, certain sustainability goals, and also other goals. At some point, there is a risk that the complexity will become so high that clear prioritisation problems, and thus a weakened incentive structure overall, arise.[459]

Here, the challenge is to find the optimal point between the complexity of goals and incentives. Both too-high and too-low complexity weaken the interest of the provider in achieving the paying party's goals. With incentives to achieve too many goals, the picture becomes too complex, and the strength of the incentives decreases. However, if the complexity is reduced too much, there is a risk that, e.g., a CEO's or service provider's incentives to achieve goals that are nevertheless important to the paying party become too weak or even non-existent. In this situation, it is complexity instead of risk allocation that risks creating a conflict of interest.

In sufficiently complex contexts, it may be more effective to find other ways to create aligned interests between the parties than to work with an outcome-based business model, which brings us to the governance model perspective below.

23.2 THE PERSPECTIVE OF FAIRNESS AND IRRATIONALITY

The description of business models above shows the opportunities and challenges of using the business model tool to create aligned interests through the contract, based on agency theory. In both the transactional and outcome-based models, it will also be important to determine which governance model the parties use. However, before turning to the matter of governance models, it is important to address another perspective on contracts, namely the perspective of fairness and irrationality. This perspective has already been referred to in Chapter 6 regarding corporate purpose since it largely undermines agency theory. In the context of contracts, this perspective also helps to create a better understanding of the governance model perspective.[460] It is also closely linked to sustainability matters, as this is very much about considering people's sense of what is fair and equitable.

In the description of the business model perspective above, the starting point was that people and organisations are entirely guided by self-interest and are completely rational. These are the assumptions made in traditional economic theory. However, practical experience and, as referred to in Chapter 6, a lot of research in so-called behavioural economics have unequivocally proven that people are not as rational as is often assumed and are not only driven by self-interest but that feelings of fairness, reciprocity, etc., also play an important role. When people are offered the opportunity to distribute money among themselves, they do not keep it all for themselves but often share it equally. For many people, it is more important to feel treated fairly and to treat others fairly than to make more money.

This fact is something that everyone who works with contracts must take into account, not least in the context of sustainability. When contracts are to be entered

459. *See, e.g.*, Holmström, B. and Milgrom, P., Multi-Task Principal Agent Analysis, 7 Journal of Law, Economics and Organization, 1991, 24-52.

460. For a more complete review of this perspective, *See* Frydlinger et al., Contracting in the New Economy – Using Relational Contracts to Boost Trust and Collaboration in Strategic Business Relationships, Palgrave Macmillan, 2021, Chapter 6 (The psychology of Contracting).

into, it is important to write agreements that make it possible for the parties to collaborate effectively in different ways. This is also very much the case when sustainability matters are important in contracts, both in sustainable financing and in supplier contracts, for example. Sustainability matters are often complex, and there is still often a lack of knowledge about what works and what does not work to create increased sustainability. This increases the importance of effective collaboration even more so that the parties can take a learning perspective. However, all of this risks being undermined if contracts are written under the assumption that all people are rational and that feelings of fairness and justice do not matter. It is therefore important not only for strictly economic reasons to consider these perspectives but also to create the conditions for greater sustainability. In Chapter 6, the danger, in general, to adopting rules on the market that assume that people follow utility maximisation was pointed out. This danger is equally relevant in a more narrow contracting context.

23.2.1 Cognitive Biases

Why choose such a strange concept as *irrationality perspective*? Simply to underline the fact that humans are far from being as rational as is often assumed, which matters for contracts and thus, for sustainability. In a well-known example, you get the following question:

(1) A bat and a ball cost EUR 1.10.
(2) The bat costs EUR 1 more than the ball.
(3) How much does the ball cost?[461]

Most people intuitively answer 10, as in 10 cents. But the correct answer is 5 cents. Had the answer been 10 cents, the bat and ball would have cost EUR 1.20. This thought experiment has been used in a wide variety of contexts, one aim of which is to show that our intuition is not always to be trusted. At the same time, of course, we can also solve this simple problem. In psychology, it is said that the human brain works with two systems – System 1 and System 2 – where System 1 is intuitive, emotional and fast, and System 2 is rational, intellectual and slow. The existence of System 1 means that all people walk around with a variety of cognitive biases. Three of them are particularly important when it comes to contracts.

Planning fallacy. All contracts require a degree of planning. More extensive contracts often require extensive planning to be able to describe what each party should do within the framework of the contractual relationship. However, people suffer from an overconfidence in their ability to plan, something that is called the planning fallacy.[462] People have a relatively poor ability to predict what will happen in the future but believe they have a good ability. A large number of construction projects with cost budgets that have been grossly exceeded are clear examples of this perennial

461. Kahneman, D., Thinking, Fast and Slow, Penguin Books, 2011.
462. *Ibid.*, pp. 201 ff.

problem. Anyone who works with contracts must be vigilant about the planning fallacy, as it contributes to an illusory feeling that the contract to be concluded regulates most of what can happen during the contract period. Those who work with contracts to achieve increased sustainability must be even more vigilant, as overconfidence in one's own planning ability can be costly from a sustainability perspective and harm others.

Probability neglect. Contracts are always, to some extent, also about risk management. Often, it is a matter of financial risks, such as higher costs or lower revenues than planned. It can also be about sustainability-related risks, such as damage to the environment or health. A risk is a function of negative impact and probability. The risk of dying from a meteorite impact is low. If a meteorite hits your head, the negative impact will be high, but the probability is vanishingly small. Thus, the risk is low. This is a calculation that most people spontaneously make. However, because people also think in terms of System 1, risk assessments are often not rational in this way. In fact, risks are often assessed emotionally, with the element of probability being denied. The greater the discomfort a person feels when thinking about a particular risk, the more likely it appears. This is called probability neglect.[463] When contracts are negotiated, probability neglect often leads to a focus on improbable issues instead of important issues, something anyone who has sat in long negotiations on liability limitation clauses instead of in equally long discussions about joint problem-solving during the contract period recognises.

Self-serving bias. If a population of people is asked how good they are at driving compared to an average driver, the result is typically that a large majority rate themselves as better than average. When couples are asked about the division of housework, the total is often well over 100%.[464] This phenomenon is usually described by the term self-serving bias. People tend to overestimate their own achievements, attributing to themselves the cause of success but external factors the cause of failure, and so on. This bias can often lead to different types of friction and conflicts, especially when two people or companies interpret events or contracts to their own advantage but in incompatible ways. The self-serving bias can create problems when using outcome-based business models, as two parties can make completely different interpretations of what has caused a certain positive or negative outcome.

23.2.2 Sense of Fairness and Justice

In the previous section, the focus was on the fact that people are not as rational as is often assumed in, for example, traditional economic theory. This theory, to simplify, assumes that people only act in their own self-interest and that matters of fairness and justice do not play a role in their actions.

463. Sunstein, C., Probability Neglect: Emotions, Worst Cases, and Law, 112(61) Yale Law Journal, 2002.
464. *See, e.g.*, Svenson, O., Are We All Less Risky And More Skillful Than Our Fellow Drivers?, 47(2) Acta Psychologia, February 1981, 143-148.

The fallacy of this assumption has been demonstrated in the field of behavioural economics, for example, in the famous Ultimatum Game.[465] An experimental person A is given a sum of money, say EUR 1,000 and is given the task of giving a proposal to experimental person B on how A and B should share the money. If B accepts A's proposal, the money is distributed according to the proposal. If B rejects the proposal, neither A nor B will receive any money.

A rational A would here propose that B receive, for example, EUR 1 and A EUR 999. A rationally acting B would accept because B would then have become richer. However, this is not how people act when the experiment is done. Many in A's position offer an equal split of the money. Equally important, many in B's position reject offers that are worse than a 70/30 split. B thus chooses to punish A for what is perceived as an unfair act, even though it means giving up money.

The Ultimatum Game is just one of many proofs that people act largely based on feelings of fairness and justice. People are ready to punish others if they feel they have been treated unfairly or if they feel someone is abusing their power against them.[466] It should be obvious that this is important when writing contracts, not least when sustainability matters are relevant. If two companies need to cooperate efficiently to, for example, limit greenhouse gas emissions or achieve better social sustainability, efficiency will be undermined if either party behaves in a way that violates the other's sense of fairness and justice.

23.2.3 The Importance of Reference Points

Another important insight from psychology relevant to contracts and sustainability is that people do not value things in absolute terms but in relation to reference points. Suppose Laura and John go to the casino one night, and they both leave with EUR 1,000 in their pockets. If Laura and John had assessed value in absolute terms, both would have been equally happy. But they do not. Laura came to the casino with EUR 100 and John with EUR 5,000. You can understand that Laura is happy and John is annoyed and angry. The value of EUR 1,000 is judged based on the reference point of how much money they had when they came to the casino.

Reference points are surprisingly important for contracts.[467] Several experiments have shown that if a buyer and seller enter into a contract, the contract as such will determine whether they later perceive that it was a good or bad deal. A buyer may have made a saving of EUR 0.5 million but still perceives it as negative because they expected a saving of EUR 1 million when entering into the contract. If the contract can be interpreted in different ways and something unexpected and costly happens during the contract period, it is easy for both parties to act according to their respective

465. *See, e.g.*, Thaler, R., The Winner's Curse: Paradoxes and Anomalies of Economic Life, Princeton University Press, 1992, pp. 21 ff.
466. *See, e.g.*, Kahneman, D., Knetsch, J. and Thaler, R., Fairness as a Constraint on Profit Seeking: Entitlements in the Market, 76(4) The American Economic Review, September 1986, 729.
467. This is based on the theory of contract as a reference point, first developed in Hart, O. and Moore, J., Contracts as Reference Points, 123(1) Quarterly Journal of Economics, 2008, 1-48, and then further developed in a series of experiments and articles.

self-serving bias, interpret the contract to their advantage and perceive the other party as unfair because of how that party interprets the contract. This then easily leads to the same punitive behaviour exhibited in the Ultimatum Game, for example, by the party who is angry starting to lower their quality, work more slowly, not try as hard, start reading the contract like the devil reads the Bible, and so on.

This shows that contracts are not just about avoiding conflicts of interest. Contracts are also very much about creating *aligned expectations* between the parties, as they can easily get angry with each other and act suboptimally if their expectations are disappointed, and they start blaming each other.

This creates a need for striking a balance between rigidity and flexibility. To create a high degree of consistency in the parties' expectations, it may be appropriate to write very rigid and detailed contracts. The purpose of this would then be to create very convergent reference points, thereby avoiding friction. This is also very common in the market. However, it is problematic in at least two respects. First, there is a risk that the party who is presented with the rigid contract will react negatively and want to punish the other party in various ways.[468] Paradoxically, the party who wants to write a detailed contract to avoid being ripped off by the other party risks provoking the other party's desire to act opportunistically.

Second, rigid contracts have the disadvantage that they often restrict the business relationship in inhibiting ways. This is particularly problematic in business deals where a lot of unexpected things can happen during the contract period, which is, of course, common. Flexible contracts are better. The problem with more flexible contracts, however, is that the parties then risk interpreting the agreement and what they are entitled to in different ways, affected by self-service bias, which gives rise to different types of friction.

23.3 THE GOVERNANCE MODEL PERSPECTIVE

Creating aligned interests is very much a matter of aligning the parties' incentives. As mentioned in the section on business models, this can be difficult to achieve only by regulating how compensation is to be paid. There is a risk that conflicts of interest will arise if too much or too little risk is allocated to one party in, for example, a supplier agreement. And the previous section showed that conflicts of interest, in fact, can be generated if one is not careful.

However, it is not only through the business model that an alignment of interests can be created. It can also be done through how the parties, on a more fundamental level, govern their relationship – hence the concept of a governance model perspective. More specifically, it is about how the parties allocate the right to make important decisions within the frame of contract. It is also about how the ownership of assets important to the contract is allocated, which in practice becomes the same as the right

468. *See, e.g.*, Erlei, M. and Reinhold, C., To Choose or Not to Choose: Contracts, Reference Points, Reciprocity, and Signaling, TUC Working Papers in Economics 0007, Abteilung für Volkswirtschaftslehre, Technische Universität Clausthal (Department of Economics, Technical University Clausthal), 2012.

to make important decisions because of the actual influence that comes with the ownership of an important asset. In a shareholders agreement, a balance can be found where the majority owner is entitled to make most decisions but where minority owners are given the right to veto on certain matters. In an outsourcing agreement, the parties can choose that either the customer or the supplier should own certain assets, such as IT equipment. These kinds of considerations have a significant impact on the interests and incentives of the parties.

Here, too, however, there is a need for trade-offs related to conflicts of interest between the parties. Here, the trade-off is instead about, on the one hand, a buyer's need not to become too dependent on a seller and, on the other hand, the seller's incentives to make investments, etc., to achieve the desired results in the business relationship.[469]

23.3.1 Balancing Control and Incentives

An example of this trade-off is a so-called impact investment, where a loan agreement is concluded between a lending investor and a borrowing company. The lender need not use an outcome-based business model, where, for example, the amortisation rate and interest rate vary depending on how the borrower performs in relation to specified sustainability parameters. Instead, the lender can, through the contract, to a greater or lesser extent, restrict the borrower's right to act freely in the conduct of its business. For example, it is fairly common for the borrower to only be entitled to dispose of substantial assets if the lender's approval is obtained in advance. From this first step of increased control for the lender, there are many steps through which control can be gradually increased to a point where the borrower cannot, in principle, act at all without the lender's consent. In practice, it can then be said that the lender has acquired the borrower.

Another example is an impact investment with equity instead of debt. The investor may try to control an entrepreneur's actions through an outcome-based incentive programme. However, the investor can also ensure that it has a high degree of influence over both the company and the entrepreneur by making sure they have far-reaching decision-making rights in investment and shareholder agreements.[470]

A further example is a supplier contract for a supply of services. The customer may want to use a transactional business model and can then manage the allocation of risk between the parties by writing a detailed contract in which the services and how they are to be performed are described in detail while severely restricting the supplier's ability to terminate the contract, replace staff and other measures.

469. The presentation is based on, among others, Grossman, S. and Hart, O., The Costs and Benefits of Ownership: A Theory of Vertical and Lateral Integration, 94(9) Journal of Political Economy, 1986, 691-719, Hart, O. and Moore, J., Incomplete Contracts and Renegotiations, 56 Econometrica, 1988, 755-786 and Hart, O. and Moore, J., Property Rights and the Nature of the Firm, 98 Journal of Political Economy, 1990, 1110-1158.

470. *See, e.g.*, Kaplan, S. and Strömberg, P., Venture Capitalists as Principals: Contracting, Screening and Monitoring, 91 American Economic Review, 2001, 426-430.

Thus, there is a spectrum of control in which a contracting party has full freedom of action at one end of the spectrum and, in principle, no freedom of action at the other end. As with different business models, there is a trade-off between risk and incentives.

To return to the earlier example of a bus operator, it is conceivable that the public transport authority uses a transactional business model and thus reimburses the bus operator for its costs plus a certain margin. In the governance model, the public transport authority can acquire very extensive decision-making powers over how bus services are to be run. The public transport authority can own the buses and be responsible for maintaining them, owning management systems, setting fares and collecting ticket revenue, exercising traffic management, and so on. This model creates low risk for the bus operator. However, it also creates low incentives for the bus operator to make any investments at all to improve or maintain the quality of service delivery. After all, all the benefits of such investments will accrue to the public transport authority. There is an obvious risk that conflicts of interest will arise between the public transport authority and the bus operator, for example, if the public transport authority feels that the bus company does not make sufficient investments to maintain quality.

At the other end of the spectrum, the bus operator can own the buses, carry out maintenance, set ticket prices, collect ticket revenue, and so on. The bus operator then carries a great risk – if people do not travel, there will be no revenue and the company risks going bankrupt. But at the same time, the bus company has very strong incentives to invest in the business to make it attractive to passengers. This is a good thing, but it is also problematic. The public transport authority faces a problem here, which is expressed in what economists call the hold-up problem. If a conflict of interests arises between the public transport authority and the bus operator during the contract period – for example, because the need for public transport in the region changes, a pandemic arises, and so on – the public transport authority will have weak negotiating power in a renegotiation. This is because the bus operator has, in principle, all decision-making and ownership rights regarding the assets used to operate the service. The bus operator will, therefore, be able to capture virtually all the added value in the event of renegotiations, i.e., hold up the public transport authority.

To avoid this hostage situation, the public transport authority can, as I have said, reverse the situation and usurp all the relevant decision-making powers. But then you are back to the previous situation, and you now realise that the bus company has a hold-up problem. This is because, in the event of a change in circumstances, the public transport authority can negotiate for itself all the value in case of a renegotiation.

As it is important, within the business model perspective, to find the optimal point in a balance between risk and incentives, it is important in the governance model perspective to find the optimal balance between the distribution of ownership/decision-making rights and incentives for investments, further development and more. This applies to employment contracts, supplier agreements, financing agreements, and so on.

23.3.2 Transactional and Relational Contract Models

In contract theory, the governance model perspective is often about where the boundaries of a company are and should be. As stated above, a party can acquire such extensive control over all relevant decision-making rights that the counterparty is, in practice, vertically integrated and instead works as an employee or subsidiary. But often, companies choose to enter into contracts with external parties instead. In the same way that there are different business models, there are different contract models, where companies need to make considered decisions to achieve the goal of creating aligned interests between the parties.

The two basic contract models are transactional and relational contract models. These contract models are described in detail elsewhere in the book and will therefore only be briefly discussed here.[471] The transactional contract is the traditional contract that is most common in the market. The relational contract has been an emerging phenomenon for many years, as companies have discovered the need to write more flexible contracts that build partnerships and aligned interests in the long term.

The difference between transactional and relational contracts is appropriately described in the five dimensions of focus, relationship, risk management, social norms and planning.[472] A general overview is given below, and each dimension is described in more detail below.

Dimension	*Transactional Contract*	*Relational Contract*
Focus	On the deal	On the relationship
Relation	Arm's length	Partnership
Risk management	Power	Creation of continuously aligned interests and expectations
Social norms	Irrelevant	Embedded in the agreement
Planning	Ambition for a complete agreement	Flexible framework

Focus. The transactional contract has a strong focus on the deal itself, for example, on the exchange of goods and services for remuneration, on loans for interest and amortisation, on remuneration for work, and so on. The essence of the contract lies in the description of, on the one hand, the goods or services to be provided or activities to be carried out and, on the other hand, the monetary payment. All the other clauses are intended, in principle, to make sure the value generated by this economic exchange is not undermined in various ways.

471. For a detailed review of relational contracts, *see* Frydlinger et al., Contracting in the New Economy – Using Relational to Boost Trust and Collaboration in Strategic Business Relationships, Palgrave Macmillan 2021.
472. For a detailed comparison, *see* Frydlinger et al., Chapter 7.

In the relational contract, there is instead more focus on the relationship between the parties themselves. It is appropriate to shift focus in this way when the business is changing over time because then the parties need to manage the changing business within which what does not change, namely that the parties have a relationship with each other. The parties then focus more on what goals or outcomes they want to achieve together, how goal achievement will be measured, what principles the parties will follow during the contract period, how the parties will manage their relationship to meet the goals, and so on.

Relationship. All contracts involve the establishment of a relationship. In the transactional contract, an arm's length relationship is created between the parties. The parties have no built-in loyalty to each other; in other words, no duty to consider the other's interests.

Instead, the relational contract creates the conditions for a partnership, which is characterised by the parties having a mutual loyalty to each other and looking out for each other's best interests.

Risk management. In the transactional contract, risks are often managed through various forms of power. The most basic fact is that the contract is enforceable in court. The risk of conflicts of interest is managed by the threat of being taken to court in case of a contract breach.

Relational contracts, in the sense in which the term is used here, are, of course, also binding and enforceable. In the relational contract, however, the focus is instead on the root cause of the problem, namely that the parties often have conflicting interests. In the relational contract, the parties instead try to manage the risks of disagreement by creating continuously aligned interests and expectations. This is done through the mechanisms described above with common goals, objectives, principles for fair behaviour and active governance of the relationship.

Social norms. In relationships based on transactional contracts, it is often accepted that the parties act in ways that would not be acceptable in many other social contexts, such as in family or friendship relationships. It is common and even expected for the parties to use power against each other, to fail to look after each other's interests, not to share all relevant information, and so on. The friction that this may cause can often be managed, not least by the parties leaving each other.

On the contrary, the relational contract is based on a high level of anchoring in social norms. There are six fundamental social norms or guiding principles:

(i) reciprocity;
(ii) autonomy;
(iii) honesty;
(iv) loyalty;
(v) equity; and
(vi) integrity.[473]

473. For a review of the precise meaning of each principle, *see* Frydlinger et al., Chapter 14.

The parties must reciprocate favours in kind (reciprocity), refrain from using power against each other (autonomy), tell the truth about facts and intentions (honesty), look after each other's interests (loyalty), apply proportionality in the allocation of risks, rewards, etc., (equity) and be consistent in their actions in accordance with these principles (integrity). These are norms common in family and friendship relationships. In many business relationships, company representatives often act according to these norms, which is natural when the same people meet frequently over a longer period.[474] An important difference between transactional and relational contracts is that, as a rule, these standards are not part of the transactional contract, whereas, on the contrary, they are an integral and central part of the relational contract.

Incorporating social norms considers people's sense of fairness and justice, as described above. This mechanism is an important tool to avoid the friction that easily arises in contractual relationships when various forms of conflicts of interest arise.

Planning. As a rule, the transactional contract claims to exhaustively manage the relationship between the parties. Often, the parties try to anticipate virtually everything that may happen during the contract period and then write contract clauses that regulate all these situations. This is often possible to achieve at least partially, especially in simple transactions. In many contexts, however, this is an unrealistic ambition. The so-called planning fallacy has been described above, which must be taken into account. Even only moderately complicated deals are impossible to capture in complete contracts. Conditions will often change over time.

In the relational contract, the difficulty of planning is taken into account and instead strives to create more of a flexible framework for the parties to operate within. However, this forces the parties to consider the balance between rigidity and flexibility described above, where flexibility is certainly positive but also risks creating friction when the parties interpret the contract in incompatible ways. One of the best ways to overcome this challenge is the guiding principles of the relational contract.[475]

The relational contract is a written, binding contract. However, due to its focus on the relationship, the weight differs from the transactional contract. As it is a matter of creating continuous alignment of interests, this contract model is based on clear and jointly agreed objectives, on the six guiding principles described above, and on the development of common structures and processes to govern the relationship.

Which contract model should be chosen in different situations from an economic and sustainability perspective is discussed in the next chapter.

474. Macaulay, S., 'Non-contractual Relations in Business: A Preliminary Study', 28 American Sociological Review, 1963, 1-19.
475. For a description of how guiding principles can assist parties in dealing with the frictions that arise from the incompleteness of all contracts, *see, inter alia*, Frydlinger, D., and Hart, O., Overcoming Contractual Incompleteness: The Role of Guiding Principles, The Journal of Law, Economics, and Organization, 2023.

CHAPTER 24
Six Steps for Due Diligence in Contracts

In light of the description of the three perspectives on contracts, the six-step process for demonstrating positive contribution and due diligence in contracts described in Chapter 23 is dealt with in more detail. There will then be a reason to go back to the description in the previous chapter. The process is generically applicable to all types of contracts:

24.1 STEP 1: ADOPT AND IMPLEMENT A CONTRACT POLICY

Like any other effort to work with sustainability and due diligence, the company's work with contracts should be based on policies adopted by the board of directors or management. Most of the company's revenues and costs are generated within the framework of contractual relations. The actions of all employees, from management downwards, are governed by contracts. All purchases, sales, investments, and so on are made within the framework of contracts. It is largely within and through their contracts that companies either operate sustainably or unsustainably. Since contracts are thus one of the company's most important instruments for conducting business, the company's processes for entering into contracts should be governed by formal policies and other governing documents. As has already been noted, companies subject to the CSRD must report on their supplier relationship management strategy.[476] Companies subject to CSDDD must base their due diligence conduct on adopted policies.[477]

There are no templates for how a contract policy should be written. However, the policy should preferably contain a clear statement of intent from the board of directors or management regarding the business-critical importance of the contracts for the company, not least regarding financial performance, financial risk management and sustainability matters. Furthermore, it is appropriate for the policy to describe how the company will work according to the due diligence norm in relation to its contracts, for example, by including the six-step process described here or an equivalent process. The policy should guide different departments – for example, procurement, sales, legal, and so on – so that a uniform approach is applied.

24.2 STEP 2: CONDUCT AN ANALYSIS OF SUSTAINABILITY-RELATED IMPACTS, RISKS AND OPPORTUNITIES

Each contract is based on some kind of business case. It is then a matter of setting a basis for making financial decisions. The economic business case includes an analysis of revenues, costs, profitability, investments, risks and so on. This must always be done and will not be discussed in detail here.

In addition, however, it is important to analyse impacts, risks and opportunities from a sustainability perspective. It is then a question of applying the double materiality analysis to contracts.[478] The company must analyse how social, environmental and governance factors may be affected by the relevant business relationship. What are the risks? What are the possibilities of achieving positive effects on these factors? Which sustainability factors create risks for the business relationship and the parties' revenues, costs, profitability and so on within this relationship?

The company should use the same tools to carry out the analysis as used to comply with CSRD's reporting requirements. For example, TCFD and TNFD frameworks can be used.[479] The analysis could be documented through a map of impacts, risks and opportunities linked to the topic-specific ESRS standards, as follows:

476. Disclosure requirement G1-2 of ESRS G1.
477. *See* Chapter 14.
478. *See* section 16.2 on double materiality analysis.
479. *See* section 15.3.

	Bidirectoral Analysis of Impacts, Risks and Opportunities				
Area	*None*	*Low*	*Medium*	*High*	*Very high*
Climate					
Pollution					
Water and marine resources					
Biodiversity and ecosystems					
Resource use and circular economy					
Own workforce					
Workers in the value chain					
Affected communities					
Consumers and end-users					
Anti-bribery					

In this way, the company can get an overview of important forms of impacts, risks and opportunities - including financial ones - in the transaction in question. Of course, the analysis does not end at this step but is an ongoing process. Not least, the counterparty in the business relationship must often eventually be included in the work on the analysis.

With the help of the map above, one can easily imagine a number of different examples with different degrees of impact, risks and opportunities regarding sustainability. In equity or debt financing, the situation will look very different depending on, for example, the operations and size of the company financed. In an industrial company with long supply chains, impacts, risks, and opportunities could be high in all of the listed sustainability dimensions. In a smaller company that provides a cloud service application, the opposite may be true. However, the latter company may also have a consumer offering based on extensive processing of personal data, which is why the sustainability impact can be high in that particular dimension. Furthermore, the map of a forestry company will look different than that of a mining company, as a bus company's map will differ from an IT consulting company's map.

It is important to understand that the map will also say something about how easy it will be for a company to transition to a sustainable business. If a company has made large investments that have not yet been depreciated, there is a risk that it will limit the pace of change, even if these investments generate high greenhouse gas emissions.

The perspectives are similar for a buying customer considering entering into a major supplier contract, for example, regarding manufacturing or outsourcing of services. The initial sustainability mapping provides important insights into which sustainability challenges will need to be addressed and what potential for sustainability improvements there is.

24.3 STEP 3: DESIGN A CONTRACT STRATEGY

In light of the analysis in step 2, the company can design a contract strategy. This is a natural part of the business case and includes a formulation of the company's main objectives with the contract. The goal description should then include both financial objectives and sustainability objectives. The company should set metrics and goals for the strategic goals. However, this is also something that the parties can agree on in step 5.

In equity financing, the investing company can, for example, set goals not only regarding sales, market shares and so on but also regarding increased gender equality and the transition to a circular business model. For example, a supplier contract may include goals for the inclusion of people with disabilities in the value chain, reduction of greenhouse gas emissions and impact on biodiversity.

24.4 STEP 4: CHOOSE BUSINESS MODEL AND GOVERNANCE MODEL

Step 4 is a crucial step, as the choice of business model and governance model will have a decisive impact on whether the parties at a later stage set the right incentives to manage the business relationship's impact, risks and opportunities on sustainability matters.[480]

24.4.1 The Business Model

The difference between transactional and outcome-based business models has been described in the previous chapter. It also stated that the outcome-based model can be divided into the two subcategories of output-based and outcome-based model, which differ based on the degree of control over the outcome that the non-wage performer has. When choosing a business model, there are a number of important factors to consider. Four factors should be highlighted.

Term of agreement. Some deals are transactional by nature. If a company buys 100 % of the shares in another company, the shares are transferred for a purchase price, and the deal is over. In such deals, it is irrelevant to consider an outcome-based model. If a company buys a machine, the money and the machine change hands, and the relationship is over, except for the warranty period. However, in other cases, a share transaction can also establish a longer relationship, for example, if the parties let the purchase price be finally determined based on how the target company performs during a certain period. A so-called earn-out mechanism is often applied, which is a form of outcome-based business model. The purchase of the machine can also involve a long-term relationship, for example, if the seller does not sell the machine but instead

480. For a detailed review of the considerations that need to be made when choosing a business and governance model, *see* Keith et al., Sourcing in the New Economy: Harnessing the Potential of Sourcing Business Models for Modern Procurement, Palgrave Macmillan, 2016. Note however that the book is focused primarily on customer-supplier relationships. In this book, I extend the framework to also cover financing contracts.

offers 'machine-as-a-service'. In such cases, outcome-based models may be considered. The point here is that the contract period matters for the choice of business model.

Potential for value creation. As a general principle, the greater the potential to create economic and sustainability value in the relationship, the more evidence suggests that some form of outcome-based model should be chosen. The concept of value creation is here used in a broad sense and may include, for example:

- cost savings;
- efficiency improvements in resource consumption;
- reduction of greenhouse gas emissions or other environmental impacts; and
- reduction of various forms of socially negative factors such as poverty, gender inequality, and so on.

The reason an outcome-based model should be used in cases of medium to high potential for value creation is that this model is often required to provide sufficient incentives for the parties to contribute to the realisation of the potential value.

The degree of control over outcomes. No matter how much potential there is for value creation, it does not matter if, for example, a supplier or an entrepreneur is unable to achieve it. For example, some suppliers have so little influence that their incentives will be reduced if they are to have to bear risks linked to the outcomes.

Business criticality. Some business relationships concern processes and other factors that are more or less business-critical for the company. In some vendor contracts, a failure to deliver services can have a significant negative impact on the company. A simple example is services related to critical IT infrastructure. As a rule of thumb, the higher the degree of business criticality, the stronger the reasons for an outcome-based business model.

The description above explains why it may be appropriate, as is also common, to use different forms of outcome-based models in so-called impact investments, incentive programs for executives, outsourcing agreements with a high impact on sustainability factors, and so on.

24.4.2 Governance Model

The choice of governance model is just as important as the choice of business model. As a first step the company needs to decide whether the relevant deal should be governed through ownership or through contracts entered into on the market. If contracts are to be entered into on the market, it is a choice between a transaction and a relational contract model.

In the same way, as with the choice of business model, there are several important factors to consider when choosing a governance model. Here, too, four should be particularly highlighted.[481]

481. For a detailed description of how the choice between the two contract models can be made, *see* Frydlinger et al., *ibid.*, Chapters 8 and 9.

Term of agreement. In the same way, as with the choice of business model, the contract period and, thus, the length of the business relationship are important in the choice of governance model. In simple purchases, there is no reason to use anything other than a transactional contract. The longer the relationship lasts, the stronger the reasons to use a relational contract. However, this criterion in isolation cannot determine the choice of governance model.

Dependency. In this context, the degree of dependency means the degree to which the parties are dependent on each other or at least one party on the other. The degree of dependency is largely about what the cost would be to break the relationship and contract with someone else. Several factors affect the degree of dependency. Maybe the parties have made investments in the relationship, for example, by a supplier building a production facility close to its customer, which has no obvious alternative uses. Another example is if a supplier has built up unique knowledge about its customer, which would be expensive to recreate.

Generally, the higher the degree of dependency, the stronger the reasons for a relational contract or that the deal should be governed through ownership. This is especially true if the risks are also reasonably high, as discussed below. If the risk of conflicts of interest and friction is medium to high, it will be problematic because the parties will not be able to leave each other without great expense. The relational contract, with the typically low level of friction it leads to, may then be a suitable choice.

Strategic impact. Some long-term business relationships have great strategic importance. It is an old truth – but one that can be questioned – that companies should focus on their core business and consider letting other activities be handled by suppliers. Core business refers to the processes in which the company creates the most value and probably also the value that makes the company unique. For a bank, this includes lending money to companies and individuals. For an industrial company, it is about the production of certain goods. What is the core business varies. In the choice of governance model, the greater the strategic importance of the business from this perspective, the stronger the reasons to use a relational contract or even that governance takes place through ownership.

Risk level. In this context, the risk level refers to the risk that the parties will end up in conflicts of interest or disappointed expectations. This level of risk increases with the economic value of the contract and the more complex and long-term the transaction is. In deals with limited dependency and risk, the transactional contract is typically enough to manage the relationship. However, as dependency and risk increase, there is increasing support for the use of the relational contract. This is largely because the relational contract has mechanisms to manage risk by creating continuously aligned interests.

24.4.3 General Principles

The choice of business and governance model is sometimes simple. Most trades that are made are simple transactions where a transactional business model and a transactional contract should be chosen.

However, in deals where there is a medium to high impact, risk or opportunity linked to one of the sustainability factors, the choice can be more complicated. Exercising due diligence, at least in a moral sense, here means making careful considerations to find the overall model that creates the best results from both an economic and a sustainability perspective.

Consider the interplay between business model and governance model. As described above, both the business model and the governance model involve trade-offs between risk allocation and incentives. It is necessary here to think in two dimensions at the same time and consider how they affect each other. Suppose an outcome-based business model is considered, such as an incentive programme, a loan agreement, or a supplier contract. As a first step, consideration needs to be given to how much risk the employee, borrower or supplier should bear, i.e., to what extent compensation or other compensation should be linked to the outcomes. Both too little and too much risk lead to too low incentives, as described above.

However, in the subsequent choice of governance model, it is important to consider that the employee, borrower or supplier must also be given the opportunity to control the outcomes. If, for example, a lender or a customer of a supplier agreement chooses a transactional contract where extensive decision-making and control rights accrue to the lender/customer, it will not matter how the balance in the first step has been made. Since the contract model deprives the borrower/supplier of the opportunity to influence the outcomes, the incentives will still be low.

Instead, suppose a company wants to build a long-term partnership with a strategically important supplier. Regardless of the business model, there are strong reasons to use a relational contract. It is then important to consider the interests and potential for conflicts of interest created by the business model. As discussed in more detail in Part V on value chains, direct conflicts of interest between the parties can be generated if a transactional business model is used. So, it is often appropriate to use some type of outcome-based model when using the relational contract.[482]

These overview examples show the importance of carefully considering how the governance model and the business model interact.

Be careful about the use of outcome-based business models and transactional contracts. It is common for outcome-based business models to be used together with transactional contracts. Examples of this are loan agreements, where the loan terms are tied to the borrower's performance in designated sustainability areas, and supplier agreements, where the supplier's payment is based on the achievement of set goals such as customer satisfaction, sustainability and so on. Another example is a supplier contract where the supplier's right to compensation is made partly dependent on factors such as end-customer satisfaction, security and other factors that are not only

482. When combining an outcome-based business model with a relational contract in a customer-supplier relationship, a good choice is to use the Vested model, developed at the University of Tennessee. *See, e.g.*, Vitasek et al., Veste: How P&G, McDonald's and Microsoft are Redefining Winning in Business Relationships, Palgrave Macmillan, 2012. Vitasek et al., Vested Outsourcing: Five Rules That Will Transform Outsourcing, 2nd edn, Palgrave Macmillan, 2013.

the supplier can influence. This combination can work but can often become problematic. The reason for this is that the outcome-based model easily creates friction when the parties, according to the description of the fairness and irrationality perspective above, interpret the outcomes and what has caused them in their own interests. A borrower may perceive the application of a loan term as unreasonable when he or she believes that the outcome has been influenced by factors beyond the borrower's control. The lender makes the opposite interpretation, and friction arises to the detriment of the business and the relationship. The same is true in supplier contracts.

It is problematic to manage this friction in the context of a transactional contract and the arm's length relationship that this contract model establishes. The parties can often manage the friction to some extent by maintaining good informal relationships, but this is rarely enough, especially if important key people leave the relationship. There is, therefore much to be said for considering the relational contract when the outcome-based model is used. The exception is where the outcomes are clearly measurable and where the performing party has very much control over the outcomes.

Consider direct and indirect impacts on sustainability factors. The two principles above apply independently of sustainability matters, and they play a direct role even if only economic efficiency and value creation are in focus. However, they become even more important to consider when entering into contracts significantly from a sustainability perspective. The degree of significance is based on the analysis from step 2.

To begin with, if there is a great potential for improvements or lower risks in sustainability matters, an outcome-based business model linked to sustainability matters should be considered. This is because the supplier can then be given good incentives to achieve set sustainability goals. The most common way to implement sustainability in contractual relationships is through a code of conduct made contractually binding. This means using the contract model to achieve sustainability, which often is a weak tool. This is often due to the customer's lack of follow-up, but often to an even greater extent due to the fact that sustainability matters are usually something that the parties must cooperate to deal with efficiently. A unilateral requirement to abide by a code of conduct will not help much. If a transactional business model is to be chosen, despite high sustainability potential, a relational contract should be used, within which the parties can work together to achieve the desired sustainability outcomes.

Another thing to keep in mind is the relationship in the contract between economic and sustainability matters. An integrated perspective should be taken, where the goal must be to maximise the economic value that can be created, but without harming sustainability matters and preferably also that positive outcomes on sustainability factors are achieved.

If an outcome-based business model is to be used, it is important to consider the relationship between outcomes linked to economics and sustainability. It is easy for the business model to be designed so the economic factors are given greater weight, which will then lead to a lower focus on sustainability matters. This can sometimes be managed to some extent through the contract model, for example, by making a supplier obliged to follow a code of conduct. However, the weakness of the code of conduct as a contractual mechanism in many cases has already been underlined above.

These and other principles are important to consider when choosing a business and contract model.

24.5 STEP 5: PROCURE, NEGOTIATE, WRITE AND ENTER INTO CONTRACTS

In the next step, the contract itself must be concluded, applying the chosen business model and contract model. How this is done depends to a large extent on the context and the type of contract to be concluded. The issue will not be dealt with in detail here.

24.5.1 The Contracting Process

It is important to emphasise that the choice of contract model should have a major impact on the actual process of entering into the contract. If a relational contract is to be entered into, a partnership must be built and then the process itself is crucial for success.[483] The parties should then wait to address purely commercial issues until a later stage and instead start building a relationship based on mutually agreed goals and guiding principles for the relationship. This applies irrespective of whether it concerns the conclusion of a supply agreement, the establishment of a loan agreement or an investment with equity.

24.5.2 Choice of Counterparty

In some deals, the company chooses a contractor based on the price quoted, on assessments of how well the contractor believes the contractor will be able to perform, and so on. This applies, for example, to procurements of goods or services or to various types of project financing. It then becomes crucial that the company considers which evaluation model should be applied and how the company should obtain information for the evaluation. Typically, the strategy from step 3 should support the evaluation and choice of the counterparty. Transactional contracts often let traditional procurement methods be used. The perspective must, however, change if a relational contract is to be used. Sustainability aspects must, of course, be considered in the evaluation model.

24.5.3 Use of Bargaining Power

An issue of particular importance is the use of power in contract negotiations. This is basically out of the question if a relational contract is used, where respecting the

483. For a detailed description of the process of entering into relational contracts, *see* Frydlinger et al., Part IV.

autonomy of the parties is one of the key guiding principles. However, it is common for bargaining power to be used in different ways when transactional contracts are to be concluded.

There isn't *one* form of transactional contract. However, it is common for parties using this contract model to try to exert various forms of power and influence to negotiate the deal. However, this is a practice that, in principle, must be abandoned when sustainability is an important issue in the relationship. This will be described in more detail in Part IV regarding supplier agreements. However, it can already be said that since sustainability is about respect for human equality and freedom, it is, of course, morally problematic if one party uses power in a way that leads to an unequal distribution of risk and that one party must accept contract terms because of the counterparty's superiority in the negotiation.

More importantly, however, using power to gain an advantage at the expense of the other party typically leads to the business becoming more unsustainable. Using your stronger bargaining power to place a risk on a counterparty without compensating them for the risk is essentially the same as creating an external effect. It is then very easy for the other party to use the same method in order not to be left with risks, i.e., to push it onto someone else without compensating for it. This may involve increasing the work pressure on employees, using unsustainable materials or resources because they have lower costs, and so on.

This means that regardless of whether a transactional or relational contract is entered into, the contractual clauses should not conflict with the six guiding principles that form an integral part of the relational contract: reciprocity, autonomy, honesty, loyalty, fairness and integrity. In the transactional contract, these principles are not included as part of the contract, but the negotiations should still follow the principles and the end result should be consistent with them.

The description above means that the methods for negotiating contracts in the market need to change fundamentally when a sustainable business is to be conducted.

24.6 STEP 6: FOLLOW-UP AND REPORT

The sixth step in the process of demonstrating due diligence in the company's contracts is follow-up and reporting. If the company has consistently followed the previous steps, this should be a follow-up of the chosen strategy, which should have been implemented in the contractual relationship. Established financial and sustainability-related targets are reported and evaluated. Within the framework of a relational contract, follow-up and reporting take place in collaboration with the aim of jointly steering the relationship towards the set goals. In the event of deviations, corrective action needs to be taken. Here, the demarcation between step 6 and step 2 becomes fluid, as the follow-up easily turns into a further analysis, which is as it should be.

CHAPTER 25

Sustainable Financing Contracts

Part II dealt with the EU sustainability laws on sustainable finance. Based on the previous chapters in Part IV, it is now possible to also address the important topic of sustainable finance contracts. The framework presented here is generic and applies equally to employment contracts, supplier agreements and various types of contracts regarding financing. The financial markets are characterised by a wide variety of contract types, which cannot be dealt with here even briefly. Instead, the focus will be on the two basic forms of sustainable finance, namely debt investments (including corporate bonds) and equity. The emphasis here will be on some aspects that financial actors that have sustainability as an objective under Article 9 of the SFDR need to take into account in relation to contracts to achieve the set objectives. However, the due diligence and contract process described above will not be repeated, as it directly applies to investment agreements.

25.1 RISKS OF CAUSING ADVERSE SUSTAINABILITY IMPACTS THROUGH FINANCING AGREEMENTS

The first ambition of a financing agreement should be to avoid creating a negative sustainability impact, in line with the due diligence norm. A sustainable investment, as defined in the SFDR, is an investment that does not cause significant harm. The investment must be made to avoid such damage. In addition, financial market participants shall disclose their policies to take into account the principal adverse impacts of investment decisions.

Insufficient consideration of the business and contracting model in a finance contract generates risk for unsustainable results. It is easiest to think in terms of a loan in project financing, where the lender receives a regular fixed income in the form of interest during the term of the loan agreement in exchange for financing a certain project. If the agreement is not designed with the most suitable business model and contract model, there is a risk that incentives are created that can lead to significant harm and that the investment is thus not sustainable. Several risks that also exist in supplier contracts recur here.

The loan terms can be written in such a way that the borrower receives a requirement for cost levels that mean that non-sustainable materials, solutions, etc., are used in the project.

The investor can also set budget requirements for the project as part of protecting their investment. This is logical, but it can lead to clearly negative consequences. If, as is common, the borrowing company engages suppliers to carry out its project, the budget requirement may lead to a requirement to enter into supplier agreements with fixed prices to create cost predictability. The problem is that in many contractual relationships, it is not possible to predict and plan what will happen during the contract period other than to a limited extent. The fixed price between the target company and the supplier will then risk creating a lot of friction between the parties. In addition, the supplier will have a clear incentive to create externalities to manage its risk, i.e., impose the risks on someone else without paying for it. The problem is propagating and risks leading to the choice of unsustainable solutions.

The challenge described above applies not only to project financing through loans but to any form of investment. Other problems may arise if outcome-based models are applied where financial incentives are tied to specific objectives in a way that neglects and perhaps harms other important areas. Certain levels of required returns can create similar problems when they mean that the target company begins to make financial decisions that do not consider sustainability factors to meet the required return on investment.

Thus, there is a risk that an investor with sustainability goals will fail because the investment agreements are written in such a way that incentives for unsustainable actions are created.

25.2 SUSTAINABILITY CONSIDERATIONS REGARDING BUSINESS AND GOVERNANCE MODEL IN FINANCING AGREEMENTS

However, the ambition of financing can be not only to avoid causing harm but also to contribute to positive effects on sustainability matters, in accordance with the norm of positive contribution. This is the purpose of so-called impact funding, which may then be classified under Article 9 of the SFDR. Impact funding is often done not only through loans or corporate bonds[484] but can also be done through equity. The purpose of the investor is to contribute to or achieve a sustainability goal. The financial return is important but not necessarily the overriding motive. A variety of environmental or social purposes can be pursued: improved health, education, biodiversity, land use, equality, and so on.

To succeed in this, the funder must consider what the contract should look like. Not least, considerations must be taken regarding the choice of business model and

484. For a good review of impact investing and loan agreements, *see* Burand, D., Contracting for Impact: Embedding Social and Environmental Impact Goals into Loan Agreements, 13 NY Journal of Law & Business, 2017, 775.

governance model discussed in Part IV, considering people's irrationality and sense of fairness. Regarding impact funding, there is also a perspective which has so far been too little discussed in contract theory, namely the fact that the investment is made to benefit a 'third party' - vulnerable people, the environment, and so on.

Section 23.3 on governance models outlined the risk-incentive trade-off that needs to be made from a governance model perspective. The starting point is that all contracts are incomplete, i.e., it is impossible to regulate in advance all conceivable situations that may arise during the term of the contract where the parties could have conflicting interests. This also applies to loan agreements and other financing agreements. When an unforeseen situation arises, the contract may need to be renegotiated. The party that is most dependent on the other risks ending up in a hold-up problem, where the stronger party can extract most of the value from the renegotiation. Alternatively, or at the same time, the parties also risk experiencing that they are betraying each other's expectations based on the reference points that the contract has created. This, in turn, risks leading to punitive behaviour between the parties, which increases the risk of conflicting interests even more.

A fairly common way to manage these risks for the investor is to write a transactional contract where the investor is given extensive control rights. This may involve regulating the target company's/borrower's right to incur certain costs, make investments or make other types of decisions. This can be done directly in a loan agreement, as veto rights in a shareholders' agreement, or in any other way. The aim is always the same, namely to restrict the freedom of action of the recipient of the financing so it does not take measures contrary to the interests of the investor.

There are at least two challenges with this approach. First, there is a risk that the investor acquires so much control that the incentives for performance by the counterparty are weakened too much. The counterparty can easily get a risk-minimising focus. Second, the investor risks disturbing the other party's sense of fairness and justice, which can give rise to a number of suboptimal behaviours.

An alternative here, of course, is to create aligned interests through the business model, for example, by linking the loan terms in a loan agreement to the target company meeting the sustainability goals that the investor wishes to achieve. But even then, the trade-off between risk and incentive described earlier in this part must be made, now tied to the business model.[485] Both too much and too little risk associated with the business model lowers the incentives for performance. In addition, the model risks creating incentives to achieve sustainability goals while creating incentives for significant harm in other ways, as described above. The problem, as is well known, is that it is easy to get what you measure, and you do not get what you do not measure but still want.

The latter problem can be avoided by combining the business and contract model, for example, by combining the outcome-based model with contractual clauses that impose certain minimum requirements on the target company, such as compliance with human rights requirements. However, this must take into account what has been

485. *See* section 23.1.

described in Chapter 24, namely the challenge of managing the risks of conflicts of interest and friction created by an outcome-based business model through a transactional contract and the inherent difficulty of directly linking the performing party's activities with the measured outcomes.

Added to these considerations is the fact that this type of agreement is entered into to create improvements for someone else – for people and/or the environment. The challenge can be easily described from the perspective of a force majeure clause. Suppose a lender has invested in a company that will provide health care. A pandemic breaks out, and the local government imposes restrictions that make it very difficult for the borrower to meet set KPIs. It is a force majeure situation (we assume). The problem is that the force majeure clauses in the contract only protect the parties – they do not breach the contract even if they fail to perform. However, the individuals who would have received health care do not benefit from it. On the contrary, they are harmed by it.

The description above points to the same factors described in Chapter 24, namely that in investments that have sufficiently high levels of risk – in terms of amounts, difficulty in predicting the future, and so on – the relational contract should be considered, where the parties manage a changing business environment through trusting cooperation within the framework of clear governance structures and processes.[486] This way of working with investments based on relational contracts is not yet common. But there are examples: Legal Innovation for Sustainable Investment.[487] For example, parties have developed a so-called term sheet for impact investing, which is intended to create the conditions for entering into a relational contract. The terms include that the parties must set up a common vision, adopt the guiding principles of the relational contract and set up decision-making forums to manage a relationship that here becomes more of a partnership than the traditional relationship at arm's length.

486. It is not uncommon for mechanisms for discussion and renegotiation to be present in sustainability-linked loans, as there is an awareness that circumstances may change during the loan period. This is a step in the direction of a more relationship-based perspective.
487. https://www.lisi-law.eu/.

PART V Sustainable Value Chains

CHAPTER 26

Beyond the Codes of Conduct

It is fairly common that companies' greatest impact on sustainability matters is generated indirectly through its value chain, for example, through greenhouse gas emissions. As stated in Part III, according to ESRS 1, companies must include information about their material impacts, risks and opportunities related to their direct and indirect business relationships in the value chain. This reporting requirement linked to the value chain recurs in several of the subject-specific standards. In addition, ESRS G1 requires companies to disclose how they manage their supplier relationships, which includes disclosing the company's supplier relationship strategy and whether it considers social and environmental criteria in choosing suppliers.[488]

Furthermore, the CSDDD, described in Chapter 14, requires large companies to which the directive is applicable to not only follow the general due diligence norm in Article 5 of the directive in its own operations but also in relation to the 'chain of activities'.

A short-term challenge for many companies that must prepare sustainability reports is the difficulty of obtaining relevant information from, for example, their suppliers, including on greenhouse gas emissions. This is often because the level of maturity in sustainability matters varies among suppliers. In the medium and long term, however, the challenges are much greater. The traditional way for larger companies to promote sustainability in their value chains is by including a code of conduct in their contracts, making this contractually binding, often linked to a right of termination if the code of conduct is not followed. Codes of conduct are general and do not aim to address specific sustainability matters in specific contracts. In addition, follow-up varies greatly. This and other reasons often make this instrument inadequate. This is evident when it is considered that the due diligence norm means that companies work according to structured processes that include:

488. Data point 14 of ESRS G1.

- incorporate sustainability due diligence into the company's governance, strategy and business model(s);
- communicate with and engage the company's stakeholders, i.e., the groups of individuals affected by the company's operations from a sustainability perspective;
- identify and assess the company's negative impact on people and the environment;
- take action to address adverse actions on people and the environment; and
- monitor the effects of the measures taken.[489]

When this process is extended to the entire value chain, a contractually binding code of conduct will often be far from sufficient. In this Part V of the book, sustainability in the value chain will be addressed. The subject is a natural part of sustainability law, as the value chain is built up by business relationships based on legally binding contracts. The presentation will be kept brief, as these are, from a legal perspective, mainly contractual issues that arise, which have been dealt with in Part IV.

489. Data point 65 of ESRS 1.

CHAPTER 27

The Value Chain

The concept of value chain was introduced by Michael Porter in the book *Competitive Advantage* 1985.[490] It is used in the ESRS to designate other companies in the supply or distribution chain of the undertaking in question, with which the undertaking may have either a direct relationship by contract or an indirect relationship by contracting with a company with which the undertaking in question has a contract. In the CSDDD, the term chain of activities is used instead. However, Porter used the concept of value chain primarily to avoid thinking in terms of individual organisational entities. The concept is part of his overall framework for understanding what creates competitive advantages for companies and how strategies can be set to create and maintain such competitive advantages.

Competitive advantage means more than temporary opportunities for companies to outperform their competitors. It can be about selling more products, having higher profitability, more customers, or other factors. Outperforming your competitors means creating more value for your customers than your competitors, where value is defined as the amount of money that customers are willing to pay for the products or services that the company sells.[491] As already described in Chapter 17, according to Porter, companies can create a competitive advantage by keeping costs lower (low-cost strategy), by providing something unique (differentiation strategy), or by focusing on a particular segment through something unique (segment strategy). Each strategy is reflected in the company's value-adding activities, which Porter generically defines as inbound logistics, production, outbound logistics, marketing and sales, and services.[492] Competitive advantages are created by the company implementing the chosen strategy within its activities and areas of activity. A group of activities can, in theory, be carried out at a significantly lower cost or to create significantly more value than the

490. Porter, M., Competitive Advantage, Free Press, 1985.
491. Porter, *supra*, p. 38.
492. *Ibid.*, p. 46.

competition. In both cases, the performance of the activities is measured in financial terms: lower costs and increased revenues, respectively.

In the ESRS standards, this theoretical background to the value chain concept is not very relevant. Quite simply, the value chain represents a company's suppliers and distributors at several levels. However, it is important to keep Porter's perspective in mind. The nature of the value chain is, or at least should be, a strategic choice. For Porter, it was a matter of optimal design to create competitiveness. This is still highly relevant from a sustainability perspective. However, as pointed out earlier[493] in the book, this perspective means that sustainability factors must be factored into the strategic work in a way that has not been common before. This also applies to the design of the value chain.

493. *See* section 12.2.

CHAPTER 28

Sustainability Shortcomings in the Value Chain and Their Causes

Many value chains show clear shortcomings from a sustainability perspective. It can range from the use of forced or child labour to pollution and waste of resources. There are many examples.

Why is the value chain so often unsustainable? Why does it so often cause negative externalities on the environment, people and society that companies do not bear the costs of? These are big questions that have not been given unambiguous answers in research. In economics, externalities are seen as so-called market failures, which means that the self-interest of companies does not coincide with the public interest (e.g., a clean environment or low levels of corruption). The questions can be answered from a variety of perspectives. Here, however, only a more limited but nevertheless very important perspective will be highlighted. It is about how contracts are written in business relationships that build up the value chain.

The considerations that need to be made when entering into a contract are discussed in Part IV of the book. An important reason for the lack of sustainability in the value chain is that companies make insufficient considerations when choosing a business and contract model. This is true from a purely economic perspective, where wrong choices often lead to economic inefficiency. But this is even more true from a sustainability perspective.

28.1 THE CHOICE OF BUSINESS AND CONTRACT MODEL

As shown in Part IV, there are two basic business models to choose from in a supplier contract: the transactional and the outcome-based models. It is furthermore appropriate to divide the outcome-based model into two sub-models: the output-based model and the outcome-based model. In addition, two contract models are available: the transactional and the relational model.

By far, the most common combination in supplier agreements on the market combines a transactional business model and a transactional contract. It is, therefore, important to look at the incentives that this model often creates and what significance it may have from a sustainability perspective.

The transactional business model means that the supplier is paid for its activities, which are often divided into individual transactions. Some examples are when a supplier is paid per hour, per produced unit of a product, per answered call in customer service, and so on. This model has advantages, mainly because it allows comparisons between the prices of different suppliers. The problem is that, as pointed out earlier, it also easily creates directly conflicting interests between the parties. This can be illustrated by the following table, which shows the incentives that the model typically creates.

	Economic value	*Creates incentives to...*
Customer	Difference between what it would have cost the company to produce itself and the price from the supplier	... Push the price per transaction ... Minimise the number of transactions ... Make sure to get as high quality per transaction as possible
Supplier	Difference between price and cost per transaction	... Increase the price per transaction ... Maximise the number of transactions ... Reducing the cost per transaction, for example, through quality degradation

A buying customer thus maximises its value through a low price per transaction, few transactions and high quality. A selling supplier maximises its value in the opposite way in all three dimensions, namely through high price, many transactions and low costs, which easily affects the level of quality. Here, the parties have opposing interests built into their relationship from the beginning.

As mentioned, this business model is most often combined with a transactional contract, even in long-term relationships with a high degree of dependency and risk. Since the parties have conflicting interests built into the deal, a situation easily arises where the parties, through power-based negotiations, try to write a contract in which they prevent each other from acting on their opposing interests. This often results in long and complicated contracts, which will still always be incomplete. They are never clear enough not to need to be interpreted at a later stage, and they never cover all situations that may arise during the contract period. This is partly a result of the planning fallacy, which was described in Part IV.[494]

Thus, the common combination of a transactional business model and a transactional contract means that the parties build a deal in which they have conflicting interests, which they then try to keep in check through a contract model based on

494. *See* section 23.2.

power. This is problematic even from a purely economic perspective, as it often leads to low efficiency, lack of innovation, etc. Here, however, the focus is on what it is that causes a lack of sustainability in the value chain. Below, a number of negative effects are highlighted.

28.2 NEGATIVE EFFECTS ON SUSTAINABILITY

Incentives for high resource use. The transactional business model creates incentives for suppliers to sell many units at a low cost per unit. This applies to both goods and services. In the case of goods, there is thus an incentive to consume a lot of resources since many goods require a high consumption of resources. This is rarely compatible with what is best from a sustainability perspective.

Incentives to drive down costs. At the same time, the transactional model creates incentives for the supplier to reduce its costs to increase margins. Thus, there is no incentive to use more sustainable solutions in the production of goods and services, as long as these solutions are not also the cheapest. Although sustainable solutions can often be more cost-effective over time, they are rarely so in the short term, which means that cost pressure easily creates incentives to use non-sustainable solutions.

Incentives to exploit externalities. However, there is an even more effective way for a supplier to increase its profits than to reduce costs, namely by avoiding costs altogether. This can be done by production based on natural resources and people, who may bear the costs while the company receives the benefits. This, then, is like creating and exploiting externalities. Costs can be avoided, at least in the short term, if measures are not taken to, for example, create more environmentally friendly production processes or a safe working environment for producing workers.

Incentives to shift risks and costs onto the weaker party. When externalities are exploited, people who are not part of the contractual relationships in the value chain are harmed. However, problems arise already at an earlier stage, namely directly in the relationship between the customer and the supplier. As mentioned, the traditional model uses the transactional contract model, in which the parties manage their risks through power. The problem of using power in contract negotiations has already been discussed in Part IV but will be further elaborated on here.[495]

Using power in a business relationship means that one company uses the weaker position of the other company in such a way that the first company can obtain an economic advantage without having to pay the true cost of that advantage.

In ESRS G1, only one possible example is clearly highlighted, namely the payment time on invoices. It is not uncommon for buying customers to apply 90 or more days of payment time to their suppliers while demanding 30 days of payment time from their customers. This is a great way to improve your working capital. But it comes with a cost to the supplier. This cost can be calculated in different ways, but a simple way to look at it is to think about the more normal situation where a 30-day

495. *See* section 24.5.

payment period applies. In the event of late payment, interest is payable. The supplier's cost from day 31 can, therefore, be calculated as the loss of interest income. From the customer's perspective, the missing interest expense is revenue received from the supplier without the customer paying for it.

There are a large number of other ways a party can obtain benefits from an opposing party through the exercise of power without paying for it. The most common is through pricing. From a customer perspective, it can be the case that they use their power to push a supplier's prices to a level where they get a long-term unsustainable margin on the deal. Other examples include imposing various forms of commercial or other risks on the counterparty. Some examples are:

- asymmetric lock-in periods, where one party is bound to the contract for a certain period while the other party is given the right to terminate the contract at any time;
- imposing risk on the counterparty for factors beyond its control, such as changes in the surrounding economic environment; and
- low limitations of liability, which means that one party takes responsibility for any damage caused to the other party only up to a low level, after which the other party must bear the cost itself.

The list goes on and on. The common denominator here is that one party uses power to gain an advantage without paying the cost of it. This is the essence of what an external effect is. Economically, the effect of using power in this way is the same as not bearing the cost of one's external influence. Morally speaking, the same is true. To use one's power in this way violates the equality and freedom of the other party. The other party's right to equal treatment is not respected by taking advantage of his lack of freedom, i.e., dependency.

This use of power risks having a direct negative impact on various sustainability matters in the value chain. A customer can, through the exercise of power, impose a cost on the supplier and bear a benefit for this without paying for it. Instead, the supplier must pay the cost, such as the missing interest, the cost of the higher level of risk, and so on. Every cost must ultimately be financed because, without funding, the supplier will eventually become insolvent. The supplier faces several courses of action. The supplier can bear the cost itself and thus lower its margin. The supplier may lower the quality of its goods and services, which leads to lower costs. In principle, this means that the cost is then charged to the customer again.

However, it is obvious that the supplier also has an incentive to do what the customer does, i.e., to try to pass the cost on to someone else without paying for it, which brings us back to the previous point where the supplier tries to take advantage of the opportunity that external effects provide.

There is a clear economic logic here, which means that a customer's use of power ultimately leads to people, the environment and society having to bear a cost that the customer does not pay for. Law professor Sara Dadush refers to this way of contracting as 'extractive contracting', which is a very accurate description.[496]

Inability to cooperate. An additional factor that complicates improvements from a sustainability perspective is the other side of the previous factor, i.e., the tendency to use power in commercial relationships. The more a company uses power, the more the ability to collaborate effectively decreases. Cooperation is based, among other things, on trust and openness. Exercising power undermines trust and creates incentives to exploit information asymmetries.

Why is collaboration important to increase the creation of sustainable value? This is simply because sustainability matters are often complicated and require many actors to act in a coordinated way. An almost too obvious example is a transition from a linear to a circular business model. If a company that uses suppliers in four tiers, has different distributors in different countries, and different segments of end customers is to carry out such a project, it is, first and foremost, a major collaboration challenge. Products must be designed for maximum lifespan and the possibility of reuse of used materials. Supply chains need to become supply circles. New business models must be found, which will create enough value for all parties that everyone is willing to participate. It is a highly complex operation, which will require acceptance of failure, innovation, risk-taking, and so on. Trying to carry out such an operation through the exercise of force is doomed to failure precisely because the exercise of power will lead to a lack of transparency, risk aversion, fear of failure, and so on.

It is against this background that the standard solution to increase sustainability in the value chain - by using a code of conduct - should be viewed.[497] Typically, the customer imposes on the supplier a one-sided obligation to follow the customers' code of conduct and to ensure it is applied back-to-back with the sub-suppliers. This is combined with a unilateral right to terminate the contract in case of breach of the code of conduct. That this mechanism is often insufficient has already been pointed out in Chapter 26. Looking closer, it is clear that the mechanism can even backfire for a number of reasons.

The code of conduct is typically imposed as part of an extractive contract, where the transaction based economic model is combined with a transactional contract. From the beginning, the incentives to use externalities are already in place, i.e., incentives to let people and the environment bear costs. Enters the code of conduct, which requires that measures will often be costly to take for the supplier. It is thus not only an interesting but also a tragic paradox that *the imposing of a code of conduct often generates incentives to generate externalities on those whom the code of conduct is supposed to protect.*

Add to this the right to terminate the agreement for breach of the code of conduct. What happens if the agreement is terminated? The supplier will lose revenues, may have to lay-off people (who were supposed to be protected by the code of conduct) and will have an incentive to let the environment carry costs.

---

496. Dadush, S, Prosocial Contracts: Making Relational Contracts More Relational (January 5, 2022). Law and Contemporary Problems, Vol. 85, No. 2, 2022, Rutgers Law School Research Paper.
497. *See* Chapter 26.

An ignorant use of the code of conduct mechanism thus runs the risk of generating the very harm it is supposed to try to avoid.

28.3 MODEL CLAUSES

The insufficiency of using a code of conduct has, of course, not gone unnoticed. In later years, a number of initiatives have been taken to produce model clauses related to sustainability being used in supply chain contracts. The American Bar Association has launched a Model Clauses for Human Rights Project.[498] The Center for Corporate Law and Governance at Rutgers Law School hosts the Responsible Contracting Project (RCP), which includes European Model Clauses.[499] A similar project focusing on climate change is the Chancery Lane Project.[500] The common aim of these important projects is to provide companies with better contracting tools to address various sustainability matters, not only by imposing, for example, obligations to combat climate change but also by introducing fairness and reciprocity throughout the supply chains. As an example, the RCP's Supplier Model Contract Clauses start by setting the tone with this clause:

> Buyer and Supplier each covenants to establish, maintain, and cooperate in a human rights and environmental due diligence process appropriate to its size and circumstances to identify, prevent, mitigate, and account for how Buyer and Supplier addresses the direct and indirect Adverse Impacts of its activities on the human rights of individuals affected by their supply chains.

The rest of the clauses impose mutual obligations of the parties to cooperate to address actual and potential adverse impacts on people and the environment. These projects are important and show a clear trend of growing awareness that contracts can not only generate sustainability problems but should also be part of the solution. It should be pointed out, however, that there seems to be a risk if such clauses are included in contracts in the standard ways that codes of conduct are often used. The fact that such model clauses are needed is the symptom of underlying problems, which often are related to the business model used in the contract, to traditional procurement practices and, of course, to the focus on shareholder value discussed in Chapter 6. A shift to sustainable supply chains requires a systemic shift in the approach to contracts and the introduction of model clauses without considering the contracting system they are used in risks, making them lose a lot of their force.

498. www.americanbar.org/groups/human_rights/business-human-rights-initiative/contractual-clauses-project/.
499. www.responsiblecontracting.org/.
500. www.chancerylaneproject.org/clauses/.

CHAPTER 29

Creating the Sustainable Value Chain

As described in the previous chapter, the combination of a transactional business model and a transactional contract thus creates incentives for high resource consumption, low and therefore not necessarily sustainable costs, shifting of risks and costs to the weaker party and thus an incentive for the latter to compensate by using externalities to avoid bearing the costs themselves. This, combined with the inability to cooperate created by a model that fundamentally creates conflicting interests and incentives to use power, naturally builds up a lot of externalities and, thus, major sustainability gaps. Model clauses such as those published by the Responsible Contracting Project are important tools to address these issues but can also be insufficient.

Creating a sustainable value chain is a vast task, and the subject goes far beyond what is possible to cover in this book. Here, a limitation is made to the sustainability law perspective since it is the rules of the game for the value chain actors that determine whether the value chain is sustainable or not. The description above shows how the choice of business and contract model in the value chain's contracts is crucial for whether the value chain is sustainable or not. It is this choice that sets the basic rules of game for the value chain. This needs to be considered if the norms of due diligence and positive contribution should be implemented in relation to the value chain.

Part IV described a process for how the standard can be applied to individual contracts. The corresponding process can be adapted to the entire value chain:

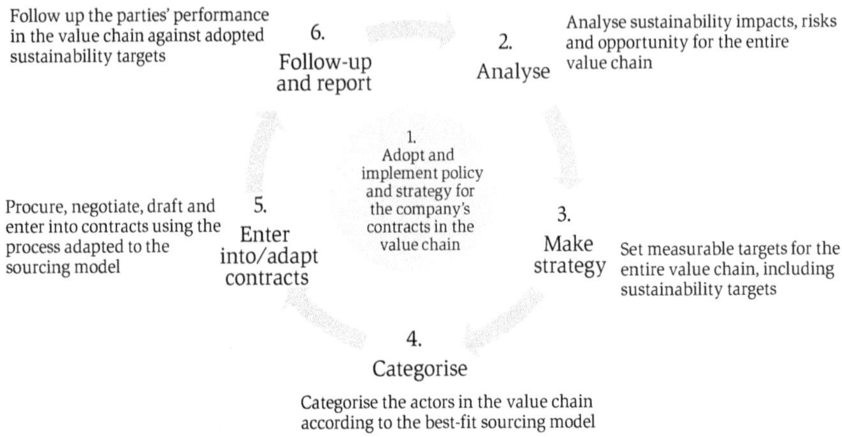

As the above process is very similar to the due diligence process described in Part IV, its details will not be further addressed. However, the fourth step - choosing your sourcing model - should be particularly highlighted. It is common for companies' purchasing departments to use various forms of supplier segmentation. Of course, these are also important from a sustainability perspective, and it is possible to envisage a segmentation according to the potential for creating positive sustainability effects and reducing negative impacts. However, the essence of step 4 is to categorise by business and contract model. It is then a question of an analysis of the current situation and the target situation. Most contracts in the value chain will be transactional and apply transactional business models. Some contracts are also likely to apply an outcome-based model. A smaller number will be relational in the sense of this book. The above description of how negative sustainability impacts are easily created by the combination of transactional business model and transactional contract shows the importance of identifying the best-fit sourcing business model for each relationship.

Ultimately, this is about making the value chain sustainable by changing the institutional set-up into a set of rules of the game that avoids negative externalities and thus respects everyone's equality and freedom.

Annexes

Annex 1

Sustainability matters to be included in companies' materiality assessment.[501]

ESRS	*Sustainability topics covered by the subject-specific ESRSs*		
	Topic	*Subtopic*	*Sub-subtopic*
ESRS E1	Climate change	- Climate change adaptation - Climate change mitigation - Energy	
ESRS E2	Pollution	- Pollution of air - Pollution of water - Pollution of soil - Pollution of living organisms and food resources - Substances of concern - Substances of very high concern - Microplastics	
ESRS E3	Water and marine resources	- Water - Marine resources	- Water consumption - Water withdrawals - Water discharges - Water discharges in the oceans - Extraction and use of marine resources
ESRS E4	Biodiversity and ecosystems	- Direct impact drivers of biodiversity loss	- Climate Change - Land-use change, fresh water-use change and sea-use change - Direct exploitation - Invasive alien species

501. Application Requirement 16 of Appendix A of ESRS 1.

ESRS	*Sustainability topics covered by the subject-specific ESRSs Topic Subtopic Sub-subtopic*		
			- Pollution - Others
		- Impacts on the state of species	Examples: - Species population size - Species global extinction risk
		- Impact on the extent and conditions of ecosystems	Examples: - Land degradation - Desertification - Soil sealing
		- Impacts on and dependencies on ecosystem services	
ESRS E5	Circular economy	- Resource inflows, including resource use - Resource outflows related to products and services - Waste	
ESRS S1	Own workforce	- Working conditions	- Secure employment - Working time - Adequate wages - Social dialogue - Freedom of association, the existence of works councils and the information, consultation and participation rights of workers - Collective bargaining, including rate of workers covered by collective agreements - Work-life balance - Health and safety
		- Equal treatment and opportunities for all	- Gender equality and equal pay for work of equal value - Training and skills development - Employment and inclusion of persons with disabilities

ESRS	*Sustainability topics covered by the subject-specific ESRSs*		
	Topic	*Subtopic*	*Sub-subtopic*
			- Measures against violence and harassment in the workplace - Diversity
		- Other work-related rights	- Child labour - Forced labour - Adequate housing - Privacy
ESRS S2	Workers in the value chain	- Working conditions	- Secure employment - Working time - Adequate wages - Social dialogue - Freedom of association, the existence of works councils and the information, consultation and participation rights of workers - Collective bargaining, including rate of workers covered by collective agreements - Work-life balance - Health and safety
		- Equal treatment and opportunities for all	- Gender equality and equal pay for work of equal value - Training and skills development - Employment and inclusion of persons with disabilities - Measures against violence and harassment in the workplace - Diversity
		- Other work-related rights	- Child labour - Forced labour - Adequate housing - Privacy

ESRS	Sustainability topics covered by the subject-specific ESRSs Topic	Subtopic	Sub-subtopic
ESRS S3	Affected communities	– Communities' economic, social and cultural rights	– Adequate housing – Adequate food – Water and sanitation – Land-related impacts – Security-related impacts
		– Communities' civil and political rights	– Freedom of expression – Freedom of assembly – Impacts on human rights defenders
		– Rights of indigenous peoples	– Free, prior and informed consent – Self-determination – Cultural rights
ESRS S4	Consumers and end-users	– Information-related impacts for consumers and/or end-users	– Privacy – Freedom of expression – Access to (quality) information
		– Personal safety of consumers and/or end-users	– Health and safety – Security of a person – Protection of children
		– Social inclusion of consumers and/or end-users	– Non-discrimination – Access to products and services – Responsible marketing practices
ESRS G1	Business conduct	– Corporate culture – Protection of whistleblowers – Animal welfare – Political engagement and lobbying activities – Management of relationships with suppliers including payment practices	
		– Corruption and bribery	– Prevention and detection including training – Incidents

Annex 2

Economic activities subject to the European Commission's technical screening criteria set out in Delegated Regulation (EU) 2021/2139 regarding substantial contributions to climate change mitigation.

1. **Forestry**
   1.1. Afforestation
   1.2. Rehabilitation and restoration of forests, including reforestation and natural forest regeneration after an extreme event
   1.3. Forest management
   1.4. Conservation forestry

2. **Environmental protection and restoration activities**
   2.1. Restoration of wetlands

3. **Manufacturing**
   3.1. Manufacture of renewable energy technologies
   3.2. Manufacture of equipment for the production and use of hydrogen
   3.3. Manufacture of low carbon technologies for transport
   3.4. Manufacture of batteries
   3.5. Manufacture of energy efficiency equipment for buildings
   3.6. Manufacture of other low carbon technologies
   3.7. Manufacture of cement
   3.8. Manufacture of aluminium
   3.9. Manufacture of iron and steel
   3.10. Manufacture of hydrogen
   3.11. Manufacture of carbon black
   3.12. Manufacture of soda ash
   3.13. Manufacture of chlorine
   3.14. Manufacture of organic basic chemicals
   3.15. Manufacture of anhydrous ammonia

3.16. Manufacture of nitric acid
3.17. Manufacture of plastics in primary form

4. Energy

4.1. Electricity generation using solar photovoltaic technology
4.2. Electricity generation using concentrated solar power (CSP) technology
4.3. Electricity generation from wind power
4.4. Electricity generation from ocean energy technologies
4.5. Electricity generation from hydropower
4.6. Electricity generation from geothermal energy
4.7. Electricity generation from renewable non-fossil gaseous and liquid fuels
4.8. Electricity generation from bioenergy
4.9. Transmission and distribution of electricity
4.10. Storage of electricity
4.11. Storage of thermal energy
4.12. Storage of hydrogen
4.13. Manufacture of biogas and biofuels for use in transport and of bioliquids
4.14. Transmission and distribution networks for renewable and low-carbon gases
4.15. District heating/cooling distribution
4.16. Installation and operation of electric heat pumps
4.17. Cogeneration of heat/cool and power from solar energy
4.18. Cogeneration of heat/cool and power from geothermal energy
4.19. Cogeneration of heat/cool and power from renewable non-fossil gaseous and liquid fuels
4.20. Cogeneration of heat/cool and power from bioenergy
4.21. Production of heat/cool from solar thermal heating
4.22. Production of heat/cool from geothermal energy
4.23. Production of heat/cool from renewable non-fossil gaseous and liquid fuels
4.24. Production of heat/cool from bioenergy
4.25. Production of heat/cool using waste heat

5. Water supply, sewerage, waste management and remediation

5.1. Construction, extension and operation of water collection, treatment and supply systems
5.2. Renewal of water collection, treatment and supply systems
5.3. Construction, extension and operation of waste water collection and treatment
5.4. Renewal of waste water collection and treatment
5.5. Collection and transport of non-hazardous waste in source segregated fractions
5.6. Anaerobic digestion of sewage sludge
5.7. Anaerobic digestion of bio-waste
5.8. Composting of bio-waste

5.9. Material recovery from non-hazardous waste
5.10. Landfill gas capture and utilisation
5.11. Transport of CO_2
5.12. Underground permanent geological storage of CO_2

6. Transport

6.1. Passenger interurban rail transport
6.2. Freight rail transport
6.3. Urban and suburban transport, road passenger transport
6.4. Operation of personal mobility devices, cycle logistics
6.5. Transport by motorbikes, passenger cars and light commercial vehicles
6.6. Freight transport services by road
6.7. Inland passenger water transport
6.8. Inland freight water transport
6.9. Retrofitting of inland water passenger and freight transport
6.10. Sea and coastal freight water transport, vessels for port operations and auxiliary activities
6.11. Sea and coastal passenger water transport
6.12. Retrofitting of sea and coastal freight and passenger water transport
6.13. Infrastructure for personal mobility, cycle logistics
6.14. Infrastructure for rail transport
6.15. Infrastructure enabling low-carbon road transport and public transport
6.16. Infrastructure enabling low carbon water transport
6.17. Low carbon airport infrastructure

7. Construction and real estate activities

7.1. Construction of new buildings
7.2. Renovation of existing buildings
7.3. Installation, maintenance and repair of energy efficiency equipment
7.4. Installation, maintenance and repair of charging stations for electric vehicles in buildings (and parking spaces attached to buildings)
7.5. Installation, maintenance and repair of instruments and devices for measuring, regulation and controlling energy performance of buildings
7.6. Installation, maintenance and repair of renewable energy technologies
7.7. Acquisition and ownership of buildings

8. Information and communication

8.1. Data processing, hosting and related activities
8.2. Data-driven solutions for GHG emissions reductions

9. Professional, scientific and technical activities

9.1. Close to market research, development and innovation
9.2. Research, development and innovation for direct air capture of CO_2
9.3. Professional services related to energy performance of buildings

Annex 3

Economic activities subject to the European Commission's technical screening criteria set out in Delegated Regulation (EU) 2021/2139 regarding substantial contributions to climate change adaptation.

1. **Forestry**
    - 1.1. Afforestation
    - 1.2. Rehabilitation and restoration of forests, including reforestation and natural forest regeneration after an extreme event
    - 1.3. Forest management
    - 1.4. Conservation forestry

2. **Environmental protection and restoration activities**
    - 2.1. Restoration of wetlands

3. **Manufacturing**
    - 3.1. Manufacture of renewable energy technologies
    - 3.2. Manufacture of equipment for the production and use of hydrogen
    - 3.3. Manufacture of low carbon technologies for transport
    - 3.4. Manufacture of batteries
    - 3.5. Manufacture of energy efficiency equipment for buildings
    - 3.6. Manufacture of other low carbon technologies
    - 3.7. Manufacture of cement
    - 3.8. Manufacture of aluminium
    - 3.9. Manufacture of iron and steel
    - 3.10. Manufacture of hydrogen
    - 3.11. Manufacture of carbon black
    - 3.12. Manufacture of soda ash
    - 3.13. Manufacture of chlorine
    - 3.14. Manufacture of organic basic chemicals
    - 3.15. Manufacture of anhydrous ammonia

3.16. Manufacture of nitric acid
3.17. Manufacture of plastics in primary form

4. Energy

4.1. Electricity generation using solar photovoltaic technology
4.2. Electricity generation using concentrated solar power (CSP) technology
4.3. Electricity generation from wind power
4.4. Electricity generation from ocean energy technologies
4.5. Electricity generation from hydropower
4.6. Electricity generation from geothermal energy
4.7. Electricity generation from renewable non-fossil gaseous and liquid fuels
4.8. Electricity generation from bioenergy
4.9. Transmission and distribution of electricity
4.10. Storage of electricity
4.11. Storage of thermal energy
4.12. Storage of hydrogen
4.13. Manufacture of biogas and biofuels for use in transport and of bioliquids
4.14. Transmission and distribution networks for renewable and low-carbon gases
4.15. District heating/cooling distribution
4.16. Installation and operation of electric heat pumps
4.17. Cogeneration of heat/cool and power from solar energy
4.18. Cogeneration of heat/cool and power from geothermal energy
4.19. Cogeneration of heat/cool and power from renewable non-fossil gaseous and liquid fuels
4.20. Cogeneration of heat/cool and power from bioenergy
4.21. Production of heat/cool from solar thermal heating
4.22. Production of heat/cool from geothermal energy
4.23. Production of heat/cool from renewable non-fossil gaseous and liquid fuels
4.24. Production of heat/cool from bioenergy
4.25. Production of heat/cool using waste heat

5. Water supply, sewerage, waste management and remediation activities

5.1. Construction, extension and operation of water collection, treatment and supply systems
5.2. Renewal of water collection, treatment and supply systems
5.3. Construction, extension and operation of waste water collection and treatment
5.4. Renewal of waste water collection and treatment
5.5. Collection and transport of non-hazardous waste in source segregated fractions
5.6. Anaerobic digestion of sewage sludge
5.7. Anaerobic digestion of bio-waste
5.8. Composting of bio-waste

5.9. Material recovery from non-hazardous waste
5.10. Landfill gas capture and utilisation
5.11. Transport of CO_2
5.12. Underground permanent geological storage of CO_2

6. Transport

6.1. Passenger interurban rail transport
6.2. Freight rail transport
6.3. Urban and suburban transport, road passenger transport
6.4. Operation of personal mobility devices, cycle logistics
6.5. Transport by motorbikes, passenger cars and commercial vehicles
6.6. Freight transport services by road
6.7. Inland passenger water transport
6.8. Inland freight water transport
6.9. Retrofitting of inland water passenger and freight transport
6.10. Sea and coastal freight water transport, vessels for port operations and auxiliary activities
6.11. Sea and coastal passenger water transport
6.12. Retrofitting of sea and coastal freight and passenger water transport
6.13. Infrastructure for personal mobility, cycle logistics
6.14. Infrastructure for rail transport
6.15. Infrastructure enabling road transport and public transport
6.16. Infrastructure for water transport
6.17. Airport infrastructure

7. Construction and real estate

7.1. Construction of new buildings
7.2. Renovation of existing buildings
7.3. Installation, maintenance and repair of energy efficiency equipment
7.4. Installation, maintenance and repair of charging stations for electric vehicles in buildings (and parking spaces attached to buildings)
7.5. Installation, maintenance and repair of instruments and devices for measuring, regulation and controlling energy performance of buildings
7.6. Installation, maintenance and repair of renewable energy technologies
7.7. Acquisition and ownership of buildings

8. Information and communication

8.1. Data processing, hosting and related activities
8.2. Computer programming, consultancy and related activities
8.3. Programming and broadcasting activities

9. Professional, scientific and technical activities

9.1. Engineering activities and related technical consultancy dedicated to adaptation to climate change
9.2. Close to market research, development and innovation

10. Financial and insurance activities

10.1. Non-life insurance: underwriting of climate-related perils

10.2. Reinsurance

11. Education

12. Human health and social work activities

12.1. Residential care activities

13. Arts, entertainment and recreation

13.1. Creative, arts and entertainment activities

13.2. Libraries, archives, museums and cultural activities

13.3. Motion picture, video and television programme production, sound recording and music publishing activities

Annex 4

Economic activities subject to the European Commission's technical screening criteria in the Delegated Regulation regarding substantial contributions to adaptation to sustainable use and protection of marine resources.

1 Manufacturing

1.1 Manufacture, installation and associated services for leakage control technologies enabling leakage reduction and prevention in water supply systems

2 Water supply, sewerage, waste management and remediation activities

2.1 Water supply

2.2 Urban Waste Water Treatment

2.3 Sustainable urban drainage systems (SUDS)

3 Disaster risk management

3.1 Nature-based solutions for flood and drought risk prevention and protection

4 Information and communication

4.1 Provision of IT/OT data-driven solutions for leakage reduction

Annex 5

Economic activities subject to the European Commission's technical screening criteria in the Delegated Regulation regarding substantial contributions to the transition to a circular economy.

1 Manufacturing

1.1. Manufacture of plastic packaging goods
1.2 Manufacture of electrical and electronic equipment.

2 Water supply, sewerage, waste management and remediation activities

2.1 Phosphorus recovery from waste water
2.2 Production of alternative water resources for purposes other than human consumption
2.3 Collection and transport of non-hazardous and hazardous waste
2.4 Treatment of hazardous waste '
2.5 Recovery of bio-waste by anaerobic digestion or composting
2.6 Depollution and dismantling of end-of-life products
2.7 Sorting and material recovery of non-hazardous waste

3 Construction and real estate activities

3.1 Construction of new buildings
3.2 Renovation of existing buildings
3.3 Demolition and wrecking of buildings and other structures
3.4 Maintenance of roads and motorways
3.5 Use of concrete in civil engineering

4 Information and communication

4.1 Provision of IT/OT data-driven solutions

5 Services

5.1 Repair, refurbishment and remanufacturing
5.2 Sale of spare parts

5.3 Preparation for reuse of end-of-life products and product components
5.4 Sale of second-hand goods
5.5 Product-as-a-service and other circular use- and result-oriented service models
5.6 Marketplace for the trade of second-hand goods for reuse

Annex 6

Economic activities subject to the European Commission's technical screening criteria in the Delegated Regulation regarding large contributions to pollution prevention and control.

1 Manufacturing

1.1 Manufacture of active pharmaceutical ingredients (API) or active substances
1.2 Manufacture of medicinal products

2 Water supply, sewerage, waste management and remediation activities

2.1 Collection and transport of hazardous waste
2.2 Treatment of hazardous waste
2.3 Remediation of legally non-conforming landfills and abandoned or illegal waste dumps
2.4 Remediation of contaminated sites and areas

Annex 7

Economic activities subject to the European Commission's technical screening criteria in the Delegated Regulation regarding substantial contributions to the protection and restoration of biodiversity.

1 **Environmental protection and restoration activities**
   1.1 Conservation, including restoration, of habitats, ecosystems and species

2 **Accommodation activities**
   2.1 Hotels, holiday, camping grounds and similar accommodation

Bibliography

Acemoglu, D. and Robinson, J., Why Nations Fail, Profile Books Ltd, 2013.

Anand, P., Foundations of Rational Choice under Risk, Clarendon Press, 1993.

Aristotle, Nicomachean Ethics, Good Press, 2023.

Ash, E., Chen, D. and Naidu, S., Ideas Have Consequences: The Impact of Law and Economics on American Justice (February 2022). NBER Working Paper No. w29788.

Bazerman, M. and Tenbrunsel, A., Blind Spots – Why We Fail to Do What's Right and What to Do about It, Princeton University Press, 2012.

BCTI, Tackling Inequality: An Agenda for Business Action, 2023.

Bebchuk, L. and Tallarita, R., The Illusory Promise of Stakeholder Governance (26 February 2020), 106 Cornell Law Review, 2020, 91-178.

Benthman, J., An Introduction to the Principles of Morals and Legislation, Good Press, 2022.

Berle, A. and Means, G. The Modern Corporation and Private Property, 2nd edn, Harcourt, Brace and World, 1967.

Bernstein, J., et al., SDGs For All: Strategic Scenarios: Earth4All System Dynamics Modelling of SDG Progress, Working Paper version 1.0, September 2023.

Brealey, R.A., et al., Principles of Corporate Finance, 14th edn, McGraw Hill, 2023.

Bourdieu, P., The Logic of Practice, Stanford University Press, 1980.

Bourdieu, P., Homo Academicus, Stanford University Press, 1990.

Bourdieu, P., The Political Ontology of Martin Heidegger, Polity Press, 1991.

Bourdieu, P., An Invitation to Reflexive Sociology, Polity Press, 1992.

Bourdieu, P., Pascalian Meditations, Polity Press, 2000.

Bourdieu, P., Science of Science and Reflexivity, The University of Chicago Press, 2004.

Bourdieu, P., Classification Struggles, General Sociology Volume 1, Polity Press, 2018.

Burand, D., Contracting for Impact: Embedding Social and Environmental Impact Goals into Loan Agreements, 13 NY Journal of Law & Business, 2017, 775.

Chancel, L., et al., World Inequality Report 2022.

Coase, R., (1937) The Nature of the Firm, 4(16) Economica, 386-405.

Collins, J., and Porras, J., Built to Last, Harper Business, 1994.

Cook, E., Efficiently Unequal: The Global Rise of Kaldor-Hicks Neoliberalism, 9(1-2) Global Intellectual History, 2024, 247-269.

Dadush, S, Prosocial Contracts: Making Relational Contracts More Relational (January 5, 2022). Law and Contemporary Problems, Vol. 85, No. 2, 2022, Rutgers Law School Research Paper,

Dixson-Decleve, S., et al., Earth for All: A Survival Guide for Humanity, New Society Publishers, 2022.

Drucker, P., The Purpose and Objectives of a Business, in The Essential Drucker, Harper, 2001.

Dworkin, R., A Matter of Principle, Harvard University Press, 1985.

Dworkin, R., Law's Empire, Harvard University Press, 1986.

Dworkin, R., Is Democracy Possible Here?: Principles for a New Political Debate, Princeton University Press, 2006.

Dworkin, R., Justice in Robes, Harvard University Press, 2006.

Dworkin, R., Justice for the Hedgehogs, Harvard University Press, 2011.

Dworkin, R., Taking Rights Seriously, Bloomsbury Academic, 2013.

Easterbrook, F.H. & Fishel, D.R., The Economic Structure of Corporate Law, Harvard University Press, 1991.

Edmans, A., Grow the Pie, Cambridge University Press, 2020.

Eisenhart, K., Agency Theory: An Assessment and Review, 14(1) The Academy of Management Review (January 1989), 57-74.

Elgar, F.J. and Aitken, N, Income Equality, Trust and Homicide in 33 Countries, 21(2) European Journal of Public Health, 2021, 241–246.

Ellickson, R., Order Without Law: How Neighbors Settle Disputes, Harvard University Press, 1991.

Erlei, M. and Reinhold, C., To Choose or Not to Choose: Contracts, Reference Points, Reciprocity, and Signaling, TUC Working Papers in Economics0007, Abteilung für Volkswirtschaftslehre, Technische Universität Clausthal (Department of Economics, Technical University Clausthal), 2012.

Fehr, D., et al., Inequality, Fairness and Social Capital, 120 European Economic Review, 2000, 120, 103566.

Fehr, E. and Schmidt, K.M., A Theory of Fairness, Competition, and Cooperation, 114(3) The Quarterly Journal of Economics, 1999, 817–868.

Fourcade, M. and Khurana, R., The Social Trajectory of a Finance Professor and the Common Sense of Capital. 49(2) History of Political Economy, June 2017, 347-381.

Fourcade, M. and Khurana, R., From Social Control to Financial Economics: The Linked Ecologies of Economics and Business in Twentieth Century America. 42(2) Theory and Society, 2013, 121-159.

Freeman, E., Strategic Management: A Stakeholder Approach, Pitman, 1984.

Friedman, M., The Social Responsibility of Business Is to Increase Its Profits, New York Times, 13 September 1970.

Frydlinger, D., et al., Contracting in the New Economy: Using Relational Contracts to Boost Trust and Collaboration in Strategic Business Relationships, Palgrave Macmillan, 2021.

Frydlinger, D. and Hart, O., Overcoming Contractual Incompleteness: The Role of Guiding Principles, The Journal of Law, Economics, and Organization, 2023

Frydman, C. and Jenter, D., CEO Compensation, 2 Annual Review of Financial Economics, 2010, 75-102.

Galliani, D. and Sened, I., Institutions, Property Rights and Economic Growth: The Legacy of Douglass North, Cambridge University Press, 201.

Gane, N., Neoliberalism and the Defence of the Corporation, 40(3) Theory Culture & Society, 2023.

Giddens, A., The Constitution of Society, University of California Press, 1992.

Grossman, S. and Hart, O., The Costs and Benefits of Ownership: A Theory of Vertical and Lateral Integration, 94(4) Journal of Political Economy 1986, 691-719.

Hansman, H. and Kraakman, R., The End of History for Corporate Law, 89 Georgetown Law Review, 2001, 439.

Hardin, G., The Tragedy of the Commons, 162(3859) Science, 1968, 1243-1248.

Hart, H.L.A., The Concept of Law, Oxford University Press, 2012.

Hart, O. and Moore, J., Incomplete Contracts and Renegotiations, 56 Econometrica, 1988, 755-786.

Hart, O. and Moore, J., Property Rights and the Nature of the Firm, 98 Journal of Political Economy, 1990, 1110-1158.

Hart, O. and Moore, J. Contracts as Reference Points, 123(1) Quarterly Journal of Economics, 2008, 1-48.

Hart, O. and Zingales, L., Companies Should Maximize Shareholder Welfare Not Market Value, 2 Journal of Law, Finance and Accounting, 2017, 247-274.

Henderson, R., Reimagining Capitalism in a World on Fire, Penguin Books, 2020.

Herrington, G. Update to Limits to Growth: Comparing the World3 Model with Empirical Data, 25(3) Journal of Industrial Ecology (June 2021), 614-626.

Herrington, G., Update to Limits to Growth: Comparing the World3 Model with Empirical Data, 25(3) Journal of Industrial Ecology (June 2021) 614-626.

Hickel, J., Less Is More, Penguin Books, 2020.

Holmström, B. and Milgrom, P., Multi-task Principal Agent Analysis, 7 Journal of Law, Economics and Organization, 1991, 24-52.

Jackson, T., Prosperity Without Growth, Routledge, 2016.

Jensen, M. and Meckling, W., Theory of the Firm: Managerial Behavior, Agency Costs and Ownership Structure, 3(4) Journal of Financial Economics, 1976, 305-360.

Jensen, M. and Murphy, K., Performance Pay and Top-Management Incentives, 98 Journal of Political Economy, 1990, 225-264.

Jolls, C., Sunstein, C. and Thaler, R., A Behavioral Approach to Law and Economics, Stanford Law Review, July 1998.

Jolls, C., Behavioral Economics and the Law, Foundations and Trends in Microeconomics, 6(3) Foundations and Trends® in Microeconomics, 2011, 173-263.

Kahneman, D., Knetsch, J. and Thaler, R., Fairness as a Constraint on Profit Seeking: Entitlements in the Market, 76(4) The American Economic Review, September 1986.

Kahneman, D., Thinking, Fast and Slow, Farrar, Straus and Giroux, 2013.

Kant, I., Critique of Practical Reason, The Big Nest, 2016.

Kant, I., Fundamental Principles of the Metaphysics of Morals, The Big Nest, 2016.
Kaplan, S. and Strömberg, P., Venture Capitalists as Principals: Contracting, Screening and Monitoring, American Economic Review, 91, 2001, 426-430.
Keith, B., et al., Sourcing in the New Economy: Harnessing the Potential of Sourcing Business Models for Modern Procurement, Palgrave Macmillan 2016.
Kraakman, R., et al., The Anatomy of Corporate Law, 3rd edn, Oxford University Press, 2017.
Langevoort, D., Cultures of Compliance, 54 American Criminal Law Review, 2017, 933-977.
Loughnan, S., et al., Economic Inequality Is Linked to Biased Self-perception, 22(10) Psychological Science, 2011, 1254-1258.
Macaulay, S., Non-contractual Relations in Business: A Preliminary Study, 28 American Sociological Review, 1963, 1-19.
MacKenzie, D., An Engine, Not a Camera: How Financial Models Shape Markets, The MIT Press, 2006
Mayer, C., *Prosperity*: Better Business Makes the Greater Good, Oxford University Press, 2018.
McLean, R.D., The Case for Shareholder Capitalism: How the Pursuit of Profit Benefits All, Cato Institute, 2023.
Meadows, D., Thinking in Systems, Chelsea Green Publishing, 2008.
Meadows, D., et al., Limits to Growth: The 30 Year Update, Chelsea Green Publishing Co., 2013.
Michanek, G. and Zetterberg, C., Den svenska miljörätten, 5th edn, iUstus, 2021.
Mill, J.S., Utilitarianism, Aeterna Classics, 2018.
Mindus, P. and Spaak, T., Cambridge Companion to Legal Positivism, Cambridge University Press, 2021.
Mirowski, P. and Plehwe, D. (eds), The Road from Mont Pelerin: The Making of the Neo-liberal Thought Collective, 2nd edn, Harvard University Press, 2016.
North, D., Institutions, Institutional Change and Economic Performance, Cambridge University Press, 1990.
Osterwalder, A. and Pigneur, Y., Business Model Generation: A Handbook for Visionaries, Game Changers and Challengers, John Wiley & Sons, 2010.
Ostrom, E., Governing the Commons: The Evolution of Institutions for Collective Actions, Cambridge University Press, 1990.
Parisi, F. (ed.), The Oxford Handbook of Law and Economics: Volume 1: Methodology and Concepts, Online edn, Oxford Academic, 2017.
Piketty, T., Capital in the Twenty-First Century, The Belknap Press, 2017.
Popper, K., The Logic of Scientific Discovery, Routledge, 2002.
Porter, M., Competitive Strategy, Free Press, 1980.
Porter, M., Competitive Advantage, Free Press, 1985.
Posner, R., The Problems of Jurisprudence, Harvard University Press, 1993.
Posner, R., The Economic Analysis of Law, Wolters Kluwer Law Business, 2014.
Putnam, R., Making Democracy Work: Civic Traditions in Modern Italy, Princeton University Press, 1994.

Randers, J. and Collste, D., The Earth4All Model of Human Wellbeing on a Finite Planet Towards 2100, September 2022.

Rawls, J., A Theory of Justice, The Belknap Press, 2005.

Raworth, K., Donut Economics, Random House UK, 2018.

Raz, J., Between Authority and Interpretation, Oxford University Press, 2009.

Robbins, L., An Essay on the Nature and Significance of Economic Science, Macmillan and Co., 1932

Robbins, L., Interpersonal Comparisons of Utility: A Comment, 48(192) The Economic Journal, 1938, 635-641.

Rockström, J., et al., A Safe Operating Space for Humanity, 461(7263) Nature, 472-475.

Rockström, J. and Gaffney, O., Breaking Boundaries: The Science of Our Planet, DK, 2021.

Rothstein, B., Controlling Corruption, Oxford University Press, 2021.

Royal Swedish Academy of Sciences, Oliver Hart and Bengt Holmström: Contract Theory, Scientific Background on the Sveriges Riksbank Prize in Economic Sciences in Memory of Alfred Nobel 2016.

Rubinstein, A., A Skeptic's Comment on the Studies of Economics, 116 The Economic Journal, March 2006, C1-C9.

Rumelt, R., Good Strategy, Bad Strategy, Profile Books Ltd, 2013.

Schoenmaker, D. and Schramade, W., Principles of Sustainable Finance, Oxford University Press, 2019.

Schwab, K., Stakeholder Capitalism, World Economic Forum, 2021.

Sjåfjell, Beate and Taylor, Mark B., Clash of Norms: Shareholder Primacy vs. Sustainable Corporate Purpose (28 August 2019). International and Comparative Corporate Law Journal, 13 (2019) 3.

Sjåfjell, B. and Mähönen, J., Corporate Purpose and the Misleading Shareholder v Stakeholder Dichotonomy, 34(2) Bond Law Review, 2024.

Stout, L., The Shareholder Value Myth, Berret-Koehler Publishers, 2012.

Stroh, P., Systems Thinking for Social Change, Chelsea Green Publishing, 2016.

Sunstein, C., Probability Neglect: Emotions, Worst Cases, and Law, 112(61) Yale Law Journal, 2002.

Svenson, O., Are We All Less Risky And More Skillful Than Our Fellow Drivers?, 47(2) Acta Psychologia, February 1981, 143-148.

Taleb, N., The Black Swan: The Impact of the Highly Improbable, Random House Trade, 2010.

Teorell, J. and Rothstein, B., What Is Quality of Government: A Theory of Impartial Institutions (January 16, 2009), 21(2) Governance: An International Journal of Policy, Administration and Institutions, April 2008, 165-190.

Terzi, A., Growth for Good, Harvard University Press, 2022.

Thaler, R., The Winner's Curse: Paradoxes and Anomalies of Economic Life, Princeton University Press, 1992.

Tosi, H., et al., How Much Does Performance Matter? A Meta-analysis of CEO Pay Studies, 26 Journal of Management, 2000, 301-339.

Turner, G., A Comparison of the Limits to Growth with 30 Years of Reality, 18(3) Global Environmental Change, 2008, 397-411.

Turner, G., Is Global Collapse Imminent? Melbourne Sustainable Society Institute, The University of Melbourne, 2014.

Wiedmann, T., et al., Scientists' Warning on Affluence, 11(1) Nature Communications, 2020, 3107.

Index

U